Hagar's Vocation

Hagar's Vocation

PHILOSOPHY'S ROLE IN THE THEOLOGY OF RICHARD FISHACRE, OP

R. James Long

THE CATHOLIC UNIVERSITY OF AMERICA PRESS
Washington, D.C.

The paper used in this publication meets the minimum requirements of American National Standards for Information Science—Permanence of Paper for Printed Library Materials, ANSI Z39.48-1984.
∞

Library of Congress Cataloging-in-Publication Data
Long, R. James (Raymond James), 1938–
Hagar's vocation : philosophy's role in the theology of Richard Fishacre, OP / R. James Long.
pages cm
Includes bibliographical references and index.
ISBN 978-0-8132-2737-5 (cloth : alk. paper) 1. Fishacre, Richard, approximately 1200–1248. 2. Theology, Doctrinal—History—Middle Ages, 600–1500. 3. Philosophy, Medieval. 4. Richard Rufus, of Cornwall, –approximately 1260. I. Title.
BX1749.F57L66 2015
230'.2092—dc23 2014038486

Contents

Acknowledgments vii

Abbreviations ix

Introduction xi

1. Richard Fishacre's Way to God 1

2. The Role of Philosophy in Richard Fishacre's Theology of Creation 12

3. Between Idolatry and Science: The Magical Arts in the Grosseteste School 21

4. Of Angels and Pinheads: The Contributions of the Early Oxford Masters to the Doctrine of Spiritual Matter 48

5. The First Oxford Debate on the Eternity of the World 63

Appendix 5A. Richard Rufus, *In 2 Sent.* 1.1; ed. Stephen F. Brown, in *MM* 21/1 (1991), 270–76 80

Appendix 5B 85

6. Fishacre and Rufus on the Metaphysics of Light 88

Appendix 6A. Richard Rufus, *In 2 Sent.* 13.1; Oxford, Balliol Coll. MS 62, fols. 131ra–32rb 100

7. The Division of the Waters (Gn 1: 6–7): The History of a Conundrum and Its Resolution by the Early Oxford Masters 110

Appendix 7A. Richard Rufus, *In secundum librum Sententiarum*, dist. 14; Oxford, Balliol Coll. MS 62, fols. 132va–134ra 127

Appendix 7B: The Summa of Alexander of Hales (*Summa Halensis*) 133

8. Adam's Rib: A Test Case for Natural Philosophy in Grosseteste, Fishacre, Rufus, and Kilwardby 134

9. Richard Fishacre and the Problem of the Soul 149

10. Interiority and Self-Knowledge according to Richard Fishacre 158

11. Richard Fishacre's Treatise *De libero arbitrio* 168

12. Undoing the Past: Fishacre and Rufus on the Limits of God's Power 181

Appendix 12A. Ricard Rufus, *In 2 Sent.* 25.1 191

13. The Virgin as Olive Tree: A Marian Sermon of Richard Fishacre and Science at Oxford 196

Appendix 13A. The Edition 203

14. Richard Fishacre's *Quaestio* on the Ascension of Christ 208

Appendix 14A. The Manuscript and Edition 222

15. Richard Fishacre's *"Super S. Augustini librum de haeresibus adnotationes"* 235

Selected Bibliography 255

Index of Names 263

Subject Index 267

Acknowledgments

I acknowledge with gratitude the editors and publishers of the following journals and books who have granted me permission to reprint studies of mine that first appeared in their publications:

"Richard Fishacre and the Problem of the Soul," *TMS* 52 (1975): 263–70.

"Richard Fishacre's *Quaestio* on the Ascension of Christ: An Edition," *MS* 40 (1978): 30–55.

"The Virgin as Olive Tree: A Marian Sermon of Richard Fishacre and Science at Oxford," *AFP* 52 (1982): 77–87.

"Richard Fishacre's Way to God," in *A Straight Path: Studies in Medieval Philosophy and Culture; Essays in Honor of Arthur Hyman*, ed. Ruth Link-Salinger, Jeremiah Hackett, Michael S. Hyman, R. James Long, and Charles H. Manekin (Washington, D.C.: The Catholic University of America Press, 1988).

"Richard Fishacre's *Super S. Augustini librum de haeresibus adnotationes*: An Edition and Commentary," *AHDLMA* 60 (1993): 207–79.

"Richard Fishacre's Treatise *De libero arbitrio*," in *Moral and Political Philosophies in the Middle Ages,* Proceedings of the Ninth International Congress of Medieval Philosophy, ed. B. Carlos Bazán, Eduardo Andújar, and Léonard Sbrocchi (Ottawa: Legas, 1995), 2:879–91.

"The First Oxford Debate on the Eternity of the World," *RTPM* 65/1 (1998): 54–98.

"Fishacre and Rufus on the Metaphysics of Light: Two Unedited Texts," with Timothy B. Noone, in *Roma, magistra mundi. Itineraria culturae medievalis. Mélanges offerts au Père L. E. Boyle à l'occasion de son 75e anniversaire*, ed. Jacqueline Hamesse, Textes et Études du moyen âge (Louvain-la-Neuve: Fédération Internationale des Instituts d'Études Médiévales, 1998).

"Of Angels and Pinheads: The Contributions of the Early Oxford Masters to the Doctrine of Spiritual Matter," *FS*: *Essays in Honor of Girard Etzkorn*, ed. Gordon A. Wilson and Timothy B. Noone, 56 (1998): 237–52.

"The Role of Philosophy in Richard Fishacre's Theology of Creation," *MM* 26 (1998): 571–78.

"Interiority and Self-Knowledge according to Richard Fishacre," in *Intellect and Imagination in Medieval Philosophy*, Actes du XIe Congrès International de Philosophie Médiévale de la S.I.E.P.M., ed. M. C. Pacheco and J. F. Meirinhos, Recontres de philosophie médiévale 11 (Turnhout: Brepols, 2006).

"Undoing the Past. Fishacre and Rufus on the Limits of God's Power," in *Laudemus viros gloriosos. Essays in Honor of Armand Maurer, C.S.B*, ed. R. E. Houser (Notre Dame, Ind.: University of Notre Dame Press, 2007).

"The Division of the Waters (Gn 1, 6–7): The History of a Conundrum and its Resolution by the Early Oxford Masters," in *Philosophy and Theology in the Long Middle Ages: A Tribute to Stephen F. Brown,* ed. Kent Emery, Russell Friedman, and Andreas Speer (Leiden: Brill, 2011).

"Between Idolatry and Science: The Magical Arts in the Grosseteste School," in *Robert Grosseteste, His Thought and Its Impact*, ed. Jack P. Cunningham, Papers in Mediaeval Studies 21 (Toronto: Pontifical Institute of Mediaeval Studies, 2012).

Abbreviations

AFP	*Archivum Fratrum Praedicatorum* (Rome)
AHDLMA	*Archives d'Histoire Doctrinale et Littéraire du Moyen Âge* (Paris)
Beiträge	*Beiträge zur Geschichte der Philosophie des Mittelalters* (Münster i. W.)
CCSL	Corpus Christianorum series latina (Turnhout)
CSEL	Corpus scriptorum ecclesiasticorum latinorum (Vienna)
FS	*Franciscan Studies* (St. Bonaventure, N.Y.)
MM	*Miscellanea Mediaevalia* (Cologne)
MS	*Mediaeval Studies* (Toronto)
NB	*New Blackfriars* (Oxford)
NS	*New Scholasticism* (Washington)
OED	*Oxford English Dictionary*
PG	Migne, Patrologiae cursus completus. Series Graeca
PL	Migne, Patrologiae cursus completus. Series Latina
RNSP	*Revue Néo-Scolastique de philosophie* (Louvain)
RSPT	*Revue des sciences philosophiques et théologiques* (Le Saulchoir)
RTAM	*Recherches de théologie ancienne et médiévale* (Louvain)
RTPM	*Recherches de Théologie et Philosophie médiévales* (Leuven)
TMS	*The Modern Schoolman* (St. Louis)
ZKT	*Zeitschrift für katholische Theologie* (Tűbingen)

Introduction

The story, and so by now its analogue, has been well aired.[1] Sara is unable to conceive so tells Abraham to lie with Hagar, the Egyptian serving girl, who promptly conceives. It is only then that Sara is able to conceive—even though she is ninety biblical years old.[2] Richard Fishacre, the first Dominican friar to incept at Oxford, finds in this story a metaphor for the relationship between philosophy and theology: the theologian must first know (in the non-Biblical sense) the natural sciences before he or she can hope to be fruitful as a theologian. This project is outlined in the sermon that inaugurates his *Sentences* Commentary, the earliest to have been written at Oxford, and a project that he outlived by only two or three years.[3]

His text here is provided by Paul's letter to the Romans: "O the depth of the riches of the wisdom and of the knowledge of God! How incomprehensible are his judgments, and how un-

1. These comments are found in an expanded form in my study "Lying with Hagar: The Role of Natural Philosophy in the Theology of Richard Fishacre," *TMS* 86, nos. 1 and 2 (2008–2009): 47–64.

2. We find the same reading of the text in one of Bonaventure's sermons, possibly influenced by his reading of Fishacre; see Stephen F. Brown, "Richard Fishacre on the Need for 'Philosophy,'" in *A Straight Path. Studies in Medieval Philosophy and Theology. Essays in Honor of Arthur Hyman*, ed. Ruth Link-Salinger, Jeremiah Hackett, Michael S. Hyman, R. James Long, and Charles H. Manekin (Washington, D.C: The Catholic University of America Press, 1988), 23n4.

3. See Long, "The Science of Theology according to Richard Fishacre: Edition of the Prologue to his *Commentary on the Sentences*," *MS* 34 (1972): 79–98. Brown traces the origin of the subordinate role of philosophy vis-à-vis theology to St. Augustine and argues that Fishacre found inspiration for his project in the pages of the *De doctrina christiana*; "Need for Philosophy," 23–36.

searchable his ways!"[4] This wisdom God in his providence has shared with us by means of three books—the book of life, the book of the scriptures, and finally the book of creation.[5] The first is the divine mind itself, in which all is written but which is closed to us who are in exile. The book of creation, moreover, while readable by humankind before the Fall, has likewise become opaque to us, heirs of Adam's darkened reason. That leaves us with the book of the divine scriptures.[6]

But wait. The scriptures need decoding, and if Aristotle is correct that all of our knowledge comes through the senses—especially the *sensus disciplinales*, sight and hearing—the book of creation again enters the picture. Just as the armillary spheres in the medieval classroom illustrate the text of Ptolemy's *Almagest*, the reading from that book, reciprocally, helps the student make sense of the model. For successful teaching, both words and examples are needed. The divine wisdom, in short, is addressed to our ears—though incompletely—in the scriptures and to our eyes in the book of creation.[7]

The science of scripture, however, has a twofold property: a *virtus motiva* and a *virtus apprehensiva*—or in Grosseteste's terminology, *affectus* and *aspectus*. The former has to do with right living and the "modern masters," as Fishacre calls them, treat moral matters in their lectures on the books of scripture. The latter, having to do with the difficult questions relating to the articles of faith, have been excerpted by Peter Lombard in his books of *Sentences* and will be the focus of the Dominican master's Commentary.[8]

4. Rom 11:33. See Long, "Science of Theology," 79.

5. Again, the notion of the three books is echoed by St. Bonaventure; Brown, "Need for Philosophy," 24n5.

6. Long, "Science of Theology," 81.

7. Ibid., 82–83.

8. Ibid., 96–97. Note that the *Sentences* are regarded as a gloss on scripture and hence part of a single science. Note also that moral matters are not wholly absent from Fishacre's Commentary; see my study, "The Beginning of a Tradition: The *Sentences* Commentary of Richard Fishacre, OP," in *Medieval Commentaries on the "Sen-*

The doctrinal part of theology itself, however, yields a further division, namely between things and signs, a distinction Peter Lombard makes in the very first line of his *Sentences*, repeating the distinction Augustine makes in the *De doctrina christiana*.[9] Signs mean the sacraments, and these Lombard (and all his commentators) deal with in the fourth book, treating the difficult things or realities in the first three.[10]

It was incumbent on the commentator on the second book of Lombard's *Sentences* to confront problems having to do with creation and the visible as well as the invisible worlds. But there is a distinction, says Fishacre, between idle seekers after curiosities (those presumably who spend their academic lives exclusively in the Arts faculty) and the serious students of the created world. The former probe the secrets of the world for their own sakes, the latter for the sake of seeing therein reflections of the creator. Only the latter can be said to have a sense of purpose and can truly be called *studiosi*, whereas the former, in the words of the psalmist, "are corrupt, and are become abominable in their ways."[11]

Although the creation material of the second book naturally offers more scope to Fishacre's project, there are certainly other examples scattered throughout the other three books. In discussing the question of the knowledge of the incarnate Word as human in book 3, for example, Alexander Eichinger, one of the Fishacre editors, has written a very interesting study on the use Fishacre makes of the optics of Alhacen to explicate the discrep-

tences" of Peter Lombard. Current Research, ed. Gilian R. Evans (Leiden: Brill, 2002), 1:355–56. Some of these *moralitates*, excerpted from Fishacre's Commentary, were in fact collected at some point, probably by a Cistercian monk, to form a work intended for the edification of the brethren; see Long, "The Moral and Spiritual Theology of Richard Fishacre: Edition of Trinity Coll. MS O.1.30," *AFP* 60 (1990): 5–143.

9. Peter Lombard, *The Sentences* 1.1.1, trans. Giulio Silano (Toronto: Pontifical Institute of Mediaeval Studies, 2007), 1:5.

10. Long, "Science of Theology," 98.

11. Richard Fishacre, *In secundum librum Sententiarum*, prologue, ed. R. James Long, part 1 (Munich: Verlag der Bayerischen Akademie der Wissenschaften, 2008), 3.

ancy between John's account of the Word being full of grace and truth and Luke's account of Jesus advancing in age and wisdom.[12] Much more broadly and with more detail than any of the earlier commentators on this particular text of the Lombard, Fishacre launches into a discussion of the sensory powers of Christ. He asks, for example, whether Christ was able to see through walls or at great distances. In brief, his answer hinges on Alhacen's theory of intussusception (the receiving of forms emitted by the object) as opposed to the earlier extromission theory of vision (that is, the sending of rays to the object which then apprehend its form): in other words, the deficiency lies with the object's inability to send its form through a solid obstruction or for a great distance rather than with the perceiving subject.[13] The same argument holds for refracted images, the oar dipped in water appearing to be bent, for example: Christ would be subject to the same optical conditions as the rest of us, while remaining free of any cognitive deficiency on his part.[14]

The most developed and dramatic examples of the Fishacrean methodology, however, are to be found in several disputed questions which were composed after he completed his Commentary in 1245 or 1246, as I have argued elsewhere.[15] These were folded into the text of later copies of the work. The questions are four in number and they are all concerned with philosophical issues prompted by the hexaëmeron, the Genesis account of the six days of creation.[16] I have included studies of most of these questions in the collection below.

12. Alexander Eichinger, "Optics and the Knowledge of Christ in Richard Fishacre," in *Intellect and Imagination in Medieval Philosophy*, Actes du XIe Congrès International de Philosophie Médiévale de la S.I.E.P.M., ed. Maria Pacheco and José Meirinhos (Turnhout: Brepols, 2006), 2:1279–90.

13. Ibid., 1282–87.

14. Ibid., 1288–89.

15. See R. James Long and Maura O'Carroll, SND, *The Life and Works of Richard Fishacre, OP* (Munich: Verlag der Bayerischen Akademie der Wissenschaften, 1999), 34–36.

16. These have been edited and appear in Richard Fishacre, *In secundum librum*

A scripture commentary was also attributed to Fishacre by early bibliographers.[17] Although this has not survived—or at least has not been identified—there are several sermons that with varying degrees of certitude are assigned to him; and here too is reflected his project of engaging natural philosophy in the service of theology. One of his sermons, the study of which appears below, compares the Virgin Mary to an olive tree. The text is from Psalm 51, "But I, as a fruitful olive-tree in the house of the Lord," and so forth. Unless one knew, for example, that the olive tree was of singular eminence—and here his source is the pseudo-Aristotelian *De plantis*—useful as it is sublime, able to reproduce itself without outside assistance, as bitter in its roots as it is sweet in its fruit, less fruitful but productive of superior fruit than the trees of the forest, and so forth—unless one knew all this, one would not fully appreciate the allegorical reference of the sacred text or perhaps miss it entirely.[18]

Finally, there are two works, both of which are included in the collection, that appear in a unique copy at the end of a Vatican manuscript, and which I argue can with some degree of certitude be attributed to Fishacre.[19] The first is a project in keeping with the original *raison d'être* of the Order of Preachers, that is, the fighting of heresy. Fishacre supplies rational arguments designed to refute six of the heresies listed and described in Augustine's *De haeresibus*. The second is a question on the Ascension of Christ, wherein he invokes the Aristotelian concepts of natural place, natural motion, gravity, and levity, and the vacuum and time to explicate this tenet of the creed.

Sententiarum, ed. R. James Long, Part 2, Band 25 (Munich: Verlag der Bayerischen Akademie der Wissenschaften, 2011), Appendices A–D, 315–63.

17. Long and O'Carroll, *Life and Works*, 31–32.

18. See Heinz Meyer, "Zum Verhältnis von Enzyklopädik und Allegorese im Mittelalter," *Frühmittelalterliche Studien* 24 (1990): 290–313, and Iolanda Ventura, "Plant Symbolism in Thirteenth-Century Biblical Exegesis and in Bartholomaeus Anglicus's *De proprietatibus rerum*," *Schola Salernitana Annali* 12 (2007): 121–34.

19. Long and O'Carroll, *Life and Works*, 33–35.

Professedly, Friar Richard was doing theology, engaged in the project of attempting to understand his faith, which entailed understanding the biblical text and using to that end whatever tools of rational analysis that were available to him. It was not, however, a one-way street. Just as (in the well-worn aphorism) extreme cases test the law, the extreme cases provided by the biblical text[20] forced Fishacre to understand the philosophy he had inherited from Aristotle in new and untrodden ways. Thorndike's apodictic statement was that "Medieval men ... studied nature from scientific curiosity and not to search for spiritual allegories."[21] On the face of it this is certainly open to challenge but it is not, in the case of Fishacre, without some measure of truth. Such an attitude of wonder toward the natural world, moreover, may very well account for the commendation of Fishacre by Matthew Paris, who was not known for lavishing praise on the mendicants, as being "pre-eminent in theology *and in other sciences* [emphasis mine]."[22]

The rationale for reprinting these several studies of Richard Fishacre and his milieu in a single volume is that many of these pieces were published originally in conference proceedings or *Festschriften*, both venues that typically are not widely circulated and hence not readily accessible to scholars. The order in which I have placed these studies in the following collection was dictated, somewhat arbitrarily, by the order in which the subjects

20. Consider, for example, the oddities presented by the days of creation: light without a body to emit the light, the division of waters such that there is water above the firmaments, which is alien to its natural place, and the formation of an adult human body out of a rib—to name only the most obvious.

21. Lynn Thorndike, *A History of Magic and Experimental Science During the First Thirteen Centuries of our Era*, corrected ed. (New York: Columbia University Press, 1929), 1:502–3.

22. Matthew Paris, *Chronica maiora*, ed. H. R. Luard, *Rerum Britannicarum medii aevi scriptores* 57 (London, 1880), 5:16. On the other hand, Gilson's judgment remains largely true, *viz.* "... the question arises whether Aristotle himself would have been able to understand the meaning of his main positions," *History of Christian Philosophy in the Middle Ages* (New York: Random House, 1955), 354.

are taken up in Lombard's *Sentences*, not by the order in which they were written. Thus, for example, the study of Fishacre's arguments for God's existence occurs toward the beginning of the first book of his *Commentary*. There are, however, exceptions. The Mother of God comes in for mention only in the third book of the *Sentences* (see especially distinctions 4 and 8); thus I have placed the sermon on the analogy between Mary and the olive tree near the end. The doctrine of the Ascension of Christ, on the other hand, is not treated by the Lombard, nor is the subject of heresy in any formal sense. These two outliers from the end of the Vatican manuscript I have therefore put at the very end.

The fact, moreover, that at this time we have published editions for only books 2 and 3 of the *Sentences* Commentary leads to some awkwardness with respect to the source of texts from the unedited books. This is especially obvious in my paper on Fishacre's "Way to God," where I draw texts of book 1 from a study published by a German scholar, from my dissertation, and from texts edited for the occasion from four representative manuscripts. Although plans are well underway for the editing of the remaining two volumes, I thought it best not to await their appearance.

I acknowledge with thanks the support I have received from the National Endowment for the Humanities and, more recently, Fairfield University for a Senior Summer Fellowship in 2012.

I would like to dedicate this collection to the team of editors, who have been laboring selflessly on Fishacre's Commentary since the Bavarian Academy of Sciences offered its sponsorship in the late 1980s: Stephen Brown, Alexander Eichinger, Joseph Goering, Hans Kraml, Gerhard Leibold, Maura O'Carroll, Klaus Rodler, and (most recently) my colleague John Slotemaker. Of this number I would like to single out Dr. Rodler, who has been on a number of occasions my host in Munich and my constant good angel. I would also like to dedicate this volume to the memory of James

A. Weisheipl, OP, who guided my first researches on Fishacre, and Leo Cardinal Scheffczyk, the late *Vorsitzender* of our Commission of the Bavarian Academy, who received me with such warm and gracious hospitality.

My youngest son, Christian, asked me one day several years ago whether I had ever thought of what Friar Richard Fishacre would say to me if I met him in the next life. I had frankly never thought about it, but I answered that I hoped he'd be pleased.

Hagar's Vocation

CHAPTER 1

Richard Fishacre's Way to God

There are some persons to whom the inquiry seeking to demonstrate that God exists may perhaps appear superfluous. These are the persons who assert that the existence of God is self-evident, in such wise that its contrary cannot be entertained in the mind.[1]

With this observation Thomas Aquinas begins his discussion of the problem of God's existence in the *Summa contra Gentiles*. Twice before he had raised the issue—in the *Scriptum super libros Sententiarum* (1252–1256) and the *De veritate* (1257–1258), and would return to it in the *Summa theologiae*, always invoking the rubric *utrum Deum esse sit per se notum* ("whether the proposition 'God exists' is self-evident"). The rubric, which was Thomas's invention—no one had, in fact, claimed that God's existence was self-evident—was a device enabling him, by denying any privileged knowledge of God's essence, to place full weight on his own *a posteriori* demonstrations for God's existence. If the exis-

1. Thomas Aquinas, *Summa contra Gentiles* 1.10, trans. Anton C. Pegis (Notre Dame, Ind.: University of Notre Dame Press, 1975), 79.

tence of God were not in any meaningful sense self-evident to us, then it could be denied prior to demonstration. A demonstration properly so-called is therefore necessary, if the human creature is to have any natural knowledge of the reality of its maker.[2]

Notwithstanding, the statement of the *Contra Gentiles* remains curiously provocative. Suppose that Thomas's concern here is not with writing history but with "borrowing themes which allow him to emphasize important points."[3] Even so, the wording suggests that he has in mind someone or some group maintaining that the existence of God was so evident that God's nonexistence could not even be thought. Who were these *asserentes*?

The question has been asked before, notably by Gilson and Chatillon.[4] The evidence they have marshaled indicates that Thomas's characterization could have represented any one or all of a group of theologians that included William of Auxerre, Alexander of Hales, Richard Fishacre, and Thomas's contemporary, St. Bonaventure, all advocates of what has been called a "theology of essence."[5] All agree not only on the thesis that the nonexistence of God is unthinkable but also on the authorities they invoke in support of their position: St. Anselm, St. Augustine (sometimes by name, sometimes not), and St. John Damascene. It is no accident that from his youthful Commentary on Peter Lombard's *Sentences* to his mature *Summa theologiae* these are the same authorities St. Thomas cites as opposing his position.

My project in this paper will be to focus on one of these al-

2. See Etienne Gilson, *The Christian Philosophy of St Thomas Aquinas*, trans. Lawrence K. Shook (New York: Random House, 1956), 46–58, and *The Philosophy of St. Bonaventure*, trans. Dom Iltyd Trethowan and Frank J. Sheed (Paterson N.J.: St. Anthony Guild Press, 1965), 107–26; Jean Chatillon, "De Guillaume d'Auxerre à saint Thomas d'Aquin. L'argument de saint Anselme chez les premiers scholastiques du XIIIe siècle," *Spicilegium Beccense* (Paris: J. Vrin, 1959): 209–31; and Pegis, "The Bonaventurean Way to God," *MS* 29 (1967): 206–42.

3. Gilson, *Aquinas*, 47.

4. Ibid., 46–58, and *Bonaventure*, 107–26; Chatillon, "Guillaume," 209–31.

5. The expression is Gilson's; See *Aquinas*, 48–54.

leged sources, Richard Fishacre, and to ask whether indeed he qualifies as one of the *asserentes*. I do not intend to claim thereby that Thomas had ever read his older Dominican confrere.[6] There is only slight evidence that he may have done so in an otherwise unsubstantiated marginal gloss in a copy of the treatise *De quatuor in quibus* to the effect that St. Thomas wished to have a copy of Fishacre's *Sentences* Commentary.[7]

Fishacre is not the first of the thirteenth-century scholastics to have exploited the arguments of Anselm, Augustine, and John Damascene.[8] However, he is the first Oxford master to have done so. Furthermore, until that time, his was the most complete and coherent treatment of the problem of the divine existence.[9] This was true in spite of some obvious parallels with William of Auxerre's *Summa aurea*. Richard's discussion is to be found in his imposing *Commentarium in IV libros Sententiarum*, the first of its

6. Indeed the Leonine editors have found only one parallel passage in Fishacre's *Sentences* Commentary (viz. *Quaestiones disputatae de veritate*, q. 27 [de gratia], art. 4, ed. Leon. [Rome: Santa Sabina, 1976], 22:3, 804).

7. Stephanus de Salaniaco & Bernardus Guidonis: "Item fr. Ricardus Fisacra, natione Anglicus, tempore s. Thome et eo antiquior, super sententias profundissime scripsit, cuius scripta s. Thomas desiderabat habere," *De quatuor in quibus Deus Praedicatorum Ordinem insignivit*, ed. Thomas Käppeli, *Monumenta Ordinis Fratrum Praedicatorum Historica* 22 (Rome: Santa Sabina, 1949), 16; textual variant to line 11. This gloss was first noted by Quétif-Échard, *Scriptores Ordinis Praedicatorum* (Paris, 1719; ed. altera A. Picard, 1910), 1:118.

8. That distinction belongs to William of Auxerre, secular master at Paris, who raises the issue in his *Summa aurea*, composed between 1215 and 1231 (Chatillon, "Guillaume," 214). The text is reprinted in Augustinus Daniels, "Quellenbeiträge und Untersuchungen zur Geschichte der Gottesbeweise im dreizehnten Jahrhundert mit besonderer Berücksichtigung des Arguments im Proslogion des Hl. Anselm," *Beiträge* 8/1–2 (Münster i. W.: Aschendorff, 1909), 25–27.

9. I omit from consideration the *Summa* ascribed to Alexander of Hales, books 1–3 of which, according to the Quaracchi editors, were composed (or assembled) between the years 1236 and 1245 at Paris (Alexander de Hales, *Summa theologica* 4.3 [Quaracchi, 1948], Prolegomena, 339), approximately the same years Fishacre was writing his Commentary at Oxford. See Chatillon, "Guillaume," 214, n. 21, and R. James Long and Maura O'Carroll, SND, *The Life and Works of Richard Fishacre, OP. Prolegomena to the Edition of his Commentary on the "Sentences"* (Munich: Verlag der Bayerischen Akademie der Wissenschaften, 1999), 39–42.

genre composed by an Oxford Dominican and very possibly the first by any Oxford master.[10] Commenting on the text in book 1, distinction 3, which the Lombard cites from the *De civitate Dei*, a text wherein Augustine discusses how the Platonists have transcended the physical world to arrive at its immaterial maker, Fishacre finds occasion to offer his own arguments.[11]

Richard constructs ten arguments in all, each of which is of the kind that Aquinas will term *a priori*. The exception is the final argument, a truncated version of a causal argument found in the *Summa aurea*.[12] Each presupposes a metaphysics of participation and exemplarism, whereby every hierarchical order of perfection leads the mind to posit the existence of a greatest. Each argument contributes more or less forcefully to the conclusion toward which Fishacre is hastening—namely, that one cannot even say in one's heart that God does not exist.[13]

The centerpiece of the Fishacrean proofs is the argument from the *Proslogion*, variations on which account for three of the ten arguments. If there be something most simple, it would be identical with its being; otherwise it would have being and something else besides and consequently would not be most simple. Therefore, if

10. Daniel Callus, "Introduction of Aristotelian Learning to Oxford," *Proceedings of the British Academy* 29 (1943): 32, and R. James Long, "Science of Theology according to Richard Fishacre: Edition of the Prologue to his *Commentary on the Sentences*," *MS* 34 (1972), 71n1.

11. "Quod autem Deus sit multipliciter ostenditur" (Daniels, "Quellenbeiträge," 21). The texts I cite in these notes derive either from the one published by Daniels, or (in the case of texts not cited by Daniels) established from four manuscripts (see below), or from my dissertation, or—when relevant—from the published text of book 2. The following are the manuscripts I use to correct Daniels and to establish a text not cited by him and their *sigla*: Bologna, Univ. MS 1546 (=*B*); Cambridge, Gonville and Caius College MS 329/410 (=*C*); London, British Library MS Royal 10.B.VII (=*R*); BAV Ottob. Lat. MS 294 (=*V*).

12. See Daniels, "Quellenbeiträge," 26; the argument ultimately owes its inspiration to John Damascene (*De fide orthodoxa*, 1.3).

13. "Hinc patet quod non potest intelligi vel cogitari non esse quia ad ipsum non esse sequitur ipsum esse. Sed dicere in corde est cogitare; ergo non potest dici in corde ipsum non esse" (Daniels, "Quellenbeiträge," 24).

anything be most simple, it would exist; but the most simple is the most simple; therefore it exists.[14]

Moreover, continues Fishacre, if God were to exist, God would be something than which nothing greater could be thought; but upon hearing this anyone would think "something than which nothing greater can be thought." If I say the words, my listeners understand them. What they are thinking exists either in their thought alone or also in fact. If the latter, then I have the conclusion I want; if the former, then something greater than this can be thought—namely, anything existing in both thought and fact.[15]

Fishacre illustrates his final working of the *Proslogion* inference with a particularly prosaic example. The "best" encompasses every good. But just as "snub nose" (*simus*) cannot be understood without also understanding "nose," neither can the best be understood without being. Therefore, if there be a best, it exists; but the best is the best; therefore it exists.[16]

Just as for Anselm before him (and for Bonaventure after him), the atheist represents an especially troublesome problem for Fishacre. If all his arguments lead him to the conclusion that God's nonexistence is unthinkable, how can he explain that someone is thinking the unthinkable? And very much like Anselm before Gaunilon pressed him on the issue, Fishacre dismisses the fool of

14. "Item, si aliquid esset simplicissimum, non differret ab esse suo, sed esset suum esse; quia si non, iam haberet esse et aliquid amplius, et tunc non esset simplicissimum. Igitur, si aliquid esset simplicissimum, illud esset; sed simplicissimum est simplicissimum; ergo est" (ibid., 23). Cf. The Bonventurean argument: "Si Deus est Deus, Deus est; sed antecedens est adeo verum quod non potest cogitari non esse; ergo Deum esse est verum indubitabile" (*De mysterio Trinitatis* 1.1.29).

15. "Item, si Deus esset, esset quo maius cogitari non potest; sed aliquis hoc audiens cogitat quid quo magis cogitari non potest; si dico verba, intelligit hoc quod ipse cogitat aut in cognitione eius tantum aut in re: si in re, hoc volui; si in cognitione tantum, iam illo cognito aliquid erit maius, quia illud quod est in cognitione et in re maius est quam illud quod est in cognitione tantum" (Daniels, "Quellenbeiträge," 23).

16. "Item, in intellectu optimi cadit esse bonum; sed hoc ipsum esse tam magnum bonum est ut illud omnes appetant: ergo in intellectu optimi est esse. Ergo sicut simus non potest intelligi sine naso, sic nec optimum sine esse: ergo si est aliquid optimum, est; sed optimum est optimum, ergo est" (ibid.).

the psalm text because he is ignorant and truly a fool. When the fool says "there is no God," he does not mean what I understand by "God," but something less than God. The atheist may be saying or thinking the words, but he does not comprehend their meaning.[17]

Lest we think, however, that we are engaged in a vain exercise by attempting demonstrations of God's existence—for John Damascene has declared that nature has implanted in every person a knowledge of God—Richard responds with a countertext from the same author: evil has prevailed over human nature to such an extent as to drag some down to the irrational and unspeakably evil pit of perdition, so that they are prompted to say that there is no God. Does not the psalmist add in the same text: "They are corrupt, and are become abominable in their ways"?[18]

Because the human mind is clouded by vice, it does not see what is otherwise radiantly clear. Therefore, the effort to argue God's existence rationally is not futile, insists Fishacre. But what about his proofs? How seriously does he take them and how seriously does he expect his students to take them? To say that they exhibit none of the intellectual rigor and almost obsessive attention to detail of the Thomistic proofs is to understate the case. Fishacre presents his arguments facilely, almost indifferently. And so the careful reader is led to suspect that there is

17. "Contra. Dixit insipiens in corde suo 'non est Deus.' Solutio. Cum hoc dicit non de Deo dicit, sed de aliquo quod est minus Deo quod comprehendit per hoc quod dico 'Deus'; sicut dicens 'dii,' non intelligit Deum sed aliquid Deo inferius, quod potest cogitari convenire pluribus" (ibid., 24).

18. "Item, si non potest cogitari non esse et etiam innata est nobis cognitio existendi Deum, ut dicit Damascenus cap. 1: 'Non dereliquit nos Deus in omnimoda ignorantia. Omnibus enim cognitio existendi Deum ab ipso [ab ipso *om.* P] naturaliter inserta est' [*De fide orthodoxa* 1.1]. Ergo probando ipsum esse stulto labore consumitur. Solutio. In tantum malitia quosdam corrupit ut quod naturaliter est certissimum fiat eis dubium. Damascenus cap. 3: 'In tantum praevaluit malitia hominum naturae, ut quosdam in irrationabilissimum et omnium malorum pessimum perditionis deduceret barathrum, ut dicant non esse Deum, de quorum insipientia ait sacrorum enuntiator David: Dixit insipiens in corde suo non est Deus' [*De fide* 1.3]. Et bene subiungitur: 'corrupti sunt et abominabiles' [Ps. 13.1]" (ibid., 24).

more here than meets the eye. There is: but to uncover it we must examine Fishacre's philosophy of knowledge.

Daniel Callus once wrote, with perhaps a touch of irony, that "it would certainly be an exaggeration to claim Fishacre as an ardent Aristotelian."[19] Nowhere is this more true than in his epistemology. The sensible species, which is like the word by which the sensible object speaks to us, reaches only as far as the inmost sentient organ, which is the common sense (*sensus communis*). At this juncture Fishacre invokes the help of Augustine (or in this case pseudo-Augustine): the soul in marvelous ways and with awesome speed produces in itself something similar to that which is in the common sense—that is, it assimilates and conforms itself to that received species, as the light to the water with which it comes in contact.[20]

There are several passages in which he sounds very much like an Aristotelian, affirming, for example, that the process of knowing begins in the senses and is deficient to the extent that sensation is deficient.[21] However, Fishacre nowhere endorses an Aristotelian theory of induction or abstraction. We find rather the often repeated conviction that the mind is not passive with

19. Callus, "Introduction," 31.

20. "Cum verbum quo se loquitur res exterior mihi, scilicet species rei, pervenerit ad intimum sentiens, non procedit ulterius ut intret gignendo se in mentem. Sed, ut dicit Augustinus [i.e., Alcher of Clairvaux, *de spiritu et anima*, cap. 25 (PL 40,798)], anima miris modis et mira quadam velocitate efficit in se simile ei quod est in organo intimo, hoc est assimulat se illi speciei susceptae et conformat, ut lux aquae cui contiguatur" (*In 1 Sent.* 2). This and the following texts from the first book of Fishacre's *Sentences* Commentary are taken from R. James Long, "The Problem of the Soul in Richard Fishacre's *Commentary on the Sentences*" (Ph.D. diss., University of Toronto, 1968), *24.

21. See, for example, the following text from book 2: "Sensibilia gignendo ex se similitudines suas, et per sensus immittentes eas in nobis, eas imprimunt in instrumento sensus communis, id est in ultimo sentiente, scilicet in corde; ex qua impressione efficitur ut anima, eo quod sit illi parti corporis maxime unita, intelligat illud cuius similitudo in corde fuit impressa. Nostra enim cognitio incipit a sensu. Et ideo dicit Aristoteles quod deficiente sensu necesse est scientiam deficere, in *Post. an.*," Richard Fishacre, *In secundum librum Sententiarum,* Part 1: Prologue, Dist. 1–20, ed. R. James Long (Munich: Verlag der Bayerischen Akademie der Wissenschaften, 2008), 134. Hereafter cited as: Fishacre, *In 2 Sent.*, ed. Long.

respect to sensation and that the latter merely provides the occasion for the soul's activity.[22]

What then is the origin of the intelligible similitude that the mind produces (*efficit*) in itself? The answer is soon forthcoming. The likenesses of things (*similitudines rerum*) have been implanted in us by nature, in such a way, however, that we can contemplate one without being aware of any other. It is at this point that the soul actually (*actu*) becomes like the object that is understood.[23] Later Fishacre reveals his sources: according to Augustine and the Platonists every truth and all things are naturally written (*scripta sunt*) in the soul, although many things in our souls lie hidden to us. This is evident from the fact that the possible intellect is in a state of potentiality with respect to all intelligibles—not only passive potentiality but rather active. If this were not the case, that saying of Aristotle's would be false—namely: "Every man by nature desires to know."[24] From the fact that he says "to know" simply—not to know this or that—it is obvious that he intends that in the human being there is an active potentiality to know all things.[25]

This attempt to enlist Aristotle in support of either Platonic innatism or Augustinian immanence is philosophically awkward and raises more questions than it answers. Indeed we are confronted here with three distinct positions with respect to the origin of our concepts, and in vain does one search the text of Fishacre's Commentary for an unequivocal statement with respect to his own preference. Perhaps, like Augustine, he simply assumes their presence in the soul without venturing an opinion as to their origin.[26]

22. The position is Augustinian; see *De musica* 6.5 (PL 32,1168).

23. "Sic in anima naturaliter insitae sunt similitudines rerum, et tamen unam earum intuemur actualiter sine alia. Et tunc quasi actu efficitur similis illi rei extra quam intelligimus," *In 1 Sent.* 2, ed. Long, "Problem of Soul," *25.

24. Aristotle, *Metaphys.* 1.1 (980a22).

25. Fishacre, *In 2 Sent.* 16.1, ed. Long, 1:332.

26. See Dorothea Sharp, "The Philosophy of Richard Fishacre," *NS* 7 (1933): 291,

Whatever the process by which they be "written" or "implanted" in the soul, however, it is clear that we become aware of the forms or the intelligibles of things only through God's power.[27] The analogy is a familiar one. If the soul can be understood as a panel (*tabula*) and the similitudes of things in it as paintings (*picturae*), God is the light illumining these paintings.[28]

Here Fishacre has entered the terrain staked out by Augustine, and the metaphor of light and illumination recurs frequently. Everything begets a species or likeness of itself, because a thing is intelligible only through the likeness it begets—and this by God's agency and gift to them (*Deo agente et eis dante*); for just as a corporeal light draws color into act, so God draws out into act every intelligible.[29] Again, in another distinction: God works on the mind as light illumines color and the eye.[30] The light, then, that is God is present to the mind, more present indeed than the mind is to itself.[31]

In a remarkable text Fishacre draws a remarkable conclusion—namely, that whoever sees something in the presence of light, sees the light more than the object. Because, therefore, God is the light of every intelligible, as sensible light is of every visible object, whoever sees anything with the intellect, also sees God

---

and R. James Long, "Lying with Hagar: The Role of Natural Philosophy in the Theology of Richard Fishacre," *TMS* 86 (November 2008): 47–64.

27. "Creata igitur cognoscuntur Deo adiuvante in quantum est natura, scilicet cognitione vespertina, non matutina," Fishacre, *In 2 Sent.* 3.5, ed. Long, 1:88.

28. "Igitur intelligo animam sicut tabulam, similitudines rerum in ea sicut picturas illuminantem," Fishacre, *In 1 Sent.* 17, ed. Long; "Problem of the Soul," *53.

29. "Unaquaeque res gignit ex se speciem vel similitudinem, quia quaelibet est intelligibilis per similtudinem quam gignit—et hoc Deo agente et eis dante. Sicut enim lux corporalis educit colorem in actum talem, sic Deus omne intelligibile," Fishacre, *In 1 Sent.* 3, ed. Long, "Problem of Soul," *43–44.

30. "Ipse enim est menti tamquam lux quae illuminat colorem et oculum," *In 1 Sent.* 32.

31. "Item, summe praesens est menti, quia praesentior quam mens sibi, ut dicit Augustinus," *In 1 Sent.* 17. And: "Sed omni menti intimior est ipsa essentia Dei quam ipsa mens sibi. Ergo sicut novit mens creaturas ei absentes similitudine earum et ea est sciens, sic Deum trinum et unum se ipso praesente ipsi menti et ipse erit sapientia qua eum sapit mens," *In 1 Sent.* 32.

with the intellect. Therefore, regardless of one's state of grace, either one understands nothing whatsoever or one sees God.[32]

Here we must exercise caution. Fishacre objects on behalf of the adversary that no one has ever seen God (Jn 1:18). Perhaps, he responds with his customary hesitation, we do see God with our minds in this life, though poorly (*tenuiter*)—so poorly, in fact, that it can rightly be judged to be nothing compared to the vision that the blessed will enjoy *in patria*, just as the earth is but a point compared to the heavens. Even the wicked can be said to see God intellectually, though they are unaware that they see God. Again, the light metaphor serves Friar Richard well; just as in seeing the color white in a strong light I indeed see the light—which I cannot gaze at directly—even though I be ignorant of the fact or inattentive to it.[33]

That not all rational creatures acknowledge the existence of the light intimately present to them, and without which they could not know intelligibles, Fishacre attributes to two causes: sinfulness and the necessity for the soul in this life to minister to the body. It is the latter that impeded our first parents, even before the Fall, from knowing God perfectly. Only when we are not only united to God by grace, but also freed from the task of managing the body, will we know God perfectly and immediately.[34]

32. "Item, quicumque videt aliquid in luce magis videt ipsam lucem. Igitur cum Deus sit lux omnis intelligibilis, sicut haec lux sensibilis est omnis visibilis, quicumque aliquid videt intellectu et Deum videt intellectu. Igitur qui habent caritatem, immo et qui non habent, aut nihil omnino intelligunt aut Deum vident," *In 1 Sent.* 17.

33. "Quid est ergo Ioan 1: 'Deum nemo vidit unquam' [1 Ioan 4:12]; Ex. 33: 'Non videbit me homo et vivet' [Ex. 33:20]; I Tim. 6: 'Quem nullus hominum vidit nec videre potest' [I Tim. 6:16] ... Solutio. Forte visione intellectuali videtur Deus in via licet tenuiter. Sed tam modica est, ut respectu illius quae erit in patria merito nulla iudicetur, sicut terra punctus est respectu caeli. De malis vero dici potest quod si vident aliquid visione intellectuali, vident et Deum, sed nescientes se videre eum, sicut videndo album in luce video lucem, nesciens nec attendens eam, quam etiam in se nunc videre non possum. Hoc tamen asserere non audeo, licet huic consonare videatur illud Iob 36: 'Omnes homines vident eum, unusquisque intuetur procul' [Iob 36:25]," ibid.

34. Fishacre, *In 2 Sent.* 23.3, ed. Long, 2:55–56. For Fishacre's dualistic view of the

What, then, is the relationship between illumination and demonstration? Does the former allow us to dispense with the latter, or does it act as its ground of certitude? If the presence of the divine light is so evident to the attentive mind (one might almost say *self-evident*), what role does proof play?

Surely, as Gilson remarks apropos of St. Bonaventure, any chain of reasoning must lose much of its significance if it makes use of some prior experience sufficient of itself to establish the same conclusion.[35] Noetically the Fishacrean proofs occupy a universe different from that of St. Thomas. It is with the God-given light of the mind that Thomas works his way from the beings that we know through our senses to the cause of those beings. Fishacre focuses on the light itself, without which the mind knows nothing, not even itself, and which therefore the mind knows to exist just as surely as it knows that it knows.

Fishacre's proofs are not superfluous only because wickedness has blinded humans to the obvious. But for the soul with charity and with sufficient attentiveness, the proofs are, strictly speaking, quite unnecessary. That is why they emit an air of nonchalance, and why a student of Thomas Aquinas must find them unacceptable.

Precisely what theologians Thomas might have had in mind when he attacked those who assert that the existence of God is self-evident we will of course never know. That Richard Fishacre in fact qualifies for inclusion among the *asserentes* is, I submit, beyond question.

---

soul, see R. James Long, "Richard Fishacre and the Problem of the Soul," *TMS* 52 (1975): 263–70.

35. Gilson, *Bonaventure*, 114.

CHAPTER 2

The Role of Philosophy in Richard Fishacre's Theology of Creation

Fishacre's theological project has been too thoroughly studied for me to rehearse it at any length here.[1] In a very rich and dense proemium to his Commentary on the *Sentences,* Fishacre borrows imagery from the book of Genesis to illustrate the relationship between *scientia* or philosophy and *sapientia* or theology. Abraham, according to the biblical account, is obliged to have sexual relations with Hagar the slave woman before he is able to impregnate Sarah. The aspiring theologian, in other words, must have commerce with the worldly sciences before he can with any hope of being productive enter the chambers of the queen of the sciences.[2]

1. See e.g., R. James Long, "Science of Theology according to Richard Fishacre: Edition of the Prologue to his *Commentary on the Sentences,*" *MS* 34 (1972): 71–98; and Stephen F. Brown, "Richard Fishacre on the Need for 'Philosophy,'" in *A Straight Path. Studies in Medieval Philosophy and Culture: Essays in Honor of Arthur Hyman,* ed. Ruth Link-Salinger, Jeremiah Hackett, Michael S. Hyman, R. James Long, and Charles H. Manekin (Washington, D.C.: The Catholic University of America Press, 1988), 23–36.

2. Long, "Science of Theology," 85. The aphorism of the schoolmen "*Non est senes-*

God's wisdom, says Fishacre, is imparted to his creatures in three books: the book of life, the book of creation, and the book of the scriptures.[3] In our fallen state, however, the first two are closed to us and we have only the Bible, the object of the theologian's study.[4] Though we cannot read the book of nature, as Adam was able to do before he sinned, it can nevertheless provide visual models that aid us in our understanding of the sacred text, very much like models of armillary spheres and astrolabes, which appeal to the sense of sight, serve to supplement the auditing of a lecture on astronomy. A flame, for example, which encompasses heat and light and splendor, illustrates the three-in-oneness of the Trinity. Conversely, those who study the book of creation without reference to sacred scripture not surprisingly have gone astray, because they are ignorant of what in the visible world is merely an analogue of a divine reality.[5]

The inaugural lecture for the second book, however, has not received the attention it deserves, although upon examination it turns out to be every bit as rich as the first. His text here is the psalm verse, "Thou art fearfully magnified: wonderful are thy works, and my soul knoweth right well."[6] Wonderful indeed are God's works, continues Fishacre, and these will be the subject of the second book.[7] The works of creation are wonderful in them-

cendum in artibus" is here echoed in Fishacre's warning that those who pursue the sciences exclusively have grown so old in the embraces of their mistress that when they finally go in to the lady of the house, they are unable to father children owing to their advanced age, just as the elderly David slept with Abisag but knew her not; ibid., 86.

3. The same metaphor, ascribed by Ruffinus to St. Anthony of Egypt ("Meus codex, philosophe, natura rerum est creatarum, quae mihi quoties verba Dei legere cupio adesse consuevit" [PL 73, 1018]), will reappear in the works of the Dominican Humbert of Romans ("Treatise on the Formation of Preachers," 9.107, 2.9, in *Early Dominicans*, ed. and trans. Simon Tugwell [Ramsey, N.J.: Paulist Press, 1982], 217) and the Franciscan Bonaventure (*Quaestio disputata de mysterio Trinitatis 1.2* [Quaracchi: Collegium S. Bonaventurae ad Claras Aquas, 1891], 5:54–55).

4. Long, "Science of Theology," 80.

5. Ibid., 81–83.

6. Ps 138:4. I use the Douay translation, which is closest to Fishacre's Vulgate text.

7. The recreation of God's works will constitute the subject of the third book, and

selves and even more wonderful to us; wonderful in themselves because they are numbered (*numerosa*), formose[8] or beautiful (*formosa*), and good: "numbered" because even the tiniest atom of earth has an infinite number of parts; "formose" because in this atom are infinite forms, matter's garments as it were, that is figures or shapes; and "good" because by that same principle by which a thing is, namely its form, it is also good. The tiniest atom of the basest body, therefore, is full of beauty and goodness and power. Does not the sacred text say: "And God saw all the things that he had made, and they were very good"?[9]

If created beings are wonderful in themselves, moreover, how much more wonderful are they to creatures capable of wonder? Here, citing Seneca, Fishacre claims that the novel is more wonderful (in the sense of provoking wonder) than the great. But in the created world there are no two species that are alike, and within the species no two individuals that are alike. Every being is unique. This uniqueness—what the poet Hopkins called "the dearest freshness deep down things,"[10] is fully intelligible, as the psalmist indicates when he says "my soul knoweth right well."[11]

But how is it, Fishacre asks, that the divine and Godtaught (*theodoctus*) David wants to know created beings "right well" (*nimis*), since it is the vocation of the theologian to know the creator rather than creatures, the latter being the business of lowly arts students (*artistarum*)? It is a rhetorical question, but Fishacre's response is telling: alluding to the wellworn Pauline metaphor, he

their glorification the subject of the fourth: "In consequentibus libris 'mirabilia opera tua et anima mea cognoscet nimis.' Mirabilia quidem opera creationis, de quibus agitur in hoc secundo; mira etiam opera recreationis, de quibus in tertio; mira opera glorificationis, de quibus in quarto in fine," Fishacre, *In 2 Sent.*, prologus, ed. Long, 1:1.

8. The word, meaning "beautiful" or "comely," is obsolete in English (*OED* 1:466). I use it here to preserve the connection which is clear in the Latin between the concepts of form and beauty.

9. Fishacre, *In 2 Sent.*, prologus, ed. Long, 1:1.

10. Gerard Manley Hopkins, "God's Grandeur," in *Poems and Prose of Gerard Manley Hopkins* (Baltimore, Md.: Penguin Books, 1963), 27.

11. Fishacre, *In 2 Sent.*, prologus, ed. Long, 1:1.

contends that just as one who cannot gaze directly at the sun is able nonetheless to see it through a mirror, so the sun that is the divine intelligence can best be seen by our weak and damaged eyes through the mirror that is the created world.[12] It belongs, for example, to the science of astrology to study the heavenly bodies. Yet the astrologer constructs wooden models for the purpose of a better understanding of the celestial spheres.[13] Thus it is that the *sphaera mundialis* is touched on by the sacred writers, so that that intelligible sphere, of which it is said that its center is everywhere and its circumference nowhere, might be proclaimed.[14]

Herein is found, says Fishacre, the crucial distinction between the idle seekers after curiosities and the serious students of the created world. The former probe the secrets of creation for their own sakes, the latter for the sake of seeing there the reflection of the creator. Only the latter have a sense of purpose and can truly be called *studiosi*. The former, in the words of the psalmist, "are corrupt, and are become abominable in their ways."[15]

In commenting on distinctions 12 to 19 of book 2 of Lombard's *Sentences*, where he takes up the hexaëmeron or six days of creation, Fishacre remains true to the course he has plotted. In order better to understand the creations of the almighty he invokes *sensibilis experientia*, "sensible experience"[16] and even *experimenta*, "observations"[17] that are close at hand. In distinction 12, for exam-

12. The mirror is of course the governing metaphor in Alexander Nequam's *Speculum Speculationum* and Vincent of Beauvais's *Speculum Naturale*.

13. Fishacre is here obviously recycling an example he uses in the first proemium; see above.

14. Fishacre, *In 2 Sent.*, prologus, ed. Long, 1:2–3.

15. Ibid., 1:3.

16. See e.g., Fishacre: "Sicut docet nos etiam sensibilis experiential"; Fishacre, *In 2 Sent.*, 14.9, ed. Long, 1:288. The point here is that just as we observe that ebony is not consumed by fire, so neither are the stars.

17. See Fishacre, *In 2 Sent.*, 31.6.3, ed. Long, 2:205, where he refers to the *experimentum nautarum*, and dist. 14, cap. 4 (ibid., Appendix D, ed. Long, 2:360), where he uses the word *experimentator*, perhaps first used by Grosseteste (*De natura locorum*, in Ludwig Baur, ed., *Die philosophischen Werke des Robert Grosseteste*, *Beiträge* 9.68). See *Dictionary of Medieval Latin from British Sources* (London: Oxford University Press, 1986), fasc. 3:857.

ple, he finds a physical phenomenon to illustrate the position that the omnipotent God and we finite creatures enjoy a shared efficacy in procreation: namely, the spectacular effect of stained glass windows on the eye, which requires both light, the active element, and the color of the glass; one without the other does not produce the desired effect.[18]

In distinction 15 he argues that God conserves the entitative composition of contingent beings just as moisture holds paint on a wall (as in the fresco technique) or keeps the earth from turning into dust.[19]

To illustrate his view that a star generates light and heat in proportion to its size and speed he invokes the example of the lead on the shaft of an arrow, which is said by Aristotle in the *De caelo* to liquefy when released from the bow with sufficient velocity.[20]

To make sense of the puzzling text of the creation account: "Let there be a firmament in the midst of the waters, and let it divide the waters from the waters. And God made the firmament, and divided the waters which were under the firmament from the waters which were above the firmament [Gn 1:6–7]," Fishacre says that the higher sphere of water does not fall to its natural place beneath the firmament, as water in a jar with an opening at the bottom but sealed at the top does not fall lest a vacuum be created.[21] And in fact it is the water above the firmament that accounts for the blueness (*lapis lazuli*) of the sky, he says, just as it does in the depths of the sea.[22]

To the point that the element water (as the other elements) assumes the figure of a sphere unless impeded, Fishacre proposes

18. Fishacre, *In 2 Sent.*, 12.6, ed. Long, 1:249.

19. Ibid., 15.6, ed. Long, 1:320.

20. Ibid., 14.2, ed. Long, Appendix C, 2:341. This was obviously not an *experimentum* that Fishacre had tried for himself.

21. Ibid., 2:343.

22. Ibid.

this observation: that a goblet in the cellar of a house, that is in a place closer to the center of the earth, holds more liquid than the same goblet on the rooftop, because the surface of the liquid in the goblet when in the cellar is a portion of a smaller sphere (being closer to the center of the earth) and therefore more swollen (*tumorosior*) and more capacious than when it is a portion of a sphere that is farther from the center.[23]

In discussing the source of the stars' light, he weighs the position that the stars are composed of the four elements, not the fifth element favored by Aristotle. His determination of the question includes a whiff of humor, rare in a scholastic text: "If we posit that [namely, that the stars are composed of the four elements of earthly experience], they will raise a cry, that crowd of Aristotelian dabblers (*scioli*), and will stone us! But before making any assertion let us cast some stones at them, though these stones be not bright and indissoluble [as were the stars according to the Aristotelians]."[24]

My claim is by no means that Fishacre was himself an experimenter. Although it is perfectly plausible that some of his *experimenta* be based on his own observations, for the most part he relies on his authorities: Albumasar,[25] Alfraganus, Alhacen, Alpetragius, Euclid, and Ptolemy.[26] His principal authority for natural philoso-

23. Fishacre, *In 2 Sent.*, 14.5, ed. Long, 1:274. What Fishacre observed may have been caused simply by surface tension, such tension being more effective in a calm environment (like a cellar) than one more exposed to the winds (the rooftop).

24. Ibid., 14.9, ed. Long, 1:287.

25. The Arab astrologer, for example, is invoked in an attempt to locate paradise; See Fishacre, *In 2 Sent.*, 17.5, ed. Long, 1:351.

26. Whether Fishacre was reading these texts directly or via a secondary source is not always easy to determine. There is no question, for example, that he had Grosseteste's *Hexaëmeron* on his desk, as Richard Dales has amply demonstrated: See "The Influence of Grosseteste's *Hexaëmeron* on the Sentences Commentaries of Richard Fishacre, O.P. and Richard Rufus of Cornwall, O.F.M.," *Viator* 2 (1971): 271–300. Many of the writers he cites, however, are not to be found in Grosseteste's work nor in any of the other proximate sources we know he uses: Euclid, for example, Alfraganus, Albumasar, Alpetragius, and Maimonides. Though I have not yet discovered Fishacre's source or sources for these writers, I have argued elsewhere that Fishacre's

phy, however, remains the "Master of those who know."[27] To be sure, he feels at liberty to disagree with Aristotle, even assigning him to eternal punishment,[28] and he certainly never prefers the Stagirite's authority to Augustine's or even the Lombard's.[29] Yet he is convinced that Aristotle is in possession of the truth about the created realm. Realizing that the sacred text can bear more than one interpretation and noting indeed that the fathers not infrequently disagree on the meaning of a text, Fishacre insists, in a startling passage,[30] that they, that is the holy expositors, [with respect to disputed passages] be mindful only that they show that whatever truth be found in the writings of Aristotle is not contrary to scripture, in order that it may thus be plain to all that this our scripture be not contrary to the truth in any detail.[31] Thus the theologian who is properly grounded in philosophy should yield to the authority of the *physicus* in the latter's own proper realm—not only better to understand the sacred text but also to deny to nonbelievers the occasion to ridicule the faith itself.[32]

Far from being confined to the hexaëmeral questions or even to the *Sentences* Commentary, there is growing evidence that Fishacre's interest in natural philosophy intensified in his post-

encounter with much of Aristotle's natural philosophy was via a *florilegium*; R. James Long, "The Reception and Use of Aristotle by the Early English Dominicans," in *Aristotle in Britain during the Middle Ages*, ed. John Marenbon (Turnhout: Brepols, 1996), 51–56.

27. See Dante, *Inferno*, 4.131.

28. "Item novimus multos sapientes perisse aeternaliter, utpote Luciferum, Platonem, Aristotelem, et forte Salomonem et multos alios," *In 1 Sent.*, 12, in R. James Long, ed., "Moral and Spiritual Theology of Richard Fishacre: Edition of Trinity Coll. MS O.1.30," *AFP* 60 (1990): 21.

29. See Long, "Reception and Use," 53.

30. So startling is this claim in fact that all of the scribes but two alter the original reading: *aliis Aristotelis* RV: *aliarum* OP; *om.* BC. For *sigla* and descriptions of the manuscripts see R. James Long and Maura O'Carroll, SND, *Life and Works of Richard Fishacre OP. Prolegomena to the Edition of his Commentary on the "Sentences"* (Munich: Verlag der Bayerischen Akademie der Wissenschaften, 1999), 49–207.

31. Fishacre, *In 2 Sent.*, 13.2, ed. Long, 1:260.

32. One is reminded here of the unfortunate Galileo case.

Commentary period.[33] There is by him a question on the Ascension of Christ,[34] a treatise on heresies,[35] and a number of university sermons.[36] All of these genres make use of the new learning to discover more about the sacred text. There are in addition four lengthy discussions of questions suggested by the hexaëmeron that were not a part of the first redaction but that were apparently composed after the issuance of the Commentary (circa 1245–1246). These discussions are on light, on the nature of the heavens, on the waters above the firmaments, and on the eternal duration of the world,[37] and were inserted into the text in four later witnesses of the Commentary. There are indications, furthermore, that they were gathered originally in a *quaternus*.[38] This was referred to by a marginal note in a Cambridge manuscript,[39] which con-

33. This intensification of interest came in large measure as a result of his having come into contact with new sources, Greek and especially Arab, which were unknown to Grosseteste. It is in his mature work that Fishacre comes into his own as a thinker and emerges from the shadow of the formidable bishop of Lincoln.

34. See R. James Long, "Richard Fishacre's Quaestio on the Ascension of Christ: An Edition," *MS* 40 (1978): 30–55.

35. See R. James Long, "Richard Fishacre's Super s. Augustini librum de haeresibus adnotationes: an Edition and Commentary," *AHDLMA* 60 (1993): 207–79.

36. See R. James Long, "The Virgin as Olive Tree: A Marian Sermon of Richard Fishacre and Science at Oxford," *AFP* 52 (1982): 77–87; and Maura O'Carroll, SND, "Two Versions of a Sermon by Richard Fishacre, OP for the Fourth Sunday of Lent on the Theme *Non enim heres erit filius ancille cum filio libere*," *AFP* 54 (1984): 113–41.

37. For an edition thereof see R. James Long, "The First Oxford Debate on the Eternity of the World," *RTPM* 65, 1 (1998): 54–98.

38. For the use of the term in the High Middle Ages see Louis J. Bataillon, "Exemplar, Pecia, Quaternus," in Olga Weijers, ed., *Vocabulaire du livre et de l'Écriture au moyen Âge*, (Turnhout: Brepols, 1989), 206–19.

39. Viz. Cambridge, Gonville and Caius Coll. MS 329/410 (=*C*), fol. 170v: "hic deest questio de creatione vel inchoatione mundi que scripta est una cum questione vel inchoatione mundi que scripta est una cum questione de luce in parvo volumine ante questionem de heresibus." In addition, a manuscript containing the same work and once belonging to the Dominican convent of San Domenico in Bologna, now Bologna, Univ. MS 1546 (=*B*), at the same place in the text reads as follows: "questionem de eternitate mundi que deest habes in alio volumine questionum ..." Several folia later (viz. at fol. 175v), *C* has the following marginal note: "hic deest questione de luce que scripta est in parvo quaterno cum questionibus de heresibus." The accuracy and thoroughness of these notes, coupled with the number and range of the textual

tains as well other questions determined during his brief regency (1245–1248). The growing sophistication of these questions bears eloquent witness to Fishacre's continued absorption with philosophy up to the time of his death.

Elsewhere, I have argued that it was this project of Fishacre's that grafted the peculiarly English interest in the natural sciences onto the scholastic methodology being developed on the continent.[40] Here my intention was merely to hold Fishacre to the test of his own methodology. At the same time, I wished to elicit an answer to the question posed by the Tenth International Congress of Medieval Studies from this earliest of the Oxford-trained Dominicans.[41] The question is, namely, what is medieval philosophy? Fishacre's answer—and indeed that of the English tradition in general—would have been that philosophy is the knowledge of the created realm, what he called *scientia*, as guided by and enlisted in the service of the Christian faith.

---

additions in *C*, lead me to believe that they may be in the hand of Fishacre himself (or at least a scribe working under Fishacre's direction). Franz Pelster had reached the same conclusion on different grounds: "Das Leben und die Schriften des Oxforder Dominikanerslehrers Richard Fishacre (d. 1248)," *ZKT* 54 (1930): 522–23.

40. Viz. at the International Medieval Congress, University of Leeds, July 10, 1996, in a paper entitled "The Debate over the Science of Theology at the Early Oxford Studium." A recent study argues reductively that the Dominicans took the lead in appropriating Aristotle's natural philosophy specifically as part of their campaign against the Cathars, whose claim was that the world was evil; Roger French and Andrew Cunningham, *Before Science: The Invention of the Friars' Natural Philosophy* (Aldershot, UK: Scolar Press, 1996), 120 et passim. Later in the book the authors do concede that a second end was "the new theology with its systematic exposition (including that of Genesis, the story of creation), its new dialectic and its need for literal exposition," 140.

41. Robert Bacon, Fishacre's master, most likely studied at Paris; see Beryl Smalley, *The Study of the Bible in the Middle Ages* (Notre Dame, Ind.: University of Notre Dame Press, 1964), 265.

CHAPTER 3

Between Idolatry and Science

The Magical Arts in the Grosseteste School

Magic has always occupied the marches between religion on the one side and science on the other. It has also served as a crossing point where popular beliefs and folk religion intersect with the religion of the elite, expressed in the theology and philosophy of the schools.[1] Attributed by tradition to the Persian Zoroastrians,[2] this loosely defined phenomenon caught the attention of the bishop of Hippo, whose writings set the tone for Christian thinking on the subject until the twelfth century.[3] With the

1. See Richard Kieckhefer, *Magic in the Middle Ages* (Cambridge: Cambridge University Press, 1989), 1–2.

2. See especially Jan N. Bremmer, "The Birth of the Term Magic," in *The Metamorphosis of Magic from Late Antiquity to the Early Modern Period*, ed. Jan N. Bremmer and Jan N. Veenstra (Leuven: Peeters, 2002), 1–11. The story appears first in Isidore, *Etymologiae* 8.9; ed. Wallace M. Lindsay (Oxford: Clarendon Press, 1911), n.p.; and is repeated by Hugh of St. Victor, *Didascalicon*, cap. 15; ed. Charles H. Buttimer (Washington, D.C.: The Catholic University of America Press, 1939), 132.

3. See Fritz Graf, "Augustine and Magic," in *Metamorphosis of Magic*, ed. Bremmer, 87–103.

influx of the scientific literature of the Arabs and newly recovered Greek materials, however, Augustine's focus on the religious connotations of the magical arts faced new challenges and was extended to new fronts.[4]

The earliest scholastic to devote serious attention to the subject was William of Auvergne, master at the university of Paris and subsequent bishop of that city. William's interest in the *opera magica* was deep and long-standing. He remembers, he tells us in his *De legibus*, having read the books of the *magi*[5] and the sorcerers (*malefici*) from the time of his adolescence.[6] The final third of the second and final book of his monumental *De universo*, moreover, is devoted to the magical arts, including discussions of demons,[7] occult powers, divination, and astrology.[8]

William served as an important conduit of occult lore to the thinkers of the High Middle Ages.[9] In addition, he contributes a

4. See Steven Marrone, "Magic and the Physical World in Thirteenth-Century Scholasticism," in *Evidence and Interpretation in Studies on Early Science and Medicine. Essays in Honor of John E. Murdoch*, ed. Edith Sylla and William Newman (Leiden: Brill, 2009), 158–85. Marrone, in this stimulating article, looks at magic through the prism of the doctrine of *actio in distans* in three thirteenth-century masters: William of Auvergne, Thomas Aquinas, and Giles of Rome.

5. The term *magus* is more value neutral than *maleficus* (which is always negative) and will be used in this chapter instead of the English term "magician." Michael Scot, for his part, notes that the word has three different significations: *illusor* (a deceiver), *maleficus*, and *sapiens*; the three Magi of Matthew's Gospel played all three roles, but following their conversion became witnesses and *doctores* of the supreme king. See Bodley Library MS Canon. Misc. 266, fol. 3ra.

6. "Et haec omnia in libris iudiciorum astronomiae, et in libris magorum atque maleficorum tempore adolescentiae nostrae nos meminimus inspexisse," William of Auverge, *De legibus*, cap. 25, in *Guilielmi Alverni Opera Omnia*, vol. 1 (Paris, 1674; repr. Frankfurt am Main: Minerva, 1963), 78a.

7. On the intense variety and hybridity of the concept "demon" see Carl S. Watkins, *History and the Supernatural in Medieval England* (Cambridge: Cambridge University Press, 2007), 55–66. See also Frederick Van Fleteren, "Demons," in *Augustine through the Ages: An Encyclopedia*, ed. Allan D. Fitzgerald, et al. (Grand Rapids: William B. Eerdmans Publishing Company, 1999), 266–68.

8. Lynn Thorndike, *A History of Magic and Experimental Science* (New York: Columbia University Press, 1923), 2:339.

9. Graziella Federici Vescovini, *Medioevo Magico. La magia tra religione e scienza nei secoli XIII e XIV* (Turin: UTET libreria, 2008), 35. Mention should also be made

distinction which enables these thinkers to treat the subject with the seriousness and dispassionate objectivity that it deserves: in addition to demonic magic, roundly condemned by Augustine and all his readers, William introduces the category of natural magic (*magia naturalis*) that the philosophers, he says, call necromancy or philosophic magic (though quite improperly, he adds) and which he counts as the eleventh part of natural science. Natural magic for William is thus no more than a kind of applied science and no more illicit.[10] Ignorance of that science, on the other hand, leads many Christians to suppose that all marvels (*mira*) are the work of demons, whereas in fact many are natural occurrences, brought about by powers invested in nature by the creator.[11] In thus misapplying *mira*, moreover, they do double injury to the creator: not only do they deny power to the Godhead, says William, they also denigrate the subject of such marvels, which is nature.[12]

In William's view, therefore, nothing in the realm of natural magic is brought about through the agency of demons. This magic is, rather, often the work of good magicians, whom we call

of the astrological and magical writings of Michael Scot, produced during the same years, but though William and Michael make use of many of the same sources, they seem not to be aware of the writings of the other; ibid.

10. Thomas B. de Mayo, *The Demonology of William of Auvergne* (Lewiston, N.Y.: Edwin Mellen Press, 2007), 60.

11. "[William's] division of wondrous events into three causal categoris—divine miracles, demonic illusion, and the occult operations of nature—remained largely unchanged into the early modern period," ibid., 218

12. "Tertia causa fuit mirificentia quorundam operum, quae revera opera naturalia sunt: verumtamen quia procuratione daemonum naturas ipsas vel coniungentium vel commiscentium vel aliter ad operandum expedientium facta sunt, opera daemonum credebantur ab ignorantibus haec. Et de operibus huiusmodi est magia naturalis, quam necromantiam seu philosophicam philosophi vocant, licet multum improprie, et est totius licentiae naturalis pars undecima. Haec igitur mirifica homines ignari scientiae istius, quae natura operabantur virtutibus sibi a creatore inditis, credebant daemones operari, et propter hoc non solum potentiam magnam, et mirificam eisdem attribuerunt; sed etiam omnipotentiam; et hoc in duplicam iniuriam creatoris. Primum quia virtutem, quae talia operabatur, ab ipso creatore removebant, et etiam ab ipsa natura; cum et ipsius creatoris esset, et auctoris dominantis, et ipsius naturae, ut proprii subiecti, et beneplacito creatoris absque ulla rebellione ac contradictione servientis," *De legibus*, cap. 24, in *Opera Omnia*, 1:69b. See Vescovini, *Medioevo Magico*, 37.

magi. Creating an etymology of which Isidore would have been envious, William says that the word *magi* is derived from *magna agentes*, "doers of great things," and not, as some have erroneously maintained, from *male agentes*, "acting evilly." Those who bring about marvels by means of demonic ministry, on the other hand, are indeed evil and must be so regarded and so labeled.[13] William, it must be remembered, is writing in his role as a theologian to those who have some learning in these matters, and he tells them not to be surprised at such wondrous feats but rather to glorify the creator, knowing that it is by God's power alone that nature operates, not only in the customary manner known to men but also in new ways, sometimes producing new realities.[14]

Scholars in recent decades have been exploring the connections between the bishop of Paris and the bishop of Lincoln.[15] In matters of the occult, however, there is—so far as I can determine—little or no discernible influence of the former on the latter. As evidence of Grosseteste's own interest in the occult, one can cite an apparently early work, printed in the Baur edition, the *De impressionibus aeris* or *De prognosticatione*, in which the

13. "Harum igitur naturarum vires, et potentias occultas, qui noverunt, multa mirifica faciunt, et multo mirabiliora efficerent, si rerum eis huiusmodi facultas et copia suppeteret, et scientia non deesset, propter quod et magi huiusmodi homines vocati sunt, quasi *magna agentes*, licet quidam male interpretati fuerint magos, quasi *malos* seu *male agentes*. Qui autem ministerio daemonum talia operantur, revera et mali et mala agentes, et habendi et dicendi sunt," William of Auvergne, *De universo*," cap. 21, in *Opera Omnia*, 1:1058b.

14. "Qua de causa ut etiam maxime vigeret, et praestaret Christiana religio, indictum est, ut si quis talia, et taliter operaretur, malus, et maleficus haberetur, et non virtute naturae alicuius; sed magis adiutorio, et potentia daemonum huiusmodi opera facere putaretur. Qui autem in his docti sunt, talia non mirantur, sed solum creatorem in eis glorificant scientes, quod sola omnipotentissima voluntate ipsius natura operatur, et iuxta consuetudinem notam hominibus, et praeter consuetudinem non solum novis modis, sed etiam res novas," William of Auvergne, *De legibus*, cap. 24, in *Opera Omnia*, 1:69b–70a.

15. See e.g., Steven Marrone, *William of Auvergne and Robert Grosseteste: New Ideas of Truth in the Early Thirteenth Century* (Princeton: Princeton University Press, 1983), and Joseph Goering, "Where and When Did Grosseteste Study Theology?" in *Robert Grosseteste: New Perspectives on his Thought and Scholarship*, ed. James McEvoy (Turnhout: Brepols, 1995), 17–51.

author undertakes to predict the weather on April 15, 1249, many years in the future, and also to predict a poor wine and fruit harvest in the autumn of 1255, which would be two years after Grosseteste's own death.[16] Richard Dales,[17] Richard Southern,[18] and James McEvoy[19] accept the work as authentic. Nevertheless, serious objections have been raised about its authorship by Cecilia Panti.[20] In the absence of agreement the prudent course is to proceed to works that are unquestionably authentic. These include Grosseteste's *Dicta*, one of which is dedicated to the proposition that those who place their trust in the *artes magicae* are permitted to be mistaken in their predictions of the future; if events always transpired as the *magi* predicted, he argues, their arts would indeed be true; because they are false arts, events sometimes turn out otherwise than predicted—even if it is by God's mercy that the hoped for results are nullified in order to wean the gullible from trust in the fallacious.[21]

In his *Hexaëmeron*, moreover, Grosseteste takes a very critical view of astrology, one of the magical arts.[22] Granting that celestial bodies have some effect on events on earth (tides are an obvious example) and even on human temperaments—views commonly held by his contemporaries—Grosseteste draws the line at the free choice of the will:

16. *De prognosticatione*, ed. Ludwig Baur, in *Die philosophischen Werke*, (Münster i. W.: Aschendorff, 1912), 50–51.

17. Richard C. Dales, "Robert Grosseteste's Views on Astrology," *MS* 29 (1967): 357–58.

18. Richard W. Southern, *Robert Grosseteste: The Growth of an English Mind in Medieval Europe* (Oxford: Clarendon Press, 1986), 107, n. 35.

19. James McEvoy, *Robert Grosseteste*, (Oxford: Oxford University Press, 2000), 79.

20. Cecilia Panti, *Moti, virtù e motori celesti nella cosmologia di Roberto Grossatesta: studio ed edizione del trattati De spaera, De cometis, De motu supercelestium* (Florence: Societá internazionale per lo studio del medioevo latino, 2001), 45–46.

21. *Dictum* 114, Oxford, Bodlieian Library MS Bodley 798 (SC 2656), fol. 95rb; www.grosseteste, com/cgi-bin/dicta. I am grateful to Professor Joseph Goering, who is editing the *Dicta*, for calling my attention to this text.

22. See Edward Peters, *The Magician, the Witch, and the Law* (Philadelphia: University of Pennsylvania Press, 1978), 85–86.

For the free choice of a rational mind is subject to nothing in the rational order of things except God alone, but is rather placed above all corporeal creatures. Therefore, since the agent is nobler than the patient, a corporeal nature cannot by its action impress passions on the freedom of the will.... Therefore, whoever posits the efficacy of the stars on free will subjects the nature of the rational soul and the dignity of the human condition to a corporeal nature. And these people are enemies of human nature, since they subject it to what is naturally subject to it and deny that it is the image of God.... They also blaspheme against God, because they take away from God his dignity when they posit that the rational mind, which they concede to be the image of God, is lower than bodies.... We wish finally to give this warning, that astrologers of this sort are seduced and seducers, and their teaching is impious and profane, written at the dictation of the devil, and therefore their books ought to be burned. And not only they, but those who consult them, are lost.[23]

The Dominican master Richard Fishacre (†1248) was one of the earliest members of the Grosseteste school and a close reader of his *Hexaëmeron*.[24] Fishacre devotes considerable attention to the subject of magic and the magical arts.[25] However, he takes his inspiration in these matters directly from the Parisian masters William of Auvergne and Hugh of St. Cher. In the seventh distinction of book 2 of his *Sentences* Commentary, the Lombard says "It is also by the knowledge and power of these evil spirits

23. Translation is by Richard C. Dales, *The Scientific Achievement of the Middle Ages* (Philadelphia: University of Pennsylvania Press, 1973), 153–55. Original text can be found in Grosseteste, *Hexaëmeron* 5.10.1 & 5.11.1; ed. Richard C. Dales and Servus Gieben (Oxford: Oxford University Press, 1982), 166–67; 170. See also Marrone, "Magic and the Physical World," 164.

24. See Dales, "Influence of Grosseteste's *Hexaëmeron*," 272–74.

25. While it is conceivable that Fishacre was also acquainted with the works of Michael Scot, the latter takes a much more negative view of magic in general and, while allowing and perhaps even practicing astrology, he never uses the term "natural magic"; see Lynn Thorndike, *Michael Scot* (London: MacMillan, 1965), 116–17. Michael Scot also insists that the *ars magica* is not a part of philosophy (*Liber particularis*, Bodleian Library MS Canon. Misc. 555, fols. 21va–22rb).

that the magical arts are practiced."[26] Fishacre is prompted to ask two questions: upon what do the *magi* rely for the revelation of things hidden, called divination, and upon what for the performing of miracles? The first question divides itself into three specific questions: how can the *magi* reveal things that are hidden; are they ever wrong and, if so, for what reasons; and lastly, how do the astrologers differ from the prophets in revealing what is hidden?

As to the first question, responds Fishacre, that which is hidden or secret is either present or future; the present, moreover, is either proximate or remote. With respect to the former, that is present secrets that are close at hand, the *magus* can often divine what is hidden, because what a person is thinking reveals itself in his or her voice or even in body language and facial expressions. Although Fishacre's principal authority in this chapter is a small pastoral piece by Augustine, entitled *De divinatione daemonum*, he transfers to *magi* powers that Augustine attributes to demons. The more remote case he illustrates by the story of the messenger, whose arrival on a certain day in Paris is known to the *magus* nearly instantaneously.[27] The Lombard attributes knowledge of both proximate and remote *occulta* to what he calls a "refinement of nature" (*subtilitatem naturae*) on the part of the *magus*, a kind of sensitivity to signs and signals which the casual observer or someone not so finely attuned would miss.[28]

26. Peter Lombard, *2 Sent.* 7.6, trans. Giulio Silano (Toronto: Pontifical Institute of Mediaeval Studies, 2008), 2:30.

27. This is perhaps a variant on the story told by William of Auvergne of the holy man who was transported by malign spirits from the region of Burgundy to Rome within the space of two or three hours; *De universo,* cap. 23, in *Opera Omnia*, 1:1064a. Another possible source is the story told by Augustine in the *De divinatione* with respect to Carthage. Speed of travel is an attribute of demons, since they are composed of the element air, the thinnest of the elements, or (as in William's view) are absolutely incorporeal. See Graf, "Augustine and Magic," in *Metamorphosis of Magic*, ed. Bremmer, 97.

28. Fishacre, *In 2 Sent.*, 7.6, ed. Long, 1:136–37. William prefers the term "sense

Future events, on the other hand, are known and revealed in many ways. *Magi* often foretell acts that they themselves intend to perform as well as those they suggest to men who are perverted and greedy for earthly gain, aware from the character of such men that they will readily comply with their suggestions. Likewise, *magi* know the future from the course of the stars or other natural occurrences, signs that cannot be discerned by ordinary mortals. Finally, *magi* know the future from a revelation made to them either from angels or from prophets, whose writings have for the most part not reached us from the heathen, or, if they have, their readers have not understood them.[29]

As to the second question, namely, why are *magi* sometimes wrong in their predictions, Fishacre answers as follows: it is the case both that demons can be wrong and that *magi* can lie. Regarding the first, God can impede demonic predictions from being realized, for even phenomena that occur according to the laws of nature can be rendered void if the coefficiency of God is withheld. As for *magi* lying, there are two causes: either things turned out otherwise than the demons, from which the *magi* learned them, believed they would; or, supposing things transpired as the demons predicted, nevertheless since they delight in deceiving men, they lied to the *magi*.[30]

Third, and lastly, *magi* differ both from astrologers (*astrologi*) and from prophets. *Magi* predict the future relying on what has been revealed to them by demons. Astrologers, by contrast, reveal what they have expertly learned from the natural course of the stars. Fishacre adds, parenthetically, that occasionally the latter, as in the case of the three who came to adore the Christ Child,

---

of nature" (*sensus naturae*): "In multis animalibus fit ligatio et congregatio vel divina virtute et miraculose, ut diximus, vel *sensu naturae*, quae est una de radicibus magiae naturalis," *De legibus*, cap. 27, in *Opera Omnia*, 1:91a. See also Kieckhefer, *Magic in the Middle Ages*, 90.

29. Fishacre, ibid., 1:137.

30. Ibid., 1:137–38.

are also called *magi*.[31] Prophets, however, have learned the future either through God's revelation or that of an angel.[32]

For Fishacre, moreover, the umbrella term "magic" covers not only divination but also the phenomenon known as miracles (*miracula*). Within this context Fishacre organizes his analysis around three questions: first, what in the miracle derives from man, what from a demon, what from other sources; second, is there an *ars magica* that is to be numbered among the arts or is "art" said here mendaciously; lastly, in what way do marvelous occurrences (*mira*) brought about by *magi* differ from those realized by the saints (for example, the staff into serpent trick carried off by Pharaoh's men and Moses)?[33]

So to his first question: what in the magical deed is from man, what from a demon, and what from another source? In the act of magic that is deemed a miracle, says Fishacre, three things concur: the first is on the part of the *magus*, the second that of the demon, the third that of nature. For example, the *magus* wants to cure someone. What transpires? He pays homage to the demons, pleases them with sacrifices, and invokes those who are thus placated, so that one of those supplicated makes himself present to the wish of the mortally ill man. To the extent that the demon knows illnesses and the medications whereby cures are engendered, he examines the patient and then applies them to the sick man, albeit undetected. The medicines by their very natures bring about health. Therefore, although it is characteristic of *magi* to invoke the help of demons, applying medicines to a sick person

31. In large measure the Vulgate's use of the term "*Magi*" to identify the wise men who followed the star to discover the infant Christ (Mt 2:1–16) made it possible to incorporate a type of *magus* within the Christian dispensation. See Valerie Flint, *The Rise of Magic in Early Medieval Europe* (Princeton: Princeton University Press, 1991), 364–75. See also Thorndike, *Michael Scot*, 117–18.

32. Fishacre, *In 2 Sent.* 7, ed. Long, 1:138. Dales cites this passage as evidence that Fishacre was unwilling to go as far as Grosseteste in his condemnation of astrology; Dales, *Scientific Achievement*, 155.

33. Fishacre, ibid.

is the work of the demons and is done imperceptibly, in keeping with their caution; but actually to effect a cure belongs to nature: just as when a sick man is cured by a medical doctor, summoning the doctor is the role of the friends of the stricken man, applying suitable medications to him the role of the physician, and effecting a cure once the medications have been applied is the role of nature.[34]

Fishacre's second question of the triad is the crucial one: can magic be considered an art? It is now apparent that the art lies neither in the first step of the process outlined above, which is the work of the *magus*, namely to invoke, nor in the third, which is the work of nature, namely to bring about healing. The comparison to medicine is instructive: the medicine applied to a sick person owes its efficacy to nature, not to art. The art comes into play in the selecting of the medication and the deciding on the dosage suitable to the malady. The devil operates like the physician in healing, only more subtly and more efficaciously.[35]

Thus it would seem in Fishacre's analysis that the term "art" is wrongly applied to magic, or if there be any truth to the expression *ars magica*, it is owing to the fact that the "art" derives from the devil's operation, which is medicinal and thus exercising art (*artificiosa*); but the predicate "magic" derives from the part played by the *magus*, which is to invoke. For I do not think, says Fishacre, that there is any kind of art in the invoking of demons, just as there is not in the invoking of God—one does it as he or she wills—unless it be the case that some invocations are perhaps written down, ready for those wishing to make supplication, just as prayers are made and written down for the calling upon God. Therefore, just as there is no art that teaches one how to pray to God, so there is no art that teaches how to invoke demons, unless taking note of those things by which individual demons are delectably enticed may perhaps be called an "art" and is

34. Ibid., 1:138–39.

35. Ibid., 1:139.

a lore which *magi* have learned from demons. Fishacre then cites Augustine, who in one of several extended passages in the *City of God* expands on his views as to how demons are attracted: not by food, says Augustine, as animals would be attracted, but "by such symbols as suit their taste, various kinds of stones, woods, plants, animals, songs, rites," and the demons in turn instruct a few disciples, the *magi*, as to the nature of their desires.[36]

Fishacre lastly inquires about the miracles wrought by saints and the wondrous deeds of *magi* and asks in what way they differ? The philosophical foundation for any phenomenon that arouses our wonder, hence a *miraculum*, lies in the doctrine of seminal reasons or natures.[37] The potency of matter, declares Fishacre, is twofold: namely a passive potency, which is receptive of form; and an active potency, which is something of form latent in matter. This latter is called by Augustine a *ratio seminalis*, and in a later passage Fishacre, following Grosseteste,[38] identifies this with Aristotle's notion of "active potency."[39] This seminal reason in matter, moreover, has a corresponding causal reason in God. It is therefore possible that a seminal reason be educed from potency into act in two ways. Either it is realized through divine causal reasons

36. Ibid. See Augustine, *De civ. Dei* 21.6 (CCSL 48, 767).

37. Fishacre employs the same principles in his analysis of the question as to whether God can undo the past in distinction 25 of the same book; see Long, "Undoing the Past: Fishacre and Rufus on the Limits of God's Power," in *Laudemus viros gloriosos. Essays in Honor of Armand Maurer, CSB*, ed. Roland E. Houser (Notre Dame, Ind.: University of Notre Dame Press, 2007), 60–62.

38. See Grosseteste, *Hexaëmeron* 3.11.2, eds. Dales and Gieben, 111. See also Dales, "Influence of Grosseteste's *Hexaëmeron*," 289–93, and Maaike van der Lugt, *Le ver, le démon et la vierge. Les théories médiévales de la génération extraordinaire* (Paris: Les Belles Lettres, 2004), 85.

39. "Cum sit triplex opinio circa exitum rerum in esse: ... tertia media, quae est Aristotelis, quae ponit nec formas omnino latere nec omnino esse ab extrinseco, sed aliquid eius latere (et hoc est potentia activa materiae, quam hic Augustinus vocat 'rationem seminalem') et aliquid eius esse ab extrinseco agente, scilicet complementum et actus. Patet quod Augustinus est huius eiusdem opinionis cum Aristotele," Fishacre, *In 2 Sent.* 7, ed. Long, 1:151. See Long, "Undoing the Past," 61. On the role of *rationes seminales* in miracles see Marcia Colish, *The Stoic Tradition from Antiquity to the Early Middle Ages* (Leiden: Brill, 1990), 2:205–6.

immediately—and when something of this nature is brought about by the prayers of the saints, it is called a "miracle"—or it is brought into act by the mediation of agents other than the saints. The latter, moreover, can be effected in two ways: either nature alone acting as a medium brings this about, and in this case the result is called "natural," not "miraculous"; or nature acts together with the principle that is the will, and this will is either good, as that of an angel, or evil, as that of a devil. Thus it is that magical acts are brought about by the agency of the devil in consort with nature, the devil educing the seminal reasons found in matter from potency to act.[40]

The efficacy of good angels is the same, says Fishacre, educing namely from potency to act in cooperation with nature, the only difference being that they can do this so much more effectively and excellently than the fallen angels. And if such marvelous and unaccustomed things come about through angelic agency, they would not be very far removed from those things that happen magically. In other words, magical happenings are explainable through a combination of nature and created will. However, those things educed from potency to act in an unprecedented manner and immediately from causal reasons are miracles in the true and proper sense.[41]

The latter scenario, moreover, can happen in two ways. There are many causal reasons that have no corresponding seminal reason in matter. There is, for example, a causal reason for woman in the divine mind, but perhaps, says Fishacre, not a seminal reason in a rib, and when miracles such as this occur, they are brought about by God alone, nature having no role to play.[42] Miracles of

40. Ibid., 140. Hugh of St. Cher, with whose *Sentences* Commentary Fishacre was familiar, likewise denies that the pharaoh's *magi* truly produced miracles; it is simply the operation of nature: *In 2 Sent.*, dist. 7, BAV MS Vat. lat. 1098, fol. 51va.

41. Fishacre, ibid.

42. See Long, "Adam's Rib. A Test Case for Natural Philosophy in Grosseteste, Fishacre, Rufus, and Kilwardby," in *Robert Grosseteste and His Intellectual Milieu. New Editions and Studies*, ed. John Flood, James Ginther, and Joseph Goering (Toronto:

this sort are considered to be the greatest. There are some, however, that are educed from seminal power into act through causal reasons alone, which nevertheless nature also is able to accomplish, as we read for example in the Gospel accounts of the multiplication of the loaves and the changing of the water into wine at Cana. These are lesser or minor miracles according to Fishacre's taxonomy. The least type of miracle (*miraculum minimum*) is the bringing about of such happenings with the help of nature, but sooner and more quickly than nature itself could realize on its own. [43] (For example, the Castilian roses miraculously bloomed in winter from the life of the recently canonized St. Juan Diego.) Fishacre admits that he does not know whether this most minor of miracles is brought about by the agency of good angels, yet he has no doubt that they can be wrought by fallen angels with, of course, God's permissive will.[44]

Fishacre comments on the lemma "that they are not creators, even though the magicians made frogs and other things through them; God alone creates."[45] Here, he distinguishes between creating and producing. To create—whether it be the rational soul or Eve from the rib—requires infinite power, but the production into act from an active potency does not entail infinite power: between such an act and such potency there is not an infinite distance, as Fishacre explains in terms of his favorite metaphor.[46] Therefore, the finite power of a good or evil will, acting in consort with nature, is capable of this production.[47]

Fishacre next raises three questions concerning the limits of

Pontifical Institute of Mediaeval Studies, 2013), 158. See also Long, "Undoing the Past," 62.

43. See Long, "Undoing the Past," 61 and n. 11. Cf. Van der Lugt, *Le ver*, 226–27, who studies the same distinction, establishing his text from two manuscripts, both of which were well chosen.

44. Fishacre, *In 2 Sent.* 7, ed. Long, 1:140.

45. Peter Lombard, *2 Sent.* 8.1, trans. Silano, 2:31.

46. See Leo Sweeney and Charles Ermatinger, "Divine Infinity according to Richard Fishacre," *TMS* 35 (1957–58): 191–212.

47. Fishacre, *Sent.*, 1:151.

demonic power. First, are demons able to bring all seminal reasons into act, if permitted, or are there some that they cannot actualize? For it seems there is a limit, taking as a test case the miracle face off in the book of Exodus: the Pharaoh's wise men, who are *malefici*, were able to bring forth serpents and frogs, but not gnats (*sciniphes*).[48] But why could they not similarly produce a cow or indeed a man, as they did serpents and frogs? This leads Fishacre to the next question: are demons able to generate human beings, as legend had it that Merlin was born of an *incubus*?[49] Lastly, he asks whether demons can restore an eye or make a mute talk; the answer seems to be in the affirmative, and the proof text is the apocryphal Acts of Peter which tells the tale of Simon Magus, who made his dogs to sing and caused a man to speak.[50]

With respect to the first question, whether demons were able to bring all seminal natures into act, God permitting, Fishacre answers that it seems both bad and good angels are able to do all these things, the reason being that they had knowledge of the quantity of each element present in any seed whatsoever and thus the proportion of each in the seminal compound. Because this knowledge extended to the human seed, the demons were able to fashion such semen and deposit it in a woman's womb or in another container with the same dispositions as the maternal womb. Thus, without the agency of a man (because in Aristotelian genetic theory the male was the crucial factor, the woman serving simply as a receptacle) demons could engender a human-demonic

48. Ex 7:11–8:18.

49. William also tells the story of Merlin, without however mentioning him by name; *De universo*, cap. 24, in *Opera Omnia*, 1:1072a. Hugh of St. Cher, quoting the *magistri*, denies the truth of the Merlin legend: *In 2 Sent.*, dist. 7, fol. 51va. It was Geoffrey of Monmouth who first claimed that Merlin was fathered by an *incubus*, from whom he learned his occult powers; see *The Historia Regum Britanniae of Geoffrey of Monmouth with Contributions to the Study of its Place in British History*, ed. and trans. Acton Griscom (London: Longmans, Green and Co., 1929), 380–82.

50. Fishacre, *Sent.*, 1:140–41.

mixed breed.[51] This is, of course, the notorious *incubus* theory, a reminder that the tradition of magic always devoted a great deal of attention to sex and generation.[52]

Later in the chapter, Fishacre returns to the question: can demons generate human offspring, as one famously reads about Merlin? It is Fishacre's position that though a demon can assume the form of a human body, it cannot unite itself to it in the sense that it can vivify it, as does the soul. Thus it cannot cause the separation of semen (*decisio*),[53] a function of the animal soul, and thereby generate a human being. It can, however, seize semen when the human male secretes it, appropriate it into a body fashioned for itself, and, by lying with some woman, it can inject it into her, so that from that seed a man is made. It is in this way that the *incubi* can produce other hybrid demons.[54] Though Fishacre does not mention the *succubus*—either out of ignorance or discretion—the next generation of theologians adds this detail, that is, a demon who takes the form of a woman. The demon in this account appears to a man in the guise of a *succubus*, obtains semen from the man in the act of sexual intercourse, then immediately transforms itself into an *incubus* and impregnates a woman.[55]

The demons, according to Fishacre, are therefore unable to produce souls, only the matter in which souls inhere. If souls are derived from elsewhere, however, demons are capable of bring-

51. Ibid., 1:141.

52. William of Auvergne, for example, gives several instances of the phenomenon: See *De universo*, cap. 8 (1029b) and cap. 25 (1070b). See Thorndike, *History of Magic*, 353.

53. See the obsolete English word "decision" as a cutting off or separation; *OED*, 661. Hugh of St. Cher also employs the word; *In 2 Sent.*, dist. 7, fol. 51va.

54. Fishacre, *Sent.*, 1:143. The generation of half-human, half-demon hybrids, however, raises questions respecting the economy of salvation; see van der Lugt, *Le ver*, 190.

55. Van der Lugt claims that the notion of the *succubus* does not become common until the second half of the thirteenth century, though it is found already in Walter Map in the twelfth century; *Le ver*, 200–201. See Kieckhefer, *Magic in the Middle Ages*, 197. This fantastical tale was based loosely on later medieval exegesis on Genesis 6, 4; ibid.

ing into being some wondrous things, such as serpents, frogs, and talking dogs—all of which are encountered in the pages of the canonical scriptures or the apocrypha. What all these phenomena have in common is that they serve no purpose; they are useless. Why is that the case? The demons envy us and therefore have no care to provide anything that will contribute to our good.[56]

Fishacre, however, is unwilling to leave it at that. Why can't the demons produce useful as well as useless things? I don't see it, he says, and asks whether it wasn't the case that the angels, both good and bad, who appeared in human guise, composed their own bodies out of the four elements. Furthermore, wasn't the body of Adam, from which our bodies derive, already present seminally in the four elements at an earlier day of creation? Yet, finally, Fishacre is unwilling to grant such power to the angels, good or bad.[57]

At this point Fishacre lights upon what is for him a useful distinction: there are in nature two modes of generation, sexual and spontaneous (as from putrefaction, for example). Moreover, both good and bad angels are capable of spontaneous generation. Hence it is that the *magi* of pharaoh, and indeed Moses and Aaron, could produce serpents and frogs. As for the apparent inability of pharaoh's team to produce gnats (*sciniphes*), they *could* indeed produce them, but were not permitted to do so by God. The generation that is effected by means of sexual coupling, however, is beyond the power of angels and demons.[58]

Ultimately, the reason demons cannot produce a human being, though they know the proportion of the elements in semen and can even produce it, is what Fishacre calls the *ultima dispo-*

56. Fishacre, *Sent.*, 1:141. Hugh of St. Cher likewise suggests that utility is the crucial difference; of what use are dogs that sing or images that walk, he asks: *In 2 Sent.*, dist. 7, fol. 51va.

57. Fishacre, *Sent.*, 1:141–42.

58. Ibid., 1:142. See Hugh of St. Cher, *In 2 Sent.*, dist. 7, fol. 51va.

sitio corporalis, which makes the body a necessity with respect to the rational soul.[59] Created spirits, angels, and demons, which have not been united to bodies, have no power over a disposition of this sort; such power resides only with God and such creatures empowered to emit semen. However, with respect to the examples in the book of *Exodus*, namely serpents and frogs, Fishacre's answer is that they belong to an intermediate range of living things: animals that come into being from putrefaction, that is, asexually, and thereafter reproduce sexually. He finds, furthermore, support for this position in Augustine: "Many animals … grow up and produce offspring by copulating, although they themselves came into being asexually."[60]

Therefore, Fishacre concludes, because the angels and demons have power over a mixture of elements and thus are able to fashion a body in the figure of a human body in which they appear, such a body cannot be properly speaking a human body. If it were integrally human, it would possess a necessity with respect to the rational soul, and thus would immediately possess such a soul.[61]

Can the demons repair an eye or restore the ability to speak, Fishacre asks. Again, the answer is that they might know the elemental composition of an eye or a tongue, but parts of the animal body or human body function as such only if united with a soul, and this, as we have seen, is beyond the power of demons. That said, Fishacre adds that there are many infirmities impeding speech and vision which the demons do know how to cure. As for the case of the talking dog, Fishacre says that it is not the dog speaking but a devil speaking through the dog's mouth, just as once in paradise the devil spoke through the mouth of a serpent and oftentimes through the mouth of those possessed, that is demoniacs. Similarly, an angel perhaps—Fishacre professes

59. See Fishacre, *In 2 Sent.* 18, ed. Long, 1:362–63.
60. Augustine, *De Trin.* 3.7 (CCSL 50, 140).
61. Fishacre, *Sent.*, 1:142-43.

not to know—spoke through the mouth of the ass of Balaam (Nm 22:28–30).[62]

Another facet of the rich and complex tradition of magic is the power of amulets and charms to summon and constrain demons. According to Augustine's catalogue these include "various kinds of stones, woods, plants, animals, songs, and rites."[63] The interesting question for Fishacre is this: if these things are indeed efficacious, does this attraction or coercion come about by the agency of nature or the agency of the will?[64]

It seems to Fishacre that the attraction does not occur through the nature of the amulet, because the attraction would then affect equally every member of the same species, as when the lodestone naturally attracts iron, it attracts not only this particular piece of iron but all iron indifferently. Therefore, if a certain herb attracts this demon, it will equally and indifferently attract every demon, since all are of the same species. Likewise, since the good and bad angels are of the same species, the aforementioned herb will attract not only every demon but every angel as well. Again, let us suppose that the aforementioned herb has attractive powers. Why then would a demon (or all the demons and angels) be drawn to the one specimen in your possession, when there are many others of the same species? Moreover, even if yours were a unique member of the species and none other existed in act, does the option remain of educing a specimen from its seminal existence in the four elements, something of which Fishacre has decided the demons are capable? After all, since the *magi* can make frogs and serpents at the behest of the pharaoh, and since every animal is nobler in kind than every plant, why are *magi* not able to produce a stone or a plant from the four elements? And, if this is so, how

62. Ibid., 1:143. Fishacre's source here may well have been Hugh of St. Cher: see *In 2 Sent.*, dist. 7, fol. 51va.

63. Augustine, *De civ. Dei* 21.6 (CCSL 48,767).

64. Fishacre, *Sent.*, 1:144.

will the demon be attracted to your herb in particular, since whenever it wishes it can produce one that is similar?[65]

Likewise, demons possess only the apprehensive or intellective power, not the sensitive or the imaginative, because they are not endowed with a sensible soul. For any being, the presence of a beloved object is a cause of delight. A corporeal thing, however, is not present to the intellect nor can it be except through its intelligible likeness (or *species*). But angels and demons, purely spiritual beings, find delight only in an intelligible species, which is neither stronger in a more proximate location nor weaker in a more remote. Therefore, it is equally present to the being in which is found only the apprehensive and intellective power; thus, a thing that is very remote is equally delectable. Unless this were the case, when the angels, who find mutual delight in the presence of other angels, are sent on a mission to earth, their pleasure would be threatened owing to their distance from other beloved angels. Therefore, states Fishacre, the aforementioned herb—or, more accurately, the intelligible species thereof—equally delights a demon at a great distance, as if it were present, and this is a further reason that it is not especially drawn by the particular herb in your possession.[66]

For that matter, says Fishacre, a pure spirit does not delight in taste as taste or odor as odor. Such responses require a sensitive soul. Instead, the pure spirit delights in corporeal things only insofar as they are intelligibly good or beautiful. But if the attractive power of an herb lies only in its goodness and its beauty, the demon can certainly discover better and more beautiful things elsewhere. Where, then, is the attraction, Fishacre asks. Likewise, the attractive object naturally acts on that which is attracted to it. Therefore, if the by now famous herb were to attract this demon naturally, it would naturally act on the demon; that is, the less

65. Ibid.

66. Ibid., 1:145.

noble would act on the nobler. But this is impossible, concludes Fishacre.[67]

Likewise, Fishacre continues, it is considered heretical to make free choice subject to the stars, to believe the stars could force someone to want to do something or in fact to do it. If free choice nevertheless is not subject to the stars, much less is choice subject to baser bodies (for example, herbs), which themselves are subject by their nature to the stars. How, therefore, are Augustine's remarks in the above mentioned passage true, that is, that demons are subject to such things?[68]

If it is the case, then, that demons are not forced or even attracted by the nature of corporeal things, Fishacre continues, does the power of amulets and talismans derive from some will? Clearly the power does not come from any human will, for the will of a man does not have power over the will of another, only over the other's body. *A fortiori*, no human will has power over the will of a demon by nature, unless it is by the power of God. Nor is a demon drawn or forced to fulfill the disordered will of the *magus* by means of a divine or angelic will, since the latter do in no way consent to the evil entailed; and although they might permit the deed, they do not lend a hand. The sole exception is conceivably a case in which an alpha demon decrees that the will of the *magus* be enacted; thus one of the subordinate demons, eager to please its superior, is drawn to act on behalf of the *magus* or is forced to do so by the dominant demon.[69]

At this point Fishacre raises ten objections to the claim that demons obey other demons, focusing on the motivation for such alleged obedience, and then answers each in turn. For example: one is moved to act either out of love or fear. In the case of the demons it is clearly not out of love, Fishacre argues, nor for that

67. Ibid. Fishacre's proof text here is the sixth book of Augustine's *De musica*.

68. Fishacre, *Sent.*, 1:145. See n. 23 above for its source in Grosseteste.

69. Ibid., 1:145–46.

matter does it seem to be out of fear, for what greater punishment can the demon suffer than eternal damnation? The demon does have something to fear, however, and that is to be stripped by the alpha demon, the devil, of the power to tempt and seduce, in which demons take their greatest delight. Why then is it necessary, he asks, for the *magus* to enlist the service of demons by means of songs or chants or adjurations, when the demons naturally take delight in human iniquity? The answer, says Fishacre, is that there is an even stronger motive in their desire for veneration and self-adulation and whatever accrues thereto. However, even the will of a demon is free and not subject to coercion. Yet the coercion in this case, while not sufficient, is efficient. It is like the situation of one in danger from the sea who is forced to jettison merchandise lest he perish (borrowing the famous example from Aristotle's *Ethics*).[70]

One of the objections raised by Fishacre has to do with the occult powers of Solomon, as related by Peter Comestor in the *Historia scholastica*. According to the story told by Peter, which is based in turn on a passage in Josephus's *Jewish Antiquities*,[71] Solomon "thought up adjurations, by which illnesses are wont to be mitigated, others by which demons are cast out, still others by which those expelled do not return. He also invented characters, which were inscribed on gems, which placed in the noses of the possessed along with the root shown to Solomon (the root of the balsam brought to him by the queen of Sheba), freed one from the demons."[72] This

70. *Eth. Nic.* 3.1 (1110a8–11).

71. Josephus, *Jewish Antiquities*, VIII, §45ff. See Thorndike, *History of Magic*, 279–84; and Thorndike, *Michael Scot*, 120.

72. Petrus Comestor, *Historia scholastica*, cap. 7 (PL 198,1352). Petrus Riga (ca. 1180–1190) repeats the same tale:

Das de carminibus milia quinque Deo.
        Quicquid in arboribus, virgultis, floribus, herbis,
Seminibusve latet in Salomone patet.
Omnes naturas pecudum cognovit et omnis
Reptilis et piscis omnis et omnis avis.

knowledge, Fishacre adds, was much valued and even necessary before the coming of Christ.[73]

With respect to these occult powers, whose existence Fishacre accepts on the authority of Comestor, he says that the demons obeyed Solomon's adjurations not for evil, but for good, because God subjected the malign spirits to his power and to the will of his holy ones, as we read for example in Luke's Gospel (10:17): "The seventy <disciples> returned saying: Lord, even the demons submit to us in your name." The gems and adjurations and the root of the balsam, moreover, were a part of the dispensation under the Old Law, as we read in John 5:2–7: When the water of the probatical pond was stirred, the first one to be immersed in it was cured, but not by the water. In like manner, it was not by the power of a root or a gem that a demoniac was cured, says Fishacre, but by the power of God and the ministry of a good angel and the secondary agency of a man.[74]

Therefore, concludes Fishacre with his accustomed modesty, "concerning these occult matters I presume to assert nothing, and yet I am not silent." Demons are summoned or conjured not by things, called amulets, insofar as amulets are natures instituted by God, but rather insofar as they are signs, not natural but conventional signs, a kind of signal system devised by the demons and revealed by them to the *magi*.[75] Moreover, because the demons envy

---

Invenit voces quibus adiurare solebat
Egrorum morbos subsidiumque dabat.
Obvia spiritibus invenit verba malignis,
Inde fugabat eos, nec remeare sinens;
Deque characteribus fuit auctor, quos pretiosis
Inscripsit gemmis, mira potenter agens;
Quas cum radice quam novit naribus egri
Ponens, pellebat demonis omne genus,

Aurora: Petri Rigae Biblia versificata, ed. Paul Beichner, Part I (Notre Dame, Ind.: University of Notre Dame Press, 1965), 291.

73. Fishacre, 1:148.

74. Ibid., 1:149–50.

75. See Kieckhefer, *Magic in the Middle Ages*, 38.

one another and find delight therefore only in their own proper veneration, lest their marks of respect be mixed together such that no one should have his own proper honors, each establishes his own proper mark or amulet that honors him and him alone in a special way. Thus, if anyone should want to honor the kind of demon that presides over lechery, for example, he must make use of the physical object that is the agreed-upon sign, which signifies the intention on the part of the devotee of venerating that particular demon.[76]

Several pages later Fishacre gives what we may regard as his final thought on the matter:

> It is clear therefore that they who have thought that the *magi* or the demons are some sort of gods, to the extent that they reveal what is hidden or were able thus to bring about wonders, have most seriously erred by paying them adoration and by sacrificing to them what is owed to God alone. For just as we do not pay divine worship (*obsequia*) to those twisted men skilled in the knowledge of the stars, even though they were able to reveal many hidden things to us, in like manner neither should we offer the same to *magi* or to demons, nor for the same reason to physicians who can foretell the health and death of many, and indeed can accomplish either by the aid of natural remedies.... Thus divine worship must not be extended to demons, because in certain operations they outstrip men, doing what we cannot do or doing more quickly what we are able to do, just as we do not show deference to animals, who in many matters surpass human beings.[77]

It is well established that Richard Rufus of Cornwall, who became a Franciscan late in life, was a close reader and constant critic of his Dominican rival, who was now at least two years in the grave. To begin with, much of Rufus's text, nearly a third, is a verbatim and unacknowledged reproduction of the Fishacre

76. Fishacre, 1:148.

77. Ibid., 1:152. Dales calls attention to the same passage; *Scientific Achievement*, 155–56.

text.[78] Most of the reproduced passages pass without comment. However, Rufus does object, usually in Augustine's name, to the extent of the powers that Fishacre grants to the demons, referring them instead to the unmediated act of God.

For example, where Fishacre attempts to explain the apparently miraculous power of the *magus*, acting under demonic inspiration to read our innermost thoughts, Rufus objects that this does not take place universally or always necessarily, citing pseudo-Augustine as his authority.[79]

Furthermore, Rufus denies that Moses (and *a fortiori* the pharaoh's team) actually turned his staff into a serpent, but only symbolically (*imaginarie*). We know this to be the case, he says, because if it had been a true metamorphosis, the staff would have remained a serpent; but, as we know from the sacred text, Moses subsequently used his staff to deliver plagues, to part the sea, to split the rock in Horeb, and so forth.[80] Augustine's rule of thumb, Rufus reminds his readers, is that a demon cannot transform any nature that nature itself cannot transform, and there is no wood found in nature that can produce a serpent.[81]

As to the question of the devil cooperating with nature in producing things out of semen, Rufus simply replies that he does not want to go there—*nec multum volo in hac quaestione sollicitari*—and invokes the authority of Augustine who says that it is impossible for a person to explore this issue.[82] He then, however, reverses himself and claims that both the staff of Moses and that of the pharaoh's *magi* were truly changed into serpents, but that this was accomplished solely by the power and the will of God.[83] The devil operates within the bounds of nature and is able merely to accomplish the same results more quickly and easily (*citius et facilius*).[84]

78. In the edited text of Rufus presented in this volume, italic font indicates these verbatim borrowings.

79. Richard Rufus, *In 2 Sent.* 7, Balliol Coll. MS 62, col. 62.

80. Ibid.

81. Ibid.

82. Ibid.

83. Ibid.

84. Ibid.

Nor does Rufus want to admit that the devil (it is always *diabolus*, never *daemon*) is able to produce semen, even though the devil knew the proportion of the elements of which it is constituted, and even though "some say the opposite." It pleases God rather that human semen be secreted from a mature man.[85]

With respect to the devil appearing in human form, Rufus again denies that the evil one himself forges a true human body out of the four elements; it is only an apparent human body. The same holds for the instances of the devil speaking through the mouth of a serpent or the mouths of demoniacs: corporeal nature obeys not the devil but God, permitting the devil's evil will to be fulfilled.[86]

Lastly, on the question of the devil generating a human being by lying with a woman, Rufus accurately quotes Fishacre's account, but expresses his unwillingness to assert anything (*in hac quaestione nolo ego aliquid asserere*). Moreover, he reminds his readers of the authoritative testimony of Augustine:

> Whether angels, inasmuch as they are spirits, could have bodily intercourse with women ... it is doubtful. However, Scripture testifies that angels have appeared to men in such bodies as could not only be seen, but also touched. There is, too, a very general rumor, which many have verified by their own experience, or which trustworthy persons who have heard the experience of others corroborate, that sylvans and fauns, who are commonly called *incubi*, had often made wicked assaults upon women, and satisfied their lust upon them; and that certain demons ... are constantly attempting and effecting this impurity is so generally affirmed, that it were impudent to deny it. From these assertions, indeed, I dare not determine whether there be some spirits embodied in an aerial substance (for this element, even when agitated by a fan, is sensibly felt by the body), and who are capable of lust and of mingling sensibly with women.[87]

85. Ibid.

86. Ibid.

87. Augustine, *De civ. Dei* 15.23 (CCSL 48,488–89). Aquinas in endorsing the notion of the *succubus* cites the same passage (*Summa theologiae* 1.51.3. ad 6).

You hear, concludes Rufus, how temperately and prudently Augustine refuses to determine this question, in favor of which nevertheless he had adduced such powerful testimony.[88] The implication is that Fishacre rashly rushes to judgment on the basis of much thinner evidence, an argument in other words *ad verecundiam*.

What is clear is that the possibility of magic as one of the legitimate arts does not fully engage Rufus: *non volo sollicitari, nolo aliquid asserere*. He pauses, moreover, in his rather desultory treatment only to correct Fishacre by appealing to the authority of Augustine.

Fishacre, for his part, is at constant pains to find natural explanations for phenomena that previous generations of theologians and certainly the popular mind tended to attribute to preternatural and even supernatural causes, in particular the demonic world. Magic and natural philosophy are old enemies, and the latter seeks always to eliminate the mysteries and irrationality of magic; as our knowledge of nature and the workings of nature grow, the scope for the preternatural diminishes.[89]

On the other hand, Fishacre the theologian is well aware of the claims of religion, in particular the testimonies of scripture and tradition, respecting phenomena that defy natural explanation and that are attributed to divine or angelic intervention—in short, the various classes of *miracula* "miracles." Paradoxically, it is by removing many marvels from the realm of demonic power that the truly exceptional nature of the miraculous is heightened and emphasized and also the author of nature further glorified.

In matters magical Fishacre is true to his stated purpose in the *Sentences* Commentary about how to explore the difficult

88. Rufus, Appendix, §32. Gervase of Tilbury, writing in the last quarter of the twelfth century, likewise supported the *incubi-succubi* phenomenon on the basis of a widespread folk belief; see Watkins, *History and the Supernatural*, 222.

89. See Flint, *The Rise of Magic*, 6–7.

questions concerning the faith.[90] He does so by making use of the latest tools of analysis, the Aristotelian categories of active and passive potencies, matter and form, and dispositions, nature, and the particulars regarding human reproduction. And because moral matters do not fall within the scope of the *Sentences*, there is no talk here of idolatry or superstition or even curiosity, all relevant categories for moral theology.

To be sure, Fishacre's demonology leaves a number of unanswered questions.[91] His philosophical analyses are also sometimes strained, which is Rufus's incessant charge. Nevertheless, there is much to admire in his attempts. If his immediate successors—Albert the Great, Bonaventura, and Thomas Aquinas—were more successful, or at least more coherent, it was the pioneering effort of Richard Fishacre that helped to show the way.

90. Richard Fishacre, *In 1 Sent.*, prologue, in "The Science of Theology according to Richard Fishacre: Edition of the Prologue to his *Commentary on the Sentences*," ed. R. James Long, *MS* 34 (1972):98. In this same prologue, however, he signals a negative assessment of things magical, commenting on the verse in the epistle of James (3:15): "For this is not wisdom, descending from above; but earthly, sensual, devilish." He says that the last category, *scientia diabolica*, encompasses heretical and magical sciences, the latter including "judgments of the stars," geomancy, all divinations and auguries and casting of lots; ibid., 79.

91. For example, Fishacre is reluctant to shed the folk belief that demons inhabit the lower air and have after the Fall aerial bodies, here invoking the authority of Isidore: "Hi corporum aeriorum natura vigent; ante transgressionem quidem caelestia corpora gerebunt, lapsi vero in aeriam qualitatem conversi sunt," Fishacre, *In 2 Sent.*, 3.4.3, ed. Long, 1:73. See also ibid., 8.1, 1:157–61, where Fishacre concludes that although demons do not have bodies naturally united to them, they don them, as we do a set of clothing. Hugh of St. Cher, commenting on the lemma SUI GENERIS, had likewise ventured the opinion that demons have "aerial bodies;" see *In 2 Sent.*, dist. 7, fol. 51rb. William of Auvergne, on the other hand, had a more forward-looking angelology, insisting that angels were completely bodiless, not made of air or ether; see de Mayo, *Demonology*, 125. On the demons inhabiting the lower air see ibid., 140.

CHAPTER 4

Of Angels and Pinheads

The Contributions of the Early Oxford Masters to the Doctrine of Spiritual Matter

Surely one of the strangest doctrines to emerge from the intense theological debates of the thirteenth century was the concept of "spiritual matter."[1] Traceable to the *Fons vitae* of Ibn Gabirol, spiritual matter (or "universal hylomorphism") in tandem with the doctrine of the plurality of forms became one of the pillars of what used to be called with such confidence "the Franciscan School."[2] In fact, as I shall argue, this terminologically gauche

1. On the face of it an oxymoron, spiritual matter is more generally referred to by historians of philosophy by the less obtrusive label, "universal hylomorphism." The most complete treatment of the issue is still the dissertation of Erich Kleineidam, *Das Problem der hylomorphen Zusammensetzung der geistigen Substanzen im 13. Jahrhundert, behandelt bis Thomas von Aquin* (Breslau Inaug.-Diss, 1930). For corrections and additions to the latter see Odon Lottin, "La composition hylémorphique des substances spirituelles; les débuts de la controverse," *RNSP* 34 (1932): 21–41.

2. See e.g., Etienne Gilson, *Christian Philosophy in the Middle Ages* (New York: Random House, 1955), 327–53, and David Knowles, *The Evolution of Medieval Thought* (London: Longmans, Green and Co., 1962), 235–48. *The Cambridge History of Later*

teaching exemplifies the occasional ill fit between the newly discovered natural philosophy of Aristotle and traditional Christian teaching.

The metaphysical testing ground par excellence for the compatibility of these two world views was the doctrine of the angels, spiritual substances that were at the same time limited and mutable. How, in philosophically coherent language, was one to account for their composition (or lack thereof) and their distinctiveness both from the incarnate spirits below them in the chain of being and the infinite spirit above them? Indeed, how account for their distinction from one another?

In the three or four decades before positions hardened into the *Wegenstreit* between the Dominicans [read "Thomists"] and the Franciscans, masters belonging to both orders, as well as secular masters, debated the issue without the constraints of following a party line. I intend here to focus on the contributions to this debate of the earliest Oxford theologians who wrote on the subject: Grosseteste, Fishacre, and Rufus—a secular, a Dominican, and a Franciscan respectively.[3]

The Fourth Lateran Council in 1215 had set the parameters for Christian belief concerning the angelic nature, that it was, namely, spiritual: "creator omnium visibilium et invisibilium, spiritualium et corporalium: qui sua omnipotenti virtute simul ab initio temporis utramque de nihilo condidit creaturam, spiritualem et corporalem, angelicam videlicet et mundanam."[4] But "spiritual" was philosophically imprecise (as imprecise as *mundanam*, "earthly," in the

Medieval Philosophy: From the Rediscovery of Aristotle to the Disintegration of Scholasticism, 1100–1600, ed. Norman Kretzmann, et al. (Cambridge: Cambridge University Press, 1982) talks of "Franciscan thinkers" and even "Franciscan thought" but avoids mention of a "Franciscan School."

3. Although one cannot ignore the influence of Parisian theologians (among them William of Auvergne, William of Auxerre, Alexander of Hales, and Philip the Chancellor) on their English counterparts, what one finds on investigation is that the distinctively empirical orientation of Oxford infuses even their angelology.

4. Conc. Lateranense IV (1215); Henricus Denzinger, *Enchiridion symbolorum,* editio no. 31, ed. Carolus Rahner (Rome: Herder, 1960), no. 428.

same formula) and needed to be translated into Aristotelian terms. And herein lay the difficulty. Did "spiritual" mean pure form, as were the separate substances in Aristotle's cosmos? If so, how account for their finitude on the one hand and for their individuation on the other hand? It was to respond to these metaphysical exigencies that the notion of "spiritual matter" was born.

Although Grosseteste's influence on speculative theology at the Oxford *studium*, especially on the Franciscans, is difficult to exaggerate, it seems that he was not responsible for the doctrine of spiritual matter. On a number of occasions, in fact, Grosseteste insists that the angels are immaterial both in their nature and their activity.[5] The sole statement of his to the contrary—namely, that in comparison with the absolute simplicity of God all creatures are material—can be explained away by the context.[6]

There is a lack of any evidence to the contrary.[7] Therefore, we can assume that the Dominican master, Richard Fishacre, was the first Oxford theologian to subscribe to the doctrine of spiritual matter with respect to angels and human souls.[8] That he gives

5. See e.g., this passage from Grosseteste's *De cessatione legalium*: "Igitur simpliciter universitatem reducere ad completam unitatem non est, ut videtur, alio modo possibile, nisi isto, videlicet ut intelligimus angelum primo creatum a Deo ex nichilo, qui non potest uniri corpori in unitatem persone nec participare cum corpore in aliqua unitate, nisi forte in unitate secundum genus. Anima autem rationalis et angelus communicant in natura rationalitatis et intelligencie, qua communicacione habent indissolubile vinculum et concatenacionem naturalis unitatis," 3.1.27; ed. Richard C. Dales and Edward B. King, Auctores Britannici Medii Aevi, British Academy (London: Published for the British Academy by the Oxford University Press, 1986), 130.

6. See James McEvoy, *The Philosophy of Robert Grosseteste*, 2nd ed. (Oxford: Clarendon Press, 1982), 133.

7. Although Roger Bacon also held a theory of spiritual matter, "there is not a single shred of evidence that Bacon returned to Oxford <as a master of Arts> and that he studied theology under Adam Marsh" (Jeremiah Hackett, "Scientia Experimentalis: From Robert Grosseteste to Roger Bacon," in *Robert Grosseteste: New Perspectives on his Thought and Scholarship*, ed. James McEvoy, Instrumenta Patristica 24 [Turnhout: Brepols, 1995], 98).

8. Unaware of its origins in the *Fons vitae*, Fishacre remains convinced that the doctrine was Augustine's. See John Wippel, "Essence and Existence," in *The Cambridge History of Later Medieval Philosophy,* ed. Norman Kretzmann, et al. (Cambridge: Cambridge University Press, 1982), 408–10.

careful consideration to the former is evident by the sheer volume of text he devotes to the subject—that is, approximately a third of the second book of his *Sentences* Commentary, from distinctions 2 to 11 inclusive.[9] In the first half of the thirteenth century only the *Summa fratris Alexandri* is comparable in terms of length of treatment.

Fishacre asks first whether angels exist and second what they are. As to the former, he furnishes the reader with no more than probable arguments. It is, however, the latter question that I would like to investigate, because that brings us to the heart of his treatment of "spiritual matter." Early in the first book (viz. at distinction 8) he had already broached the subject. The angel and the human soul, he asserts, are composed substances, composed namely of matter and form. For if the angel were a form without matter, it would be mutually penetrable with other spiritual substances, that is, the angel itself, not merely a similitude, would be in the mind of one understanding it.[10] The upshot is that if one angel understands all the other angels, they will all be in that one angel.[11] Indeed, according to this metaphysics the demons cannot

9. This constitutes 209 pages in the printed edition. The outline of Fishacre's treatise on angelology is to be found in the *arbor ramificata* (the schematic outline characteristic of the Fishacre manuscripts) at the beginning of the second chapter of the second distinction: namely, whether angels were created before the world or with the world or after the world; and whether in the empyrean heaven or elsewhere; whether they were created among natural beings only or also among the graced; whether some are given power over others; and finally what the mission and custodial duties of the angels were; see Fishacre, *In 2 Sent.* 2, ed. Long, 1:25–26.

10. "Hic esset ostendendum quod anima habet compositionem in substantia, ut quod constat ex materia et forma. Et similiter angelus. Si enim angelus esset forma sine materia, ipsa esset in mente intelligentis eum, non similitudo eius aliqua, quae non sit ipsa," *In 1 Sent.* 8.4. The texts for book 1 (given the fact that this book of the Commentary has not yet appeared in print) have been prepared from six manuscripts: *BCOPRV*. For the *sigla* and descriptions of the manuscripts they represent see R. James Long and Maura O'Carroll, SND, *The Life and Works of Richard Fishacre, OP. Prolegomena to the Edition of his Commentary on the "Sentences"* (Munich: Verlag der Bayerischen Akademie der Wissenschaften, 1999), 78–197.

11. "Et etiam illud in quo prima forma et similitudo eius conveniunt forma est. Illa aut habet similitudinem a se diversam aut non. Si habet, erit similitudo similitudi-

be cast out of heaven, if they are understood by the good angels; the soul of the reader will be in hell, if thought by a demon—and other absurd consequences.[12] This is on the face of it a most curious argument and makes sense only if Fishacre is understanding matter here as having some measure of actuality.

Likewise, Fishacre continues, every action is attributed to form and every passion to matter. But the soul and the angel are naturally passible, that is, subject to change. Therefore they have matter, since matter is the cause of every change.[13]

Likewise, Aristotle maintains that a chest without matter exists only in the mind of the artisan, and from this it must be inferred that a soul without matter would have existence only in the mind of God.[14]

Likewise, every individual is an individual through matter. If the angel is the same in this and that property, what will you add to it that it might be *this* particular angel? It is either an accident or a (specific) difference or matter: these are the choices. If an accident, then individuals differ by accidents alone. And if substances can be imagined without accidents (the implication is that they can), they will be the same substance. If, however, angels differ by specific difference, then each angel will belong to a distinct species.[15] This is an option Fishacre refutes at some length

---

nis et forma formae in infinitum. Ergo ipsa forma substantialis angeli est in intellectu intelligente eam. Ergo cum unus angelus intelligat omnes angelos, si totaliter sunt forma vel substantialis vel accidentalis, erunt omnes in uno quolibet," *In 1 Sent.* 8.4.

12. "Item, omnes in mente mea, immo et omnes in inferno, et omnis anima iam in caelo, immo et ubique, ut Deus, quia ubique similitudo eius quae esse non potest nisi ipsum, si non est nisi forma. Sic anima tua in inferno, et daemones in caelo, unde proiecti sunt. Et non possunt inde proici, quia intelliguntur a bonis," ibid.

13. "Item, omnis actio formae et passio materiae attribuuntur. Sed anima et angelus natura passibiles. Ergo habent materiam. Et etiam omnis mutationis causa materia est. Ergo cum sint mutabilia, non carent materia," ibid.

14. "Item, Aristoteles: si esset arca forma sine materia, vere esset arca in mente artificis. Ergo similiter si anima est forma sine materia, vere est in mente Dei intelligentis eam," ibid.

15. "Item, omne individuum est individuum per materiam. Quid enim, cum angelus sit idem in hoc et in illo, addes tu ei ut fiat iste angelus: aut accidens aut dif-

in book 2, distinction 3.[16] By process of elimination he decides that individuation—including angelic individuation—has to be through matter.[17]

Fishacre then cites Augustine's commentary on the Genesis text *in principio fecit caelum et terram*, understanding *terram* to mean the *matter* of heaven and earth, that is to say, the created universe, intelligible and corporeal. Therefore, not only is it the case that created spirits have matter, indeed it is the *same* matter as that of bodies. For Augustine says *materiam* [singular], not *materias* [plural].[18] Yet in glossing the predicate *immaterialis* in the second book of the Lombard text, he says that angels are immaterial only in the sense that they lack the matter that is the cause of generation and corruption in the things here below—that is, corporeal matter—just as Aristotle says that the heavens do not have

ferentiam aut materiam? Si accidens, ergo individua differunt solis accidentibus. Et si imaginarentur substantiae sine accidentibus, essent eadem substantia. Et etiam prius natura est substantia quam accidens. In illa ergo prioritate naturae quid separavit substantias singulares ab invicem? Si differentia substantialis, igitur quilibet angelus erit diversae speciei ab altero, quia habet differentiam constitutivam diversam," ibid.

16. Fishacre, *In 2 Sent.* 3.2.3, ed. Long, 1:63–64.

17. "Ergo omne individuum habet materiam qua potest esse et non esse. Unde Aristoteles: Omne individuum habet materiam qua potest esse et non esse," *In 1 Sent.* 8.4. Later, in the text cited in the previous note, Fishacre provides an argument against specific differences among angels: the specific difference would either be nobler or less noble than the angelic form. But it cannot be nobler because the angelic form is the noblest. Nor can it be less noble, for how can the less noble perfect the more noble? It is the sensible that is superadded to the vegetative, and the rational to the sensible. Therefore, all angels belong to the same species. See Fishacre, *In 2 Sent.* 3.2.3, ed. Long, 1:63–64. He reverts to the problem for a final time in 4.44, where his view was challenged by the authority of Porphyry, who claimed that individuation was had through accidents like time and place; Fishacre distinguishes between individuation (*individuatio*) and the diversity of individuals (*diversitas individuorum*). Perhaps it was the latter that Porphyry intended, says Fishacre rather disingenuously (*In 4 Sent.* 44). The whole problem of individuation, it must be concluded, remains unfocused in Fishacre.

18. "Item, Augustinus *Super Genesim ad litteram*, qui accipit 'in principio (id est primo) fecit caelum et terram,' non habet quomodo veraciter intelligat caelum et terram nisi materiam caeli et terrae, id est universae intelligibilis corporalisque creaturae. Ergo non tantum spiritus creati habent materiam, immo et eandem cum corporibus. Dicit enim *materiam*, non *materias*," *In 1 Sent.* 8.4.

matter, because they lack the matter of corruptible things.[19] This apparent inconsistency can be resolved only if we assume that in the first case Fishacre has in mind *materia* as a *genus generalissimum*, matter prior to its division into spiritual and corporeal, and in the second case matter after its division.[20] The question of the numerical sameness of matter, however, was much debated even among proponents of universal hylomorphism.[21] It is not clear that Fishacre is fully aware of the difficulty.

In attempting to explain John Damascene's definition of the angel ("an angel is an intellectual substance, always changing, free to choose, incorporeal," and so forth), Fishacre says that in the angels there is little of matter and much of form (*modicum est de materia et multum de forma*). Moreover, in a connection that would have pleased Grosseteste, but which Fishacre does not exploit, he says that since all form is light, and because the angel is almost wholly form, then it is almost wholly light.[22]

Although the angel has matter, it is incorruptible because of its form. From this latter principle derives the corruption of any material composite, because its form is not so noble that it terminates and completes every inclination of matter to another form. The form that is intellect, however, is so noble that it altogether completes matter, so that now there is left in it no inclination to another form. Thus, by the nature of their form spiritual substances are incorruptible. On the other hand, just as the nature of matter accounts for the dissolubility of composite things, so too the same principle accounts for the mortality of living things.

19. Fishacre, *In 2 Sent.* 3.1.2, ed. Long, 1:57.

20. See Roger Bacon, *Opus tertium*, cap. 38, ed. John S. Brewer, *Fr. Rogeri Bacon opera quaedam hactenus inedita* (London: Longman, Green, Longman and Roberts, 1859), 1:122. Bacon's exposition of the doctrine of spiritual matter is the most extensive of any of the Franciscan masters; see my article "Roger Bacon on the Nature and Place of Angels," *Vivarium* 35 (1997): 266–82.

21. Bonaventure himself acknowledges the perplexity of the question; see Wippel, "Essence and Existence," 409.

22. Fishacre, *In 2 Sent.* 2.1.2, ed. Long, 1:29–30.

Every composite being, insofar as it has matter, is dissoluble; every living being, insofar as it has matter, is mortal. Therefore God alone, lacking all matter, is among living things immortal *simpliciter*. But angels, just as they are naturally mortal according to their matter, are also naturally immortal according to their form.[23]

As to the location of the angel, Fishacre makes his own contribution to the old chestnut concerning the number of angels that can dance on the head of a pin.[24] To the Lombard text, *Ubi angeli mox creati fuerint: in empyreo scilicet, quod statim factum, angelis fuerit repletum*, he raises a contrary argument. A point (*locus punctalis*) suffices as the place of an angel. But even in the shortest lines there is an infinite number of points; therefore the shortest lines will not be filled up except with an infinite number of angels. How much more is it the case that the empyrean will not be filled up except with an infinite number of angels?[25] The implication is that there is not an infinite number of angels, and if that's the case, as he argues below, what a waste of space!

One can in fact distinguish three questions that can be raised concerning the locus of spiritual creatures: whether the spirit is in a place according to its substance; whether many can be in the same place; and whether there is a place natural to them determined by nature.[26] As to the question of the angels being in a place, Fishacre raises a number of objections. A point is not a place; place is a surface. Citing Damascene's definition that place is a bodily boundary which contains that which is contained,

23. Ibid., 2.3.3, ed. Long, 1:66.

24. Apparently the first to put the question in precisely those terms was the Cambridge Platonist, Henry More, who in his *The Immortality of the Soul* (published in 1659) writes as follows: "that it may stop the mouths of them that, not without reason, laugh at those unconceivable and ridiculous fancies of the Schools; that first rashly take away all Extension from Spirits, whether Souls or Angels, and then dispute how many of them booted and spurr'd may dance on a needle's point at once." I am grateful to Professor Edith Sylla for this reference.

25. Fishacre, *In 2 Sent.* 2.4.3, ed. Long, 1:38.

26. Ibid.

he concludes that angels cannot be in a place according to their substance.[27] Likewise, it seems that a body needs place, or place body, much more than a spirit needs place; but since there is at least some body without place, namely the ultimate heaven (because there is no *continens*), an *a fortiori* case can be made for a spirit to be without place.[28]

To the second question, whether there could be two spirits in the same place, he ventures an affirmative answer. In fact, it happens in nature that two bodies occupy the same place, namely light and air.[29] And in demonic possession the demon occupies the same body as the soul.[30] This view falls, however, in the face of the authority of Augustine.[31]

To the third question, whether there is a natural place for the angels, Fishacre says that it is the heavens. The more noble the creature the higher its natural place, and heaven is higher than the place of fire, and fire than air, and so on. So if there is a natural place that has been determined, this can only be the heavens.[32]

Here again, however, Fishacre finds a contrary position. Can beings that are separated from their natural place be happy, he asks. If not, angelic messengers sent to us could not then be completely happy. Moreover, movement away from one's natural place would be violent. Yet scripture testifies to angels ascending and descending (Jn 1:15 and Gn 28:12) without an agent forcing such movement.[33]

As evidence in support of the contrary position, Fishacre cites certain authorities (clearly the Aristotelians) to the effect that

27. Ibid., 1:38–39.

28. Ibid., 1:39. This text is unique to *O*.

29. Ibid.

30. Ibid.

31. Ibid. In fact, the authority in this case is pseudo-Augustine (the *De fide ad Petrum*).

32. Ibid., 1:39–40

33. Ibid., 1:40.

composed being is here and now by reason of its matter and not by reason of its form. What is solely form is not here and now—God, for example, or a universal—but everywhere and always.[34]

Again the authority is Damascene: God as an immaterial being is not in a place. It follows therefore that every created spirit, since it has matter, is not only here and now by its operation but also by its substance, because matter is part of its substance. Since, moreover, matter is defined by Aristotle as having parts outside of parts, it has parts outside of parts in actuality only owing to form. Hence, if it were possible to be wholly matter without any form, it would occupy only a punctal place (*locum punctalem*). Matter on its own would seek only a point. Only by reason of form, which extends matter and causes it to have parts outside of parts in actuality, does the substance seek a larger place. If therefore matter were granted some form that was not the cause of its having parts outside of parts, that composite could still be in a point. Therefore, since the form of the spiritual creature does not extend its matter so that it produces parts outside of parts, the spiritual creature will be here in this place by reason of its matter. By reason of such a form, however, it occupies only a point; but by reason of its operation it can occupy a larger space.[35]

The spiritual creature is thus in a place in two ways: by its substance (then it is only a point) and by its operation. A point is not comprehensible by sense but only by the mind—an intelligible, not a sensible place. Glossing the Damascene text that the angel is in a place because it is present *intelligibly*, Fishacre claims that this place is a point, because the Damascene immediately adds: "It is circumscribed where it operates." Only the latter, corporeal sense, is properly speaking "place," because here there is surface.[36]

It is entirely possible, he says in response to an objection, that

34. Ibid.

35. Ibid., 1:40–41.

36. Ibid., 1:41–42.

two or more spiritual creatures occupy the same point and yet remain distinct, not being within one other, but being coterminous.[37]

To another objection he says: given the nature of its matter, the angel is necessarily somewhere. The nature of its form, moreover, dictates that it occupy the highest place. But the principle of angelic action is not only nature but will, and in fact the latter is more powerful than the former. There is, however, for the will no place that is determined. Since nature and will are naturally united in the angel, its nature is nowhere violently where it is voluntarily.[38]

Finally, however, Fishacre finds against the position that the angel is located in a place:

> I don't assert this opinion [he says], in fact, I bring forward the opposite opinion in which I am able to place greater credence, namely the view of those who claim that a spirit is not in a place essentially. Therefore, although arguments have been put forward for the second opinion and contrary to the prior … we are adding more <arguments for the first>, so that anyone who pays attention to these will know that the former should be doubted and consequently will not shrink from positing that to which manifold reason concludes.[39]

Fishacre follows with ten new arguments directed against the position that angels are circumscriptively in a place.[40] He concludes with a consideration based on the plurality of forms:

37. Ibid., 1:42.

38. Ibid., 1:42–43.

39. Ibid., 1:43.

40. Among the ten arguments which Fishacre adduces against the angels being in place are the following: 1) If angels were created before every corporeal creature (citing Damascene and Gregory Nazianzus), they were also complete in their essence before any body was created. Therefore a spirit existed altogether without body, and thus without place and site and position according to Aristotle's rule in the *Physics*. 2) If there is but one body which contains all bodies (viz. the outer heaven), and this is sufficient that there be a proper or common place, why not similarly one spirit, namely God, supplying sufficient place for all spirits? 3) If it is a sufficient condition for a punctal location that it have matter, which has extension not of itself but

> Another opinion which posits that a spirit needs a punctal place (*loco punctali*), because it has matter through which it is here and now, which, without form extending it, is punctal I reckon to be false. For this matter now under a corporeal form, if it were to be despoiled of everything as far as the form of bodiness (*forma corporeitatis*) and to this point it perhaps still has position and is localized and punctal according to the imagination. But the form by which it is localized may be further despoiled and it will remain not yet altogether denuded. For [the spirit] still has the first form [viz. substantial form], which is as it were the unity among the forms, by which it is one and without position. For unity is substance without position. Being thus constituted, matter is clothed with a spiritual form, and thus a spirit of its own essence is perhaps not able to be localized (*situalis*).[41]

Not unlike peeling away the layers of an onion, the forms of the spiritual being are stripped away until all that is left is the substantial form, which, although it has matter, lacks both the form of corporeity and, by extension, location.

Although the Franciscan master Richard Rufus disagreed with Fishacre on details, he too embraced the doctrine of spiritual matter. In his typical disengaged engagement he introduces the topic thus: "This is a big [*magna*] question with some people, whether namely the angel has matter or not."[42]

Following his own methodology, Rufus raises a total of seven-

---

from corporeal form, without the latter the place of the material thing is like a point. Therefore everything that has this matter will be local and in some place, even the ultimate heaven. Therefore, if extended matter is not in a place, how much more is it the case that nonextended matter is not in a place? 4) In a curious argument, Fishacre talks about the amount of wasted space in the empyrean, if in fact an infinite number of angels can be located in a single atom. In an analogy suggested by Bede, it would be an empty city if all its inhabitants could live in a single small house (*domuncula*).

41. Fishacre, *In 2 Sent.* 2.4.3, ed. Long, 1:46. Dorothea Sharp in the first English language study of Fishacre, published in 1933, concluded that "a *forma corporeitatis* receives no recognition in the philosophical system of Fishacre" ("Philosophy of Fishacre," 286), a comment repeated by Gilson in his *History of Christian Philosophy in the Middle Ages*. Such an observation is patently wrong and is testimony to philosophical judgments arrived at without benefit of a reliable text.

42. *In 2 Sent.* 3 (Oxford, Balliol Coll. MS 62, fol. 108va).

teen objections to his position, then immediately refutes each.[43] In his response to the fourth argument, for example, Rufus replies that natural forms necessarily demand matter in which to inhere. The alternative is to place abstracted forms in the soul (as if in matter), as in Aristotle's teaching, or outside the soul, as in the Platonic Forms, an obviously erroneous view.[44]

From the point of view of matter, Rufus's position is that form-matter composition is simply entailed in mutability. Glossing the Lombard text *Creatura quoque spirituali*, Rufus argues as follows: "Nothing simple is mutable. But every creature is mutable. Therefore no creature is truly simple.... Therefore if matter is either the cause of mutability or is itself mutability, since the angel is mutable like any other creature ... every angel will have matter."[45]

These appeals to reason are followed in the text of the Rufus commentary by arguments from authority, the foremost among them St. Augustine.[46] Rufus concludes without much apparent conviction: "What may I say to so many and such great questions? I do not know. To raise doubts about individual issues is not without its usefulness, those issues namely that are not about the articles of faith. But I do not see what profit my assertion could possibly be to me or to others.[47] A bit later in the text, moreover, there

43. A total of four arguments are *ex parte agentis*, eight *ex parte angelorum*, and five *ex parte materiae*.

44. "Et videmus quod formae naturales necessario exigunt materiam in qua. Nam aut sunt actualiter abstractae, et tunc sunt in anima ut in materia, licet spirituali, sicut ait Philosophus, aut sunt in individuis extra animam. Imponitur autem Platoni error ex hoc quod posuit ideae habere esse per se extra materiam et extra particularia. Patet ergo quod forma creata quae non habet materiam ex qua non potest habere esse per se," *In 2 Sent.* 3, Balliol MS, fol. 110va.

45. "CREATURA QUOQUE SPIRITUALI. Nihil simplex mutabile est. Omnis autem creatura mutabilis est. Ergo nulla creatura vere simplex est.... Ergo si materia vel causa mutabilitatis est vel ipsa mutabilitas, cum angelus mutabilis sit, sicut quaelibet creatura, ... habebit omnis angelus materiam," ibid., fol. 109rb.

46. Like Fishacre, Rufus attributes the doctrine of spiritual matter to Augustine, not to Ibn Gabirol.

47. "Quid ad haec tot et tanta dicam? Nescio. Dubitare de singulis non est inutile,

comes this grudging conclusion: "Since this matter is not among the articles of faith, I do not yet see that it could not be more probable that it be posited that the angel has matter than not."[48]

On related issues Rufus sometimes agrees with Fishacre (angels are not in place circumscriptively) and sometimes disagrees (angels and human souls for Rufus do not constitute a single species). In general, however, when set against the perspective of the theologians of the following generation, these two Oxonians occupy a common ground. Indeed, common to both is confusion with respect to the concept of matter. Neither seems to grasp the Aristotelian sense of *hyle* as pure potentiality. They are both apparently conceiving of matter in the sense of what Aristotle would consider quantified or second matter, a kind of stuff, having some actuality.

Such confusion is in part testimony to that generation's incomplete absorption of Aristotle's natural philosophy. I have argued this elsewhere with respect to Fishacre[49] that, although he cites the *Physics* a total of fourteen times in his hexaëmeron, ten times by name, most of the references can be found in a florilegium, his probable source. In other words, Fishacre's penetration of the new learning was necessarily shallow, because for the most part (I make exceptions for the logic and the biological works) he was not reading the Aristotelian text itself but collections of aphoristic sayings excerpted from the Stagirite's text. As an Arts master, Rufus had at least read the text, though the commentary on the *Physics*, recently attributed to him, was most probably not his.[50]

---

scilicet quae non sunt de articulis fidei. Nec video quid mihi vel aliis prodesse posset mea assertio," *In 2 Sent.* 3, Balliol MS, fol. 110ra.

48. "Et cum istud non sit de articulis fidei, non adhuc video quod non possit probabilius poni angelum habere materiam quam non habere," ibid., fol. 110vb.

49. See R. James Long, "Reception and Use of Aristotle by the Early English Dominicans," in *Aristotle in Britain during the Middle Ages*, Proceedings of the international conference at Cambridge, April 8–11, 1994, ed. John Marenbon (Turnhout: Brepols, 1996), 51–56.

50. Silvia Donati, "The Anonymous Commentary on the Physics in Erfurt, Cod. Amplon. Q.312 and Richard Rufus of Cornwall," *RTPM* 72,2 (2005): 232–359.

The strange doctrine of spiritual matter became in the following generation one of the issues that separated the two mendicant orders. The Dominicans, following St. Albert and St. Thomas, rejected the teaching; the Franciscans[51] embraced it, although—as in the case of Bonaventure—not always with enthusiasm. Bonaventure's final position on spiritual matter in the angels, in fact, was that even if it were not true, it is less dangerous to claim that the angel is composed rather than simple. Therefore, he maintains this position, he says, out of piety, not wishing to ascribe to the creature what belongs to God alone.[52]

In the end, the doctrine of spiritual matter proved to be a thought experiment, which despite its perceived virtues collapsed under the weight of its metaphysical tensions, the fault lines of which are already apparent in the writings of the two Oxford friars, Richard Fishacre, OP, and Richard Rufus, OFM.

51. Viz. Alexander of Hales, Roger Bacon, St. Bonaventure, John Peckham, William of la Mare, Richard of Middleton, and later in the fourteenth century by Gonsalvus of Spain; see Wippel, "Essence and Existence," 408.

52. "Minus est periculosum dicere quod angelus sit compositus, *etiam si verum non sit* [emphasis mine], quam quod sit simplex: quia hoc ergo attribuo angelo nolens ei attribuere quod ad Deum solum aestimo pertinere, et hoc propter pietatem quam habeo ad reverentiam Dei," *Collationes in Hexaëmeron* 4.12, ed. Ferdinand M. Delorme (Quaracchi: Collegium S. Bonaventurae ad Claras Aquas, 1934), 5:351.

CHAPTER 5

The First Oxford Debate on the Eternity of the World

In a Paris manuscript containing a copy of Richard Fishacre's *Sentences* Commentary[1] there appears at book 2, distinction 12, chapter 3, a lengthy treatment of the problem of the eternity of the world.[2] The same text, with only minor variants, is found at the very end of a copy of the same commentary in a London manuscript.[3] Although missing from all the other manuscripts containing the second book of the Fishacre commentary, seven in number, a marginal comment in a Cambridge manuscript (*C*) notes its absence: "Hic deest questio de creatione vel inchoatione mundi, que scripta est una cum questione de luce in parvo volumine ante questionem de heresibus."[4] The treatise on heresies to

1. Viz. Paris, BNF MS lat. 15754.

2. Technically the question turns on the unending duration of the world, not its eternity (in the Boethian sense). However, common usage dictates that the latter term be retained.

3. Viz. London, BL MS Royal 10.B.VII, fols. 386rb–388va.

4. Viz. Cambridge, Gonville and Caius Coll. MS 329/410, fol. 170v. In addition, a

which the note refers is in all probability the opusculum by the same Fishacre, which survives only in a Vatican manuscript.[5]

In the following distinction, also at chapter 3, the above-mentioned Paris manuscript (*P*) features a question on light, likewise omitted from all other manuscripts save the London witness (*R*), where it again appears at the very end of the codex. This time *C* has the following marginal note opposite the place in the text where the insertion begins in *P*: "hic deest questio de luce que scripta est in parvo quaterno cum questionibus de heresibus."[6] Based on all the evidence, my conjecture is that this "small *quaternus*," which is a kind of unbound notebook,[7] and which either has not survived or has not as yet been identified, is the repository of several of Fishacre's opuscula, representing the fruits of his activity during the years following the completion of his *Sentences* Commentary (ca. 1245) and his death in 1248.[8] These writings are occasional in nature and most probably extracurricular, not forming a part of his lectures as regent master. This particular question on the eternal duration of the world would then have been copied from the *quaternus* onto several spare folia at the end of *R* and later still inserted into an appropriate place in the Commentary on the Lombard's text by the scribe of *P*.[9]

---

manuscript containing the same work and once belonging to the Dominican convent of San Domenico in Bologna, now Bologna, Univ. MS 1546 (*B*), at the same place in the text reads as follows: "questionem de eternitate mundi que deest habes in alio volumine questionum." I have elsewhere referred to this *volumen* as the Q Text; see Fishacre, *In 2 Sent.*, ed. Long, 1:35*–36*

5. See my edition, "*Fishacre's Super S. Augustini librum de haeresibus adnotationes:* An Edition and Commentary," *AHDLMA* 60 (1993), 207–79.

6. *C*, fol. 175v.

7. For the use of the term in the High Middle Ages See Louis J. Bataillon, "Exemplar, Pecia, Quaternus," in *Vocabulaire du livre et de l'écriture au moyen âge*, ed. Olga Weijers (Turnhout: Brepols, 1989), 206–19.

8. For the dates of Fishacre's Commentary See R. James Long and Maura O'Carroll, SND, *Life and Works of Richard Fishacre, OP, Prolegomena to the Edition of his Commentary on the "Sentences"* (Munich: Verlag der Bayerischen Akademie der Wissenschaften, 1999), 39–42.

9. The more customary place in Lombard's work for such a discussion was the

The discovery of this hitherto unknown treatise on the world's eternity, as it turns out, enables us at last to complete the account of the earliest recorded discussion at Oxford of what was later at Paris to become a litmus test for philosophical leanings. Significant portions of this text, moreover, are cited *verbotenus* by Fishacre's nemesis, Richard Rufus of Cornwall, in his own (first) Commentary on the *Sentences*.[10] This fact provides us with both a *terminus ante quem* and further evidence of Fishacre's authorship.[11]

As with so many other issues, the earliest Oxford master to venture an opinion on the question of world's eternity was Robert Grosseteste.[12] In the course of commenting on the opening verses of Genesis in his *Hexaëmeron* Grosseteste finds occasion to respond to an opinion voiced most likely by a fellow Englishman Alexander of Hales, then Master of Arts at Paris.[13] In a question on the eternity of the world, still unpublished, Alexan-

---

first distinction of the second book, not the twelfth; See Richard C. Dales, *Medieval Discussions of the Eternity of the World* (Leiden: Brill, 1990), 37–38.

10. For a detailed description of this unique witness see Peter Raedts, *Richard Rufus of Cornwall and the Tradition of Oxford Theology* (Oxford: Clarendon Press, 1987), 20–21.

11. See italicized text in Appendix 5A.

12. Given the fact that Grosseteste's contribution to the question has been thoroughly studied, I will attempt here no more than a brief review of the current scholarship. The scholar to whom we are most indebted for our knowledge of the question is Richard Dales, whose many studies culminated finally in the book, *Medieval Discussions* (see n. 9 above), and its companion volume of texts, edited with Omar Argerami, *Medieval Latin Texts on the Eternity of the World* (Leiden: Brill, 1991). Among his other studies see especially: Dales, "Discussions of the Eternity of the World During the First Half of the Twelfth Century," *Speculum* 57 (1982): 495–508; Dales, "Robert Grosseteste's Place in Medieval Discussions of the Eternity of the World," *Speculum* 61 (1986): 544–63; and Dales, "Time and Eternity in the Thirteenth Century," *Journal of the History of Ideas* 49 (1988): 27–45. Stephen Brown goes over much of the same ground in "The Eternity of the World Discussion at Early Oxford," in *Mensch und Natur im Mittelalter, MM* 21/1, ed. Albert Zimmermann and Andreas Speer (Berlin: De Gruyter, 1991), 260–63.

13. There exist two extant versions of a disputed question which have been provisionally attributed to Alexander; see Dales, "Robert Grosseteste's Place," 549, and Victorinus Doucet, "The History of the Problem of the Authenticity of the *Summa*," *FS* 7 (1947): 26–41 and 274–312. These questions have been edited as part of an unpublished doctoral dissertation: Donald M. Nathanson, "Alexandri de Hales, *Quaestiones 'De eternitate, evo, et tempore' et 'De duratione mundi'*" (Ph.D. diss., University of Southern California, 1986), 21–115.

der argues that Aristotle's view could be reconciled with Christian belief in the temporal origin of the universe:

It is true that the view is attributed to Aristotle that the world was able to be perpetual and always to have existed. But it should be known that the phrase "the world always existed" can be understood as meaning that it never had a beginning, and in this sense it is not true; or it can be understood as meaning that the world is commensurate with the whole of time, and in this sense it is true that the world has always existed; *and this is what Aristotle believed* [emphasis mine]. For thus the adverb "always" refers only to the totality of time.[14]

To Grosseteste this smacked of false syncretism, and he initiates his treatment of the question in his *Hexaëmeron* with a solemn warning against

certain moderns ... who said that Aristotle in particular had not felt that the world lacked a beginning of time but agreed with the Catholic faith on this point and posited a beginning of time and of the world ... [and] who try, against Aristotle himself and his Commentator, and also the holy commentators, to make a Catholic of Aristotle the heretic, thinking with amazing blindness and presumption that they are able to understand more clearly and interpret more truly the meaning of Aristotle from corrupt Latin versions than could the philosophers, both pagan and Catholic, who knew the entire, uncorrupted, unexcerpted Greek text. And let them not deceive themselves and sweat in vain to make Aristotle a Catholic, lest they uselessly waste their time and mental powers ... and make heretics of themselves.[15]

This uncompromising view respecting the Philosopher's position on the eternity question forms the background for Grosseteste's own exposition. His first argument is from authority and

14. Paris, BNF lat. MS 16406, fol. 7vb, and Bologna Univ. MS 2554, fol. 5vb; cited from Dales, "Grosseteste's Place," 549.

15. Grosseteste, *Hexaëmeron* 1.8.2–4; eds. Richard C. Dales and Servus Gieben (Oxford: Oxford University Press, 1982), 58–61; again the translation is for the most part Dales's ("Grosseteste's Place," 547–48). Roger Bacon later was to echo these same sentiments, with a particular animus directed toward the *summa* of Frater Alexander.

from his catholic and omnivorous reading he marshals his sources, Greek and Latin, which he claims had access to the *uncorrupted* text of Aristotle. These sources, which include Boethius, Augustine, Ambrose, Pliny, John Chrysostom, John Damascene, and an unidentified *Hexaëmeron*, ascribed to both Jerome and Bede, constitute almost the complete stock of authorities utilized by later writers on the subject.[16]

Following upon the arguments from authority, Grosseteste fashions several arguments from reason to show that the universe could not have been eternal, as Aristotle and his followers claimed. First, he points to confusion in the minds of the "ancients" between eternity properly so-called and endless duration or perpetuity. Because their minds' gaze (*aspectus mentis*) had not been purged of love for temporal things, the pagans could not think of eternity except by analogy with temporality. Perpetuity, however, a temporal mode, upon examination is revealed to be an impossibility, the analogies to the contrary notwithstanding.[17]

The pagans and their Christian fellow travelers, moreover, fail to understand that cause and effect with respect to eternity and time fall under two distinct measures. Therefore, says Grosseteste, analogies such as the footprint in the dust are not valid when applied to the eternal:

> If the cause and what is caused (*causatum*) do not share in the same kind of measure of being, this rule does not apply to them, namely that if the cause exists, the caused necessarily coexists. Therefore, since God is eternal, and the world and motion and time are temporal, time and eternity are not of the same kind of measure.... The eternal God is the cause of the temporal world and time, but He precedes them not with respect to time, but with respect to simple eternity.[18]

16. Dales, "Grosseteste's Place," 551–52.

17. Grosseteste, *Hexaëmeron* 1.8.5, eds. Dales and Gieben, 61.

18. Ibid.. 1.8.6, 61–62; See Dales, "Grosseteste's Place," 554, and Dales, "Time and Eternity in the Thirteenth Century," *Journal of the History of Ideas* 49 (1988): 32. Cf. Augustine, *Conf.* 12.29 for the possible inspiration for the argument. It is, however, un-

Grosseteste's final argument in the *Hexaëmeron* was a commonplace in the Islamic-Jewish tradition.[19] This argument runs as follows: if the world were eternal and if the human race were coeternal, either an infinite number of human souls would have by now been generated or a single soul would serve for all bodies or souls would be recycled into other bodies—each of which is clearly impossible.[20]

When Fishacre composed his extracurricular question on the eternity of the world, he clearly had Grosseteste's *Hexaëmeron* before his eyes.[21] The piece opens with a reflection on the first verse of Genesis, "In the beginning God created the heavens and the earth," a text which is cited by the Lombard and which thereafter provided the occasion for all of his commentators to discuss the question of the world's eternity. Observing that the literal sense of the scriptures is manifold, Fishacre wonders about the many meanings of "beginning" (*principium*). Reflecting on the beginning of time, moreover, he asks with Grosseteste why the world was created at the vernal equinox and not at the autumnal, here adding original arguments of his own.[22]

---

clear precisely what Grosseteste means here by God's preceding the world with respect to simple eternity; he was to clarify the issue somewhat in his later *De finitate* (see n. 20 below), a work to which Fishacre may possibly have had access (see n. 34 below).

19. The argument is to be found in Algazel, Avicenna, and Maimonides; "Grosseteste's Place," 557. See also Richard Sorabji, *Time, Creation and the Continuum. Theories in Antiquity and the Early Middle Ages* (Ithaca, N.Y.: Cornell University Press, 1983), 202–3.

20. Grosseteste, *Hexaëmeron* 1.8.7, ed. Dales and Gieben, 62; cf. Dales, "Grosseteste's Place," 557–58. It should be added that Grosseteste entertains the same question on the world's duration in a little treatise, written about the same time as the *Hexaëmeron* and later appended to his *Physics* commentary, namely the *De finitate motus et temporis*; see the edition of Richard C. Dales, "Robert Grosseteste's Treatise 'De finitate motus et temporis,'" *Traditio* 19 (1963): 245–66. For Richard Rufus's use of the same work see Rega Wood, "Richard Rufus of Cornwall on Creation: The Reception of Aristotelian Physics in the West," *Medieval Philosophy and Theology* 2 (1992): 25.

21. See Dales, "Influence of Grosseteste's *Hexaëmeron*," 271–300. Cf. R. James Long, "Richard Fishacre's Treatise *De libero arbitrio*," in *Moral and Political Philosophies in the Middle Ages*, ed. B. Carlos Bazán, Eduardo Andújar, Léonard Sbrocchi (Ottawa: Legas, 1995), 2:879–91, for other instances.

22. Fishacre, *In 2 Sent.*, Appendix A, ed. Long, 2:316–17.

The philosophical issue is joined, however, when Fishacre names the thinkers (Aristotle, Plato, Apuleius, and Pliny) who held that the world was eternal, having neither beginning nor end, and therefore coeternal with God. Departing now from the Grosseteste text, Fishacre distinguishes several variants of the proeternity position: first, that the world is coeternal with God in such wise that it is in no way *ab alio* and therefore is not created; second, that the world is coeternal with God, yet is made by God—eternally. The latter has two subspecies: that the world is from an unwitting God, a God who necessarily emanates being; or that the world is made by a God who wills that the world be coeternal with Him.[23]

Fishacre's methodology will be to rehearse the arguments in favor of the first variant, that the world namely is uncreated and therefore eternal, then to refute them one by one, and then finally to offer some arguments that demonstrate the contrary, namely that the world is temporal in origin. In part borrowed from Maimonides[24] and Alexander of Hales,[25] the arguments that Fishacre finds in support of the world's eternal duration are eight in number. God is, to begin with, the supreme good (and the good is according to the prevailing myth self-diffusive); since God is also eternal, and hence his goodness is eternal, this is sufficient cause of an eternal effect, which is the world.[26]

23. Ibid., 2:319.

24. See Moses Maimonides, *The Guide of the Perplexed* 2.14, trans. Shlomo Pines (Chicago: University of Chicago Press, 1963), 2:285–89. Although it cannot be established that Fishacre had access to the work, Wolfgang Kluxen has argued convincingly that there existed a Latin version of Maimonides's *Guide* as early as 1230–1235; see Kluxen, "Literargeschichtliches zum lateinischen Moses Maimonides," *RTAM* 21 (1954): 23–50. Fishacre refers to Maimonides only once by name (viz. "Rabbi Moyses") in the second book of his *Sentences* Commentary (2.14.4)—and it is by way of reporting (not quoting) Rambam's view on the impossibility of comparison except within the same species—but a number of times in books 3 and 4.

25. See note 13 above.

26. Fishacre, *In 2 Sent.*, Appendix A, ed. Long, 2:320. Cf. Alexander of Hales, *De duratione mundi*, ed. Donald Nathanson (Ph.D. diss., University of Southern California, 1986), 69–70.

Furthermore, continues Fishacre, since the eternal is better than the noneternal, either God could have created a world coeternal with himself or not. If he could not, he was not omnipotent. If he could, but willed not to, he was envious—which likewise violates the Platonic myth. Therefore, God could and did create eternally.[27]

Thirdly, three things are required for action: power, wisdom, and will. God not only has these three requisites, he *is* omnipotence, omniscience, and supreme will. But infinite power produces finite act instantaneously. Therefore, if an agent of infinite power is also eternal, its act is coeternal.[28]

The fourth argument he extracts from the *Metaphysics*, the fifth from the *Physics*. If, according to the latter, motion began to be when previously there was no motion, a mover also began to be where before there was no mover. But the nature of the divine substance precludes coming-to-be. If, however, this substance is first not moving, then moving, we say that it has undergone a change. Therefore there can be no first mover. This, however, is impossible. Therefore, the divine substance, which for the Christian is God, is always moving.[29]

The sixth argument is similar. If God is ever the same, what reason can be assigned that he is creating now rather than before, or indeed before that? On the part of the creator there is no reason why creation takes place at this instant rather than before, and of course there could be no reason on the part of that which is to be made, since before it was made it was nothing. Thus either God never created—and therefore there is nothing now in being—or he created from eternity.[30]

27. Ibid.

28. Ibid. Cf. Maimonides, *Guide,* trans. Pines, 288, and Alexander of Hales, *De duratione* (68–69).

29. Fishacre, *In 2 Sent.,* Appendix A, ed. Long, 2:320. Cf. Maimonides, *Guide,* trans. Pines, 286. Cf. also Philip the Chancellor, *Summa de bono,* q. 3, ed. Nicolas Wicki (Berne: Francke, 1985), 1:47–48.

30. Fishacre, *In 2 Sent.,* Appendix A, ed. Long, 2:321. Cf. Maimonides, *Guide,* Pines, 287–88.

Seventh and most subtly, of everything that has a beginning it is true to say that it once did not exist. Therefore if there is a first instant of time, in that instant which we will call *a*, it is true that the world exists. The proposition "the world does not exist" is thus true either in the same instant or in another. That it is true that the world in the same instant both exists and does not exist, however, is impossible. But affirmation and negation as the termini of generation are less distant than those which are the termini of creation. The former have in common at least matter, the principle of potentiality; the latter, since creation is *ex nihilo*, have nothing in common. If therefore the being and nonbeing which are the termini of generation cannot coexist at the same time, how much less can the absolute being and absolute nonbeing which are the termini of the act of creation? Therefore it is true that nonbeing is at another instant preceding the first instant, and between these, as between any two instants whatsoever, the medium is time. Therefore, before the first instant of time … is time. Therefore—the only way out of the muddle—the world has existed from eternity.[31]

In reply to the first argument, predicated on the necessary self-diffusiveness of the good, Fishacre distinguishes two causes or principles, the natural and the voluntary: the former is "precipitate" (*impetuosum*), the latter is "reflective" (*considerosum*). The very positing of a sufficient natural cause, therefore, entails immediate action, whereas such is not the case with a voluntary cause, which is characterized not by necessity but by contingency. Thus the will is always empowered to opt for the opposite (*valet ad opposita*), empowered namely to act or not to act. It does not therefore follow that a sufficient, eternal cause necessarily entails an eternal effect.[32]

With respect to the second argument, the argument based on the *Timaeus* account, Fishacre denies that God's "inability"

31. Ibid.
32. Ibid., 2:322.

to create a world or any creature coeternal with himself connotes impotence; the opposite is rather the case. If God were to produce the creature from his own substance, as the Father generates the Son, it would indeed count as a defect if the product did not measure up to the producer. But God creates not out of himself but out of matter or out of nothing. The noneternity of the world, therefore, is a deficiency not on the part of the agent but rather on the part of the product.[33]

The third objection is joined on two fronts. As above, God's causality is voluntary, and thus his act is not necessarily coexistent with himself. In addition, there are "those of great authority"[34] who point out that time and eternity are different measures, and therefore a temporal effect is not necessarily conterminous with an eternal cause, no matter the infinite power of the latter.[35]

To the fourth and fifth objections, Fishacre insists on the distinction between motion and the mover. The former begins to be, because it is not first by nature; the latter by contrast had no beginning, being by nature first. The eternity of the mover, moreover, does not at all entail the eternity of motion. Just as the sun can now illumine an object which before was not illumined without any change in the sun (as when a thing is conveyed from some sheltered place into the sun's light), so too an agent can effect a change without itself undergoing a change.[36]

To the sixth argument Fishacre responds in two ways. First, the reason God created when he did and not before (as he cre-

33. Ibid.

34. "Those of great authority" are most likely Grosseteste, *Hexaëmeron* 1.8.6, ed. Dales and Gieben, 61–62, and Alexander of Hales, *De eternitate,* ed. Nathanson, 58. Richard Dales (in a private correspondence) saw in this passage a reference to Grosseteste's *De finitate,* ed. Dales, 260–61.

35. Fishacre, *In 2 Sent.,* Appendix A, ed. Long, 2:322–23.

36. Ibid., 2:323–24. See the explanation below: "sicut sol posset incipere illuminare nec tamen incipere lucere, et hoc non per suam sed rei illuminatae mutationem, sic Deus incepit esse movens et movere sine sui mutatione per mutationem mobilis. Neque tamen incepit intelligere, neque novo sed aeterno consilio fecit omnia quae temporaliter facta sunt," ibid., 323. Cf. Alexander of Hales, *De duratione*, ed. Nathanson, 95.

ates this soul now and not before) is because it was best that it be done this way. Why? It is because God willed it. God does not will something because it is good—as is our mode of operating—but something is good precisely because God wills it.[37]

The second response of Master Richard is that the question ("why did God make the world now and not before") is based on a false imagination, imagining namely that there is time *before* the world's creation. It is as mindless as asking why the world was made here in this place rather than somewhere else, again falsely imagining that beyond this world there is infinite space.[38]

To the seventh and subtlest of the objections it must be noted, says Fishacre, that although other verbs consignify time, the verb *est* does not.[39] One must rather discern whether the word "now" (*nunc*) signifies the "now" of eternity or the "now" of time. For unless the "now" of time is meant, this sentence would be false: "a man is." However, unless the now of eternity is meant, this would be false: "God is," and God therefore would not have said "I am who am" (Ex 3:14).[40] If therefore in every created thing nonbeing precedes being, in some of them nonbeing precedes being in temporal sequence (as in the souls that are now being created), but in others nonbeing precedes being only with respect to nature. The proposition "nonbeing is prior to being," therefore, is not affirmed and denied with respect to the same measure.[41]

Since at the first "now" of time there was true being and since being implies nonbeing, the question is whether there was nonbeing at the same instant or at another. The answer for Fishacre

37. Ibid., 2:324–25. Cf. Maimonides, *Guide* 2.18, trans. Pines, 301–2.

38. Ibid., 2:325. The implication here is that place is defined by the ultimate containing sphere, the empyrean, so that beyond the *ultimum continens* talk of place is unintelligible. See Edward Grant, *Physical Science in the Middle Ages* (New York: Wiley, 1971), 73–74.

39. Cf. Peter Lombard's discussion regarding the consignification of nouns and verbs (1 *Sent.* 44.2.1–4), Fishacre's likely source. On the truth value of propositions with the verb "is" see Sorabji, *Time, Creation and the Continuum*, 50–51.

40. Fishacre, *In 2 Sent.*, Appendix A, ed. Long, 2:325.

41. Ibid.

is *both*. But the *other* "now" is not of the same genus; it is namely the "now" of eternity, different from the "now" of time.[42]

Regarding the objector's conclusion that between any two instants the medium is time, Fishacre notes that this is true only within the same genus. Between the "now" of time and the "now" of eternity, however, there is no *medium*, since the "now" of eternity is whole and complete in any "now" of time, just as the soul is whole in any part of the body. Fishacre is here worth quoting: "I said above, and I think what I said is true, that in the same 'now' the being and the non-being of the first creature exist simultaneously; and generally speaking in all those things created from nothing, although nonbeing precedes being according to nature, they exist nevertheless at the same time, that is in the same instant of time."[43] Therefore in the first instant of time it was true that the first creature existed and did not exist; nevertheless nonbeing is prior in nature to being, just as the same light in the same "now" of time is in the east and west, yet is prior by nature in the east.

The objection that the being and nonbeing which are the extremes of creation are more distant than the extremes of generation is thus solved. Although the extremes of generation are indeed less distant, nevertheless they do not share the same "now" of time, because they exist by reason of different "nows" of time. For different beings cause different "nows." But in the nonbeing that is one extreme of generation is a different being from that being which is the other extreme of generation. But extremes

42. Ibid. As Dales explains with respect to a similar argument in the *De finitate*: "But if the non-being of the world is in eternity and its being in time, it would seem that from the standpoint of the eternal (i.e., God) the world *is* not, unless one introduces 'before and after' into eternity," *Medieval Discussions*, 74.

43. Fishacre, *In 2 Sent.*, Appendix A, ed. Long, 2:326. Rufus characterizes this argument as a subtlety which by his lights is not true: "isti idem addunt aliquid de subtili quod non verum esse intelligo," Appendix 5A, §12. Rufus, however, could have found the same "subtle" argument in the *De finitate*; see Grosseteste, *De finitate*, ed. Dales, 260–61.

of creation, namely being and nonbeing, indeed share the same "now" of time, because, as has been said, they do not exist in any way by reason of diverse "nows"; for in the nonbeing, which is the extreme of creation, there is no being (not even potential being). Moreover, although created being necessarily requires an instant of time, the nonbeing preceding creation, to the extent that it is a pure nothing (*pure nihil*), just as necessarily requires that it not be measured by an instant.[44]

Now that Fishacre has disposed of the arguments in favor of the world's eternity, he finds ten arguments in support of the position that the world was created in time. There is little that is original in these arguments, most being restatements of the tradition from Alexander to Philip the Chancellor. Most, moreover, will resurface again in the writings of Bonaventure and other anti-Aristotelians. The first argument is simply the opposition between time and eternity. On no less an authority than St. Augustine, the world is temporal, measured by time, and therefore not eternal.[45]

Second, on the authority of Aristotle being and possibility in perpetual beings are identical. *A fortiori* it is the case in eternal beings. This means that such beings are immutable, otherwise they would not be everything that they *can* be. But the world is in constant flux. Therefore, and so forth.[46]

The third is the well-worn *versio* argument, attributable originally to John Damascene.[47] The argument states, namely, that everything that is reducible to nothing was nothing before it was something. But the world is reducible to nonbeing, because on Plato's authority everything that is joined together is by nature dissoluble. Therefore the world had nonbeing before being. But this would have been impossible had it been eternal. Therefore, and so forth.[48]

44. Ibid

45. Ibid., 2:327.

46. Ibid.

47. See Dales and Argerami, *Medieval Latin Texts*, 91.

48. Fishacre, *In 2 Sent*., Appendix A, ed. Long, 2:327–28.

Fishacre follows with several *per impossibile* arguments that are likewise commonplaces. If, for example, humankind existed from the beginning (here echoing Grosseteste), there would by now have been born an infinite number of human beings.[49] There would then be an infinite number of souls in existence (*per impossibile* according to Aristotelian canons) or else there would be one single soul for all mankind (as per Averroes) or a finite number of souls would successively occupy different corruptible bodies (as per Plato)—all of which are *impossibile*.[50]

Likewise, if Aristotle is correct, moderns are more perceptive than their forebears; but after an infinite duration our contemporaries should by this argument be infinitely perceptive—which of course belies experience. Therefore, and so forth. Also, humans are decreasing in size generation by generation, and although any quantum is infinitely divisible, a certain modicum is necessary to preserve corporeity. Therefore, and so forth. Lastly, the population is increasing over time; over an infinite duration humans would have fully occupied the finite space on the planet.[51]

In his seventh argument Fishacre maintains that any infinite series of agent causes is reducible to three orders, each succeeding the prior: call them *a*, *b*, and *c*, *b* deriving of *a*, and *c* deriving of *b*. It is agreed that without *b* there would be no *c* and without *a* no *b*. Therefore, without a first none of the remaining (even if the series be infinite) would exist. Therefore, the world had a first, a beginning.[52]

The eighth and ninth arguments make essentially the same point. For his tenth argument, however, Fishacre considers the grades of being: those that have neither beginning nor end (God), those that have both beginning and end (plants), and those that have a beginning but no end (human souls). The remaining kind,

49. Cf. Wood, "Rufus on Creation," 10–12.

50. Fishacre, *In 2 Sent.*, Appendix A, ed. Long, 2:328.

51. Ibid., 2:328–29.

52. Ibid., 2:329–30.

those with an end but no beginning, is unknown. Therefore, if all the heavenly revolutions which have taken place end with the present revolution, they necessarily had a first.[53]

Therefore, (paraphrasing Grosseteste) with a single word, *principium*, Moses has destroyed the errors of the philosophers, all of whom posited many *principia*.[54]

He [Moses] by a single letter shattered the errors of all of these <philosophers>, namely the final letter of this word, *principio*, by which is designated a singular number. Marvelous indeed is the inscrutable depth of this wisdom[55] which by a single letter lays low a host of errors. Nor is it necessary to press for the destruction of these errors, since they are mutually self-destructing.[56]

The next Oxford master to take up the question of the world's eternal duration was the Franciscan master, Richard Rufus.[57] Although he honored the scholastic convention of not referring to his opponent by name—Fishacre is referred to simply as *aliqui* or even *quidam*—Rufus clearly has the Fishacre text before him together with Grosseteste's *Hexaëmeron*.[58] Rufus's approach is to articulate the arguments opposed to creation—seventeen by one reckoning.[59] He then responds to each in turn. Of these arguments, three are quoted *verbotenus* along with their proposed solutions from Fishacre's treatise, while two others are paraphrased.

53. Ibid., 2:330. Cf. Philip the Chancellor, *Summa de bono*, q. 3, ed. Wicki, 51.

54. Ibid., 2:330–31.

55. The allusion here is to the text with which Fishacre begins his inaugural lecture and which opens his Commentary, "O altitudo divitiarum sapientiae et scientiae Dei" (Rom 11:33).

56. Fishacre, *In 2 Sent.*, Appendix A, ed. Long, 2:331.

57. See the recent edition by Brown, "The Eternity of the World," 269–80. See also Raedts, *Richard Rufus of Cornwall*, 187–200, and Wood, "Rufus on Creation," 23–30, and "Richard Rufus: Physics at Paris before 1240," *Documenti e studi sulla tradizione filosofica medievale* 5 (1994): 87–127.

58. I have reproduced the Rufus text in Appendix 5A, italicizing the portions that are quoted from Fishacre. I also made several corrections to the edited text after examining the manuscript *in situ*.

59. Raedts, *Rufus*, 193.

To the argument that a full and total cause necessarily produces a similarly eternal and therefore coexistent effect, Fishacre had wondered whether Grosseteste's solution had been sufficient, "since a temporal cause can make it such that its act or motion is contemporaneous with it. If I claim that the latter were a sufficient cause, why cannot it be similarly the case that an eternal sufficient cause be able to produce its act coeternally with itself, since an eternal cause is infinitely more powerful than a temporal cause?"[60] Fishacre, in short, as Maimonides before him and Thomas Aquinas after, was distinguishing causal from temporal sequence: the creator could have caused the world to be coeternally with Himself. Rufus's response to Fishacre's animadversion, however, is abruptly dismissive: "This question seems to me a nullity, since this is to ask why God could not make the temporal eternal."[61] This is of course to miss the point, as is clear from Rufus's alternate response, which stresses the voluntary nature of the divine cause.[62]

Rufus likewise objects to Fishacre's response to the objection that if there is no good reason why God should not have created the world earlier (or later), the world was eternal. Fishacre had argued that the problem was based on a false imagination.[63] This question is likewise a nullity, responds Rufus. The more fundamental question is why God did not create the world from eternity. The answer is that such was God's eternal will, namely that the world come to be in time.[64]

Fishacre's seventh argument, moreover, Rufus also cites *verbotenus*, but objects again to his response: "But these same <masters> add something subtle which I understand not to be true, for they say that 'in the first "now" of time the being and the nonbeing of the first creature exist simultaneously.'"[65]

60. See Appendix 5A, §6.
61. Ibid.
62. Ibid., §7.
63. See Fishacre, *In 2 Sent.*, Appendix A, ed. Long, 2:325.
64. Rufus, Appendix 5A, §10. Cf. Raedts, Rufus, 194. Raedts, however, mistakenly attributes the source of the argument to an anonymous commentary on the *Metaphysics*.
65. Ibid., §12.

Equally objectionable to Rufus is Fishacre's view that nonbeing is prior in nature to being, as illustrated by light being at the same instant in the east and the west, though by nature prior in the east. He has refuted this view in the first book of his Commentary, says Rufus: presence in more than one place at the same time is impossible both for light and for angels.[66] Rufus is also bothered by what he sees as Fishacre's claim that affirmation and negation can both be true of the same object at the same time. The mind cannot in any way grasp this (*nec hoc capit intellectus aliquis omnino*), he says.[67]

Rufus has obviously subjected the Fishacre text to a close reading. Agreeing with his conclusions, Rufus feels nevertheless that several of his rival's arguments are defective—or at best so subtle that they lose any pedagogic value. In at least one instance, Rufus simply fails to understand the argument.[68] To what extent he regarded his role as defending the views of Grosseteste vis-à-vis Fishacre's corrections remains a matter of conjecture.

What is noteworthy about Fishacre's extracurricular treatise on the eternal duration of the world is the witness it bears to an active interest and lively debate regarding the subject on the part of the earliest Oxford masters. The Fishacre contribution provides the missing link between the rather less tolerant views of Robert Grossteste and the rebuttal of Richard Rufus, which was aimed at Fishacre, possibly for his implicit criticism of Grosseteste.

While the Fishacre arguments are neither terribly remarkable nor altogether original, they provide further evidence of the brisk exchange of texts between Paris and Oxford and the continued currency of arguments mounted by Maimonides and later by Alexander of Hales and Philip the Chancellor. They also bear witness to a theologian with an extremely subtle mind, who took seriously the scholastic enterprise and contributed to its advance.

66. Ibid.
67. Ibid., §13.
68. I refer to Fishacre's argument allowing for the possibility of an eternally created world.

APPENDIX 5A

Richard Rufus, *In 2 Sent.* 1.1; ed. Stephen F. Brown, in *MM* 21/1 (1991), 270–76.

[Quaestio prima: An sit creatio?]

§1. Sit ergo nobis quaestio in medio proposita in principio: an sit creatio omnino aut non sit.

§2. Quod[69] non sit videtur, nam omne quod fit fit a et ex sibi convenienti. Non est autem convenientia inter nihil et aliquid. Ergo ex nihilo non fit aliquid. Et hoc est quod posuerunt fere omnes philosophi, scilicet "ex nihilo nihil fit." Quid autem est creatura? Augustinus, *Contra Felicianum*: "Creatura est, ex eo quod adhuc non est, aut aliquando non fuit, rei cuiuslibet corruptibilis, quantum in se, est Dei Patris omnipotentis voluntate facta substantia." —Sed puto ad praedictum argumentum quod illa[70] propositio "quod fit fit" etc., in causa agente per se, et non secundum accidens, sive mediata sive immediata, universaliter vera est. Sed non in genere causae materialis universaliter est vera: non enim omne quod fit ex materia fit. Et cum dicimus aliquid fieri ex vel de nihilo, non notatur ibi circumstantia causae materialis, sed accipitur ibi "ex," id[71] est "post," sicut: "ex" nocte fit dies.

§3. Item, actio non exigit quid agat, sed in quid; ita dicit Philosophus. Ex quo videtur quod creare exigat materiam substantialem, et ita ut prius. —Sed puto quod illud intelligendum est de actione artificis diminuti, qui scilicet indiget necessario materia subiecta. Non est autem hoc nomen de actione Dei, scilicet creatione; sed econverso illa exigit quid agatur et non in quid.

§4. Item, posita tota et plena causa alicuius, necesse est totum et plenum effectum eiusdem causae simul cum ea coexsistere. Deus autem talis causa est, quia omnipotens est, cui nulla accidit nova condicio vel sapientiae vel potentiae vel voluntatis. Ergo si mundus ab eo factus est, semper simul cum eo coexsistit, et est aeternus.

§5. Hic solvunt aliqui quod haec ratio necessaria est in his quae participant mensuram eiusdem generis, utpote quod ambo sint temporalia vel ambo aeterna. "Si autem causa et causatum non participent eiusdem generis essendi mensuram non potest eis coaptari illa regula, ut dicatur: 'exsistente causa, necessario coexsistit causatum.'"[72] Tempus vero et aeternitas non sunt eiusdem generis mensurae, et ideo in his non tenet. Sed in Patre

69. quid *ed.*

70. *om. ed.*

71. id est post: [ex] I Posteriorum *ed.*

72. Grosseteste, *Hexaëmeron* 1.8.6, eds. Dales and Gieben, 62.

et Filio "quorum uterque aeternus, et Pater causa Filii, secundum Augustinum, Damascenum et Chrysostomum,"[73] ambo coaeterni sunt. Sed "Deus aeternus causa est mundi temporalis et praecedit mundum non tempore sed simplici aeternitate."[74]

§6. Sed contra hanc responsionem quaerunt quidam: "*cum causa temporalis possit facere suum causatum esse simul tempore cum ipsa, quare non similiter causa aeterna sufficiens possit facere suum causatum sibi coaeternum, cum causa aeterna in infinitum sit potentior causa temporali?*"—Sed haec quaestio mihi videtur nulla, nam hoc est quaerere quare Deus non possit facere temporale aeternum.

§7. Respondi tamen potest ad praedictam quaestionem aliter, ut videtur, quod dupliciter est causa vel principium rei: principium naturale agit sine ratione et agit necessitate. Et ideo posita tali causa sufficiente, statim ponitur effectus. Causa autem voluntaria non agit necessitate sed pure voluntarie et cum potestate rationabili quae semper valet ad opposita. Et praeterea, nulla necessitas accidit in Deo; unde in ipso non tenet propositio praedicta.

§8. Item, sicut arguit Augustinus, *Contra Maximinum*, ut habitum est I libro, d. 20, quaero: Deus aut potuit creare mundum sibi coaeternum aut non? Si non, impotens fuit. Si sic: aut noluit, et tunc invidit; aut voluit, et tunc fecit. —Sed ad istud iam responsum est, ut videtur, quia hoc posse esset posse facere temporale aeternum et creaturam Deum, et hoc est potius[75] non posse.

§9. Item, idem eodem modo se habens semper natum est idem facere. Ergo Deus qua ratione tunc fecit mundum et semper fecit et faciet. Et sic videtur quod aut numquam creandus fuit mundus aut ab aeterno, quia ex parte Dei non est ratio aliqua, ut videtur, quare nunc et non prius, cum omnino similiter semper se habeat; nec in re facienda erat causa quia ipsa nihil fuit.

§10. Ad istud respondent aliqui quare "*tunc et non prius creavit mundum, quia sic fuit optimum.*" Et quare hoc? "*Quia Deus sic voluit, cuius voluntatis causa alia non est.*" Vel aliter: "*haec quaestio fundatur super falsam imaginationem qua imaginatur tempus fuisse ante mundum.*" Et hanc quaestionem recitat Augustinus, *De civitate Dei* libro XI, cap. 5, dicens: "Ita quaeritur cur potius tunc et non antea factus sit mundus, quemadmodum quaeri potest cur hic potius ubi est et non alibi. Nam si infinita spatia temporis ante mundum cogitant ... cogitent similiter extra mundum infinita spatia locorum. Nunc autem nec extra mundum est locus, nec ante mundum fuit tempus." Unde Augustinus, libro eodem et capitulo eodem: "Quis non videat quod tempora non fuissent nisi creatura fieret, quae aliqua motione mutaretur?" —Omnino mihi videtur, ut prius, quod haec quaestio nulla est: quare, scilicet, tunc et

73. Ibid.

74. Ibid

75. post *ed.*

non prius fecit mundum? Hoc est enim quaerere quare non ab aeterno fecit mundum: nihil enim prius mundo nisi aeternum. Ab aeterno ergo voluit Deus voluntate incommutabili mundum esse non ab aeterno, sed ex tempore, hoc est quando mundum esse possibile est. Cum ergo quaeritur an fuit causa in Deo quare non prius fecit mundum, verum videtur quod in ipso fuit causa. Haec enim videtur causa, quia scilicet ipse solus est[76] aeternus. Unde sua aeternitas et sua incommutabilitas videtur causa quare non fecit mundum ab aeterno. Unde Augustinus, libro eodem, cap. 4: "Sic credant et mundum ex tempore fieri potuisse, non tamen ideo Deum in eo faciendo aeternum consilium voluntatemque mutasse."

§11. Item, si mundus incepit, prius fuit verum mundum non esse et postea fuit verum mundum esse; "prius" autem et "posterius" sunt differentiae temporis; fuit igitur tempus ante mundi creationem. Aut aliter ducitur haec oppositio: "*si est primum instans temporis et mundi, in illo instanti quod vocetur 'a,' verum fuit mundum esse et prius fuit verum mundum non-esse. Aut ergo in eodem instanti aut in alio. Si in eodem, contra: affirmatio et negatio quae sunt termini generationis minus distant quam quae sunt termini creationis; illae enim causae habent saltem materiam; secundae vero nihil omnino, quia creatio est ex nihilo. Cum igitur esse et non esse quae sunt termini generationis in eodem instanti simul esse non possint, multo magis esse et non-esse quae sunt termini creationis simul esse non poterunt. Igitur, ambo ista 'mundum esse' et [mundum] 'non esse' non sunt vera in primo instanti temporis; igitur 'mundum non esse' fuit verum in alio instanti praecedenti primum instans. Et inter haec duo instantia erit tempus medium; ergo ante primum instans temporis <tempus> est; quare tempus est ab aeterno.*"

§12. Hic respondetur quod in omni creato non-esse praecedit esse; sed in quibusdam non-esse praecedit esse tempore, ut in animabus quae nunc creantur; in quibusdam vero non-esse praecedit esse solum natura seu aeternitate. Cum ergo in primo creato dicitur prius non-esse quam esse non affirmatur et negatur esse respectu eiusdem mensurae, sed esse negatum dicit nunc aeternitatis, esse affirmatum primum nunc temporis. Unde inter ista duo "nunc" non est tempus medium. Isti responsioni hucusque consentio. Sed isti idem addunt aliquid de subtili quod non verum esse intelligo. Dicunt enim quod "*in primo nunc temporis simul sunt esse et non esse primae creaturae, et generaliter de omnibus creatis de nihilo.*" Consimile[77] dant iudicium quod putant probare sic: Omne quod est solum natura prius alio, nihil prohibet ipsum esse simul tempore cum illo. Sed non esse primi creati solum natura prius est quam esse eiusdem; ergo etc. —Non credo quod istud teneat. Non enim sequitur nisi si [illud quod] est solum natura prius non

76. es *ed.*
77. consimilem *ed.*

est tempore prius. Sed ultra non sequitur: "non est tempore prius illo, ergo potest esse tempore simul cum illo," nam non-esse nec est prius tempore, nec simul tempore cum illo. Magis adhuc conantur explanare quod dicunt: *"non-esse, cum sit pura negatio, de se nullam quaerit mensuram; esse vero quaerit. Igitur esse et non-esse, si quaerunt distinctionem secundum tempus, hoc non erit nisi quia illud non-esse ponit aliquid, scilicet aliquod esse aliud ab esse negato. Ita est in extremis generationis,"* nam ibi est primo quidem esse in potentia, deinde vero esse in actu, et ista esse diversa sunt causae diversorum nunc temporis. Sed non-esse quod est extremum creationis[78] [est] pura negatio, et non ponit aliquod esse; unde non est causa alicuius nunc temporis. Sed aliud extremum creationis, scilicet esse est causa unius nunc temporis. Sic ergo in his utrisque sufficit unum nunc temporis, et compatiuntur se in uno. Et exemplificat in hoc de luce: quod ipsa eodem numero "*in eodem nunc temporis est in oriente et occidente, tamen prius natura in oriente.*" —De hoc exemplo dictum est primo libro, dist. 37M, quod falsum est quod hic dicitur de luce, et similiter de angelo.

§13. Item, satis mirum[79] videtur quod dicunt non-esse quod est pura negatio et esse de eodem subiecto simul esse vera, cum[80] affirmatio et negatio de nullo eodem simul sint verae. Nec hoc capit intellectus aliquis omnino, scilicet quod de eodem simul affirmatio et negatio.

§14. Item, non esse quod est extremum generationis, si supponit aliquod esse, ergo non est simpliciter negativa, quia ex pure negativa numquam sequitur affirmativa. Quod si hoc, non contradicit esse affirmato. Ergo, si debet contradicere, omnino nihil ponet.

§15. Item, si negatio potest esse vera cum contradictoria affirmatione, pari ratione poterit affirmatio esse vera cum contradictoria negatione. Si enim compatiuntur se in eodem nunc temporis, possunt et se compati in nunc aeternitatis. Ex quo sequitur quod mundum esse fuit verum ab aeterno. Distinguit Augustinus, in libro *Confessionum* XII G, "prius" et "posterius" quattuor modis: aeternitate, tempore, electione, origine. Aeternitate, sicut Deus omnia; tempore, sicut flos fructum; electione, sicut fructus florem; origine, sicut sonus cantum. —Haec praedicta mihi non placent, sed magis videtur quod non-esse mundi, si praecedit[81] esse, non tempore praecedit, nam non est tempus ante mundum; sed praecedit natura seu aeternitate, quia ab aeterno verum fuit non esse mundum, et esse[82] mundum est posterius, tempore scilicet, nam et ipsum tempus posterius est aeternitate. "Posterius," dico, se ipso tempore, ut iste ablativus designet rationem mensurae, et aeternitas est prior tempore, se ipsa aeternitate. Nec sequitur: *a* est

78. dictionis *ed.*
79. manifestum *ed.*
80. tamen *ed.*
81. praecederet *ed.*
82. *om. ed.*

aeternitate prius ipso *b*; ergo *b* est aeternitate posterius ipso *a*; et hoc tum quia in aeternitate non est prius et posterius, tum quia aeternitas non communicatur ab utroque, scilicet *a* et *b*.

§16. His ergo dimissis, redeamus ad obiectiones.

§17. Si mundus finem non habet, ergo nec initium, nam dicit Ambrosius *Hexaëmeron*, homelia prima: "Quae initium habent, et finem habent; et quibus finis datur, initium dari constat." Ecce quod convertuntur "habere initium" et "habere finem."

§18. Et idem[83] Basilius, in *Hexaëmeron* homelia prima: Omnia quae ex tempore ceperunt, necesse est tempore terminari. Si est initium temporale, de fine non dubitatur.[84]

§19. Unde Damascenus: Omne quod incipit et finitur per naturam.

§20. Sed puto quod haec intelligenda sunt secundum naturam[85] ipsorum creatorum. Sunt tamen aliqua quae habent initium et non finem. Sed hoc est per conditoris voluntatem, ut innuit illa sententia Platonis supra. Et idem Plato in *Timaeo*: "Corpora caelestia natura sunt dissolubilia, voluntate autem conditoris indissolubilia."

§21. Item, si est creatio, creat Deus postquam non creavit, et movet postquam non movit; ergo factus est de non-movente movens; ergo est mutabilis. Aut si ab aeterno movet, movere autem et moveri correlativa sunt et simul natura, ergo ab aeterno est motus.

§22. Hic iterum dicunt aliqui quod Deus fuit motor ab aeterno et movens. Unde motor vel movere non incepit esse. Sed tamen motus incepit esse: movere enim natura prius est quam moveri, sicut actio quam passio: est enim eius causa. —Istud iterum mihi non placet, quia Deus incepit esse Dominus, sicut docet Augustinus, sic et incepit creare et movere et agere. Unde Augustinus, *Confessionum* libro XI: "Audenter dico 'antequam faceret Deus caelum et terram, non faciebat aliquid.' Si enim faciebat, quid nisi creaturam faciebat? Sic ergo incepit creare, movere, et agere." Sed haec verba "movere," "agere," non proprie dicuntur de Deo, sicut hic docet Magister in secunda parte distinctionis: non enim agit Deus instrumentis corporalibus sed verbo—"dixit enim et facta sunt." Ab aeterno autem dixit, ut fieret mundus tunc quando esse incepit. Ipse ergo semper uniformiter se habuit et ante et post: non enim aliter movit vel fecit cum creavit quam ante. Sed tunc factum est quod non ante. Ex his patet quod nulla est in ipso mutatio etsi nunc quidem sit creans, prius vero non. Sed in ipso creato est mutatio, scilicet de non-esse ad esse.

§23. Item, si creat et agit Deus, erit ibi actio, ergo et passio et patiens; quare et passivum sive passibile. Est autem natura prius passibile quam pa-

83. ideo *ed.*

84. est dubitandum *ed.*

85. natura *ed.*

tiens, sicut combustibile quam combustum. Quaero ergo: Potentia quae notatur in hoc ipso passibile, ratione cuius est passibile[86] prius natura quam patiens, in quo est inquam[87] haec potentia? Aut in aliquo aut in nihilo? Si in aliquo, ergo prius fuit aliquid antequam crearetur. Si in nihilo, ergo ipsum nihil est passibile, et erit patiens. Quare, ipsum nihil creabitur et fiet. —Hic puto quod istud passibile non est priusquam patiens, nec proprie dicitur hic[88] passibile vel patiens; —sed dicatur creabile et creatum. Et puto quod creabile non est prius creato natura vel tempore, sed aut[89] solum secundum modum intelligendi. Talis enim regula, puto, non tenet nisi in eis quae sunt[90] prius in potentia, deinde in actu; hoc est in eis quae habent causas seminales in materia praeiacenti. Ipsa autem prima creatura non prius fuit creabilis, nec in potentia, nec passiva nec activa, nam ipse Deus etiam non potuit prius creare primam creaturam: hoc enim esset ab aeterno creare—hoc opposito in adiecto. Melius sic dicitur: mundus fuit creabilis ab aeterno, hoc est, fuit subiectus scientiae Dei et tale esse habuit. Sed non fuit creatus ab aeterno, id est, non habuit esse in materia. Et est unum prius altero; et est haec positio in mundo et in aliquo. Nec tamen mundus est ab aeterno nisi praedicto modo.

APPENDIX 5B

Two more friars pronounced on the problem in the 1250s, but that they should still be under the thrall of Grosseteste is a stretch for my thesis. Notwithstanding, their views on demonstrating the creation in time of the world are remarkably similar to their Oxford predecessors.

Robert Kilwardby, Dominican, probably arriving at Oxford too late to have incepted under Fishare, begins the second book of his *Quaestiones* on Lombard's *Sentences* (at least three years after Grosseteste's death) with three questions: first, whether a creation *ex nihilo* were possible, second, whether in fact things were created, and lastly whether things could have been created eternally.[91] With respect to the last question Kilwardby distinguishes three positions: the world is coeternal with God, unmade and uncreated; the world is coeternally created by God (as the eternal foot eternally makes an eternal footprint); and lastly the world is eternally created by God, but unwittingly (as a shadow results from a body). None of these

86. passibibile (sic) *ed.*

87. in quantum *ed.*

88. hoc *ed.*

89. *om. ed.*

90. sunt … in eis quae *om. ed.*

91. Robert Kilwardby, *Quaestiones in librum secundum Sententiarum*, qq. 1–3, ed. Gerhard Leibold (Munich: Verlag der Bayerischen Akademie der Wissenschaften, 1992), 3–16.

opinions can stand, insists Kilwardby, and he finds arguments against all three. What ultimately deceived the philosophers (read: the Aristotelians)? They were unable to understand a first instant except with this qualification: before this there was nothing—in other words, they could not understand "before" and "after" (*prius et posterius*) except in terms of time.[92]

At the very same time as Kilwardby was giving his lectures on the *Sentences*, the Franciscan Thomas of York (who apparently was assigned to the Franciscan chair at Oxford over Rufus) wrote his *Sapientiale*, a treasure trove of contemporary sources, the edition of which scholars have been awaiting since 1948, when it was first announced. In book 2 (in a work containing a hefty seven books) he deals in subsequent chapters with questions revolving around the metaphysics of creation and the possibility of the eternal duration of the world: in chapter 4, for example, he gives the arguments for the antiquity of the world; in chapter 5 he focuses on the authorities who argue for Aristotle's position regarding the antiquity of the world and responses to these arguments; in chapter 6 he gives seven arguments for the *novitas mundi*, featuring Moses Maimonides.[93] As with other issues, Thomas has read everything—Plato, Aristotle, Maimonides, Algazel, Avicenna, Averroes, Alexander, Albumasar, Gundissalinus, Hermes Trismegistus [which he might have read in Bacon] as well as the fathers—and digested very little: at least he doesn't make it easier for his reader.

Citing the authority of Maimonides, Thomas lists three positions: the world was created from nothing (the position he ultimately argues for), the world was made from preexisting matter (famously, Plato's position), and the world existed eternally.[94] For the last position he finds five arguments in Aristotle, several in Algazeli, Avicenna, and especially Averroes.[95]

In the following chapter, he cites Maimonides's view that Aristotle thought he was giving only probable arguments for the world's eternity, not demonstrations properly so-called.[96] The lengthiest part, however, is reserved for arguments—seven in all—lifted from the *Guide* of Maimonides, in support of the newness of the world.[97] Ultimately an eternally *ex nihilo* causing God (again the metaphor of the foot in the dust is invoked) won't hold up to scrutiny because, says Thomas, the thing caused cannot be coterminous with the cause which has fulfilled its nature of cause. In short, "cause" is a relative term demanding something that is caused. A cause *qua* cause cannot exist without an effect.[98]

92. Ibid., 11–12.

93. See edition in Ephrem Longpré, "Thomas d'York et Matthieu d'Aquasparta," *AHDLMA* 1 (1926–1927): 273–93.

94. Ibid., 273.

95. Ibid., 274–79.

96. Ibid., 279.

97. Ibid., 284–86.

98. Ibid., 289.

Six more arguments follow, none of them new, none of them demonstrative, including the variant on the infinite number of souls: the Christian and Jewish doctrine of the resurrection of the body would entail having not only an infinite number of souls (for which there would be room) but also an infinite number of bodies—for which there would not be space.[99]

What conclusions can we draw from approximately a quarter of a century of speculation on the subject? First, that the issue of the eternal duration of the world and the corresponding metaphysics of creation was a lively topic of debate at the Oxford studium—and this absent the threat that was posed by the Latin Averroists at Paris, beginning in the 1260s. Second, as with other issues this question bears ample evidence of a lively and prompt flow of texts between the studium at Paris and that at Oxford. Lastly, there is not only a common fund of arguments that keep getting repeated with only minor variations, but also the conclusions reached are invariably the same and reflective of Grosseteste's passionately held views. The eternal creation of the world is rationally untenable, and therefore creation in time (the *novitas mundi*) is the only sound position, not only according to faith but also according to reason.

99. Ibid., 289–92.

CHAPTER 6

Fishacre and Rufus on the Metaphysics of Light

In one of the witnesses of Richard Fishacre's *Sentences* Commentary there occurs in a later hand the following marginal note at book 2, distinction 13, chapter 2: "hic deest questio de luce que scripta est in parvo quaterno cum questionibus de heresibus."[1] Although the *quaternus*[2] or gathering to which the note refers has not been recovered, the *questio de luce* does appear, once at the end of a British Library copy of the Fishacre Commentary[3] and a second time in a Bibliothèque nationale de France copy of the same work.[4] Both appear at the same place in the text where the marginal note appears in *C*. There are a number of indications that this question on light belongs to the period of Fishacre's re-

1. Viz. Cambridge, Gonville and Caius Coll. MS 329/410 (*C*), fol. 175va.

2. On the use of the term in the thirteenth century see Louis J. Bataillon, "Exemplar, Pecia, Quaternus," in *Vocabulaire du livre et de l'écriture au moyen âge*, ed. Olga Weijers (Turnhout: Brepols, 1989), 206–19.

3. Viz. London, BL MS Royal 10.B.VII (*R*), fols. 388va–389ra.

4. Viz. Paris, BNF MS lat. 15754 (*P*), fols. 91rb–vb.

gency, following the completion of his Commentary in ca. 1245[5] and before his death in 1248. To begin with, neither the *questio de luce* nor the question on the eternal duration of the world[6] are to be found in any of the remaining seven manuscripts which contain the second book of the Fishacre Commentary. In *R*, moreover, the earlier of the two manuscripts containing the *De luce* text,[7] the question occurs at the very end of the codex; only in *P* is the question inserted in the text itself, at the place where the lemma from the Lombard's work occurs.

In addition, other marginal jottings provide further hints as to the composition of the aforementioned *quaternus*. A second note in *C* records the fact that the question on the creation or beginning of the world is also to be found along with the question on light in the litte volume "before the question on heresies."[8]

That Fishacre should have turned his attention to the subject is not surprising, given the fact that light was so central a theme in the thought of Robert Grosseteste, who had so decisively set his stamp on the Oxford studium.[9] In a short treatise entitled *De luce*, he crafted an entire world-system, a veritable "metaphysics of light,"[10] which James McEvoy has called "perhaps the only scientific cosmogony written between the *Timaeus* and early

5. For the dating of the Commentary see R. James Long and Maura O'Carroll, *Life and Works of Richard Fishacre, OP: Prolegomena to the Edition of his Commentary on the "Sentences"* (Munich: Verlag der Bayerischen Akademie der Wissenschaften, 1999), 39–41.

6. See R. James Long, "First Oxford Debate on the Eternity of the World," *RTPM* 65/1 (1998): 54–98.

7. Ibid., 54, n. 4.

8. For the details see chapter 5 in this volume, "The First Oxford Debate on the Eternity of the World," 63–87.

9. See James McEvoy, *Gli inizi di Oxford. Grossatesta ed i primi theologi* (Milan: Jaca Book, 1996), 72–78; and Klaus Hedwig, *Sphaera Lucis. Studien zur Intelligibilität des Seienden im Kontext der mittelalterlichen Lichtspekulation*, in *Beiträge* N.F. 18 (Münster i. W.: Aschendorff, 1980), cap. 5: "Robert Grosseteste: Sphaera Lucis."

10. The expression, which has not been without its challenges, was first coined by Clemens Baeumker in *Witelo, Ein Philosoph und naturforscher des XIII. Jahrhunderts*, in *Beiträge* 3.2 (Münster: i. W.: Aschendorff, 1908).

modern times."[11] He later engaged the same metaphysics to explicate the Genesis account of the creation of light[12] in his magisterial *Hexaëmeron*.[13]

Unexplored by Grosseteste, however, is the question which Fishacre asks in his *De luce*: is light a substance or an accident?[14] Fishacre's point of departure is the Lombard text: "Si quaeritur qualis illa lux fuerit, corporalis scilicet an spiritualis."[15] Lombard, says Fishacre, decided that light is a body, but the question is a matter of considerable dispute among the *moderni* as it was with the ancients.[16]

Conflating the questions of whether light is body or spirit and whether substance or accident, Fishacre adduces five arguments to establish his position that light is not a spirit or an accident, but that it is a corporeal substance. He then raises four contrary arguments to the above position and finally replies to each *contra* argument in turn.

Light in air, says Fishacre, is not caused by the air but by the

11. James McEvoy, *Philosophy of Grosseteste,* 2nd ed. (Oxford: Clarendon Press, 1982), 151.

12. Viz. Gn 1:3–4: "Fiat lux. Et facta est lux. Et vidit Deus lucem quod esset bona et divisit lucem a tenebris."

13. See Robert Grosseteste, *Hexaëmeron* 2.1–11, ed. Richard C. Dales and Servus Gieben (Oxford: Oxford University Press, 1982), 85–101.

14. The same question was taken up by Bartholomaeus Anglicus in book 8, chapter 40, of his *De proprietatibus rerum* (Frankfurt, 1601), 425–30. Although the *DPR* and Fishacre's question are nearly contemporaneous—in the latest scholarly estimate Baudouin Van den Abeele places the completion of Bartholomaeus's monumental work in the decade of the 1240s; "Introduction générale," Bartholomaeus Anglicus, De proprietatibus rerum, vol. 1 (Turnhout: Brepols, 2007), 4—the remarkable similarities between the two accounts tempt one to conclude either that one author read the other or that both were dependent on a hitherto unknown common third source.

15. Peter Lombard, *Sententiae in IV libros distinctae.* 13.2; ed. Ignatius Brady, Spicilegium Bonaventurianum 4 (Grottaferrata: Collegium S. Bonaventurae ad Claras Aquas, 1971), 1:389.

16. For a recent study of the controversy see David Park, *The Fire within the Eye. A Historical Essay on the Nature and Meaning of Light* (Princeton: Princeton University Press, 1997).

sun. Thus light is not in air as in a subject and is therefore not an accident.[17]

Furthermore, when light traverses air, as at dawn for instance, either it is the same in number in the east and west, or else the eastern light reaches the west by successively generating new light as it progresses. Both opinions have their supporters, claims Fishacre, but both would deny accident status to light. In the first case, light would completely alter (*permutat*) its subject, something that accidents never do. In the second, light by generating light would be performing an act beyond the capacity of its subject (air), again something contrary to the nature of an accident.[18]

Likewise, never are two accidents of the same speices found in the same part of the same subject at the same time. For example, two whitenesses cannot inhere in the same part of the same subject simultaneously. However, on the authority of Alhacen,[19] two beams of light from two different sources, from two candles say, do intersect and continue their separate ways past the point of intersection. Therefore, light cannot be an accident.[20]

Finally, Fishacre constructs a rather curious thought experiment having to do with the vacuum. Light, he says, is impeded only by an opaque object and therefore is able to penetrate a vacuum. But there can be no accident in a vacuum, because an accident must be in a subject, and if there were also a subject in the vacuum, it would by definition no longer be a vacuum.[21]

In the arguments *contra*, Fishacre finds both John Damascene and Aristotle denying that light has subsistence and corporeity. If light is a body and air is likewise a body, two bodies

17. See Fishacre, *In 2 Sent.*, Appendix B, ed. Long, 2:334.

18. Ibid.

19. Fishacre always refers to Alhacen simply as *auctor Perspective*. I am following in this paper the spelling of the Latin version of al-Haytham's name suggested by David C. Lindberg (*Roger Bacon and the Origins of "Perspective" in the Middle Ages* [Oxford: Clarendon Press, 1996], xxxiii, n. 75).

20. Fishacre, *In 2 Sent.*, Appendix B, ed. Long, 2:334–35.

21. Ibid., 2:335.

would occupy the same space, thus violating a fundamental principle of Aristotelian physics. In fact, they would not be two bodies but one: two lines of equal length in the same place become a single line.[22]

Moreover, if light were a body, it would be composed of matter and form. But light is continually being generated; the light of a moment ago no longer exists, it corrupts as soon as it is generated. If light emanates from the sun with respect both to its form and matter, something of the sun is continually perishing and will soon be reduced to nothingness. In fact, Fishacre adds, it is surprising that it has not yet happened.[23]

But what if one were to argue that light receives its matter from other bodies? The difficulty here is that matter has but a single substantial form and receives another only at the expense of the corruption of the first. Therefore, air's matter cannot receive the form of light unless the form of air be corrupted; the same thing cannot be both air and light at the same time. Since, moreover, the generation of light is instantaneous, the corruption of air must be equally so; and the generation of air must likewise be instantaneous to replace the instantaneously corrupting light, otherwise there would be a vacuum. Although Fishace does not explicitly say as much, the implication is that he finds this situation *inconveniens*. If, in addition, light is generated in the heavens, something of the heavens must be corrupted in order that light be the new form—a position clearly contrary to Aristotle's cosmology.[24]

Fishacre's solution is to assert that "light" is used equivocally of substance and accident, and that difficulties arise only when we fail to distinguish between the two usages. Sometimes "light" is the name given to the subtlest of bodily substances; sometimes the same name designates the accident caused by light, namely lighting up or illumination.[25]

22. Ibid.

23. Ibid.

24. Ibid., 2:335–36.

25. Ibid., 2:336.

Thus the answer to the conflicting authorities is clear: Damascene and Aristotle are referring to illumination, not to light-as-substance, in the passages cited. Augustine, by contrast, is alluding to the latter in the four passages quoted at the beginning of the treatise.[26]

Fishacre, moreover, finds nothing incompatible in two or more rarefied bodies occupying the same space or even one rarefied body occupying the same space as a grosser body: examples from the scriptures abound, as in the resurrected Christ passing through closed doors to appear to his disciples.[27]

In his most novel (and most vulnerable) position, Fishacre contends that the matter of light-as-substance neither emanates from the sun nor is bestowed by the air, but is unceasingly being created by God. A parallel case is the soul, whose matter[28] is created *de novo*, though this does not entail a creation of a new nature that was not a part of the six days: indeed the matter of the soul (and of light) now being created is generically the same as the soul (and light) created in the beginning. There is, however, this difference between the two cases: the entire soul—form and matter—are created together and simultaneously; when light is made, only the matter is created, the form being generated by the luminous body. Thus the sun confers light on matter which is the ongoing effect of the creative action of God.[29]

Indeed, some things that have been generated have only their matter from their *generans*, as is the case with human progeny, who receive only their matter, not their form, from their parents. Other things, namely angels, emanate directly from the creator,

26. Ibid.

27. Ibid., 2:336–37.

28. Fishacre, like the majority of his contemporaries, embraced a doctrine of spiritual matter (or universal hylomorphism); see R. James Long, "Richard Fishacre and the Problem of the Soul," *TMS* 52 (1975): 267–69, and "Of Angels and Pinheads: The Contributions of the Early Oxford Masters to the Doctrine of Spiritual Matter," *FS: Essays in Honor of Girard Etzkorn*, ed. Gordon A. Wilson and Timothy B. Noone, 56 (1998): 239–52. See chapters 9 and 4 in this voume, pp. 149–57 and 48–62.

29. Fishacre, *In 2 Sent.*, Appendix B, ed. Long, 2:337.

form, and matter.[30] The principle of plenitude, therefore, would demand the existence of the only remaining possibility; beings whose matter is supplied by the creative act of God and whose form is provided by another creature, namely the sun.[31]

A survey of his usual sources—William of Auxerre, Alexander of Hales, and, of course, Robert Grosseteste—discloses that Fishacre's little treatise is quite original, notwithstanding its Grossetestean inspiration. In fact, it was precisely Fishacre's original solution to the problem of light's ontological status that provoked a response from his chief critic, the Franciscan Master Richard Rufus.

In Rufus's first attempt at composing a Commentary on Lombard's *Sentences,* preserved in Oxford, Balliol College MS 62,[32] he takes issue with the centerpiece of Fishacre's light metaphysics, namely, the question of the substantial or accidental nature of light.[33] Employing many of the same sources as Fishacre did, Rufus proceeded to introduce an element of his own metaphysical thought, *forma-habitus*, to resolve the issue of whether light is a substance or an accident, after first reviewing the merits of Fishacre's reply.

Clearly, Rufus's use of authorities is derived in the main from both Grosseteste and Fishacre. Many of the same texts of Augustine and John Damascene are referenced and the same example of intersecting light rays from Alhacen makes its appearance, though in Rufus's appropriation the source of the example goes

30. Angels, like human souls, are for Fishacre composed of form and matter: see Long, "Angels and Pinheads," 239–45. See pp. 48–62 in this volume.

31. Fishacre, *In 2 Sent.*, Appendix B, ed. Long, 2:337.

32. For a detailed description of the Balliol manuscript (=*Ba*) See Peter Raedts, *Richard Rufus of Cornwall and the Tradition of Oxford Theology* (Oxford: Clarendon Press, 1987), 20–21; Roger A. B. Mynors, *Catalogue of the Manuscripts of Balliol College, Oxford* (Oxford: Clarendon Press, 1963), 42–43; and Franz Pelster, "Der älteste Sentenzenkommentar aus der Oxforder Franziskanerschule: Ein Beitrag zur Geschichte des theologischen Lehrbetriebs an der Oxforder Universität," *Scholastik* 1 (1926): 68–71.

33. This section of our collaborative study was contributed by Professor Timothy Noone, who has most generously given me permission to reproduce it here.

unmentioned. Yet the sources are not wholly identical; Rufus introduces Aristotle's *De anima* and Averroes's commentary on the *De anima* as texts providing key notions in developing his own solution to the problem of light.

Having introduced his authorities, Rufus proceeds first to summarize and then to criticize Fishacre's position. As Rufus interprets his views, Fishacre's basic contention is that we should distinguish between light-as-substance and light-as-accident; that is, we should not confuse light as the substantial form of the sun and light as the accident of the air which is illumined. We may be tempted to do so, quite naturally, owing to the proximity of the proper accident to the substantial form in the case of light, since we never think of light without also thinking of its presence in the medium. But if we keep in mind the distinction between light as such (*lux*) and the lighting up of the medium (*illuminatio*), Fishacre contends, we shall perceive that Aristotle and the Damascene on the one hand, and Augustine on the other, are saying things equally true but pertaining respectively to light as an accident and light as a substance.[34]

Rufus raises two fundamental problems with Fishacre's solution thus understood. First, he does not see how Fishacre's views allow for the claim that light, even as a substance, is a body, for form is the principle of operation and it is light as form that causes the activities associated with light in all of its manifestations. Second, Rufus fails to grasp how the distinction between *lux* and *illuminatio* really helps much. *Illuminatio* does not seem to be an accident of the light-as-substance which is found in the sun, since the lighting up and the light of the sun seem identical and not distinct. Yet, if we do countenance such a distinction, as we must in the case of the medium, the lighting up as received is found in the thing illumined and is not an accident of the light, that is, the sun's light, from which it has emanated. Furthermore,

34. See below, Appendix 6A, §33.

the light in the medium is obviously not a function of the nature of the medium, for example the air, since it does not arise from the principles of such a substance. Therefore, it cannot be counted as an accident of the medium.[35]

In concluding his criticism of Fishacre's distinction between *lux* and *illuminatio*, Rufus wonders whether it is really more impertinent than incorrect, for even if the distinction is admitted, one would be merely led to inquire about whether illumination as activity and illumination as received are identical; the real issue, however, concerns the very nature of the light that lightens and whether it is a substance or an accident.[36]

Apart from these fundamental problems with Fishacre's distinction between *lux* and *illuminatio*, Rufus also thinks unsatisfactory his Dominican contemporary's efforts to cope with the objection drawn from Aristotle's natural philosophy, namely that no two bodies can simultaneously occupy the same space, by appealing to the example of the glorified body of Christ.[37] Yet he finds even more suspect Fishacre's argument that light must be the third type of substance, one whose matter is continuously created by God but whose form is caused by another creature, needed to bring to fulfillment the ontological possibilities of the universe—the principle of plenitude. The matter of the light substance may not, Rufus claims, even be capable of existing without such a form, and hence, instead, the form and matter may need to be concreated if the substance of light is to exist at all.[38]

But Rufus is not really all that concerned with such arguments. What is of greater importance to him is first to acknowledge the peculiar characteristics of light that render it difficult to categorize it as either a substance or an accident, in other words the really mysterious nature of light;, and second to explore the nature of light in the medium, a topic that Rufus finds more con-

35. Ibid., §34–36.

36. Ibid., §37.

37. Ibid., §38, 40.

38. Ibid., §41–43.

genial to him and one that allows for the application of one of his metaphysical novelties, *forma-habitus.*

The thematic position in terms of which Rufus chooses to discuss the unique characteristics of light is announced by a *videtur*, but it is one that Rufus is inclined to accept notwithstanding its problems, probably out of deference to Grosseteste.[39] The position assigns light an overarching cosmic role. Light is an incorporeal substance unceasingly emanating from its source, coming to be in the medium, and abiding virtually in all visible objects; light is the bond between body and soul and assists the soul in all its powers: vegetative, sensitive, and intellective.[40]

Rufus is aware of the many difficulties consequent upon this cosmological picture of light. For example, if light is truly incorporeal, it should be unaffected by the motion of bodies. But, in fact, light changes directions whenever it strikes bodies that obstruct its path or repel it. Likewise, anything that is not corporeal is incapable of producing a body, whereas light is quite capable of producing fire, provided that concave mirrors are arranged in the correct order. Furthermore, nothing truly incorporeal has the mode of its diffusion depend upon whether a medium is filled or remains a void. Light does, however, since it generates itself instantaneously in a medium, but either would not generate at all in a void or would do so only once. Finally, light in the medium

39. Throughout the *Sentences* Commentary, as Raedts so clearly shows (*Rufus*, 67), Rufus tends to employ disclaimers regarding the tenability of the very opinions he endorses. Hence we should not be surprised that similar reservations are expressed in the text below. Another prominent theologian of the same period, Albert the Great, was also inclined to insert disclaimers whenever he discussed controversial philosophical matters, whether out of modesty or real uncertainty remains unclear. See James A. Weisheipl, "Albert's Disclaimers in the Aristotelian Paraphrases," in *Proceedings of the Patristic, Mediaeval, and Renaissance Conference* 5 (1980), 1–27. Evidence for Rufus's dependence on Grosseteste can be seen in the studies of Raedts, *Rufus*, 117–51; Rega Wood, "Richard Rufus of Cornwall on Creation: The Reception of Aristotelian Physics in the West," *Medieval Philosophy and Theology* 2 (1992): 1–30; and Timothy B. Noone, "Richard Rufus of Cornwall and the Authorship of the *Scriptum super Metaphysicam*," *FS* 49 (1989): 55–91.

40. Appendix 6A, §49.

certainly must be corporeal since it produces sensible species.[41]

Rufus supports the view that light is not, properly speaking, a body, notwithstanding these difficulties, as well as the paradoxical characteristics of light.[42] If we assume that the sun is something that enjoys hylomorphic composition like any other natural substance, light would be the substance in the sense of the form of the sun. Only on the supposition that the sun did not have matter at all—in other words, if the sun were pure form—would Rufus allow the claim that light is a body.[43]

What holds Rufus's interest more than the status of light at its origin in the sun is the status of light in the medium, since the medium is something that falls within the ordinary realm of our experience. Fishacre introduced his distinction between *lux* and *illuminatio* to cope with the difficulties associated with light in the medium, but Rufus chooses instead to extend to light his own account of sensible species. In several of his earlier writings, the *Quaestiones de ideis*, the *Scriptum super Metaphysicam*, and the *Speculum animae*, Rufus advanced the view that sensible species are not properly substances or accidents.[44] Somehow a given sensible species, say the species of this whiteness in the medium, is not another individual instance of the specific nature of whiteness found in the surface of a body, but neither is it distinct in kind, since it is not found in another one of the predicamental categories. Rather the species in the medium is closer in identity to the whiteness from which it originates than merely being specifically the same, yet is further removed in difference than by that characteristic of numerical difference within a species. The

41. Ibid., §52–55.

42. Among the latter, Rufus notes, is the fact that the whole essence of light is contained in a single point, although light continually regenerates itself in any suitable medium.

43. Appendix 6A, §59.

44. For an analysis of Rufus's notion of *forma-habitus* in the *Speculum animae*, see Rega Wood, "Richard Rufus's 'Speculum animae': Epistemology and the Introduction of Aristotle in the West," *MM* 23 (1995), 90–93, 101–2.

reason for this, Rufus explains, is that, although the species in the sensible object and the species found in the medium are related as source and offspring, the latter no longer partakes of the definition and essence of its parent, since it has acquired a wholly different and more noble mode of being.[45] This mode of being renders such sensible species impervious to the kind of categorical analysis that pertains to the things of nature, allowing them to transcend the distinction between substance and accident.

Reversing the direction of the analogy he employed in his earlier *Speculum animae*, Rufus contends that we should think of light in the medium in much the same way that he encourages us to think of colors in the medium. Such colors have lost the essence of colors as they are found in the natural world since, unlike their originative counterparts, they do not inhere in the subject that causes them and are instead found in a distinct subject, namely the medium, as one of its perfections but not one of its ontological constituents. Rufus earlier coined the term *forma-habitus* to describe such a form that originates from one subject, yet functions as the secondary perfection of another subject; here in the Balliol *Sentences*, Rufus uses the example of the habitual form of knowledge as found in the knower, while citing the authoritative texts of Aristotle and Averroes as assurances for the philosophical pedigree of his doctrine.

Applying the notion of *forma-habitus* to the case of light, Rufus claims we can say that the light found in the sun is the form of the sun after the manner of other natural substances.[46] However, it is also found in the medium as its perfection. Since, in the latter case, light is a secondary perfection, it may be termed an accident of the medium in a certain sense, even though it does not flow from the principles of the medium; indeed, claiming

45. Appendix 6A, §63.

46. Aquinas cites this opinion, which he finds impossible to maintain, in *ST* 1.67.3c: "Alii vero dixerunt quod lux est forma substantialis solis. Sed hoc etiam apparet impossibile propter duo," etc.

for light the status of a secondary perfection of the medium allows Rufus to obviate the philosophically awkward consequence mentioned by Fishacre that light would become present in the medium only by means of the instantaneous corruption of air. Furthermore, we can understand how the term "body" might be extended to the medium, even though light is really a form, since the corporeal substance of the sun is the origin of the light in the medium, and offspring are always closely akin to their source.[47]

The seriousness and ingenuity of the Fishacre-Rufus exchange testifies to the persistence of the tradition of light speculation at the Oxford *studium* in the period immediately following the departure of Grosseteste. In the hands of subsequent masters such as Roger Bacon, John Peckham, and Witelo ontological speculation about the nature of light tended to devolve into a mathematical investigation of the phenomenon of light and its applications to optics. Notwithstanding the greater complexity and sophistication of their doctrines and their ever increasing use of Greek and Arabic sources, the focus of these later thinkers had moved away from the metaphysical problems that had so engaged Grosseteste and Fishacre and Rufus. Never again, in fact, would the debate on the nature of light burn with such intensity.

APPENDIX 6A

Richard Rufus, *In 2 Sent.* 13.1; Oxford, Balliol Coll. MS 62, fols. 131ra–132rb

§1. [fol. 131ra, col. 111] De luce hic in medio non loquitur Magister in hac distinctione sed de illa primo die condita. Et de illa supponit quod fuerit corpus. De ista autem magna est dubitatio quid ipsa sit, an substantia vel accidens.

§2. Quod accidens videtur: quia ipsa est per se et immediate visibilis; color autem mediante luce. Omne autem sensibile est qualitas [fol. 131rb,

47. Appendix 6A, §64.

col. 112] de tertia specie qualitatis. Unde substantia visiblis non est, nisi per accidens.

§3. Item, quia lux de essentia coloris et de essentia cuiuslibet sensibilis secundum Augustinum *Super Gen. ad litt. 2*, qui ait: "Visus agit luce pura, auditus luce incorporata in subtilissimo aeris. Deinde lux mixta cum aere calignoso, deinde cum corpulento humore, deinde cum terrena crassitudine, et sic quinque sensus efficit."[48]

§4. Ad oppositum. Accidens si est, alicuius erit per se accidens et erit inseparabile ab illo subiecto et causabitur a forma substantiali illius subiecti. Quod non est de hac luce et aere, ergo aeris non erit per se accidens. Sed nec solis a quo gignitur. Nam quidquid nobilius in sole est, ipsa est.

§5. Et universaliter: cum ipsa sit creatura corporalis nobilissima, impossibile ipsam accidens esse.

§6. Procedo. Si est ipsa substantia, aut corporea aut incorporea. Non incorporea, tunc enim esset spiritus, vel vegetabilis vel sensibilis vel intelligibilis, quorum quodlibet est falsum.

§7. Istud non videtur tenere. Non est enim omnis substantia aut corpus aut spiritus. Multae enim sunt formae substantiae quae nec sunt spiritus nec sunt corpora, sicut sunt formae corporum non viventium.

§8. Sed si ipsa est forma substantialis corporea, ex ipsa et materia componitur substantia et erit ipsa forma materialis creata in sua materia, virtute, et situ. Et non poterit extra suam materiam multiplicari, quod est falsum de ea.

§9. Ex his videtur quod haec sit substantia corporea et ita corpus.

§10. Quod satis videtur per Augustinum in *Epistula ad Volusianum*, tertia scilicet epistula: "Hominum, inquit, iste sensus est nihil nisi corpora valentium cogitare sicut ista grossiora, scilicet humor aut humus sive subtiliora sicut aeris et lucis, sed tamen corpora."[49] Et post in eadem epistula: "Duo liquores ita miscentur ut neuter servet integritatem suam, quamquam in corporibus ipsis aeri lux incorrupta misceatur."[50]

§11. Idem, *De libero arbitrio* lib. 2: "In corporibus lux primum locum tenet."[51]

§12. Idem, *Super Genesim ad litteram* lib. 5: "Anima quoniam res est incorporea per corpus quod incorporeo vicinum est, sicuti est ignis vel potius lux et aer primitus agit. Et per hoc cetera quae crassioris sunt corporis."[52]

§13. Et in eodem post: "Anima omnem corpoream naturam naturae

48. Augustine, *De Gen. ad litt.* 12.16 (CSEL 28.1,401)
49. Augustine, *Epist.* 137.2.4 (CSEL 44,100-01).
50. Ibid., 137.3.11 (CSEL 44,110).
51. Augustine, *De lib. arb.* 3.5 (CCSL 29,284).
52. Augustine, *De Gen. ad litt.* 7.15 (CSEL 28.1,213).

dignitate praecellit. Per lucem tamen et aerem, quae in mundo praecellentia sunt corpora, corpus administrat.[53]

§14.Idem, libro 12: "Lux est subtilissimum in corpore et ob hoc animae vicinissimum.[54]

§15. Ad oppositum. Damascenus, cap. 8: "Lumen qualitas naturalis ipsius ignis est." Et post: "Non dicimus alterius substantiae ignem esse et alterius lumen. Sed dicimus propter lucem quod ex ipso provenit lucere ignem. Et non ponimus ministeriale organum ignis esse quod ex ipso est lumen; virtutem vero magis naturalem."[55]

§16. Idem, cap. 21: "Non aliud est ignis nisi lumen."[56]

§17. Hic accipe quod lumen accidens ignis non est sed aliquid ipso nobilius. Forma ergo et virtus eius naturalis.

§18. Ad idem. Si lux corpus est, non est ipsa nobilissima creatura corporalis. Omni enim corpore naturali est forma substantialis nobilior et dignior.

§19. Item, luci opponitur aliquid privative, scilicet tenebra. Ergo ipsa non est corpus; nulli corpori opponitur privatio, nam nullum corpus est habitus.

§20. Et Philosophus: "Lux non est corpus neque defluxus corporis."[57]

§21. Item, si sic, duo corpora sunt in eodem loco, quod habet Philosophus pro improbabili, nec mirum, quia si sunt in eodem loco, iam non duo erunt corpora, sed unum. Linea enim longitudinis utriusque erit una quia simul sunt, quia linea lineae superposita non est nisi linea. Similiter linea latitudinis; similiter spissitudinis. Et sic totae tres dimensiones sunt una dimensio trina et sunt unum corpus.

§22. Re vera in mixto plura corpora sunt in eodem loco, sed quaedam in potentia solum, unum vero in actu, scilicet ipsum mixtum. Et communicant omnia quinque unam et eandem materiam. Ubique enim in mixto est ignis, ubique aqua, et ita de aliis. Sed diversa corpora propriis terminis terminata, non sibi admixta, non confusa, qualiter erunt in eodem loco? Qualiter capiet unum alterum? Materia enim unius videtur <materiae alterius> repugnare. Duae enim materiae propriis et actualibus formis diversis terminatae non

53. Ibid., 7.19 (215–16)

54. Ibid., 12.16 (401).

55. John Damascene, *De fide orthodoxa,* cap. 8, ed. Eligius Buytaert, (St. Bonaventure, N.Y.: Franciscan Institute, 1955), 34.

56. Ibid., 21 (84).

57. Aristotle, *De anima* 2.7 (418b13–17), ed. René Gauthier in *Lecturam in librum De anima* cuiusdam Anonymi (Grottaferrata: Collegium S. Bonaventurae ad Claras Aquas, 1985), 303: "Quid igitur lumen et quid sit lucidum, dictum est, quia neque ignis est neque omnino corpus neque defluxus corporis ullius: esset enim corpus aliquod et sic aut ignis aut huiusmodi alicuius praesentia in lucido: neque enim duo corpora simul possibile est in eodem esse."

se compatiuntur. Lux autem et aer se simul compatiuntur sine confusione; et diversae luces a diversis stellis in eodem puncto aeris [fol. 131va, col. 113] sine confusione se compatiuntur et numerosae. Alioquin omnia viderentur confuse et nulla distincte.

§23. Item, in puncto aeris est lux; nullum corpus est in puncto; ergo lux non est corporis.

§24. Item, si sunt in eodem loco et tamen actu distincta et diversa corpora, signemus in illis duo puncta, *a* et *b*. Verbi gratia: in aere illuminato signentur haec puncta; a puncto ad punctum rectam lineam ducere. Ducatur et sit linea *a-b*. Linea aut est utriusque corporis aut alterius tantum. Si utriusque, ergo eadem ratione ubicumque fiat signatio talis. Et sequitur quod linea longitudinis utriusque sit una et eadem et sic quod <non sit> dimensio nisi unica et corpus unicum.

§25. Si alterius tantum, sit aeris. Aut ergo potest duci linea lucis recta a puncto *a* ad punctum *b*, aut non. Si potest, ducatur haec. Si alia est a prima, duae lineae rectae concludunt superficiem, quod non contingit. Si autem non potest linea lucis ab *a* in *b* duci, ergo lux non est in *a* nec in *b*. Et eadem ratione de aliis punctis aeris, et ita nusquam simul sunt lux et aer.

§26. Item, sit lux quae in aere corpus compositum ex materia et forma. Quaero: illa forma aut potest se multiplicare extra suam materiam, aut non potest. Si non potest, potest autem aer, cum agit in aquam, suam virtutem multiplicare extra suam materiam et immittere eam in partes aquae patientis. Ergo secundum hoc erit lux corpus ignobilius et magis materiale quam aer vel quodvis elementum, quod non convenit. Si autem potest, quaero: illa virtus multiplicata extra materiam corporis lucis, quid est? Et iam corpus non est et ipsa creatura corporalis est. Ergo videtur quod lux est. Ergo haec lux corpus non est. —Eadem ratione videtur quod ponendum sit de prima luce, quia ipsa multiplicata est extra corpus luminosum solare.

§27. Alio modo obicitur hic. Si lux est corpus et constat ex materia et forma, cum lux continue exit a sole, ergo continue aliquid solis deperit. Et sic tandem redigetur sol in nihil. Immo mirum est quod nondum redactus sit in nihil. Continue enim exit ab eo corpus replens mundum. Non est autem in infinitum dividere corpus naturale per partes secundum speciem; contingit autem per partes secundum materiam.

§28. Dicitur autem quod si lux propriam non habeat materiam, sed ipsam materiam aeris recipientis, tunc materia aeris non recipiet formam lucis nisi aeritas corrumpatur. Et ita in qualibet parte aeris habentis lucem, aliquid de ipso corrumpetur. Et cum lux subito fit in toto aere, aer totus subito corrumpetur.

§29. Istud non placet. Nam bene compatiuntur se in una materia forma aeris et lux, si lux corpus non est. Aer enim ipse naturaliter est susceptivus lucis, et possibilis et formabilis per lucem.

§30. Et si lux corpus non est, dico lumen hic receptum in aere, non videtur mihi quod proprie corrumpatur vel cedat in nihil. Sed quod vel redeat per reflexionem in suam originem et hoc dico quando radii incidunt super corpora plana—ibi enim potest esse reflexio—aut dico ubi non est reflexio luminis quod modo est in hac parte aeris, erit iam in alia parte aeris. Videtur enim quod radii illi suo modo moveantur comproportionaliter motui ipsius solis, scilicet sicut sol circa terram, sic isti radii corpori solis continui mutant locum et illuminant diversas partes aeris. Et ita neutro istorum modorum videtur lumen corrumpi nec aliquid deperit soli secundum hunc modum, nec minus habet modo de lumine in se quam habuit in principio.

§31. Sed lumen ignis corrupto igne videtur corrumpi per accidens; non quod cedat in pure nihil sed quod salvetur in potentia illa materia in qua salvetur et forma ignis. Eadem enim materia quae est in potentia ad formam ignis est et in potentia ad lumen et luminosum.

§32. Idem dicerem de lumine candelae extinctae. Ipsa enim generativae actionis indeficiens motio, qualitas est substantiae indeficienter sese generantis. Motus enim in genere qualitatis est.

<Opinio Fishacre>

§33. Respondetur ad quaestionem principalem quod hoc nomen 'lux' dicitur aequivoce, scilicet ipsa aeris vel obiecti illuminatio; aliter autem ipsa substantia a qua est ipsa illuminatio. Alioquin enim eodem nomine signamus substantiam et proprium accidens causatum ab illa substantia et hoc, [fol. 131vb, col. 114] vel quia formas substantiales ignoramus, vel propter propinquitatem substantiae et talis accidentis. Damascenus et Aristoteles loquuntur de luce uno modo; Augustinus vero vocat lucem ipsam substantiam a qua est illuminatio.

§34. Sed adhuc secundum hoc non videbitur lux esse corpus, sed forma aliqua; proprie enim formae debetur operatio.

§35. Item, ista illuminatio accidens ipsius lucis esse non videtur. Nam aut est illuminatio actio aut passio; lux, lucere, illuminare eiusdem naturae sunt; ergo illuminatio-actio non est accidens lucis substantiae, sed nec illuminatio-passio, ut videtur—nam idem est secundum rem illuminatio-actio et illuminatio-passio. Nam hoc quidem lumen datum, illud vero lumen acceptum dicit. Eadem autem natura luminis est dati et accepti; et lumen in dante lumen in accipiente eiusdem naturae sunt.

§36. Iterum illuminatio-passio in illuminato est et non in ipsa luce substantia. Ergo eius accidens non est. Sed nec ipsius illuminati accidens est, quia de principiis illius non causatur.

§37. Item, non loquimur de his relationibus illuminare-illuminari, sed circumscriptis his de ipsa natura absoluta quae data est et accepta. Quaero quid ipsa sit, an substantia an accidens.

§38. Dicunt etiam isti quod multa corpora substantialia possunt esse simul in eodem loco, et etiam in eodem loco cum corpore grossiori. Quod exemplificant in corpore Christi et aliis corporibus glorificatis, quod scilicet Salvator, ianuis clausis, intravit.

§39. Et dicunt quod non est eadem linea longitudinis utriusque corporis, sed duae, quia formae corporum quorum sunt lineae—formae, dico, ultimae, ut forma lucis et aeris—sunt naturaliter diversae. Quia igitur ab eodem habet res quod sit et quod unum sit; hoc autem habet a sua forma substantiali ultima; patet quod, cum sint horum formae ultimae diversae, sunt non una, sed duae lineae eorum.

§40. Istud omnino non satisfacit ad illa obiecta.

§41. Dicunt etiam, sed sine praeiudicio, quod materia huius lucis neque de sole exit neque est aliquid de materia aeris, sed continue creatur materia huius lucis, sicut quando creatur anima, creatur et materia animae, non quia nova natura modo creetur quae non fuit creatura in primis sex diebus; eiusdem enim generis est materia animae vel lucis nunc creata cuius est materia vel lucis tunc creata. Sed in hoc videtur differentia lucis et animae nunc creatae, quod anima tota, scilicet forma eius et materia creatur cum creatur anima. Cum autem gignitur lux, materia eius tantum creatur; forma vero gignitur a corpore luminoso. Et hoc est lucem generari a sole: solem dare formam materiae quae aliunde est.

§42. Si enim aliqua sunt creata a Deo ratione materiae et formae, ut angeli; et aliqua ratione formae, scilicet animae, ut homo, quare non erit tertium creatum a Deo ratione materiae tantum, scilicet lux? Alioquin universum non est completum. Vel sic. Cum sit aliquid habens nec formam nec materiam a creatura, ut angeli, aliquid etiam habens materiam tantum a creaturis, ut homo ab homine—anima enim a Deo est—quare non erit tertium habens formam tantum a creatura sicut lux?

<Recensio opinionis>

§43. Ista non placent. Nam forte nec materia quae per se subsistere non poterit sine forma creatur sine illa forma, nec econverso. Sed semper concreantur talis materia et talis forma. Et non multum curo de hoc.

§44. Lux[a] non est corpus mathematicum, quia lux natura est et addit super mathematicum, sicut linea radiosa super lineam mathematicam. Ergo si est corpus, est naturale. Sed omne corpus naturale est naturaliter mobile motu aliquo proprio naturali. Lux autem non, sed in instanti mutatur.

§45. Item, nulla duo corpora sibi impermixta neque se invicem augmentantia possunt esse in eodem loco. Lux et aer non sunt maius in quantitate quam aer per se.

§46. Item, corpus est substantia facta; lux autem in medio habet esse in fieri tantum.

§47. Item, lux naturaliter diffundit se in omnem partem et tamen non incedit nisi secundum rectum. Omne autem corpus naturale mobile motu recto in unam partem tantum naturaliter movetur.

§48. Item, nulla forma est corpus. Lux est forma, quia ipsa est actus lucidi et multis aliis modis posset hoc ostendi.

<Opinio propria et dubitationes de eadem>

§49. Videtur ergo quod lux est substantia incorporea in origine sua indesinenter scaturiens, in medio diaphono semper fiens, [fol. 132ra, col. 115] in corporibus obiectis virtualiter manens; et, cum sit talis, videtur media esse inter animam et corpus, ipsa adinvicem coniungens. Et est intellectivae partis animae tamquam occasionalis pedisequa; sensitivae vero quasi ministra necessaria; vegetativae vero quasi comes et in coniugium sibi associata. Et haec satis patent ex sententia beati Augustini in multis locis, et etiam ex philosophia. Quod enim occasionale obsequium pareret etiam intellectui, etsi aliunde non sit manifestum, ex hoc liquere potest: quod eius ministerium inferioribus partibus animae, scilicet vegetativae et sensitivae, sine quibus in hac vita non est intelligere, vel si paucis, est tam multipliciter necessarium.

§50. Item, motus primi mobilis est mensura cuiuslibet motus corporis. Ergo est velocior omni motu corporis. Non est autem velocior motu lucis. Ergo motus lucis non est motus corporis.

§51. Ad idem. Nullum corpus naturale movetur in omnem partem naturaliter et secundum rectum. Lux diffundit se undique naturaliter et secundum rectum. Ergo lux corpus naturale non est; sed nec mathematicum. Ergo omnino corpus non est.

§52. Contra. Impossibile est non-corpus corpore moveri; lux movetur corpore obstante et repellente ipsam; ergo lux non est non-corpus.

§53. Ad idem. Nullum non-corpus generat corpus in actu. Lux generat corpus in actu. Nam lux generat ignem in actu; speculis enim concavis ad solem positis, ignis accenditur, ut habetur in libro *De speculis*.[58]

§54. Item, nullius <non->corporis est multiplicata generatio vel non multiplicata ex medio pleno vel vacuo. Lucis generatio est multiplicata vel non multiplicata ex medio pleno vel vacuo. Quod patet ex hoc quod in medio pleno in uno instanti est multiplicata lucis generatio; in vacuo autem, si fuisset, aut penitus generatio lucis non esset aut si esset tantum semel et unica fuisset.

58. The title given to the twelfth-century Latin translation of Euclid's *Catoptrica*; see Kenichi Takahashi, "The Medieval Latin Traditions of Euclid's *Catoptrica*: A Critical Edition of *De speculis*, with an Introduction, English Translation and Commentary" (Higashi-ku, Fukuoka-shi, Japan: Kyushu University Press, 1992).

§55. Sed modo omne quod supra sensum positivum sentitur species est sensibilis; lux in medio est talis; ergo lux in medio species est sensibilis.

§56. Quid ergo in his et tantis dicam? Nescio imprimis an lux ista seu lumen dupliciter dici possit et accipi, scilicet aut ipsa essentia lucis simplex, situalis tamen, aut ipsa eadem expansa superficialiter sive eiusdem expansio lux dicatur, et quod ultimo modo dicta lux accidens sit.

§57. Sed cuius? Ipsius essentiae lucis quae indifferenter esse potest expansa et non expansa, sed tamen utroque modo situalis? Accidit enim suae essentiae expansio in superficie. Unde tota essentia eius salvatur in puncto.

§58. Et secundum hoc non sit ipsa accidens ipsius aeris suscipientis, sed ipsius suae simplicis essentiae, ut dixi. Et sic qualitas, sic sensibilis, sic forte accidens dici possit.

§59. Alio modo, scilicet essentia lucis hic genita, quid de hac dicam? Nescio. In origine sua considerata ibi dicerem quod si sol componitur ex materia et forma quod lux est substantia: forma, non corpus. Si autem sol materiam omnino non haberet, dicerem quod lux ibi substantia et corpus est.

§60. Sed mihi videtur quod sol et omne corpus naturale necessario materiam habet, quia secundum Boethium[59] forma substantia non est subiecta accidentibus nisi eis prius fuerit materia subiecta. Ergo dimensionibus ipsius solis necessario est materia subiecta. Ergo in sole forte dicerem quod lux est substantia forma, non corpus.

§61. Sed hic de lumine in medio quid dicam, nescio. Quid de specie coloris hic in medio dicam? An color est? Nec color nec alia natura quam color; non res alterius praedicamenti. Haec species albedinis non est res alterius speciei specialissimae quam sit haec albedo a qua gignitur. Non est individuum sub specie specialissima albedinis; non sunt co-individua eiusdem speciei—haec species proles et illa albedo parens. Magis tamen sibi approximant in convenientia naturae quam una albedo et alia albedo. Unde magis conveniunt quam unitate in specie et minus differunt quam differentia simpliciter numero; et tamen non sunt omnino idem numero.

§62. Haec species nomen et definitionem amisit albedinis, [fol. 132rb, col. 116] scilicet parentis, propter esse alterum, scilicet spirituale, quod comparative habet in medio, et adhuc magis spirituale in organo et sensu.

§63. Vide an possit dici quod haec species propter praedictam convenientiam sit color, quia, scilicet non alterius naturae est. Possit etiam insimul

59. Boethius: "Quocirca hoc vere unum in quo nullus numerus, nullum in eo aliud praeterquam id quod est. Neque enim subiectum fieri potest; forma enim est, formae vero subiectae esse non possunt. Nam quod ceterae formae subiectae accidentibus sunt, ut humanitas non ita accidentia suscipit eo quod materia ei subiecta est, dum enim materia subiecta humanitati suscipit quodlibet accidens, ipsa hoc suscipere videtur humanitas," *De Trinitate,* cap. 2 (PL 64,1250; ed. H. F. Stewart, 10–11).

dici quod non sit color eo quod nomen et definitionem coloris amisit; et hoc, quia nobilius esse adquisivit.

§64. Adapta. Vide an tali modo possit dici de lumine proiecto a corpore solari, an ipsum dici possit species illius lucis quae substantia et forma est in corpore solis. Sed esse alterum his; et ideo hic suscepta in medio nec proprie nomen substantiae nec accidentis retinens. Sed quia nulla creatura similior aut aeque similis est suae origini, scilicet corpori solari (et maxime unde corpus solare activum est et operativum), ideo possit nomen corporis admittere. Nihil enim similius est colori quam praedicta eius proles. Et ideo si eius nomen huic attribuatur, non mirandum. Similiter corpori luminoso nihil tam simile quam hoc lumen ab ipso proiectum. Et ideo si hoc lumen corpus dicatur, nequaquam est mirandum.

§65. Praeterea, minus dicitur cum dicitur lumen esse corpus quam si diceretur lumen esse sol. A sole autem omnino habet hoc lumen quod est, non ita tamen quin ex Deo.

§66. Quid ergo, si forte beatus Augustinus intellexit hac intentione lumen corpus esse eo quod eiusdem naturae cum sole et universaliter cum corpore luminoso? Damascenus autem negat eo quod materiam habet corpus luminosum a quo gignitur lumen quod materiam non habet; nec tamen alterius naturae quam illud corpus luminosum a quo gignitur iuxta illud Damasceni supra.[60]

§67. Omnia haec sine praeiudicio et assertione dicta sunt, et relinquo maiorum arbitrio. Huic tamen sententiae videntur illi philosophi concordare: Aristoteles scilicet qui dicit lumen actus lucidi est.[61] Lumen contrarium est tenebrae. Est autem tenebra privatio huius habitus ex lucido. Quare manifestum est quod huius, scilicet habitus, praesentia lumen est.[62]

§68. Et super hoc Averroes.[63] Lux est praesentia intentionis in diapho-

60. See above, n. 55.

61. Aristotle: "Lumen autem est huiusmodi actus lucidi secundum quod est lucidum," *De anima* 2.7 (418b12–13). Resp. Anonymus, Magister Artium (c. 1245–1250), *Lectura in librum De anima: quodam discipulo reportata*, lectio 13, ed. René Gauthier (Grottaferrata: Collegium S. Bonaventurae ad Claras Aquas, 1985), 303.

62. Cf. Anonymus: "Videtur autem lumen contrarium esse tenebrae; est autem tenebra privatio huiusmodi habitus ex lucido; quare manifestum est quod et huiusmodi praesentia lumen est," ibid., (418b18–19).

63. Averroes: "Id est, declaratur igitur ex hoc, scilicet quod obscuritas est privatio lucis in diaphano, quod lux non est corpus, sed est praesentia intentionis in diaphano, quod lux non est corpus, sed est praesentia intentionis in diaphano cuius privatio dicitur obscuritas apud praesentiam corporis luminosi. Et hoc quod dixit manifestum est, quoniam subiectum obscuritatis et lucis est corpus et est diaphonum; lux autem est forma et habitus istius corporis et si esset corpus, tunc corpus penetraret corpus," *Commentarium magnum in Aristotelis De anima libros* 2, t. 70, ed. F. Stuart Crawford (Cambridge, Mass.: Medieval Academy of America, 1953), 237.

no apud praesentiam corporis luminosi. Quid hic nisi quod hoc lumen sicut forma-habitus suscipiatur in aere et non sit proprie dicta substantia nec accidens, sed forma-habitus? Exempli gratia, sicut scientia in anima. Et est, ut dixi, et ut hic signat Philosophus[64] praesentia intentionis in diaphono, hoc est intentio praesens in diaphono. Intentio, id est species. Cuius? Corporis, scilicet luminosi in diaphono, id est lucido in potentia, scilicet aere et obiecto. Species, dico, et proles genita a corpore luminoso praesens hic facta in diaphono.

§69. Haec, ut prius dixi, non definio. Quod autem supra dixi, an sit lux accidens, forte aliter posset exponi et dici absolute quod non. Sed ipsa recipit esse aliquid ex admixtione et incorporatione per quod esse ipsa est sensibilis. Non tamen multum curo de hoc.

§70. Sed si esset vacuum inter centrum et terram, utrum lux a sole pertingeret et illuminaret terram.

§71. Nescio. Sed ad praesens videtur mihi quod non, quia dicit Augustinus, *Conf.* 12, in principio: "Ubi lux esset, si esset, nisi superesset eminendo et illustrando?"[65] Videtur quod natura luminis sit superesse et in alio suscipi, quando, dico, ex fonte originali producitur et gignitur.

§72. Dubitatur tamen in hoc. Ponatur enim quod sit sol et nullum aliud corpus omnino et stet per se. Iam omnino non emittit radium. Quomodo est hoc? Habet potestatem emittendi et non emittendi radios. Potestas quae valet ad opposita rationalis est. Et sic videtur sol rationem et liberum arbitrium habere.

§73. Nescio. Aut forte praesente et tangente aliquo corpore naturaliter susceptivo luminis, innata est soli necessitas emittendi et communicandi; deficiente autem omni susceptivo, innata est ei possibilitas ut terminetur sua virtus in se et in sua materia. Et si praesente et tengente susceptivo haberet potestatem naturalem non-emittendi, sequeretur quod esset potestas rationalis, non autem alio modo.

[a] Quaere de ordine huius articuli usque ad finem quaestionis *add. marg. Ba*

64. Aristotle: "Declaratur igitur ex hoc quod lux est praesentia istius intentionis," *De anima* 2, t. 70, ed. F. Stuart Crawford apud *Commentarium magnum Averrois* (Cambridge, Mass.: Medieval Academy of America, 1953), 236; on c. 7 (418b20).

65. Augustine, *Conf.* 12.3.3 (CCSL 27,217).

CHAPTER 7

The Division of the Waters (Gn 1:6–7)

The History of a Conundrum and Its Resolution by the Early Oxford Masters

One of the oddest passages in the Genesis account of creation is surely the event of the second day: "And God said: Let there be a firmament made amidst the waters: and let it divide the waters from the waters. And God made a firmament and divided the waters that were under the firmament from those that were above the firmament. And it was so."[1] The Fathers of the Church valiantly engaged the problem, but for the most part their efforts were desultory, and they ended by declaring the event a mystery, beyond human ken, and moved on to the third day. Ambrose, for example, asked:

Why do you wonder that above the firmament of heaven water can be suspended by an action of such great majesty? You can gather it from

1. Gn 1:6–7. The English translation here and throughout is that of Douay-Rheims.

other examples, from things which human eyes have seen, as when at the crossing of the Jews the waters were divided. Ask the reason for that happening! It does not happen naturally, that water should divide itself from water, and in the midst of the deep where water flows land should be separated ... But what is impossible to the one who gave power to whomever he wanted? Or to the one who gave power to weaknesses, so that a weak man might say "I can do all things in him who strengthens me."[2]

Augustine, as with so many other issues, was the exception. For him the Genesis story was an endless source of wonder, and he returned to the subject in no fewer than four of his writings. In his most extensive treatment, the *De Genesi ad litteram*, he wrestles with the separation of the waters for six chapters, rehearsing arguments that will be cited by many of those who came after him. Notwithstanding, he concludes his discussion by refusing to determine the question, invoking faith in the face of such a mystery:

In whatever form, however, waters may be there, and of whatever kind, let us have no doubts at all that that is where they are; the authority of this text of Scripture, surely, overrides anything that human ingenuity is capable of thinking up.[3]

In his earlier and briefer treatment of the subject, the *De Genesi contra Manichaeos*, he cannot resist taking up the mystery, even though he admits that he cannot recall the Manichees raising any issue with it. Here he allegorically reads the waters below to represent visible matter and those above incorporeal and thus invisible matter; and as beautiful as the heavens are, invisible

2. Ambrose, *Hex.* 2.3.10–11 (CSEL 32.1,49); quoted in Robert Grosseteste, *Hexaëmeron* 3.3.5, trans. Christopher Martin (Oxford: Oxford University Press, 1996), 104–05.

3. Augustine, *De Genesi ad litteram* 2.5 (CSEL 28.1,39), in *The Works of Saint Augustine XIII: On Genesis*, trans. Edmund Hill (Brooklyn, N.Y.: New City Press, 2002), 196. Cf. Robert Grosseteste., *Hexaëmeron* 3.3.7, ed. Richard C. Dales and Servus Gieben, ABM VI (Oxford: Oxford University Press, 1982), 105.

creatures are even more beautiful, and it is *perhaps* for this reason that they are above. At this point, however, he abruptly concludes the discussion: "we should not rashly affirm anything about this, for it is obscure and remote from the senses of men. Whatever the case may be, before we understand it, we should believe."[4]

Among the Greek fathers, Origen opted immediately for an allegorical interpretation: the waters above represented the celestial powers and those below the infernal, though the suggestion that the waters below signified evil spirits was to give offense to later Christian writers.[5] One of those taking exception was Basil the Great, who dismisses such explanations as "dream interpretations and old women's tales."[6]

For his part, Basil urges the use of our God-given reason to understand the separation of the waters and, uniquely among the fathers, offers the following architectural explanation:

> Before we touch upon the meaning of the writings, let us attempt to solve the arguments brought against it from other sources. They ask us how, if the body of the firmament is spherical, as sight shows it to be, and if water flows and slips off high spots, it would be possible for the water to lie on the convex circumference of the firmament. What, then, shall we say to this? First of all, that, if some body appears circular to us because of an inner concavity, it is not necessary for the outer surface to be made completely spherical, and the whole to be perfectly rounded and smoothly finished. Let us look, indeed, at the stone vaults of the baths and the structures of cave-like buildings which, rounded to a semicircular form according to their interior ap-

4. Augustine, *De Genesi contra Manichaeos* 1.11, in *Saint Augustine on Genesis*, trans. Roland Teske, The Fathers of the Church 84 (Washington, D.C.: The Catholic University of America Press, 1991), 65.

5. Augustine, e.g., belittles the view in *De civ. Dei* 11.34 (CCSL 48, 354). Cf. Lynn Thorndike, *A History of Magic and Experimental Science* (New York: Columbia University Press, 1923), 1:458.

6. Basil, *Homeliae in Hexaëmeron* 3.9, in *Saint Basil Exegetic Homilies*, The Fathers of the Church, trans. Agnes C. Way (Washington, D.C.: The Catholic University of America Press, 1963), 46:52.

pearance, often have a flat surface on the upper sections of the roof. Therefore, let them cease making trouble for themselves or for us, alleging that water cannot be kept in the upper regions.[7]

Perhaps the first serious treatment, dating from the eleventh century at the earliest, appears in a work called *De mundi caelestis terrestrisque constitutione*; there the author, now known simply as the Pseudo-Bede, lists four hypotheses. On the outer surface of the heavens there are low lying places (*subsidentia*) which, as in Basil's explanation, can contain water, but they are being whipped around with such speed that they do not fall down (as can be demonstrated with a vessel filled with liquid). Second, the waters are being kept there in a vaporous state, just as clouds here below. Third, owing to their distance from the sun, the main source of heat, the waters form into ice and in that hardened form stick to the heavens; and that is why Saturn, the planet closest to the icy waters, is the coldest. Lastly, these waters are being held above by the inscrutable will of God: why? Perhaps for the use of celestial beings, perhaps as a means of moderating the heat of the heavens. We just don't know.[8]

The scholastic theologians of the High Middle Ages, however, were not about to dismiss the matter as a mystery known only to God and relegated for us who are *in via* to a blind and uncomprehending faith. They had after all rediscovered Aristotle, and Aristotle had an answer for everything in the natural world. Everything had its proper place, a place dictated by nature, and motion to that place was termed "natural"—hence the motion of a stone thrown into the air, as long as it was upward bound, was deemed "violent," its fall back to the center "natural." The physical universe, in short, was intelligible, and the pagan

7. Ibid., 3.4 (42).

8. Pseudo-Bede, *De mundi celestis terrestrisque constitutione. A Treatise on the Universe and the Soul,* ed. and trans. Charles Burnett (London: Warburg Institute, University of London, 1985), 44.

Aristotle had given theologians the tools to understand it. But what natural explanation could there possibly be for waters that were outside their natural place, and—if the text of Genesis be credited—remained there? Here was the conundrum.

Who were the earliest Schoolmen to engage the problem? From the time of the arrival of the first translations of Aristotle, the theologians of the fledgling university at Paris were wrestling with the dividing of the waters. William of Auvergne, William of Auxerre, Alexander of Hales, and Philip the Chancellor all tried their hands, with varying degrees of engagement.

William of Auvergne is uncharacteristically terse on the topic. His most convincing argument is the assertion that water above the firmament is no more amazing than fire that is found beneath the earth and even beneath the seas and therefore likewise removed from its natural place; he mentions as examples Mount Etna, Mount Vulcan in the Aeolian chain, and Mount Chimaera or Ctesias in Turkey.[9] He adds, unhelpfully, that the firmament had to have been created between the waters, because one could not explain how it could have been moved there.[10]

William of Auxerre puts the question in this way: if waters are naturally located immediately above the earth, and thus below air and fire and *a fortiori* beneath the firmament, how are they then located above the firmament, as Moses wrote? The answer: miraculously.[11]

Alexander of Hales, in his *Gloss on the Sentences*, contents himself with recording all of the statements of Augustine on the subject without adding any comment of his own.[12]

9. William of Auvergne, *De universo* 1.1, in *Opera Omnia* 1 (Paris, 1674; repr. Frankfurt am Main: Minerva, 1963), 633b.

10. Ibid., 632a.

11. William of Auxerre, *Summa aurea* 2.1, ed. Jean Ribaillier (Grottaferrata: Collegium S. Bonaventurae ad Claras Aquas, 1982), 2:190.

12. Alexander of Hales, *Glossa in IV libros Sententiarum* 2.14 (Quaracchi: Collegium S. Bonaventurae ad Claras Aquas, 1952), 2:131.

Of all the Parisian masters Philip the Chancellor ventures the most complete accounting, although he labels it mere *opinio physica*, not truth.[13] Invoking the authority of Augustine, he says it seems that the waters above are not altogether of the same nature as the waters of our earthly experience and thus would not fall, even absent their congealing in the form of a crystalline sphere. Nor is Basil's explanation sound, namely, that the function of the waters above is to cool the heat of the luminous bodies, since God has willed the nature of the celestial bodies to be incorruptible and nonconsumable, unlike the inflammable bodies that we experience here below.[14]

Nor does the purpose of the cooling of Saturn make sense. Bodies higher in the hierarchy of natures are not acted upon by those that are inferior; according to this opinion, moreover, the firmament would be even colder than Saturn, which is unseemly since the firmament is the principle of the conservation of the being of bodily things which are generated and corrupted. But heat, not cold, conserves and nourishes.[15]

On the other hand, Philip has no patience with those who retreat from any attempt at a rational account, consigning the issue to the impenetrability of the divine knowledge, and quotes with approval the saying of Augustine: "Our business now, after all, is to inquire how God's Scriptures say he established things according to their proper natures, and not what he might wish to work in them or out of them as a miracle of his power."[16]

No Parisian theologian, however, could match the thoroughness and seriousness of treatment that the topic received at the hands of the theologians at the first English university. From

13. Philip the Chancellor, *Summa de bono. De bono naturae* q. 11, ed. Nikolaus Wicki (Berne: Francke, 1985), 1:140.

14. Ibid., 1:139–40.

15. Ibid., 1:140.

16. Augustine, *De Gen. ad litt.* 2.1, in *The Works of Saint Augustine XIII: On Genesis*, trans. Hill, 190.

early in the twelfth century, English scholars were engaged in the whole process of *translatio studii*, convinced that knowledge of the natural world cannot help but illuminate the sacred page. But the man who set the tone for several generations of Oxford theology that were to follow was Robert Grosseteste, who himself had come to the sacred science late in life, having as Arts master made significant contributions to the science of his time, including what has been termed the first cosmogony since the *Timaeus*.[17]

In the third book of his *Hexaëmeron* Grosseteste sets the scene: by "the firmament" is understood the heaven in which the stars are located (the *caelum stellatum*) and above which the waters were placed by the creator. Augustine had shown that this scenario was not improbable,

> for if the waters which we see can be divided into so many very small particles and be made so subtle and—by the power of heat being impressed into them, or by some other means—can be made so light as to be suspended above our air in the clouds, in a vaporous state, by a parallel reasoning the same waters, divided up into yet smaller particles, with greater subtlety and lightness, in proportion as the place above the firmament is higher than the place of the clouds, can be suspended up there.[18]

And because the power that renders them subtle is unchanging, so too is their positioning.

Grosseteste's proof that this is so is the coldness of Saturn.[19] Owing to the extended orbit of this outermost of the planets, it is required to move that much more swiftly to traverse its circuit and should thus by rights be hotter than the others, that is, if its heat were not cooled by the waters above it.

17. James McEvoy, The *Philosophy of Robert Grosseteste*, 2nd ed. (Oxford: Clarendon Press, 1982), 151.

18. Grosseteste, *Hexaëmeron* 3.3.1, eds. Dales and Gieben, 103; trans. Martin (adapted).

19. Ibid., 3.3.2.

There is another possibility.[20] Grosseteste records, without endorsement, the idea that the waters above are not vaporous but just the opposite: a crystalline solidity (here alluding to another puzzling phrase from the book of Ecclesiasticus).[21] And because crystal is a solid, it is a whole, encasing the earth, at every point equidistant from its center, and thus held immobile "by its own tendencies," as Grosseteste says.[22]

As to the usefulness of creating water above the firmament, Grosseteste ventures several guesses, again without endorsing any of them. Josephus thought it was the source of rain showers on earth, while others thought it was the source of the waters of the Great Flood (though Grosseteste is troubled by the consideration of the vacuum it would leave in the heavens—an impossibility according to Aristotle's physics). Still others thought that the waters are there to cool the heat of the stars and the ether.[23]

Having tried his best to explain in natural terms the suspension of the waters above the firmament, Grosseteste abruptly asks, citing Ambrose: "But why do we seek for nature in these things?"[24] God is the author of nature and his will is its law. A parallel case, which Grosseteste mentions here, is the dividing of the waters of the Red Sea from the book of Exodus.[25]

What then is the point of even attempting to find natural ex-

20. The *aliqui* referred to by Grosseteste would include Bede, whose commentary is incorporated into the *Glossa ordinaria* (ed. princeps: Strassburg, 1480; repr. Turnhout: Brepols, 1992), 1:11 and repeated in Peter Lombard, *Sententiae* 14.2, ed. Ignatius Brady (Grottaferrata: Collegium S. Bonaventurae ad Claras Aquas, 1971), 1:395.

21. Viz. "The cold north wind bloweth and the water is congealed into crystal; upon every gathering together of waters it shall rest and shall clothe the waters as a breastplate," Eccli. 43:22.

22. Grosseteste, *Hexaëmeron* 3.3–4, trans. Martin, 104.

23. Ibid., 3.10.1–2, 109–10. It should be noted in passing that Grosseteste argues the *usefulness* of supracelestial waters, not the necessity thereof. The (Pseudo-)*Summa fratris Alexandri* was to take it a step further and argue its *necessity* (*Summa teleologica* 2.1.3.2, q. 2, tit. 2, cap. 4, ed. Bernardin Klumper [Grottaferrata: Collegium S. Bonaventurae ad Claras Aquas, 1924], 2:340–41). See also Appendix 7B below.

24. Grosseteste, *Hexaëmeron* 3.3.5, trans. Martin, 104.

25. Ibid.

planations, since they surely cannot all be true? It is, says Grosseteste, for apologetic reasons: namely, to give an answer to those who claim that there cannot possibly be waters above the heavens. Grosseteste (and the rest of the "holy commentators") simply shows the various ways by which what scripture says to be true can in fact be the case.[26] In other words, what one is asked to accept on faith is at the very least not contrary to reason.

If Grosseteste took the issue of the division of the waters seriously, the matter was taken even further by his School.[27] That the Dominican Richard Fishacre had Grosseteste's *Hexaëmeron* open on his desk when he wrote his own account of the six days in his *Sentences* Commentary has been amply established.[28] Fishacre expands on Grosseteste's views in a question that he probably disputed after the first redaction of his magisterial Commentary, and which was added by scribes in spare folia of the earliest copies of the Commentary.[29] Let us ask three things, he says: whether there are waters above the firmament; and if they are there, why are they there; and lastly (a question Augustine said should not be asked), how are they there? After marshaling all of the authorities, both scriptural and patristic, Fishacre amasses no fewer than twenty-three arguments, many of them borrowed, some original or at least recast, in support of the reasonableness of the Genesis text.[30]

26. Ibid., 3.3.6, 105.

27. I take "school" to mean two or more thinkers between whom there is contact and similarity of outlook. See Thomas Mautner, *A Dictionary of Philosophy* (Oxford: Blackwell Publishers, 1996), 385–86.

28. Richard C. Dales, "Influence of Grosseteste's Hexaëmeron on the Sentences Commentary of Richard Fishacre, O.P. and Richard Rufus of Cornwall, O.F.M.," *Viator* 2 (1971): 47–48.

29. R. James Long and Maura O'Carroll, SND, *The Life and Works of Richard Fishacre, OP. Prolegomena to the Edition of his Commentary on the "Sentences"* (Munich: Verlag der Bayerischen Akademie der Wissenschaften, 1999), 36. Cf. R. James Long, "The Beginning of a Tradition: The *Sentences* Commentary of Richard Fishacre, OP," in *Medieval Commentaries on the "Sentences" of Peter Lombard, Current Research*, ed. Gilian R. Evans (Leiden: Brill, 2002), 1:348–49.

30. Fishacre's treatment of the subject as a whole is longer and more comprehensive than anything written to date, to be surpassed only by the monumental tome known as the *Summa fratris Alexandri*.

Making use for the first time (at least the first at Oxford) of the cosmology of the Arab Al-Faraghani (or Alfraganus), Fishacre recounts the ordering of the celestial bodies; immediately following the sun in magnitude, according to this account, are five fixed stars, brighter than any of the planets, yet of more tempering action; this would not be possible without an accompanying cooling agent, that is, water.[31]

A number of the arguments are of the *a fortiori* variety: for example, water can now be found in the bowels of the earth, in other words outside of its natural place, which is covering the earth; if water can be found below its natural place, why not above?[32]

Citing the authority of Aristotle's work on animals, Fishacre says that while a moderate depth of water appears grayish, deeper water takes on the color of lapis lazuli, that is, blue. But when we look at the sky on a clear day, what color is it? Our vision, moreover, cannot be arrested by the heaven of the fixed stars, which has to be transparent in order to transmit their light. The only possible explanation for the sensation of the color blue is a great quantity of water above the sphere of the fixed stars. And if you don't accept that, he adds, you are denying the evidence of your senses.[33]

Furthermore, given the positing of waters above the firmament (by the creative act of God), what makes them stay there? Well, if they were to fall, the event would create a vacuum, which, until Pascal proved otherwise, was universally regarded as an impossibility. Fishacre suggests an experiment to illustrate this principle: seal the top of a vessel filled with water, then poke a hole in the bottom: the water will not exit (or will exit only slowly), lest a vacuum be produced.[34]

31. Fishacre, *In 2 Sent.*, Appendix C, ed. Long (Munich: Verlag der Bayerischen Akademie der Wissenschaften, 2011), 2:342.

32. Ibid. Fishacre's source here is very possibly William of Auvergne (see n. 9 above).

33. Fishacre, *In 2 Sent.*, ed. Long, 2:343.

34. Ibid. Fishacre's experiment is a variation on the observation suggested by Augustine (*De Gen. ad litt.* 2.2 [CSEL 28.1, 33–34]).

The phenomenon of tides provides yet another illustration. If the distant moon, the smallest of the celestial bodies and according to the calculations of Albumasar 94,198,000 miles from the surface of the earth, can cause the oceans and seas to rise, what is so outlandish about supposing that the fixed stars can hold water aloft?[35]

The Aristotelian distinction between substance and accident furnishes the tools for another argument. God surely can withhold from its form the resultant action of gravity.[36] This is the case with glorified bodies. The story told by Varro and repeated by Augustine of the vestal virgin who proved her innocence by filling a sieve with water from the Tiber and carrying it to her judges without a single drop leaking provides a dramatic example; in this case the miracle was effected by a demon, but it makes the point nonetheless: waters above are no more contrary to nature than water remaining in the sieve in defiance of gravity.[37] The theology of the Eucharist, moreover, recently formulated at the Fourth Lateran Council, proclaims the distinction between the accidents of bread and the substance of the Sacrament.[38] It is applicable here as well. Sacred history also supplies an example: just as God kept fire from burning Daniel and his companions who had been thrown into the oven, a miracle entailing the separation of the power to burn from the substance of fire, so too can God separate water's *gravitas* from its substance.[39]

Water, furthermore, is naturally spherical and assumes that shape unless constrained otherwise by its container. But water here below is prevented from assuming a spherical form by the interposition of land masses. A natural desire, however, again ac-

35. Fishacre, *In 2 Sent.*, ed. Long, 2:343–44.

36. *Gravitas*, literally "heaviness," was not of course gravity in the Newtonian sense.

37. Fishacre, *In 2 Sent.*, ed. Long, 2:344.

38. Ibid.

39. Ibid., 2:345.

cording to Aristotele, cannot be eternally frustrated. Therefore, water in the shape of a sphere is achieved elsewhere, that is, in the waters above the starry heaven.[40]

Contrary to the view he embraces, Fishacre finds four objections. The first is the conviction of the natural philosophers, schooled in their Aristotle, who reason that nothing violent is lasting. But any element outside of its natural place is there violently. Therefore, waters cannot perpetually be outside their natural place.[41]

Fishacre responds that he has offered many arguments in support of the natural position of waters above the firmament, and thus the first objection has no force. Even accepting the supposition, however, that the waters are there violently, the objection is not fatal. The divine dispensation, for example, could have endowed the waters of our experience with an inclination to the second sphere, but the waters above were not endowed with the same form. Or it could be the case, as with the damned in hell, that a violent state can indeed be everlasting.[42]

A second objection is that the firmament is as it were glorified and thus neither gives place to nor resists elements invading it, but instead shares space with, for example, light and air. Thus the firmament would offer no resistance to waters placed above it, which would thus fall through it unimpeded.[43]

But, responds Fishacre, if the waters be above naturally, they would not descend, even though the heavens offer no resistance. If, on the other hand, they are there violently, they are retained there by the divine power, as in the examples of the parting of the Red Sea and the halting of the Jordan River.[44]

Thirdly, every place is natural to some body. But since water above the firmament is the same element as that beneath, the

40. Ibid.

41. Ibid., 2:345–46.

42. Ibid., 2:347.

43. Ibid., 2:346.

44. Ibid., 2:347.

place above the firmament is natural only to the heavenly element. To read the Genesis account literally, therefore, would entail the heavens being perpetually outside their natural place—which, states the objection, ought not to be conceded.[45]

Again, if the waters are above naturally, the objection falls; if violently, it is not unfitting that the firmament suffer violence to some extent (*pro parte*), though not totally (*pro toto*), just as the waters here below occupy their natural place only in part. Fishacre doubtless has in mind the protrusion of land masses above the water or the location of fire, as in the case of volcanoes, beneath the water.[46]

Lastly, rapid motion causes heat, and the intriguing example proffered is that of the lead on the point of an arrow which liquefies—so the claim goes—when shot from a strong bow.[47] Since diurnal motion, that is, the orbit of the sun, is both the swiftest and tightest (*minimus*) of all circular movements, it is the measure of all other motions. However, the motion of the ninth sphere, immediately contiguous to the waters above the firmament, since it describes a wider and hence swifter orbit, would *a fortiori* be at least equally as fast and therefore exceedingly hot, and thus would heat the waters, so the argument goes, to the point of evaporation. Water in the gaseous state, however, occupies a greater space and would encroach into the empyrean heaven itself or, failing that, the ninth sphere.[48]

Fishacre's response is multiform. First, the ninth sphere is not

45. Ibid., 2:346.

46. Ibid., 2:348.

47. This curious notion, though never verified experimentally, was widely believed by the ancients; one can find it in Aristotle, Lucan, Lucretius, Ovid, Seneca, and Virgil. Fishacre's source was probably Aristotle, *De caelo* 2.7. (289a20–28). See Aristotle, *On the Heavens*, trans. William K. C. Guthrie (Cambridge, Mass.: Harvard University Press, 1953), 180, n. a.

48. Fishacre, *In 2 Sent.*, ed. Long, 2:346. Augustine makes much the same argument and is undoubtedly Fishacre's inspiration here; See *De Gen. ad litt*, 2.5 (CSEL 28.1, 38–39).

as efficacious with respect to what is above it as with what is below. Indeed, the waters might as reasonably be rendered immobile under the influence of the empyrean with which it is contiguous on its upper part rather than mobile, owing to the ninth sphere immediately beneath it. Or the divine power could render it immobile as it does the earth (in the Ptolemaic system) or the sun, as we read in the book of Joshua or, as many believe, the starry heaven at the final Judgment.[49]

Having exhausted the *how* of the division of the waters, Fishacre next grapples with the *why*. Here he invokes the saints (Basil, Ambrose, Bede, and John Damascene), who concur that the waters have a cooling effect on the intense heat of the sun and the ether and temper the calefaction of the firmament.[50]

In answer to the question as to whether the waters are above the firmament naturally or violently, Fishacre adduces the example of the lodestone or magnet (*adamas*): iron is moved to the stone naturally, that is, in accordance with the nature of the magnet, but also violently, that is, contrary to the nature of the iron. In like manner, as he thinks he has established, there is an attractive power in the heavens, which tends to retain the waters—naturally—yet still contrary to the nature of water. In short, the retention of water above the firmament is ultimately by the will of God and therefore, in the context of the natural, clearly a miracle.[51]

As to the relationship between nature and the divine will, Fishacre articulates the following principle: God established nature according to his will, and it is not the case that he wills as he wills because it is according to nature. Indeed, it is according to nature because God wills it so. As Ambrose had stated, a principle he repeated no fewer than five times, the word of God is the origin and efficient cause of nature.[52]

We do not yet know how many readers Fishacre had; judging

49. Ibid., 2:348.

50. Ibid.

51. Ibid., 2:350–51.

52. Ibid., 2:345.

by the number, approximate dates, and provenance of the manuscripts, we can conclude that his work did not enjoy a long shelf life. But we do know of one reader, Richard Rufus of Cornwall, who subjected the Dominican (whom he consistently refers to simply as *aliquis*) to incessant criticism. It is no less true with respect to this issue. Against the literal truth of waters above the firmament, Rufus asserts, every philosophy and every human reason cries out. Not surprisingly. There is a natural place assigned to each natural body, and the natural place of water is not above the firmament.[53]

From this point the structure of Rufus's argument is difficult to discern. He seems on the one hand to be objecting to Fishacre's analysis that natural philosophy can aid in the understanding of this mystery. On the other hand, he constructs a patchwork of lengthy passages from Augustine, Ambrose, John Damascene, and Jerome—all of which he could have found (and probably did find) either in Grosseteste's *Hexaëmeron* or Fishacre's Commentary or both—which attempt to explain the Genesis text.[54] But then he reminds his students that the philosophers regard all these accounts as vain and frivolous, because they all presume in some fashion that the heavenly body or firmament is composed of the elements of our experience, whereas Aristotle teaches that the heavens are in no way alterable and are therefore incorruptible.[55] The well-worn arguments that the waters are intended as a cooling agent to the intense heat of Saturn or of the sun or the ether do not survive scrutiny.

In a curiously opaque syllogism Rufus argues that waters would be retained above, an unnatural place for them, only by violence or, in other words, by a disorder. But disorder did not predate the first sin. If therefore the waters had to be retained above by violence, either they are not there at all (contrary to the literal

53. Appendix 7A, §1.

54. Ibid., §2, 5–8.

55. Ibid., §9.

meaning of scripture) or they were always there.[56] The hidden premise seems to be that, if they were there from the beginning, it was not a violation of the order of nature.

At this point, he says, "some people" (Fishacre) respond with an example, which attempts to reconcile nature and violence: namely, magnetic attraction. The example does not work, says Rufus: the question is or should be whether the iron is moved naturally or violently by the lodestone, not whether the lodestone attracts naturally. Rufus's view is that some moving force (*vis motiva*) emanates from the lodestone, passes through a medium, and enters parts of the iron, there being perhaps some nature in the iron compatible with this power and thus receptive of it. And the latter is moved and stirred up by the former, that is, the force emitted from the lodestone. This power of the iron, having itself been moved, in turn moves. And this is the intrinsic principle that is called "nature," and thus it appears that the motion of magnetic attraction is wholly natural—not in the least violent.[57]

Since therefore philosophy cries out that an element outside its natural place can be there only by doing violence to nature, is it then the case that it is purely miraculous that waters are above? In response, Rufus invents a distinction between two senses of nature: proper or particular and general. The latter is nothing more than the law of obedience to its creator.[58] Under this rubric fall the classic examples from the Old Testament: the parting of the Red Sea and the reversing of the waters of the Jordan River.[59]

If there is some sense of nature, however, that can be reconciled with what is ordinarily termed the miraculous, it is certainly beyond our philosophy, and Rufus concludes with the oft quoted assertion of Augustine's that the authority of scripture is superior to every capacity of the human genius.[60]

56. Ibid., §12.
57. Ibid., §13–14.
58. Ibid., §20.
59. Ibid., §21–22.
60. Ibid., §24–25.

Yet Rufus cannot resist adding, almost as an afterthought, his endorsement of the view of Hugh of St. Victor to the effect that before the second day of creation water and the heavens were identical and the distinction did not arise until God placed the firmament between the waters. There can be no question, therefore, that the waters were held above by violence: they were there from the beginning before there was an above and below.[61] Rufus claims that he does not say this by way of assertion, however; even the saints do not make assertions in these matters, but simply suggest some of the possible ways in which the truth of the sacred text might have been enacted.[62]

What are we to make of this discussion? Professedly these men were doing theology; they were trying to understand their faith, which entailed understanding the biblical text, using whatever tools of rational analysis were available to them. But it was not a one-way street. Just as (in the well-worn aphorism) extreme cases test the law, the extreme cases provided by the biblical text forced the scholastics of the High Middle Ages to understand the philosophy they inherited from Aristotle in new and untrodden ways: to look at gravitational pull, for example, or the truth of the received cosmology, or the workings of tides and of the vacuum, or the nature of magnetism, and so on. In short, in their theologizing, they were at the same time advancing their knowledge of this world, advancing, in other words, the cause of science.

In the prologue to his Commentary, Richard Fishacre calls his readers' attention to another passage in the book of Genesis, the story of Abraham being commanded by God to have sex with Hagar, the serving girl, as a condition for his impregnating his wife Sarah. Abraham obeys and the rest, as they say, is sacred history. For Fishacre, Hagar represents natural philosophy (or what we would call "science"), Sarah theology. The message is clear: the

61. Ibid., §26–28.
62. Ibid., §30.

aspiring theologian must first lie with the sciences, master the knowledge of this world, before he can be a productive theologian. However, what Fishacre overlooks is that Hagar too begets a child as part of the bargain.

APPENDIX 7A

Richard Rufus, *In secundum librum Sententiarum*, dist. 14; Oxford, Balliol Coll. MS 62, fols. 132va–134ra

§1. Super primam partem distinctionis de aquis: quod non sint ad litteram supra firmamentum clamat omnis philosophia, omnis ratio humana. Nec est mirum; locus enim naturalis determinatus est unicuique corpori naturali. Unde locus naturalis huius elementi proximus terrae est, quia hoc elementum terrae proximum est in pondere naturaliter. Duo enim elementa sunt gravia et duo levia.

§2. Contra. Augustinus, *De civitate Dei* lib. 11, cap. 34: "Hi, qui in nomine aquarum angelos, qui supra caelos sunt, intelligi volunt, ponderibus elementorum moventur et ideo non putant aquarum fluidam gravemque naturam in superioribus mundi locis potuisse constitui; qui secundum rationes suas, si ipsi homines facere potuissent, non flegma quod tamquam in elementis corporis nostri aquarum vicem obtinet, in capite [fol. 132vb] ponerent. Ibi enim sedes flegmatis, secundum Dei opus utique aptissime, secundum autem istorum coniecturam tam absurde ut, si hoc nesciremus et in libro similiter scriptum esset, quod Deus humorem fluidum et frigidum ac per hoc gravem in superiore omnibus ceteris humani corporis parte posuerit, isti trutinatores elementorum nequaqum crederent."[63]

§3. Sunt enim quam plures qui nullo modo litteraliter has aquas intelligi volunt. Quidam enim purificatorias virtutes interpretati sunt aquas quae supra caelos sunt, ut ait Ambrosius, *Hexaëmeron*, homel. secunda prope finem.

§4. Alii vero exponunt hoc caelum pro aere et hoc confirmant per Scripturas, ut cum dicitur "volucres caeli" in Psalmis [8:9 et 103:12]. Et in Luc. 8 [5]: "Volucres caeli comederunt illud." Et item, Luc. 12 [56]: "Faciem caeli et terrae nostis probare."

§5. Sed iudicio Augustini et aliorum expositorum nomine "firmamenti" hic intelligitur caelum in quo locata sunt sidera, super quod veraciter sunt aquae positae.[64] Et hoc non esse improbabile nititur Augustinus probare

63. Augustine, *De civ. Dei* 11.33 (CCSL 48,354)

64. See Augustine, *De Gen. ad litt.* 2.10 (CSEL 28.1, 48)

Super Genesim ad litteram lib. 2[65] sic:[66] "Si aquae istae quas videmus in tantas minutias possunt dividi et tantum subtiliari, et aliqua vi impressi caloris vel alio modo in tantum levigari, ut super hunc aera possint vaporaliter in nubibus suspendi, eadem ratione aquae minutius divisae magisque subtilitate et levigatae secundum proportionem qua locus superior firmamento altior est loco nubium, ibidem suspendi poterunt. Et si virtus ea subtilians et levigans sit virtus fixa et manens, ibidem perseveranter manere poterunt."[67]

§6. Iterum, quod ibi sint et ad quid ibi sint docet Augustinus et alii expositores per frigiditatem stellae Saturni, "quae stella, propter situm quem habet ceteris sex planetis excelsiorem, et propter motum quem habet ex rotatione caeli ab oriente in occidentem ceteris velociorem, deberet esse ceteris planetis ferventior, nisi aquis illis superioribus temperatus esset eiusdem stellae fervor. Ipsarumque namque aquarum naturalis frigiditas admisceri videtur virtuti eiusdem stellae calescenti, sicut hic videmus quod positis iuxta se duobus corporibus, altero fervente et reliquo algente, aer circumstans minus fervet ex corpore fervente propter vicinitatem corporis algentis et minus alget ex corpore algente propter vicinitatem corporis ferventis, commixtis videlicet utrorumque corporum activis virtutibus et utraque virtute ex alterius commixtione in sua actione imminuta."[68]

§7. Hanc eandem causam assignat Ambrosius operi secundae diei: "Cum ipsi dicant volvi orbem caeli stellis ardentibus refulgentem, nonne divina providentia necessario prospexit, ut intra orbem caeli et supra orbem redundaret aqua, quae illius ferventis axis incendia temperaret? Propterea, quia exundat ignis et fervet, etiam aqua exundat in terris, ne assurgentis solis et stellarum micantium ardor exureret, et tenera rerum exordia insolitus vapor laederet."[69]

§8. Ecce hic habes causam aquarum inferiorum et superiorum. Basilius etiam, *Hexaëmeron* homel. tertia: "Aquarum abundantia valde fuit necessaria, ut incessabiliter et sine intermissione pastum sibi ignis de his attraheret."[70] Iohannes quoque Damscenus, cap. 23: "Cuius gratia super firmamentum aquam Deus[71] imposuit, propter solis et aetheris calidissimum fervorem. Mox enim post firmamentum aether expressus est. Sed sol et luna cum stellis in firmamento sunt. Et nisi superiaceret aqua, inflammatum iam utique

65. See ibid., 37–38.

66. de hoc insuper col. proxima *add. i. marg.*

67. Grosseteste, *Hexaëmeron* 3.3.1., eds. Dales and Gieben, 103.

68. Ibid.

69. Ambrose, *Hex.* 2.3.12 (CSEL 32.1, 50); *coll. ex* Grosseteste, *Hexaëmeron.* 3.10.2, eds. Dales and Gieben, 109–10.

70. Basil, *Hexaëmeron* 3.5.11, ed. Emmanuel Amand de Mendieta and Stig Rudberg (Berlin: Akademie-Verlag, 1958), 38; *coll. ex* ibid., 110.

71. *rep.*

esset a calore firmamentum."[72] Beda etiam dicit quod ibi positae sunt ad mundationem diluvii.[73] Iosephus vero dicit quod inde sunt pluviae.[74]

§9. Omnia ista habent philosophi tanquam vana et frivola, quia stella et corpus caeleste nec est elementum nec ex elementis, nec generabile, nec corruptibile, nec alterabile, nec corruptivum, nec passivum; nec sunt calida, nec frigida in actu, sed efficiunt [fol. 133ra] calorem in haec inferiora per virtutem suorum luminum et motuum. Unde dicunt quod nihil est dictum "aquam temperare ardorem stellae." Si calorem haberet stella et esset illa stella corpus alterabile, quare et corruptibile.

§10. Sed deest quaestio, scilicet an corpus caeleste eiusdem naturae sit cum corpore gravi et levi an omnino alterius. Et de hoc inferius forte aliquid dicetur.

§11. Aliter obicitur hic: si sunt ibi, per violentiam sunt ibi. Nam contra suam naturam propriam quod patere potest per Damascenum qui describit aquam, cap. 23: "Aqua est elementum frigidum, humidum, grave et deorsum ductile."[75]

§12. Item, duo elementa sunt naturaliter gravia et duo alia naturaliter levia. Ergo si ibi sunt, violenter detinentur—quod videtur inconveniens. Violentia enim contra naturam est, et inordinatio quaedam esse videtur. Nulla autem inordinatio fuit ante primum peccatum. Istae autem aquae, si ibi sunt ante primum peccatum, ibi fuerunt. Sic ergo dicerent philosophi: non decet illas ibi per violentiam detineri, et aliter ibi esse non possunt. Ergo ibi omnino non sunt.

§13. Hic tamen respondent aliqui per exemplum. Si quaeritur utrum ferrum moveatur ad adamantem naturaliter vel violenter, id est contra naturam ferri. Similiter si est ibi aliqua virtus activa et retentiva aquae, potest dici quod est ibi aqua contra naturam aquae, sed tamen naturaliter, id est per naturam illius virtutis.

§14. Non satis bene videtur dici de exemplo proposito. Nam ferrum est quod movetur, de quo est quaestio an movetur naturaliter an violenter. Et non est quaestio utrum adamas attrahat naturaliter. Verum enim est quod ex propria sua natura attrahit adamas ferrum et non quodvis aliud metallum. Est ergo ferrum ferrum, et ferrum est grave. Unde ipsum est grave. Iste eius motus videtur violentus. Unde ipsum est ferrum, videtur magis naturalis. Aliqua enim vis motiva egreditur ab adamante per medium usque ad ferrum et ingreditur partes ferri; et est forte aliqua natura in ferro conveniens

72. John Damascene, *De fide orth.*, cap. 23.1, ed. Eligius Buytaert (St. Bonaventure, N.Y.: Franciscan Institute, 1955), 98–99; proxime *coll. ex* ibid.

73. See Beda, *De natura rerum* 7 (PL 90, 200–1); *coll.ex* ibid., 109.

74. See Josephus, *Ant. Iud.* 1.1.1.30 (ed. Franz Blatt), 127); *coll. ex* ibid.

75. John Damascene, *De fide orth.*, cap. 23.1, ed. Eligius Buytaert (St. Bonaventure, N.Y.: Franciscan Institute, 1955), 98.

huic virtuti. Et haec movetur et excitatur ab illa virtute. Et haec mota movet. Et haec est principium intrinsecum quod dicitur "natura"; et sic videtur ille motus naturalis esse.

§15. Suppositae autem rationi ab Augustino respondent philosophi quod non possent aquae in tantum subtiliari. Nec posset divisio in tantum procedere, ut salvata specie aquae possent sursum naturaliter collocari. Sed in tantum posset talis divisio procedere quod salveretur species et corrumperetur aqua.

§16. Iterum est quaestio: si stant ibi, aut congelatae aut fluidae. Et in hoc sunt opiniones. Quidam enim dicunt quod glaciali soliditate. Nec mirum, ut dicunt. "Cum lapis crystallus, cuius magna est firmitas et perspicuitas, de aquis per congelationem est factus, sic aquae illae in unum magnum crystallum sunt consolidatae. Et sive quaelibet pars huius crystalli sit ponderosa sive levis, cum medium eius sit centrum terrae quo tendunt omnia ponderosa et a quo nituntur omnia levia, ipsum totum crystallinum necesse est suis propriis nisibus immobiliter librari et super stabilitatem suam fundari, sicut terra suis ponderibus librata est et super propriam stabilitatem fundata. Si autem gravitate et levitate careat, patet quod nec sursum et deorsum moveri debet."[76]

§17. Praeterea posito quod ponderosae sint et fluidae, nulla necessitas compellet eas deorsum fluere, cum sit secundum Philosophum corpus caeli, neque rarefactibile, neque condensabile, neque per alterius corporis penetrationem divisibile.[77]

§18. Quaeritur etiam utrum sint ibi mobiles vel immobiles—Et videtur quod mobiles motu circulari, scilicet per motum caeli ab oriente in occidentem. Sed nihil, ut videtur, cogit illas aliquorsum super firmamentum decurrere, cum extima firmamenti superficies ubique sit a centro mundi aeque distans, planitiem habens [fol. 133rb] sphaericam in nullo loco magis quam in alio depressam.

§19. Sed semper in omnibus his clamat philosophia quod nonnisi per violentiam et contra naturam haec stare possent. Et ideo quaeritur utrum tantum miraculose ibi sint, et violenter et contra naturam. Quod videtur velle Ambrosius, opere secundae diei, dicens: "Si naturam elementorum consideres, quomodo inter aquas solidatum est firmamentum? Illae profluunt, istud constringitur; illae currunt, hoc manet."[78] Et super illud "dividat aquas ab aquis" [Gen. 1:6]: "Quomodo iubet quod scit secundum rationem elementorum esse contrarium? Sed cum sermo eius ortus naturae sit, iure usurpat dare legem naturae qui originem dedit."[79]

76. Grosseteste, *Hexaëmeron* 3.3.3, ed. Dales and Gieben, 104.

77. See Aristotle, *De caelo* 1.3 (270a12–15). Cf. *Auctoritates Aristotelis, De caelo et mundo* #15, ed. Jacqueline Hamesse (Louvain: Publications Universitaires, 1974), 160.

78. Ambrose, *Hex.* 2.2.4 (CSEL 32.1, 44)

79. Ibid.

§20. Iste sanctus videtur innuere quod contra naturam sint ibi, sed tamen cum distinctione naturae. Duplex enim videtur esse natura alicuius creaturae, propria scilicet et particularis, et alia generalis. Et haec nihil aliud est nisi lex oboediendi suo Creatori. Ergo contra naturam primo modo dictam ibi videntur esse; contra naturam secundo modo dictam, non.

§21. Idem Ambrosius in eodem opere post sic ait: "Cum ipse facit quasi potens et quasi virtus, quid miraris si supra firmamentum caeli potuit tantae maiestatis operatione unda suspendi? De aliis hoc collige; de his quae viderunt oculi hominum, quomodo ad Iudaeorum transitum, si rationem quaeris, se unda diviserit. Non solet hoc esse naturae, ut aqua se decernat ab aqua. Sed aqua confundere non decernere solet. "Gelaverunt," inquit, "fluctus" [Ex.15:8] et specie firmati cursum suum in solito fine frenarunt. Nonne potuit etiam aliter Hebraeum populum liberare? Sed tibi voluit ostendere, ut eo spectaculo etiam ea quae non vidisti estimares esse credenda. Iordanis quoque reflexo amne in suum fontem revertitur. Haerere aquam, cum labitur, inusitatum, rursus redire in superiora sine ullo repagulo impossibile habetur. Sed quid impossibile ei qui dedit posse quibus voluit, dedit posse infirmitatibus, ut infirmus dicat: "Omnia possum in eo qui me confortat?" [Phil. 4:13].[80]

§22. "Credibile satis est quod, sicut dominus statuit ad horam aquas Rubri Maris et Iordanis 'quasi in utre' [Ps. 77:13], contra solitum cursum naturae, sic etiam multa faciat perpetue manentia contra et supra solitum cursum naturae."[81]

§23. Sed[82] quod non sint ibi aquae miraculosae videtur velle Augustinus, *Super Genesim ad litteram* lib. 2: "Multi," inquit, "asserunt super sidereum caelum aquas esse non posse, eo quod sic habeant ordinatum pondus suum, ut vel super terram fluctent vel in aere terris proximo vaporaliter ferantur, neque quisquam istos debet ita refellere, ut dicat secundum omnipotentiam Dei, cui cuncta possibilia sunt, oportere nos credere etiam aquas tam graves, quam novimus atque sentimus, caelesti corpori, in quo sunt sidera superfusas. Nunc enim quemadmodum Deus instituerit naturas rerum, secundum scripturas eius nos convenit quaerere, non, quid in eis vel ex eis ad miraculum potentiae suae velit operari. Neque enim, si vellet Deus sub aqua oleum aliquando manere, non fieret; non ex eo tamen olei natura nobis esset incognita, quod ita facta sit, ut appetendo suum locum, etiam si subterfusa fuerit, perrumpat aquas eisque se superpositam collocet."[83]

§24. Ecce ut videtur quod non sunt ibi solum miraculose. Quid ergo in

80. Ibid., 2.3.11 (49); *coll. ex* Grosseteste, *Hexaëmeron* 3.3.5, ed. Dales and Gieben, 104.

81. Grosseteste, *Hexaëmron* 3.3.5, ed. Dales and Gieben, 104–5.

82. quod non sint an aquae miraculosae *add. i. marg.*

83. Augustine, *De Gen. ad litt.* 2.1 (CSEL 28.1, 32–33).

omnibus his dicamus? Nescio. Nisi cum Augustino in eodem libro: "Quocumque modo et qualeslibet aquae ibi sint, esse ibi minime dubitemus. Maior est quippe Scripturae huius auctoritas, quam omnis humani ingenii capacitas."[84]

§25. Non debet homo in hac materia multum sollicitari. Ubi sola fides et auctoritas Scripturae cogit confiteri esse ibi aquas. Ratio autem humana omnino[85] contradicit.

§26. Tamen unum est quod monet me, quod docet Hugo, *Didascalicon*: Quomodo possunt aquae super caelum consistere? Glacialiter. Vel, quod magis credibile est, ad similitudinem illius primae caliginis fumaliter suspenduntur pendulae ad modum nebulae levis, qualis in principio natura omnium aquarum fuisse putatur.[86] Nam ut idem [fol. 133va] Hugo ait parum ante: Illa prima caligo terram ambiens tantumdem spatii sursum occupabat, quantum et nunc universitas[87] creaturarum complectitur.

§27. Et idem Hugo, *Sacramentorum*[88] lib. 1, pars prima, cap. 6: Ante primum diem nec sub caelo "nec supra caelum aquae erant."[89] Sed nec ante secundum diem, "quia ipsum caelum aquae erant; totum aquae et totum caelum, quia idem aquae et caelum. Secunda die factum est firmamentum et divisit inter aquas et aquas, quae prius aquae erant, factae sunt aquae et aquae."[90]

§28. Ex his accipe quod, si ante secundum diem non erat aqua per violentiam sursum, quod nec nunc est. Et ut videtur. Tales nunc sunt ibi aquae, quales et tunc fuerunt secundum Hugonem, scilicet nec congelatae nec fluidae, sed tertio modo praedicto. Et quod ut hic in littera dicit Magister in sexta parte distinctionis: Rariores fuerunt primariae aquae quam sint modo istae.[91] Et quod ex eadem materia factum fuit firmamentum et istae aquae inferiores et quod non magis contra naturam sunt illae aquae superius quam sit firmamentum in suo loco. Unde non videntur omnino easdem proprietates et condiciones habere quas habent istae, quia nec fluiditatem nec gravitatem.

§29. Sed numquid propter hoc non erunt eiusdem naturae? Nihil prohibet, ut videtur, esse eiusdem naturae. Nam quattuor elementa in corpore glorificato et non glorificato eiusdem sunt naturae.

§30. Sic ergo, ut dixi, tales et nunc sunt ibi, quales et fuerunt in principio. Et ibi steterunt cum ex illa caligine factae fuerunt diversae naturae corporales. Et haec dixi sine assertione; non enim ipsi sancti hic faciunt assertiones, ipsi enim scripserunt in talibus. Non tam[92] ut unum aliquod assererent, quam ut modos plures possibiles ostenderent quibus hoc Deus potuit facere, quod Scriptura dicit factum esse.

84. Ibid., 2.5 (39).

85. *corr. ex* non.

86. Locum non inveni.

87. Locum non inveni.

88. Sententiarum MS.

89. Hugo de St. Victore, *De sacramentis* 1.1.6 (PL 176,191).

90. Ibid.

91. See Peter Lombard, 2 *Sent.* 14.8, ed. Ignatius Brady, 398.

92. *corr. ex* tam

APPENDIX 7B

The Summa of Alexander of Hales (*Summa Halensis*)

The hodgepodge that goes under the name of the *Summa Halensis*, that is, the Summa of Alexander of Hales, parts of which began to circulate before Fishacre finished his Commentary, contained the lengthiest treatment of the subject. The Alexandrine contributors divide the issue into five questions or chapters: whether there are waters above (there are!) and what they are, whether these waters are gathered in the form of a circle (yes, they are), whether they move in a circular fashion (again, yes), whether *of necessity* waters are constituted above the firmament (the pseudo-Alexander grants the utility, but leaves the necessity to the inscrutable designs of the creator), and lastly, in what way those waters can be called the crystalline heaven.[93] Although the *Summa Halensis* breaks no new ground, it does articulate clearly the distinction between utility and necessity: it finds a number of considerations to show that it is useful for God to have created supernal waters; but was it necessary? Does it in other words meet the demands of an Aristotelian science? Here the "Summa of Hales" falls back on the conjunctive properties of water and therefore the necessity of conveying the motion of the First Mover from the empyrean and starry heaven to the lower heavens; water has both an active principle and a passive principle—it can be moved and in turn moves, and in this way conserves things in being.[94]

93. Alexander of Hales, *Summa theologica* 2.1.3.2.2.2, caps. 1–5, ed. Quaracchi, 336–41.

94. Ibid., cap. 4; 340–41.

CHAPTER 8

Adam's Rib

A Test Case for Natural Philosophy in Grosseteste, Fishacre, Rufus, and Kilwardby

For the natural philosopher the Genesis account of the six days of creation, or hexaëmeron in the coinage of St. Ambrose, is replete with mind-bending puzzles: how can there be light without a heavenly body to emit that light, or how can there be waters above the firmament, not to speak of the concept of creation itself, abhorrent to all ancient Greek thinkers.[1] Ranking high among these philosophical puzzles is the account of the making

1. See, for example, Parmenides: "One way only is left to be spoken of, that it is; and on this way are full many signs that *what is* is uncreated and imperishable, for it is entire, immovable and without end. It was not in the past, nor shall it be, since it is now, all at once, one, continuous; for what creation wilt thou seek for it? How and whence did it grow? Nor shall I allow thee to say or to think, 'from that which is not'; for it is not to be said or thought that it is not. And what need would have driven it on to grow, starting from nothing, at a later time rather than an earlier?" Geoffrey S. Kirk and John E. Raven, eds., *The Presocratic Philosophers* (Cambridge: Cambridge University Press, 1964), 273.

of Adam's mate, the first woman, from his rib (Gn 2:21–22).[2] It is thus not a little surprising that Robert Grosseteste's restlessly inquisitive mind should not have been engaged by this problem in his own commentary on the *Hexaëmeron*.[3] What we find instead is first an awareness of a difference in terminology between the two creation accounts: "creavit Deus hominem" (Gn 1:27) in the first chapter of Genesis, but "formavit Deus hominem de limo terrae" (Gn 2:7) in the second.[4] Grosseteste notes that there are some who suspect that creation, which is *ex nihilo*, must refer to the soul only; but *formavit*, or according to another translation *finxit* or *plasmavit* (to form, to mold, to fashion), presumes materials; it is a "making" and here, says Grosseteste, the reference is to the body, the "vasum fictile" spoken of by Paul in 2 Cor 4:7).[5] Hence, when the text says "the Lord God formed man of the slime of the earth, and breathed into his face the breath of life,"

2. This chapter is much indebted to a fine study on what is called technically "the truth of human nature" and cognate problems: Philip Lyndon Reynolds, *Food and the Body: Some Peculiar Questions in High Medieval Theology*, Studien und Texte zur Geistesgeschichte des Mittelalters 69 (Leiden: Brill, 1999). This, in turn, was inspired by work the author had done with the late Walter Principe. My focus here will be considerably narrower, that is, the questions asked by the natural philosopher: the nature of matter, manner of expansion, rarefaction and condensation, and the like.

3. The answer of course may lie in the nature of the Grossetestean corpus itself. Richard W. Southern, for example, makes the following observation: "Grosseteste was not a careful or self-conscious writer.... Even a relatively carefully composed work like his *Hexaëmeron* shows a marked deterioration in argument in its final sections, and it was never brought to a definite conclusion." Southern, *Robert Grosseteste: The Growth of an English Mind in Medieval Europe* (Oxford: Clarendon Press, 1986), 27.

4. Notwithstanding some modern scholarly opinion to the contrary, Grosseteste and the medievals in general viewed the Genesis account as a single narrative emanating from a single author, namely Moses. Even more problematically, Grosseteste was also convinced that other biblical texts referring to creation (e.g., Sirach 18:1, Wisdom 11:18, and John 5:17) were also divinely inspired and had to be reconciled; cf. Roland Teske, "Genesis Accounts of Creation," in *Augustine Through the Ages: An Encyclopedia*, ed. Allan D. Fitzgerald (Grand Rapids: Eerdmans, 1999). Quotation from the Vulgate is taken from *Biblia sacra iuxta vulgatam versionem,* 4th ed. (Stuttgart: Deutsche Bibelgesellschaft, 1994).

5. Robert Grosseteste, *Hexaëmeron* 8.18.1, ed. Richard C. Dales and Servus Gieben, ABM VI (Oxford: Oxford University Press, 1982), 243.

the breath here would be the soul already created.[6] But then he observes that Augustine rejects this view, owing to the fact that the text of the first chapter also says "male and female he created them" and sexual differentiation belongs to bodiness.[7] The text will not bear the interpretation that God first created bodiless souls.[8]

Next, Grosseteste frames the second creation account in terms of the mode of creation and that mode entails a temporal sequence: in other words, the man and the woman were both created on the sixth day; but was it, he asks, according to their perfected form or causally and potentially only? If the latter, then the purpose of the account in Genesis 2 would have been the detailing of the mode of bringing each to his or her perfected form.[9] Hence the text "then the Lord God cast a deep sleep upon Adam" (Gn 2:21) clearly suggests a process in time: Adam was awake, then he slept. And prior to this the Lord had brought the beasts of the earth and the fowls of the air to Adam for naming, further extending the passage of time beyond the sixth day (Gn 2:19). But here Grosseteste is content to leave the matter, notwithstanding the invitation the text offers to speculate on the physics of Eve's formation from Adam's rib.

Grosseteste's influence, however, extends beyond what he himself carved out the leisure to write. Grosseteste was rooted in the distinctly English and nonscholastic study of the natural sci-

6. Ibid., 10.7.1, 300.

7. Ibid., 8.18.2–3, 243–44. Grosseteste cites Augustine's *De Genesi ad litteram*, 3.22. Cf. Augustine, *De civitate Dei* 13.24.

8. Fishacre, on the other hand, commenting on the Lombard text, "For Augustine, *De Genesi*, hands down that the soul was created with the angels and without a body," allows that either God created everything in the first instant of time or that the soul was created without the body with the angels, until the body should be made. Richard Fishacre, *In secundum librum Sententiarum*, ed. R. James Long (Munich: Verlag der Bayersiche Akademie der Wissenschaften, 2008), 1:344

9. Recall here that the text of Sirach 18:1 also had to be reconciled, viz. "He that lives forever created all things together."

ences, pioneered by such Englishmen as Adelard of Bath, Daniel of Morley, and Alfred of Shareshill.[10] When in his middle years he turned his attention to the sacred science, Grossetteste did not lose his orientation nor his conviction that the knowledge of the natural world elucidates the scriptures. In the words of the late James McEvoy: "In approaching the sacred text Grosseteste fully expected that whatever was true and certain in philosophy or astronomy was already present, implicitly at least, in the text whose chief Author is also the Writer of the book of nature."[11] This conviction could not but have influenced his contemporaries at the Oxford *studium* and those of the generation immediately following. Such an orientation, I submit, can be called the Grossetestean school (I take a "school" to mean a minimum of two or more philosophers among whom there is some contact and similarity of outlook).[12]

Richard Fishacre

The Dominican Richard Fishacre (d. 1248), though he most probably never studied under Grosseteste directly, certainly felt his influence in most profound ways. Much of this influence has only recently been documented.[13] It was Fishacre who articulated

10. See Southern, *Robert Grosseteste*, 85–92.

11. James McEvoy, *Robert Grosseteste*, Great Medieval Thinkers (Oxford: Oxford University Press, 2000), 81.

12. For "school" see, Thomas Mautner, ed., *A Dictionary of Philosophy* (Oxford: Blackwell Publishers, 1996), 385–86. McEvoy, for his part, although conceding that "Grosseteste certainly set part of the agenda for the generation that succeeded him at Oxford (Marsh, Rufus, and York among the Franciscans; Fishacre among the Dominicans," insists that "no school formed around his major impulses." James McEvoy, *Robert Grosseteste* (Oxford: Oxford University Press, 2000), 138. I can only conclude that McEvoy set the bar higher than I do.

13. See, for example, Dales, "The Influence of Grosseteste's *Hexaëmeron* on the *Sentences* Commentary of Richard Fishacre, OP and Richard Rufus of Cornwall, OFM," *Viator* 2 (1971), 271–300; R. James Long, "The Beginning of a Tradition: the *Sentences* Commentary of Richard Fishacre, OP," in *Medieval Commentaries on the*

in the prologue to the first book of his Commentary on the *Sentences* the essential feature of the Grossetestean school: as Abraham was required first to bed the serving girl before he could father a child by Sarah, so must the aspiring theologian master the natural sciences before advancing to the queen of the sciences.[14]

Fishacre's point of departure in this instance is the Lombard text "that by God's power, she [Eve] was made from [Adam's] rib, without the addition of anything extrinsic, just as five loaves of bread were multiplied from themselves."[15] But here precisely is the problem: increase in volume is achieved either by addition (*appositio*)—which the Lombard denies in this case—or by thinning out.[16] Thinning out or rarefaction, however, to the extent needed in this situation-that is, from the dimensions of a rib to that of an adult female body—would seem to entail a transformation (for example, earth to water), and would not include flesh or bone or nerves; the volume of a fistful of earth increased tenfold would result in a volume of water.[17]

"Sentences" of Peter Lombard, vol. 1, *Current Research,* ed. Gilian R. Evans (Leiden: Brill, 2002), 345–57, at 351.

14. R. James Long, "The Science of Theology according to Richard Fishacre: Edition of the Prologue to his *Commentary on the Sentences*," *MS* 34 (1972): 85–86. In the same prologue Fishacre talks about the three books, a trichotomy repeated by Bonaventure: the book of life, the book of creation, and the book of sacred scripture (ibid., 80).

15. Peter Lombard, 2 *Sent.,* 18.4.1, trans. Giulio Silano (Toronto, Pontifical Institute of Mediaeval Studies, 2008), 2:78.

16. The primary meaning of *appositio* is "placing," "application," or "affixing" and I think the nuance is not unimportant: that is, there is a base which is being added to, rather than the coming together of disparate elements. See E. L. Roger, *Revised Medieval Latin Word-List from British and Irish Sources*, vol. 1 (London: Oxford University Press for the British Academy, 1965), 25. Lombard denies the possibility of addition when he writes, "If God added anything extrinsic in making the body of the woman, then the addition would be greater than the rib itself; and so the woman should rather be said to have been made from what was added, from which she had received greater part of her substance than from the rib." Peter Lombard, 2 *Sent.*18.4.1, trans. Silano, 2:78.

17. Fishacre, *In 2 Sent.*, 18.3, ed. Long, 1:368–69. Cf. an earlier text: "Et dico minimas partes quae, si ulterius dividerentur, formam pristinam non retinerent—ut est minimus aer qui in duo divisus iam non aer, sed ignis potius erit." Ibid., 12.5, ed. Long, 1:245–46.

Fishacre at this point modestly admits that he would rather be taught than teach. But he does have a solution to propose, and it derives from his version of hylomorphism. Although some modicum of matter is needed to anchor and individualize a substance, three-dimensional extension, he asserts, originates from form, not matter. In fact, a mere point of matter is sufficient as a base for infinite extension.[18] Earlier in book 2, in the context of his teaching on the angels, Fishacre had developed his teaching on matter in spiritual substances, sometimes called oxymoronically "spiritual matter."[19] According to this teaching, both the angel and the human soul are substances composed of matter and form.[20] But that matter should be extended (that is, that it should have, according to Aristotle's definition, "parts outside of parts"), it has from form. Indeed, were it possible for a substance to be wholly matter without any form, it would occupy only a point (*locum punctalem*).[21] Alternatively, if matter were granted some form that did not cause parts outside of parts (a form in other words that is other than a *forma corporeitatis*), that composite could still be located in a point—in short, an angel.[22]

If matter does not account for extension, what then is its nature and its function?[23] That depends, says Fishacre, on the kind of matter, for matter exhibits a twofold potentiality: a passive potency, which is simply receptivity to form; and an active potency,

18. Fishacre, *In 2 Sent.*, 18.3, ed. Long, 1:369.

19. See R. James Long, "Of Angels and Pinheads: The Contributions of the Early Oxford Masters to the Doctrine of Spiritual Matter," *FS: Essays in Honor of Dr. Girard Etzkorn,* ed. Gordon A. Wilson and Timothy B. Noone, 56 (1998): 237–54.

20. Unaware of its origins in the *Fons vitae* of Ibn Gabirol's and unaware that the *De ecclesiasticis dogmatibus* is not authentic, Fishacre remains convinced that the doctrine is Augustine's.

21. The reader will recognize the old chestnut: how many angels can dance on the head of a pin? This question, however, does not predate the seventeenth century; see Long, "Of Angels and Pinheads," 245n23.

22. See Fishacre, *In 2 Sent.*, 2.5, ed. Long, 1:40–41.

23. Here Reynolds expresses his puzzlement: "Whether Fishacre has a coherent theory of matter and quantity is unclear, but if he does, it is certainly quite unlike Aristotle's" (Reynolds, *Food and the Body*, 182). Indeed.

which is something of form latent in matter. This latter Fishacre identifies with the Stoic and Augustinian concept of seminal natures or seminal reasons (*rationes seminales*), the hidden seeds of all beings of God's creation and the principle of their eventual development; these in turn correspond to causal natures in God.[24] Matter in the sense of passive potency is one in number, whereas matter in the sense of active potency is plural; there are at least as many active potencies as there are forms.[25]

To return for a moment to the comparison that Peter Lombard makes between the expansion of Adam's rib into the dimensions of Eve's body and the multiplication of the five loaves of bread into thousands: Fishacre, unlike the Lombard, sees the two miraculous acts as different. Fishacre does identify the latter as a miracle, but a "lesser" miracle, because it was one in which causal reasons alone were able to reduce from potency to act: hence actualities which nature would also be capable of producing, absent divine intervention (he also includes here the changing of the water to wine from the Gospel of John).[26]

The production of Eve's body from Adam's rib, however, stands among the greatest miracles, that is, those in which there is no *ratio seminalis* in the matter corresponding to the *ratio causalis* in the divine mind: the first woman, he says, did not have a seminal nature in the rib of the first man. Nature alone cannot bring about this kind of miracle.[27] Yet, if this *miraculum* be not in violation of nature, Fishacre must provide an accounting. What he has sup-

24. Fishacre, *In 2 Sent.*, 7.6, ed. Long, 1:140. In a subsequent chapter Fishacre explicitly connects the Augustinian and Aristotelian doctrines: "Et tertia [opinio] media, quae est Aristotelis, quae ponit nec formas omnino latere nec omnino esse ab extrinseco, sed aliquid eius latere (et hoc est potentia activa materiae, quam hic Augustinus vocat 'rationem seminalem') et aliquid eius esse ab extrinseco agente, scilicet complementum et actus," Fishacre, *In 2 Sent.*, 7.8, ed. Long, 1:151.

25. Fishacre, *In 2 Sent.*, 7.8, ed. Long, 1:151–52.

26. Fishacre, *In 2 Sent.*, 7.6, ed. Long, 1:140. I take it that Fishacre would allow for the influence of art as well as nature, much in the same way as Kilwardby in the passage below, n. 50.

27. Fishacre, *In 2 Sent.*, 7.6, ed. Long, 1:140.

plied thus far is a passive potency—a nonopposition, as it were, to any form whatsoever—and a form that accounts for its increase in volume: "The potency of matter is twofold: namely passive, when nothing whatsoever of the form that has to be brought to fulfillment is in matter, but only the potency to receive form is there; such was the case perhaps of the woman with respect to Adam's rib."[28]

Fishacre sees an illustrative case in the presence of the whole soul to every part of the body; the soul, having only a modicum of matter, is able to expand to the farthest extremity of the living body; *just as*, he says, light immediately floods a room as soon as the windows are opened without suffering a transformation. Reynolds remarks at this point that "Fishacre probably has in mind a cosmogony like that of Grosseteste," that is, a metaphysics of light.[29] While it is true that, unlike Grosseteste, Fishacre never claims that light is the *forma corporeitatis*, he does say that the nature of light is such that it can elicit act from potency, *just as* when the house is closed, light does not enter; but when a window is opened, light occupies a greater place than before.[30] This is increase of volume not by addition or thinning out, but multiplication. But whether light is capable of infinite expansion is a question concerning which he expresses ignorance:

Since increase that is possible for the body is threefold, namely by addition (and of this kind even the vilest body is capable, namely an

28. "Duplex est potentia materiae: scilicet passiva, cum omnino nihil formae faciendae est in materia, sed est ibi tantum potentia recipiendi formam; sic fuit mulier in costa forte," Fishacre, *In 2 Sent.*, 18.3, ed. Long, 1:373. See: "Unum ergo de duobus est, scilicet quod summum ad quod homo potest est natura, scilicet ad quod habet rationem seminalem est posse non mori. Nec habet rationem seminalem ad gradum superiorem, scilicet non posse mori, sed tantum respectu huius habet potentiam passivam, sicut costa Adae respectu mulieris," Fishacre, *In 2 Sent.* 19.1, ed. Long, 1:386.

29. Reynolds, *Food and the Body*, 182.

30. See the opening of Grosseteste's, "Tractatus de luce secundum Lincolniensem," now critically edited by Cecilia Panti in *Robert Grosseteste and His Intellectual Milieu*, ed. John Flood, James R. Ginther, and Joseph W. Goering (Toronto: Pontifical Institute of Mediaeval Studies, 2013), 226–38.

> opaque body, for example earth, which is increased by addition) and by rarefaction (and for this kind a diaphanous body is capable, namely water and also air, which is increased by rarefaction of itself); it remains the case that there cannot be a third kind, with the exception of light or a luminous body ... [which can] increase by means of multiplication, and that this is nobler than any body, namely a kind of spiritual nature. And thus it seems that the nature of light could educe matter from potency into such an act, as is evident when a house is closed, such that not even light enters; but then when a window is opened, light occupies a greater space than previously. Nor is it the case that there is something added to it; nor is that which was present earlier made rarer, but rather multiplied. But whether light is able to educe matter from potency to a kind of act without end, I do not know.[31]

It must, however, be admitted that by comparison with Grosseteste's lucid little work on the subject Fishacre's exploitation of an illuminationist metaphysics to explain the expansion of matter is disappointingly vague and underdeveloped.

Leaving aside the theological aspects of the question with its implications respecting the transmission of original sin (all of which is fully and insightfully dealt with by Reynolds), let me return to the issue of matter: does Fishacre have a coherent theory of matter? What can be said, I think unequivocally, is that—whatever it is—it is not Aristotle's *hyle*, a principle of pure potentiality. Richard Dales, seeking to find an appropriate word for the Fishacrean

31. "Cum triplex sit augmentatio corpori possibilis, scilicet per appositionem—et in hanc potest etiam vilissimum corpus, scilicet corpus opacum, ut terra, quae augetur per appositionem; et per rarefactionem—et in hanc potest corpus diaphanum, scilicet aqua et etiam aer, quae augentur per rarefactionem sui; restat ut tertium non possit nisi lux et corpus luminosum, scilicet in augmentum per multiplicationem, et quod est corpore noblius, scilicet natura spiritualis quaelibet. Et ita videtur quod natura lucis possit educere materiam de potentia in actum talem, ut patet cum clausa est domus, nec intrat lux; deinde aperitur fenestra, lux occupat maiorem locum quam prius. Nec ei additum est aliquid; nec quae prius erat rarefacta est, sed potius multiplicata. Sed utrum possit educere materiam lux de potentia in actum talem in infinitum, nescio." Fishacre, *In 2 Sent.*, 30.15, ed. Long, 2:197. Twice, in different contexts, Fishacre makes the statement that "omnis forma lux est" without, however, expanding on that provocative claim. See Fishacre, *In 2 Sent*, 2.2, ed. Long, 1:30, and 34.5, ed. Long, 2:235.

conception, settles on the term "dross," originally a scum formed on the surface of molten metal, and by derivation a kind of worthless stuff.[32] This may be the case, perhaps, but it is imprecise. Writing of Grosseteste's concept of matter, McEvoy states that "one is entitled to suppose that Grosseteste is thinking of matter as composed of contiguous, indivisible atoms."[33] My claim is that we are entitled to think of Fishacre's concept in the same way, and in fact there is solid textual warrant for such an interpretation.[34] At one point Fishacre even refers to Democritus by name, the knowledge of whom was probably derived from Aristotle's *Metaphysics*.[35]

To what extent Fishacre consciously and explicitly held a doctrine of atomism it is difficult to say. That he was implicitly an atomist, however, there is no question, as was Grosseteste before him.[36] Matter for Fishacre, then, is manifestly not Aristotle's prime matter, but more like what the latter would term secondary or extended matter, even though that extension is limited to a point of no dimensions.[37]

32. Richard C. Dales, *The Problem of the Rational Soul in the Thirteenth Century* (Leiden: Brill, 1995), 54.

33. McEvoy, *Philosophy of Grosseteste*, 154n16.

34. For example, Fishacre's claim that there are an infinite number of points in an atom: "Si sufficeret locus punctalis spiritui, omnes creati spiritus angelici et in infinitum plures possent esse in una atomo, quia sunt in ea puncta infinita, immo et partes corporales infinitae." Fishacre, *In 2 Sent.*, 2.5, ed. Long, 1:45. See also, "Et dico crementum vel augmentum maioris loci occupationem; igitur cum ex semine primi hominis habente quantitatem modicam. Et ideo contento loco modico provenerit tota hominum multitudo, ut non fuerint tot atomi in illo semine quot homines inde processerint." Fishacre, *In 2 Sent.*, 30.15, ed. Long, 2:193.

35. For example, Fishacre's claim that there are an infinite number of points in an atom: "Si sufficeret locus punctalis spiritui, omnes creati spiritus angelici et in infinitum plures possent esse in una atomo, quia sunt in ea puncta infinita, immo et partes corporales infinitae." Fishacre, *In 2 Sent.*, 2.5, ed. Long: 1:45. See also, "Et dico crementum vel augmentum maioris loci occupationem; igitur cum ex semine primi hominis habente quantitatem modicam. Et ideo contento loco modico provenerit tota hominum multitudo, ut non fuerint tot atomi in illo semine quot homines inde processerint." Fishacre, *In 2 Sent.*, 30.15, ed. Long, 2:193.

36. See Bernhard Pabst, *Atomtheorien des lateinischen Mittelalters* (Darmstadt: Wissenschaftliche Buchgesellschaft, 1994), 255–68.

37. Callus's statement, "It would certainly be an exaggeration to claim Fishacre

Richard Rufus of Cornwall

We do not yet know how widely Fishacre's Commentary was read, but we are sure of at least of one very attentive reader, the Franciscan Richard Rufus of Cornwall (fl. 1238–59).[38] One scholar has gone so far in fact as to describe Rufus's own *Sentences* commentary as nothing more than a revised and corrected version of Fishacre's.[39] While this is surely an exaggeration, there is no doubt that Fishacre's work was open on Rufus's desk and that his reading of Grosseteste was mediated through it.

Rufus's methodology is to state Fishacre's position, pose objections to it, then offer his own solutions. Reynolds is of the view that "Rufus's treatment is lucid only as long as he is rehearsing Fishacre's views; his own objections and solutions are often obscure and sometimes incomprehensible."[40] In his own commentary on Lombard's distinction 18, Rufus begins by restating—almost *verbatim*—Fishacre's treatment of the problem of the expansion of Adam's rib into the dimensions of Eve's body as well as the solution Fishacre proposes.[41]

But, Rufus claims, there are two problems with Fishacre's

---

as an ardent Aristotelian," seems in retrospect almost coy. Daniel Callus, *Introduction of Aristotelian Learning to Oxford, Proceedings of the British Academy 29* (repr., London: H. Milford, 1944), 31–32.

38. See, for example, Richard Raedts, *Richard Rufus of Cornwall and the Tradition of Oxford Theology* (Oxford: Clarendon Press, 1987), 27; R. James Long, "The First Oxford Debate on the Eternity of the World," *RTPM* 65/1 (1998): 54–98; R. James Long and Timothy Noone, "Fishacre and Rufus on the Metaphysics of Light: Two Unedited Texts," in *Roma, magistra mundi. Itineraria culturae medievalis. Mélanges offerts au Père L.E. Boyle à l'occasion de son 75e anniversaire*, ed. Jacqueline Hamesse, Textes et Études du moyen âge (Louvain-la-Neuve: Féderation Internationale des Instituts d'Etudes Médiévales, 1998), 517–48.

39. See Jeremy I. Catto, "Theology and Theologians 1220–1320," in *The History of the University of Oxford: Vol. 1, The Early Oxford Schools*, ed. Jeremy I. Catto (Oxford: Oxford University Press, 1984), 471–518, at 489.

40. Reynolds, *Food and the Body*, 191.

41. Rufus, *In secundum librum Sententiarum*, 18; Oxford, Balliol College, MS 62, fols. 148rb–va (hereafter "Rufus, *Sent.*").

analysis of rarefaction and condensation. First, the limitations Fishacre proposes for the expansibility of the various elements do not take into account the power of the Divine Word, for which the earth and the other elements in Adam's rib suffice for the transformation.[42] Yes, of course, one is tempted to say, but this is hardly philosophically satisfying. Thus, Rufus provides a second refutation that he regards as fatal: Fishacre's elemental equivalencies—a fistful of earth yielding ten of water, one of the latter yielding ten of air, and so forth—should be reversible. Yet it seems that a single measure of water cannot be reconverted to earth; it requires, insists Rufus, at least ten measures.[43]

Rufus's own solution is found in a distinction: namely, the division *secundum speciem* and *secundum materiam*. The latter is infinitely divisible while the former has limits: that is, the element earth can be expanded or thinned out only so far before it is transformed into another species; the same holds for contraction. Perhaps, he speculates, it is according to a division *secundum materiam* that God formed the first woman from the rib of Adam? Or perhaps it was according to an infinite number of other ways which had not yet occurred to him?[44]

Returning to the question in distinction 30, where the issue is the matter of Adam's semen, Rufus repeats Fishacre's arguments virtually word for word, pausing occasionally to quibble or to insist on God's absolute power to accomplish whatever is not in the power of nature.[45] Notwithstanding the fact that Rufus makes an issue of rejecting Fishacre's attempted reconciliation of Peter Lombard (semen is entirely from the father) and Aristotle (semen is entirely the superfluity of food), he does in the end accept Fishacre's mixed solution (*sanius videtur ponere*), that is, that the flesh *secundum speciem* is from the father, the flesh *secundum materiam* is from nutriment. There remains the possibility of course—

42. Rufus, *Sent.* 18, fol. 148va.

43. Ibid.

44. Ibid.

45. Rufus, *Sent.* 30, fols. 175a–va.

and this is at issue in the expansion of Adam's rib and the multiplication of the loaves—that God can act instantaneously, though not contrary to nature:

Here some [namely, Fishacre] respond, agreeing with the Master, and respond in this way to the authorities Augustine and Aristotle: when the father emits semen that is suitable with respect to offspring, there is found something of the essence of the parent's body and something of food, and so in this case something of the body of Adam and something of food, just as in an egg it is apparent that there is a twofold substance that is distinct according to the senses, namely white and yellow, and the chick is produced from the white, but the yellow is a kind of nutriment for it. Similarly, in human semen there is a twofold substance, although not perceivably distinct, namely something of the body of the father and something of food. And perhaps it is the case that the latter is the greater part with respect to quantity, just as in an egg the yellow is greater than the white. And thus perhaps Augustine and Aristotle are saying that the semen that is emitted is the substance of food rather than the substance of the father, for the whole is sometimes denominated from the greater part. Thus there is no opposition between the Master and these authorities, for part of the seed is from the body of the father—and this is what the Master intends, and the greater part of it is from food ... However, if it were as the Master claims, God alone would bring to pass that multiplication, and without doubt it would take place instantaneously, as that which is in the rib of Adam and that which is in the breads of the Gospel [Mt. 14:16–21]. And God, as the Master says, would be able to multiply that semen by itself alone without any additive. But that would not be a natural operation; indeed divine alone. But it would not be contrary to nature.[46]

46. "Respondent hic aliqui [viz. Fishacre] consentientes Magistro, et respondent auctoritatibus Augustino et Aristoteli sic: cum parens descindit semen aptum respectu prolis, ibi est aliquid de veritate corporis parentis et aliquid de alimento, et ita aliquid de corpore Adae et aliquid de alimento, sicut in ovo patet quod est ibi duplex substantia sensibiliter distincta, scilicet album et citrinum, et pullus fit de albo; citrinum vero est ei quasi pro nutrimento. Similiter in semine humano est duplex substantia, licet non sensibiliter sint distinctae, scilicet aliquid de corpore paterno et aliquid de

It is from this point, as Reynolds notes, that Rufus goes his own way.[47] He shows no interest in explanations predicated on the self-diffusiveness of light, and although he adopts the other part of Fishacre's explanation, pertaining to the quantitative indeterminacy of matter, he develops it differently (I might add parenthetically that Rufus's response to Fishacre's rather odd conception of matter is itself by no means authentically Aristotelian).[48]

Robert Kilwardby

Although the Dominican Robert Kilwardby (ca. 1215–79) probably began his theological formation too late to incept under Fishacre, one finds in his *Quaestiones* on the *Sentences* an afterburn of the heated exchange between his older confrere and Rufus.[49] In question 88 of the second book of his commentary he finds nothing remarkable in the multiplication of the loaves. From a single seed innumerable loaves can be produced both by nature and by art: one presumes here that it is a seed that is planted, producing other seeds, which are then harvested, ground by the miller and baked into bread by the baker. But whatever nature and art can accomplish successively (*successive*) God can accomplish instantaneously. And this is the extent of the miracle.[50]

alimento. Et forte maior pars secundum quantitatem est de alimento, sicut in ovo maius est citrinum albo. Et ideo forte Augustinus et Aristoteles dicunt semen descisum esse substantiam alimenti potius quam substantiam parentis. Totum enim aliquando a maiori parte denominatur. Et sic non est contrarietas inter Magistrum et illos. Pars enim seminis est de corpore paterno—et hoc intendit Magister. Et maior eius pars est ex alimento.... Si autem esset sicut dicit Magister, solus Deus operaretur illam multiplicationem, et sine dubio fieret in instanti, sicut illa quae in costa Adae, et illa quae in panibus evangelii [Mt 14:16–21]. Et posset Deus, sicut dicit Magister, multiplicare illud semen per se solum sine aliquo adiecto. Sed non esset operatio naturalis, immo divina tantum. Nec tamen contra naturam." Rufus, *Sent.* 30, fols. 175va-vb.

47. Reynolds, *Food and the Body*, 194.

48. Rufus, *Sent.* 30, fols. 175va–vb.

49. Robert Kilwardby, *De ortu scientiarum*, ed. Albert G. Judy, ABMA IV (London: The British Academy, 1976), xv–xvi.

50. Robert Kilwardby, *Quaestiones in librum secundum Sententiarum*, ed. Gerhard

But is there a seminal reason in the rib of Adam from which Eve was made? In the proper sense, no; but by extension (what Kilwardby calls "*communiter*")—that is, from an eternal causal reason—yes.[51] In terms of the material cause of Eve, Kilwardby does not have the same worries as Fishacre. Adam's rib was a mixed body and the mixture of elements was congruent with that of the human body. It just needed the transforming command of God.[52] There is no talk here of the difficulties of the extension of matter, and so forth; it is almost as if Kilwardby were totally detached from the tradition that preceded him. Indeed, it must be said that as soon as masters of theology were able to absorb and adopt the principles of Aristotle's natural philosophy and in particular his notion of matter as pure potentiality, the problem of Eve's formation for the most part dissipated. Expansion could take place only by adding new material, which came either *ab extra* or through creation. Since the latter was unlikely, it was clear that nutrition played a vital part in the process.[53] Up to this point, however, the influence of Grosseteste on the Oxford thinkers who came under his sway was wide and deep. Even in the case here presented, a problem not dealt with by Grosseteste himself, it was his inspiration and methodology that enabled members of his school to examine and debate questions that transcended his own interests.

Leibold, Band 16 (Munich: Verlag der Bayerishen Akademie der Wissenschaften, 1992), 245.

51. Kilwardby, *In 2 Sent.*, 85, ed. Leibold, 240.

52. Kilwardby, *In 2 Sent.*, 87, ed. Leibold, 243.

53. See, for example, the lucid treatment of the question in Thomas Aquinas, *Summa theologiae* 1.92.3.

CHAPTER 9

Richard Fishacre and the Problem of the Soul

The translation of the natural philosophy of Aristotle into Latin in the late twelfth and early thirteenth centuries presented the philosophers of that age with a radical alternative to the traditional Platonic-Augustinian system. With respect to Christian doctrine, moreover, few options were as crucial as the respective positions regarding the human soul. For Augustine (as for Plato) the soul was a substance, simple, complete, incorruptible, and related to the body as agent to instrument. It was a view that had behind it the weight of centuries of Christian speculation as well as spirituality.

In Aristotelian psychology, on the other hand, the soul was a part of nature and as such an object of scientific investigation. Such investigation, moreover, revealed that the rational soul bore the same relation to the body as the form of any other material composite bore to its matter. The human soul, in other words, existed only for and in the body. Thus on the one hand the unicity of man was affirmed, and on the other his personal immortality was denied.

One of the earliest Christian thinkers to respond to the Aristotelian challenge was the Oxford Dominican, Richard Fishacre, who formulated his teaching on the soul in his *Sentences* Commentary.[1] The soul, says Fishacre, is joined to a body *secundum esse*, that is, according to its existence or activity, but separate according to its essence.[2] In other words, the soul considered in itself (essentially) is a substance; yet existentially, in its incorporated state, it fulfills the function of life-giving form.

Fishacre, however, was neither unique nor original in suggesting this compromise. Among his contemporaries, the same position was espoused by William of Auvergne, John of La Rochelle, Albert the Great, and Roger Bacon—all of whom derived their inspiration ultimately from the Persian philosopher Avicenna. It was to the treatises of the latter that the early scholastics turned for help in understanding the obscure Stagirite and it was also Avicenna, because of his Neoplatonism, who made Aristotle more palatable to Christian philosophers steeped in the same philosophical tradition. For many of Fishacre's contemporaries Avicenna was, in the words of Roger Bacon, the leader and prince of philosophers after Aristotle.[3]

In his *Liber sextus de naturalibus* Avicenna affirms with Aristotle that the soul is the form of the body; more precisely, he defines the soul as the "perfectio corporis naturalis instrumentalis habentis opera vitae."[4] But this, maintains Avicenna, defines

1. On the dating of Fishacre's *Sentences* Commentary see R. James Long and Maura O'Carroll, SND, *The Life and Works of Richard Fishacre, OP. Prolegomena to the Edition of his Commentary on the "Sentences"* (Munich: Verlag der Bayerischen Akademie der Wissenschaften, 1999), 39–42.

2. Fishacre, *In 2 Sent.* 2.2, ed. Long, 1: 28

3. Roger Bacon, *Opus maius*, ed. John H. Bridges (Oxford, 1900; Frankfurt: Minerva, 1964), 3:14.

4. Avicenna Latinus, *Liber de anima seu sextus de Naturalibus*, ed. Simone Van Riet (Louvain: Peeters, 1972), 1:29.

the soul's function, not its nature. Similarly, when we call a man a "worker" we describe only what he does, not what he is in himself, namely a man.[5]

In order to demonstrate that the soul is by its very nature independent of the body Avicenna introduces the example of the "suspended man." He imagines the case of a man created in an adult condition, who from the very moment of his creation is deprived of any sense experience and who has therefore no notion even of his own body; such a man, insists Avicenna, would still be able to affirm that he exists. Since that which is affirmed is other than that which is not affirmed—a fundamental of Avicennian logic—the essence of the soul is wholly other than that of the body.[6] In other words, where there are two completely distinct notions, there are two really distinct entities.

This Avicennian dualism runs throughout Richard Fishacre's Commentary. In book 2, distinction 19, for example, he speaks of the soul being properly the name of that life which we have in common with the animals. Hence we are called *animales*, since we stand in need of the operations of this life principle, namely nutrition, growth, and generation. We have, however, another life, a life which is spiritual and which we possess in common with the angels; the principle of this life is the rational soul, which is free of the demands of the body.[7]

In another passage, this duality is described in terms of two forms. The soul, says Fishacre, has one form which is common to itself and to the angels by which it is a rational spirit, and it has another form by which it is devoted to the body and by which it is properly a soul.[8] This second form is later in the same distinction termed the *anima brutalis sive sensibilis.*[9] Fishacre is here

5. Ibid., 26–27.
6. Ibid., 36–37.
7. Fishacre, *In 2 Sent.* 19, ed. Long, 1:388.
8. Ibid., 24.5.1, ed. Long, 2:103.
9. Ibid., 24.5.2, 2:107.

seeking metaphysical justification for the duality of the soul in a favorite thesis of the Augustinian school, the plurality of forms.

This thesis, traceable to the eleventh-century Spanish Jew Ibn Gabirol, states that for every essential perfection in the individual there is a corresponding form. The human soul, then, while remaining substantially one, would contain a vegetative, a sensible, and a rational form in a sort of hierarchical arrangement. The body, of course, has its own form, the *forma corporeitatis*, which gives to it the perfection of bodiness.[10]

Historians of medieval thought have found Fishacre either ambivalent on the question of plurality or else favorable to the unity thesis.[11] Indeed, after describing the three contemporary opinions and the objections to each, he himself hesitates to embrace any of the three—*definire non audeo*, he says.[12]

In practice, however, the texts reveal Fishacre to be a pluralist—or at least a dualist.[13] For example, one of his proofs that all angels are members of the same species runs as follows. The noblest acts are understanding and love; therefore, the form from

10. Avicenna affirms a *forma corporeitatis*, although he firmly maintains the unicity of the human soul; see Daniel Callus, "The Origins of the Problem of the Unity of Form," in *The Dignity of Science*, ed. James A. Weisheipl (Washington, D.C.: Thomist Press, 1961), 127–28.

11. Martin and Lottin conclude that Fishacre was no advocate of the pluralist position in the sense in which Kilwardby and Peckham later were: R. M. Martin, "La question de l'unité de la forme substantielle dans le premier collège dominicain à Oxford (1221–1248)," *RNSP* 22 (1920): 112; Odon Lottin, *Psychologie et morale aux XIIe et XIIIe siècles* (Louvain: Abbaye du Mont-César, 1948), 1:477–78. Théry, Meersseman, and Callus number Fishacre among the supporters of the unity thesis: Gabriel Théry, "L'augustinisme médiéval et le problème de la forme substantielle," *Acta hebdomadae augustinianae-thomisticae* (Rome: Marietti, 1931), 163, 198; Gilles Meersseman, "Die Einheit der menschlichen Seele nach Albertus Magnus," *Divus Thomas* 10 (1932): 82; Daniel Callus, *The Condemnation of St. Thomas at Oxford* (Oxford: Aquin Press, 1955), 22. See also Dorothea E. Sharp, "The Philosophy of Fishacre," *NS* 7 (1933): 285–87.

12. Fishacre, *In 2 Sent.* 22.4, ed. Long, 2:101.

13. Franz Pelster says that Fishacre does not explicitly include the vegetative principle in the sensible-rational soul because "er das vegetative Geschehen nicht als eigentliches Leben ansieht"; "Das Leben und die Schriften des Oxforder Dominikanerlehrers Richard Fishacre († 1248)," *ZKT* 54 (1930): 550.

which they proceed is the noblest form, that is, the *forma rationalis or intellectualis*. But if angels were to differ specifically, they would have to differ by means of a form superadded to the rational form. But this form would necessarily be less noble, giving rise to the absurd situation of a less noble form perfecting one more noble. Then Fishacre adds: "Cuius contrarium videtur in aliis: quia vegetabili superadditur sensibilis, et huic rationalis—et non e contrario.[14]

Elsewhere he speaks of the form by which the soul is *intellectualis,* being nobler than that by which it is devoted to the body. Nature, however, always subordinates the less noble form to the more noble, and conversely. Therefore, the form by which the soul understands is "superordinated" to that by which it is devoted to the body.[15] This is surely to posit the coexistence of at least two forms in the soul, namely the rational and the sensible.

Why then is Fishacre so hesitant in proclaiming himself a pluralist? A possible answer lies in an objection he finds against the pluralist position; Fishacre quotes the *De ecclesiasticis dogmatibus*, whose author he presumes to be St. Augustine, in saying that there are not two souls in man, one by which the body is animated and another by which man is rational, but rather one soul which performs both functions.[16] It might be argued that this does not constitute a valid objection against pluralism, since the pluralists did not support two souls but rather several forms constituting the one substance. In the present context, however, the point is academic. Fishacre in fact read it as an objection and was reluctant to contradict the putative authority of the great bishop of Hippo.

Fishacre was also a firm advocate of the other half of the so-called *binarium famosissimum*, namely universal hylomorphism. This thesis extended matter-form composition to spiritual sub-

14. Fishacre, *In 2 Sent.* 3.2, ed. Long, 1:63.
15. Ibid., 24.5, 2:105.
16. Ibid., 24.4, 2:101.

stances, that is, to angels and human souls. This too was stock-in-trade doctrine for thirteenth century Augustinians and originated with the same Ibn Gabirol.

Commenting on the Lombard's text *Manifestum est non simplicem sed multiplicem esse naturam animae* (book 1, distinction 8), Fishacre develops no fewer than ten arguments to support the hylomorphic composition of the soul, including several of dubious philosophical merit. He insists, however, that among creatures the human soul has the least amount of matter (*minimum habet de materia*). The nobler the creature, the less it has of matter. But the human soul is the noblest form; therefore, it has the least amount of matter. If the soul were outside the body, in fact, it would occupy only a point, a *punctum de loco*.[17] In the body, however, the soul occupies as much space as the body itself, because it is wholly in the entire body.[18]

The soul occupies the space of the body not by rarefaction or substantial change, as is the case for example with water, which is changed into a gas when it occupies a greater space. The soul's mode of occupying space is rather like that of light, which occupies less space with the windows closed than with the windows open. Thus it follows that in the case of light and the human soul a little matter can occupy as much space as more matter can, the form remaining the same.[19]

Furthermore, the soul in itself is immutable. As a consequence of its conjunction with a body, however, the soul changes according to the rhythm of change in the body it occupies. Again, light serves as a model: light is immobile when it touches either

17. The angels are "almost wholly form" and occupy a "*locus punctalis*"; Fishacre, *In 2 Sent.* 2.4, ed. Long (Munich: Verlag der Bayerischen Akademie der Wissenschaften, 2008) 1:45–46. One is reminded of the question that has been used so often to parody the philosophy of the Middle Ages—how many angels can dance on the head of a pin; see my paper "Angels and Pinheads," in *FS: Essays in Honor of Dr. Girard Etzkorn*, ed. Gordon A. Wilson and Timothy B. Noone, 56 (1998), 237–52.

18. Fishacre, *In 2 Sent.* 18.4, ed. Long, 1:369.

19. Ibid., ed. Long, 1:369–70.

nothing or some immobile object; when, however, it is contiguous to water or some other *mobile*, the light itself becomes mobile—that is, it moves in motions similar to those according to which the water has been moved. So also it seems that the soul, when it is not "incorporated" (to use Fishacre's word), remains immutable according to its nature; it will also be immutable when joined to an immutable body—that is, a glorified body.[20]

The degree of the soul's mutability, moreover, depends on that of the particular body it occupies. Fishacre cites Virgil's verse that woman is ever "*varium et mutabile*," and gives as a reason that woman's flesh is more fragile. The implication is that the feminine soul is more mutable than the male soul owing to the fact that her body is more subject to change than is the male's.[21]

The chronic problem of the Platonic-Augustinian psychology, according to which the soul is a complete substance, separate from the body, has been to account for soul-body interaction. Fishacre attempts to bridge this gap by positing a medium, which following Robert Grosseteste he calls "light."[22] Light is the noblest of bodies because it is nearest to the spiritual creature, which is nobler than any corporeal creature. Therefore, light is suited both by its nature and its situation to be the medium between soul and body. Light is as it were the *vinculum* or bond between soul and body. It is through light that the soul performs its operations in the body.[23]

This bifurcation in man between a soul, which is a substance in itself, and the body it animates Fishacre attempts to minimize by stressing the natural appetite the former has for the latter. Such in fact is the soul's *affectio ad corpus* that if the soul lacked

20. Ibid., 21.12, ed. Long, 2:14.

21. Ibid.

22. Alistair C. Crombie, *Robert Grosseteste and the Origins of Experimental Science* (Oxford: Clarendon Press, 1953), 163n4. See also Dorothea E. Sharp, *Franciscan Philosophy at Oxford* (London: Oxford University Press, 1930), 28.

23. Fishacre, *In 2 Sent.* 13.1, ed. Long, 1:253.

a body eternally, it would be eternally miserable. Indeed, even if the soul of Adam had foreknowledge of the fall and its reparation, he would still more willingly have chosen to enter a body than to be eternally disembodied. Should not one rather choose, asks Fishacre, that misfortune which can be repaired than that which cannot?[24] Furthermore, this *affectio* of the soul is not for any body whatsoever, but for one suitable to itself, even as to shape.[25]

It is this affection for a body that constitutes the difference between angels and human souls. No angel—good or bad—is thus favorably disposed toward a body.[26] But is this difference accidental or essential—that is to say, does this *affectio ad corpus* constitute the human soul as a species distinct from the angel? Fishacre admits he does not know but thinks that it does not.[27]

In the same distinction, moreover, he quotes with approval Augustine's statement that the rational soul and the angel are equal as to their natures, though unequal as to their office. But to be equal in nature is to have the same ultimate constitutive difference—that is, to belong to the same species. Angels, then, and human souls are specifically the same.[28]

Man himself, finally, is neither primarily body nor primarily soul, although at times the composite is referred to by one name, sometimes by the other. For example, scripture often speaks of man as "flesh"; likewise he is sometimes spoken of as "soul"—and with more reason, for the soul is the nobler part. This mode of naming, however, is obviously a figure of speech, the use of the part for the whole. There are some thinkers, nevertheless, who hold that man is truly a soul and that the flesh is but a garment. Fishacre names Avicenna and Hugh of St. Victor as representatives of this group. This opinion Friar Richard rejects as patently false.[29]

24. Ibid., 17.2, ed. Long, 1:346.

25. Ibid., 21.12, ed. Long, 2:14.

26. Ibid.

27. Ibid., 3.2, ed. Long, 1:64.

28. Ibid., 1:63.

29. Ibid., 31.2, ed. Long, 2:201.

In the final analysis, Fishacre's conception of the soul as both substance and form of the body is dualistic and finds its logical corollary in his teaching on the plurality of forms. Such a vision of the soul, which drew its philosophical justification from Ibn Gabirol, in general prevailed until the bold and innovative rethinking of the problem by Friar Thomas Aquinas. Although philosophically awkward, Fishacre's thesis was an attempt to satisfy both the biological exigencies of the Aristotelian soul and the spiritual needs of the Platonic-Augustinian soul.

CHAPTER 10

Interiority and Self-Knowledge according to Richard Fishacre

Any account of Fishacre's view of interiority and self-knowledge must begin with an examination of his view of the soul and its powers. Since, moreover, he never wrote a treatise that was professedly a *De anima* or even a *quaestio* that formally addressed the subject, one is forced to pick one's way through his major work, his *Sentences* Commentary, much of it in the context of a literal gloss on the Lombard's text.

As early as the third distinction of the first book, Fishacre addresses the structure of the human soul and its powers. Between the soul itself and its actions stand the faculties or *virtutes*, essentially and permanently ordered to some definite operation. Commenting on the Lombard's lengthy citation of Augustine's *De Trinitate*, Fishacre likewise finds the trinitarian three powers in the soul: the memory, the intelligence, and the will. Since the first two are collapsible into a single apprehensive power, Fishacre is able to save the Grossetestean dyad of *aspectus* and *affectus*, "seeing" and "feeling."[1] The distinction between the latter, Fishacre claims, is conceptual only, a claim he supports with no fewer than eight arguments.[2]

1. "ECCE ERGO MENS. Anima primo dividitur in virtutem apprehensivam et motivam sive rationem et voluntatem sive aspectum et affectum. Et apprehensiva subdividitur in apprehensivam intellectivam et apprehensivam retentivam, sive intellectivam habitualem, quod est memoria, vel actualem, quod voco 'intelligentiam.' Primo videamus quomodo se habeant primae divisionis dividentiam, deinde quomodo subdivisionis. Et ponitur quod prima dividentia, scilicet apprehensiva et motiva, sunt essentialiter differentia," *In 1 Sent.* 3.8, in R. James Long, "The Problem of the Soul in Richard Fishacre's *Commentary on the Sentences*" (Ph.D. diss., University of Toronto, 1968), *26–27.

Later, at chapter 12, Fishacre lists some definitions: "Meminisse est rei similitudinem tenere. Nosse est in illa similitudine rem videre. Cogitare est eandem notam ab aliis notis discernere," ibid., *38.

Still later, at 2.24, he says that this division is quite sufficient: "quippe sufficienter dividitur anima in aspectum et affectum; et affectus est voluntas, et aspectus ratio," Fishacre, *In 2 Sent.* 24.3, ed. Long, 2:72.

2. "Potentiae cognoscuntur per actus, et actus per operationes, et operationes per obiecta. Ergo si obiecta sunt idem in essentia, et potentiae; sed horum obiecta sunt verum et bonum, quae non differunt nisi sicut aliquid in se absolutum et idipsum ad aliud comparatum. Ergo similiter potentiae. Item, cognitio praecedit amorem in eodem ipso. Non enim quia ego cognosco, ideo tu amas; ergo idem sunt. Non enim potest aliqua potentia amare, nisi ipsa eadem cognoscat. Item, cum potentiae ordinantur ad invicem diversae essentialiter, actio ultimae non necessario est cum actione prioris. Verbi gratia: cum prius sit vegetativa, deinde sensitiva, tertio intellectiva potentia, non exigitur quod, quandocumque sentit sensitiva, vegetet vegetativa, neque quando intelligit, sentiat; sed quandocumque amat, intelligit. Ergo non sunt potentiae diversae. Item, quicquid est in anima aut est materia aut forma aut accidens. Sed constat quod haec nec sunt materia nec accidentia—ut probat Augustinus, *De Trin.* lib. 9, cap. 4—quia amor extendit se extra subiectum et cognitio. Amo enim aliquid extra me et novi. Accidens autem non extenditur extra subiectum. Augustinus ibidem: 'Non amor et cognitio tanquam in subiecto insunt menti; sed substantialiter etiam ista sunt'. Quomodo ergo nisi sicut forma insunt animae essentialiter? Ergo forma. Aut eadem (et haec volui) aut diversa. Si sic: tunc cum posterior sit voluntas, erit ipsa secundum ordinem naturae nobilior quam ratio, et ultima creaturae rationalis perfectio. Et sic magis ab illa deberet dici et denominari quam rationalis a ratione. Item, si essent potentiae diversae, sicut non audio saporem nec gusto sonum, sic nec cognoscerem bonum nec amarem verum in quantum verum. Quod falsum est. Sed si unica forma substantialis animae est, et unica virtus vel potentia est affectus et aspectus, quia 'idem non est natum nisi facere idem', unica ergo actio cognoscere et amare. Quod verum est, ut mihi videtur—licet aliter videatur multis. Non enim est aliud amare nisi cognoscere cum cuiusdam comparationis additione: sicut unica est actio solis lucere et illuminare, sed illuminare superaddit comparationem ipsi essentiae actionis quae est lucere. Similiter calefacere et liquefacere non sunt actiones ignis diversae, licet prius

But what is the distinction between the two powers of the "aspective" part of the soul, namely the memory and the intelligence? Some claim, says Fishacre, that they differ as act (the intelligence) and disposition (memory). That claim represents the view that the intelligence is simply the fulfillment or actualization of what is contained in the quasi-permanent disposition which is the memory.[3] But there are persuasive arguments to the contrary. Our memory, for example, seems clearly posterior to the knowledge which is intelligence. The turning back of the soul upon itself in the act of remembering, which is the special mark of the intellectual creature, presupposes that the species of things representing realities outside the understanding are already present in the soul.[4] Otherwise, *what* is it that we are recalling?

---

sit calefacere quam liquefacere, et licet multotiens calefaciat quando non liquefacit. Actio enim prius natura est in se quam cum respectu vel circumstantia. Similiter non est alia actio amare et cognoscere, ut videtur. Nec est aliquid amplius de actione in eo quod est amare quam in eo quod est cognoscere. Sed cognoscere dicitur apprehendere rem in se absolutam, amare vero comprehendere eam ad aliud comparatam, ut scilicet communicantem se alii, quod non est nisi comprehendere eam bonam," *In 1 Sent.* 3, in Long, "Problem of Soul," *27–*29. See Pius Künzle, *Das Verhältnis der Seele zu ihren Potenzen: problemgeschichtliche Untersuchungen von Augustinus bis und mit Thomas von Aquin* (Freiburg, Switzerland: Universitätsverlag, 1956), 158–59.

3. Who it is that holds this view Fishacre does not say.

4. "Sed quae est diversitas subdividentium? Et dicitur quod non differunt nisi sicut actus et habitus. Sed contra. Cum sit in angelis intelligentia et memoria, patet quod eorum memoria semper est in actu, non in habitu tantum. Item, si differunt sicut actus et habitus, cum similiter possit esse amor habitualis et actualis, iam non esset tantum trinitas sed quaternitas in anima. Item, memoria habitualis gignitur potius ab intelligentia, et est posterior quam e contrario. Sed memoria, ut hic dicit, gignit intelligentiam, non e contrario, et est prior. Alioquin memoria non esset vestigium Patris. Ergo memoria non dicit habitum. Ideo dico quod cum sola intellectualis creatura sit redibilis super se ipsam, potest ipsa mens se ipsam continentem in se plures species intelligibiles inspicere—quod non est aliud nisi ipsam gignere suam speciem, alias species continentem in se. Ipsa ergo inspecta, sic habens rationem gignentis, dicatur 'memoria.' Ipsa inspiciens vel speciem suam suscipiens dicatur 'intelligentia.' Sed duo videntur esse contra hoc. Unum: quod haec memoria adhuc videtur esse ab intelligentia. Prius enim est secundum speciem fieri in mente a re extra, quod est intelligere, quam animam convertere se supra se iam habentem illam speciem rei. Unde *Super Eccli.* 17 ('Secundum imaginem suam fecit illam') *Glossa*: 'Sicut ex Patre <generatur> Filius, et ex utroque Spiritus Sanctus, ita ex intellectu voluntas et ex utroque memoria,'" ibid., in Long, "Problem of Soul," *29–*30.

The answer lies in a distinction: there are two kinds of memory, a memory of the possible intellect, the other of the active intellect. The former is memory in the ordinary sense. The intelligible species is first received in the understanding or intelligence, is then loved, then finally recovered and held on to by the memory.[5]

The other power that is also termed "memory" is the *habitus* of all intelligible forms in the mind—at least in the angelic mind, Fishacre pointedly adds—from its creation; and this is the memory of the agent intellect in us. And it is this kind of memory, says Fishacre, which Augustine is talking about in the *De Trinitate*, where he seems to be referring to self-knowledge.[6]

But this is precisely Fishacre's problem here: how reconcile Augustine's view of the immediate presence of the I to itself with his own view to the contrary? The line preceding the first text of Augustine's that Fishacre quotes is after all unequivocal: "The mind knows nothing so well as what is present to it, and nothing is more present to the mind than itself."[7] This is of course one of

5. "Solutio. Duplex est in nobis memoria: una quae fit ex speciebus primo receptis in intelligentia, et deinde in memoria repositis; et haec est memoria intellectus possibilis. Et haec sequitur intelligentiam et voluntatem, quia quod primo intelligo et deinde amo, memoriter teneo," ibid., *30. See: "Dictum est supra quod duplex est memoria: una praecedens intelligentiam, et de hac hic; haec enim omnium universaliter; alia sequens, et haec praeteritorum. ALIOQUIN NON SE CAPERET, quia si esset tantum praeteritorum et non praesentium, cum ipsa sit praesens sibi, non se caperet," ibid., *37.

6. "Alia est habitus omnium formarum intelligibilium in mente, saltem angelica, ex condicione sua; et haec est memoria intellectus agentis in nobis. Et de hac dicit Augustinus, *De Trin.* lib. 14, cap. 5: 'Ipsa mens infantis nosse se credenda est, sed intenta nimis in eas res quas per corporis sensus tanto maiore quanto noviore coepit delectatione sentire, non ignorare se potest, sed potest non cogitare?' Et eiusdem 10 lib., cap. 8: 'Cognoscat semetipsam anima, nec quasi absentem quaerat, sed intentionem voluntatis qua per alia vagatur, statuat in se ipsam, et se cogitet. Ita videbit quod numquam se non amaverit, numquam nescierit; sed aliud secum amando cum eo se confudit et concrevit quodam modo,'" ibid., *30. See: "INTELLIGERE ME SCIO, habitualiter, QUICQUID AUTEM SCIO MEMINI. Contra. Si nunc primo intelligo quiddam, nondum est in memoria, quia memoria est praeteritorum. Solutio. Memoria hic dicitur, ut supra dictum est, memoria intellectus agentis, non possibilis. Et haec memoria est respectu omnis temporis," ibid., *34.

7. Augustine, *De Trinitate* 14.2; trans. Edmund Hill, OP (Brooklyn, N.Y.: New City Press, 1991), 375.

the *loci classici* expressing Augustine's conviction that the soul is transparent to itself. What Fishacre seizes upon, however, is the line that follows:

> So what then is to be said about the mind of an infant which is still so small and sunk in such vast ignorance of things that the mind of a man which knows anything shudders at the darkness of that infant mind? Must we perhaps believe that it too knows itself, but that it is wholly preoccupied with the things it is beginning to perceive through the senses of the body with a delight that is all the greater for being new; and so it is not a question of its being able to be ignorant of itself, but of its not being able to think about itself?[8]

Augustine thus shows Fishacre a way to answer Augustine: the soul is indeed transparent to itself—theoretically. The problem is that *in via* we are forced to endure the distraction of the senses. Even without the crippling effects of the Fall, the very necessity of administering a body constitutes an impediment to the soul's knowing everything, a hope it continues to cling to with respect to the next life.[9]

The second text Fishacre cites, this from book 10 of *De Trinitate*, makes precisely this point:

> Let the mind then recognize itself and not go looking for itself as if it were absent, but rather turn on to itself the interest of its will, which had it straying about through other things, and think about itself. In this way it will see that there never was a time when it did not love itself, when it did not know itself. What it did was to mix itself up with something else that it loved together with itself and to coalesce with it in some way or other; and as a result, by comprising divergent things as a unity in itself, it came to think that these things which really are divergent were one with itself.[10]

8. Ibid.

9. Fishacre, *In 2 Sent.* 23.3, ed. Long, 2:55–56. Cf.: "Unde si sine corpore esset, actu eas [i.e., species] perciperet, nisi culpa eam obscuraret," ibid., Long, "Problem of Soul," *31.

10. Augustine, *De Trin.* 10.3, trans. Hill, 295.

Perfect knowledge of the self and of all other things was enjoyed by the angels immediately upon their creation, repeats Fishacre, and likewise ("*perhaps*," he adds) the soul of Adam before the Fall. How else would human beings even in their fallen state desire actually to know all things—the reference is of course to the first line of the *Metaphysics*—unless in some way it already possessed all things. Therefore, to return to the original problem, in one sense intelligence precedes memory and in another memory precedes intelligence.[11]

Fishacre's attempt to enlist the authority of Aristotle to the contrary notwithstanding, his noetic is ultimately alien to Aristotle's. In its present condition the intellect must begin with sense experience, and the senses apprehend only material things.[12] However, the sensible species thus obtained, which Fishacre calls the "word by which the exterior thing speaks to me," reaches only as far as the innermost sentient power or common sense—but no farther. Since it is axiomatic that the inferior cannot act on the superior, this *verbum* cannot beget itself in the mind. Rather, and here Fishacre invokes the authority of Augustine, "the soul in marvelous fashion and with equally marvelous speed produces in itself a similitude of that species which is in the common sense—that is, it makes itself like and conforms itself to that received species, just as light conforms itself to the water with which it comes into contact."[13] Since there is nothing common between the physical and the spiritual, the similitude of the sensible species within the soul is the product of the soul itself.[14]

11. "Sic angeli creati statim se et omnia noverunt, et anima Adae forte se et alia. Et haec memoria omnem amorem et intelligentiam praecedit. Quomodo enim naturaliter desideraret scire omnia actu, nisi aliquo modo haberet omnia? Ergo potest dici quod est intelligentia praecedens memoriam, et est alia sequens memoriam. Hic autem loquimur de illa quae sequitur. Vel melius: anima a creatione sua habet forte in se multas species rerum, ut videtur dicere Augustinus, *Retract.* lib. 1, cap. 9," ibid., *30–*31.

12. Fishacre, *In 2 Sent.* 18.6, ed. Long, 1:374.

13. Fishacre, *In 2 Sent.* 7.4, ed. Long, 1:135.

14. "Igitur, cum assimulatio sit dupliciter, scilicet per aliquid communiter com-

As a given piece of wood is able to be configured in an infinite variety of ways, and as intuiting even one of those in act belongs to the artisan, so likewise infinite likenesses of things are part of the natural endowment of the soul, stored in the memory of the active intellect, and yet like the artisan the soul comes to awareness of one likeness at a time while leaving all the others out of its consideration.[15]

But this is still to indulge in metaphorical talk. What precisely is the mechanism? The answer seems to be that the soul is stimulated or excited by the sensible species to turn its gaze inward toward the intelligible counterpart.[16] The division of labor is something like the following: the sensible species is reproduced within, as the soul, directed by the will, focuses on the array of intelligible species available to it and "remembers" the particular intelligibility aroused by the sense percept. For example, a friend returns from a visit to the ocean, which (let's suppose) I have never seen, and tells me about it.[17] The sound of the storyteller's words reach-

municationem ab utroque similium, et hoc dicitur per participationem, vel per imitationem, ubi nihil est commune similibus, patet quod anima similis sit rei extra vel speciei in intimo instrumento, non per hoc quod habet aliquid commune, sed per imitationem. Et ita haec similitudo fundatur non super aliquid in anima quod sit commune ei et speciei vel rei, sed super ipsam animam. Se ipsa enim similis est. Et ita patet quod propter verbum in mente non est ibi aliquid plus quam prius cum non inerat verbum, nisi similitudo qua se ipsa anima assimulatur rei vel eius speciei.... Sic ergo patet quod anima habens multas veritates numerosior est, non tamen compositior, ut probat ratio illa," *In 1 Sent.* 2.1, in Leo Sweeney and Charles J. Ermatinger, "Divine Infinity according to Richard Fishacre," *TMS* 35 (1958): 228–29.

15. "Quod autem dico animam miris modis assimulare se rei extra visae vel eius similitudini in intimo organo, sic intelligo: sicut atomus habet in se infinitas figuras, vel lignum aliquod, sed sentire eas est ab actu artificis; et tunc cum una sentitur, est ipsum lignum imago alicuius extra ad cuius similitudinem nitebatur artifex, nec est ipsum lignum compositius, cum iam una figura est ita in actu, quam prius; sic in anima naturaliter infinitae sunt similitudines rerum, et tamen unam earum intuemur actualiter sine alia, et tunc quasi actu efficitur similis illi rei extra quam intelligimus," ibid., 229.

16. "Cum ergo species sensibiles veniunt ad cor, excitatur anima per has ad intuendum species intelligibiles in se ipsa; et sic prius est ipsam inspicere se habentem speciem alicuius rei quam intelligere rem ipsam," *In 1 Sent.* 3.6, in Long, "Problem of Soul," *31.

17. The reader will recognize the example from Augustine's *Confessions*, 10.8.

es my innermost sense. I can conceptualize what is being related, that is I can form a concept of ocean though it is not a part of my sense experience, because I have in the storeroom of my memory images of bodies of water as well as the concept of boundlessness or enormity or perhaps comparatives like greater or vaster. I can thus construct or reconstruct out of my own resources a meaningful interpretation of the words concerning the ocean. I would fail to understand her words only were my memory to fail me or were my will inattentive.[18]

As Fishacre says, he recognizes that Aristotle would not have approved this limited role assigned to the sensible species—*aliter sit secundum Aristotelem.*[19] Fishacre here again manages to co-opt Aristotle's authority. The soul, he says, is able to read the sensible likenesses impressed on the instrument of the common sense, the heart, and in this way it can be said that "all of our knowledge begins from the senses," and thus also "to the extent that our senses fail us to that same extent will our knowledge be deficient."[20]

Notwithstanding, Fishacre remains deeply committed to an Augustinian doctrine of innate ideas, or to be more precise, the *habitus* of all the intelligible forms in the mind from the time of

18. Cf. Brian Stock, *Augustine the Reader* (Cambridge, Mass.: Harvard University Press, 1996), 274–75.

19. "Nec species genita a corpore subintrat mentem, sed sistit in intimo sentiente, licet aliter sit secundum Aristotelem," *In 1 Sent.* 3.19, in Long, "Problem of Soul," *43.

20. "Sensibilia gignendo ex se similitudines suas, et per sensus immittentes eas in nobis, eas imprimunt in instrumento sensus communis, id est in ultimo sentiente, scilicet in corde; ex qua impressione efficitur ut anima, eo quod sit illi parti corporis maxime unita, intelligat illud cuius similitudo in corde fuit impressa. Nostra enim cognitio incipit a sensu. Et ideo dicit Aristoteles quod deficiente sensu necesse est scientiam deficere, in *Post. anal.*... Novit anima nostra creaturas corporales per earum similitudines cordis intimo impressas, cui maxime anima unitur," Fishacre, *In 2 Sent.* 7.5, ed. Long, 1:134–35. Cf. *In 1 Sent.* 36: "Res vel forma gignit similitudinem suam in sensum vel potius in intellectum, quae tamen est ab idea sua in mente divina; et ita est similitudo aliqua ipsius formae et ideae et eiusdem formae et vestigii eius in mente creata intelligente eam. Sed aestimo quod similitudo formae et ideae quod est multo maior quam formae et similitudinis eius in mente. Quippe potentior supra modum est idea ad exprimendum sibi simile vestigium, scilicet formam, quam forma ad exprimendeum sibi vestigium, scilicet simile in mente," in Long, "Problem of Soul," *54.

its creation. If angels and humans before the Fall were created not knowing everything, he argues, in other words if we did not have habitual knowledge of everything, how could Aristotle assert that we had the desire to know everything?[21] Fishacre is here interpreting Aristotle's remark as a desire to know actively or explicitly what we already know implicitly.[22]

Furthermore, if again Aristotle is correct in claiming that to know something is to know its cause, we must consider the causes of that thing: the first cause (God) and the proximate cause (the substantial form of the thing). Hence it is that there is a double knowledge on the part of the creature: in God and in the existence of the form of the same creature in the created mind. But since understanding is not had by *extramission*, as in the senses, but by an "inward-receiving" (*intussusceptio*) or—better—an "inward-dwelling" (*intushabitatio*), the knowledge which is termed "wisdom" is not received from the existence of the form in the thing known.[23] This is only *scientia*. The nobler knowledge, *sapientia*, is developed by the created intellect by knowing everything in itself. Augustine calls this "evening knowledge."[24]

The figure that Fishacre chooses to illustrate his theory is very telling. The soul, he says, is like a *tabula* "a writing tablet," but not—it should be noted—a *tabula rasa*. In fact, on the tablet of the soul are to be found the likenesses of things, like pictures, which are illuminated by the divine light. In this life, however, the soul focuses on the images, not on the canvas, much less the light: the soul, in other words, knows neither itself nor God directly.[25] It is,

21. Fishacre, *In 2 Sent.* 16.1, ed. Long, 1:332.

22. See Dorothea E. Sharp, "The Philosophy of Richard Fishacre," *NS* 7 (1933): 290.

23. Fishacre, *In 2 Sent.* 15.5. ed. Long, 1:315.

24. Fishacre, *In 2 Sent.* 24.3, ed. Long, 2:104.

25. "Igitur intelligo anima sicut tabulam, similitudines rerum in ea sicut picturas, Deum ut lucem has picturas illuminantem. Et sicut anima in hac vita non videt se ipsam, sed has picturas in se, et ita per consequens se—sed non attendit—sic et lucem hanc forsitan," *In 1 Sent.* 17.1, in "Problem of Soul," *53. See this unequivocal text:

however, owing to the presence in the soul of all forms that Aristotle can say: "The soul is in a way all existing things."[26]

But, says the adversary, if all possible forms are present in the human soul, the human creature would know all things. Fishacre's response is that all truths are indeed in the soul, as Augustine and the Platonists affirm, but they are latent; in the same way, the passive intellect is in a state of active potency with respect to all intelligibles.[27]

In the present dispensation, Fishacre concludes, the human soul is not transparent to itself and comes to know itself only through its actions, a position that will be argued at some length by his younger confrere, Thomas Aquinas.

"Sic prius est ipsam inspicere se habentem speciem alicuius rei quam intelligere rem ipsam," ibid., 1.3.6, *31.

26. Fishacre, *In 2 Sent.* 16.2, ed. Long, 1:332.

27. Ibid. See the following text from *In 1 Sent.* 3.9: "SIMILITER CUM HAEC TRIA. cap. 9. TOTA SIMUL INTELLIGO. Sed cum omnia, ut iam dictum est, sint in memoria intellectus agentis insita ex condicione, multa autem sunt quae non intelligo. Quomodo est haec vera? Intelligentis capit totam memoriam. Solutio. Intellige hic quando anima intelligit se ipsam, non in alio casu. Vel melius: sicut tu sumis memoriam intellectus agentis, non possibilis, sic sume intelligentiam intellectus agentis et non possibilis. Quae intelligentia, si esset in nobis sicut est in angelis, ita esset quod totam memoriam caperet intelligentia," in Long, "Problem of Soul," *34–*35.

CHAPTER 11

Richard Fishacre's Treatise
De libero arbitrio

That the human creature has the freedom to choose and that therefore we bear the moral responsibility for our actions was an issue central to Christian philosophy from at least the time of St. Augustine.[1] It is then not surprising to find resurfacing in the discussions of the Schoolmen of the High Middle Ages the issue of free choice.[2]

The first formal treatise on the subject in the thirteenth century was that composed by William of Auxerre (d. 1231) as part of his *Summa aurea*. It was William who appropriated the Lom-

1. See especially the first book of the *De libero arbitrio* and the eighth book of the *Confessions*.

2. Peter Raedts has argued for the use of the more current English term "free will" instead of the more contrived (his expression) "free choice" or "free decision" in *Richard Rufus of Cornwall and the Tradition of Oxford Theology* (Oxford: Clarendon Press, 1987), 201n1. "Free will" is, however, tendentious and renders awkward the discussion of the relationship between this power and the faculties of reason and will. In the interest of faithfulness to the thought of the scholastics I will, therefore, use the less common expression "free choice" to English *liberum arbitrium*.

bard's definition of *liberum arbitrium* as *facultas voluntatis et rationis*, a faculty of the will *and* the reason, which he wrongly attributed to St. Augustine.[3] In the following decade and a half, Roland of Cremona, Hugh of St Cher, Philip the Chancellor, Alexander of Hales, and John of La Rochelle all wrote substantively on the issue of *liberum arbitrium*.[4] All were masters of theology at Paris.

By comparison with Paris the young *studium* at Oxford was provincial, unsure of itself, intellectually gauche.[5] The one advantage enjoyed by the English university, however, was that its academic curriculum had not yet hardened, and masters and students alike retained the freedom to develop in new and hitherto uncharted directions.

The master who quickly established himself as the dominant force at the Oxford school was a humbly born cleric who only late in his middle years took up the study of theology, Robert Grosseteste.[6] Among the many works that issued from his decade-long stint as Oxford master is a treatise on the free choice of the will, that in size as well as in power of thought dwarfs any of the treatises produced by the Paris masters of the same period.[7] Possibly taking its origin as a disputed question, as some of the language would suggest, and possibly also intended along with four other short treatises of this period to form a part of a larger *summa* of

3. Odon Lottin, *La théorie du libre arbitre depuis S. Anselme jusqu'à S. Thomas d'Aquin* (Saint-Maximin: École de Théologie, 1929), 49. In addition, the three formulae to describe freedom—namely, *privatio coactionis*, *flexibilitas in utramque partem* and *flexibilitas in id quod vult habens liberum arbitrium*—were all creations of William; ibid.

4. See ibid., 55–94.

5. See Richard W. Southern, *Robert Grosseteste: The Growth of an English Mind in Medieval Europe* (Oxford: Clarendon Press, 1986), 59–61.

6. Ibid., 70–82.

7. Grosseteste's *De libero arbitrio* was not only influential in his own time, but continued more than a century later to influence such diverse thinkers as Thomas Bradwardine, Thomas Buckingham, and Wyclif; See Daniel Callus, "Robert Grosseteste as Scholar," in *Robert Grosseteste Scholar and Bishop: Essays in Commemoration of the Seventh Centenary of his Death,* ed. Daniel Callus (Oxford: Clarendon Press, 1955), 29.

theology,[8] the work was at some later date revised by its author, with economy and clarity of expression the beneficiaries.[9] Neil Lewis has argued for a *terminus a quo* of about 1225 for the earlier recension and 1230 for the second.[10]

The first question Grosseteste faces is whether human freedom of choice can exist. Immediately two *aporiae* arise. The first is the necessity imposed by God's foreknowledge.[11] The second (the one not dealt with by Boethius) is the necessity imposed by God's predestinating will. The latter leads Grosseteste into an analysis of the relationship between divine and human causality. The necessity of divine causality is by God's own ordination a contingent necessity, presupposing the assent of human choice.

8. See Daniel Callus: "The *De libero arbitrio* in the form in which we now have it suggests the technique of a treatise. Yet the structure of the arguments against and in favor of the thesis, and certain phrases ... may possibly hint at disputations," "The *Summa Theolgiae* of Robert Grosseteste," in *Studies in Medieval History presented to F. M. Powicke,* ed. Richard W. Hunt, William A. Pantin and Richard W. Southern (Oxford: Clarendon Press, 1948), 191.

9. In an excellent article Neil Lewis edits the earlier recension, extant in only one manuscript: "The First Recension of Robert Grosseteste's *De libero arbitrio,*" *MS* 53 (1991):1–88. Details of the differences between the two versions he recounts on pages 2–4. Because Fishacre's references are to the second recension, it will not be helpful to give the page references to the Lewis edition.

10. Ibid., 25–26. Cf. S. Harrison Thomson, who suggests the same date for the first recension in *The Writings of Robert Grosseteste, Bishop of Lincoln 1235–1253* (Cambridge: Cambridge University Press, 1940), 90–91. See also Southern, *Growth of an English Mind,* 71, 113.

11. Robert Grosseteste, *De libero arbitrio,* cap. 1, ed. Ludwig Baur, in *Die philosophischen Werke des Robert Grosseteste, Bishopf von Lincoln, Beiträge* 9 (Münster i. W.: Aschendorff, 1912), 150–52. Grosseteste's tack here turns on the two kinds of necessity: one kind, "*necessitas simpliciter,*" can never be its opposite, neither now nor ever, as for example the proposition "two and three are five"; the other kind is what may be called "contingent necessity," that is, once constituted it cannot become its opposite (for example, that "the antichrist is coming"), but *sine initio* it could have been otherwise. It is the second kind that is at issue. Ibid., cap. 6, 168–69. He cites Anselm's example: a man before he wills is able not to will; but once he wills in actuality, it is no longer possible that he not have willed; he necessarily becomes a willer (*fit volens necessario*). Ibid., cap. 8, 181. This last chapter also includes a lengthy excursus (181–96) on the nature of truth propositions, a discussion with parallels in both the *De veritate* and the *De veritate propositionis* or *De veritate futurorum contingentium* by the same author. See Thomson, *Writings of Robert Grosseteste,* 119–20.

A couple of examples will clarify: a ray of the sun's light passes through a colored window and produces in the object a colored radiance and a radiated color (*radiositas colorata et color radiosus*); there is nothing in the radiated color that is not effected by the color and that is not effected by light—both simultaneously. He also adds the pseudo-Augustine's example of the rider and the horse, both of whom complete the journey—together.[12]

Would not a universe devoid of the ability to sin be better than a universe (such as we have) that includes such an ability? In other words, was it fitting that God grant to humans the ability to sin? Yes, responds Grosseteste, and this is evident when one takes the macrocosmic view. The ability to sin is the price of voluntariness, and a universe that includes creatures endowed with freedom is clearly better than a universe that lacks such beings. The eye has in absolute terms more dignity than the finger, but the whole man would suffer if he were all eye and lacked fingers.[13]

Grosseteste follows with a number of moral arguments for the free choice position. Commands and precepts would be in vain were there no freedom. All acts would be necessary and therefore none praiseworthy. Nor would it be just to punish anyone for his or her deeds. There would be no cause to blush, even as did our first parent at the exposing of his genitals, were such happenings unavoidable. In fact, (here citing Anselm) the following are all arguments for the freedom of choice: precepts, prohibition, counsel, praise and blame, punishment and reward, reproof, reproach, shame and confusion at evil, the flight of conscience, and so on at length.[14]

Is the ability to sin entailed in free choice? God and the angels confirmed in grace do not have the *potestas peccandi*. According to Grosseteste, however, "freedom of choice is not free generally

12. Grosseteste, *De lib. arb.*, cap. 10, ed. Lewis, 202. Martin Luther will make very different use of the same metaphor in his *De servo arbitrio* (*Weimarer Ausgabe*, 635).

13. Grosseteste, *De lib. arb.*, cap. 12, ed. Lewis, 207–9.

14. Ibid., cap. 15, 212–16.

to pursue whatever it wills, but to will what it ought to will."[15] He adds the word "generally" to allow for an exception: namely, the will of God, which is free both to will what it ought and to pursue what it wills. Do Anselm's characterizations of flexibility and mutability (*flexibilitas et vertibilitas*) belong to the quiddity of free choice? So think some of the usual authorities, including the Master of the *Sentences*.[16] Such mutability, however, does not include the *potestas peccandi*, Grosseteste insists, and those authorities who claim that it does mean it only in an accidental sense.[17] He concludes that, in the creature, free choice, which he defines as the faculty of the rational will to choose good with the help of grace and evil with the same grace desisting, is, as Anselm would have it, mutable.[18]

Grosseteste's view is that the "choice" in "free choice" belongs to the reason, the "free" to the will. While it is the reason's part to apprehend and to judge whether true or false, good or evil, better or worse, and to propose to the will what to choose and what to avoid, such judgment places the will under no necessity and leaves it free to follow or reject the opinion of the reason. Choice is precisely free because it does not force him who submits himself to the choice of the judging faculty to carry out its determination.[19]

Having discussed freedom of choice, Grosseteste now turns his attention to freedom itself. True liberty is in fact moral liberty, entailing a perfect symmetry of the self with the good. God is thus supremely free, for his total being is commensurate with his will. In human beings, it is the will that takes priority, for in willing first and *per se* properly does beatitude consist, not in knowing.[20]

15. Ibid., cap. 17, 221.

16. See Lombard's definition: "Liberum arbitrium est facultas voluntatis et rationis, qua bonum eligitur gratia assistente, vel malum eadem desistente," *2 Sent.* 24.3, ed. Ignatius Brady (Grottaferrata: Collegium S. Bonaventurae ad Claras Aquas, 1971), 1:452–53.

17. Grosseteste, *De lib. arb.*, cap. 17, ed. Lewis, 224–26.

18. Ibid., 225.

19. Ibid.

20. Ibid., caps. 17–18, ed. Lewis, 229–31. Here Grosseteste shows himself a true son of St. Augustine.

He distinguishes three kinds of freedom in the human creature: freedom of nature or freedom from necessity, freedom of counsel or freedom from sin, and freedom of the reconciled or freedom from misery.[21] Having discussed which of these freedoms was enjoyed *in patria*, he then asks about the efficient cause of free choice and answers that it is God, the possibility of the will's corruption notwithstanding.[22]

Finally, can free choice on its own will a good that is meritorious? The finding both of our faith and reason is that it cannot. To avoid prolixity turning into boredom Grosseteste offers to forego discussion of the remainder of his agenda, which consists of an additional eleven questions. He enumerates the latter, he says, lest anyone think that he had said all that can and should be said, since he had been "disputing" so long on the subject.[23]

The next recorded discussion of the free choice issue at Oxford is at the hands of the Dominican Richard Fishacre, who has the distinction of having composed the first *Sentences* Commentary at that university, a move that aroused the spirited opposition of Grosseteste, by then bishop of Lincoln.[24]

Fishacre's discussion, which constitutes the lengthiest chapter in the whole of his Commentary, can truly be called a treatise in its own right. His views on free choice are rich and nuanced but, to be fully appreciated, must be located within the early thirteenth-century discussions on the topic at both Oxford and Paris, in particular the above-reviewed treatise of Robert Grosseteste, from which it draws heavily.[25]

21. Ibid., cap. 18, ed. Lewis, 232–34; See *2 Sent.* 25.8–9, ed. Ignatius Brady (Grottaferrata: Collegium S. Bonaventurae ad Claras Aquas, 1971), 466–69.

22. Ibid., caps. 19–20, ed. Lewis, 234–36.

23. Ibid., cap. 21, ed. Lewis, 237–41.

24. See R. James Long, "Science of Theology," *MS* 34 (1972), 72–74.

25. Approximately four and a half pages of text or 10 percent of the total is either quoted directly or closely paraphrased from Grosseteste's treatise. It is clear, moreover, that the recension to which Fishacre had access was the later of the two printed by Baur. It was Callus who first suggested Grosseteste's influence on Fishacre's Commentary; See Callus, "Robert Grosseteste as Scholar," 29–30.

Without so much as a nod in the direction of the Lombard text on which he is professedly commenting, Fishacre proceeds to a division of the question: first, the definition of free choice; secondly, the name. To define free choice, however, it is necessary first to define *ratio*, then *voluntas,* and finally to establish the relationship of free choice to both of these faculties. Borrowing taxonomy from Grosseteste, Fishacre claims that the term "reason" encompasses three distinct acts: the power to apprehend the true and the good, to discern good from evil, and to determine what should be chosen and what avoided. Reason in this context, however, will be taken only in the sense of the first of these powers, the apprehensive.[26]

The will, on the other hand, is taken in both a broad and narrow sense: strictly speaking, it is that which moves toward the true good. But it cannot here be taken in that sense, because then free choice would not exist in evil persons.[27] The will then will be taken in its broad sense: namely, the appetite of the reason either according to nature or contrary to it, either to good or to evil. As Damascene said, the will is the appetite of reason capable of deliberation.[28]

The third thing to be established, according to Fishacre, is a weighty question: namely, how is that power which is called *liberum arbitrium* related to reason and will? This power can be conceived either as anterior to reason and will, or as subsequent to them, or as identical with one of them, or finally as a third faculty or part of the soul.[29] The last two options, however, are untenable. As its very definition implies, *liberum arbitrium* embraces both faculties, and the soul is completely constituted by these two powers alone. Therefore, it is either anterior to or posterior to the two faculties. Now the majority (*fere omnes*), including the Lom-

26. Fishacre, *In 2 Sent.* 24.1, ed. Long, 2:71.

27. Ibid., 2:72.

28. Ibid.

29. Ibid.

bard, think that free will is posterior to reason and will and is rooted in them.[30]

To this opinion several objections can be raised. First, reason and will are not one "something" but are distinct. Therefore, if free choice were rooted in them, it would not be one power but two. And if you say that these two faculties have but one root, then it should rather be said that free will was anchored in that root than in these faculties.[31]

Likewise, reason is the apprehensive power of the rational soul, and will the motive power of the same. But in the sensible soul there is also a motive and an apprehensive power. Therefore, if *liberum arbitrium* were rooted in these powers, the animals would also have free choice. Animals, however, do not possess the freedom to choose or anything analogous to it. Therefore, free choice is not rooted in these faculties.[32]

The last objection points the way to a solution. Since free choice is in the intellectual creature but not in the brute, it will be rooted properly in that element by which the former is superior to the latter. But that which is proper to the intellectual creature is its ability to bend back upon itself—that is, to "re-flect" on itself. This ability the animal does not possess. Therefore, the root of free choice or free choice itself is this power of reflecting upon or returning upon itself.[33]

Therefore, says Fishacre,

> I think that the soul or the intellect, insofar as it is capable of returning upon itself, is called free choice. But you will say: if free choice is thus defined, then any bending back upon oneself will be an act of *liberum arbitrium*. Therefore, if the soul understands itself—which is accomplished only by a reflection upon itself—this self-understanding will be the work of free choice.... Therefore, all understanding is a turning of the soul upon itself and thus the work of free choice—which is false.[34]

30. Ibid., 2:72–73.
31. Ibid., 2:73.
32. Ibid.
33. Ibid.
34. Ibid.

Thus it seems, says Fishacre, that our definition was too general. Free choice is not a matter of a purely speculative return. It is rather the power to bend back upon ourselves at the precise moment when we are disposed to some act, without however being entirely decided. The act of free choice, therefore, is the turning back on oneself in the act of willing or on its own incomplete will and passing judgment on it.[35]

This then is the order of actions that constitutes the *actus humanus*. First the reason apprehends and then is attracted—incompletely—to the object apprehended. From this attraction the soul is incited to turn back on itself so disposed to judge whether it *ought* to be attracted or not. If it so decides, the completed will-act follows, which is the same as consent.[36]

From the foregoing it is obvious how *liberum arbitrium* is related to the will. The act of free choice is posterior to the incomplete act of the will, prior however to the complete act or consent. Furthermore, *liberum arbitrium* is nobler than the will, because it passes judgment on it. This is the Augustinian principle that the superior always judges the inferior, never conversely.[37] It is thereby evident that free choice is not grounded in the will. The relationship between free choice and reason also becomes evident from the preceding. Since the return of the intellect upon itself as willing is nothing other than the apprehension of itself willing or of its own will, it is obvious that *liberum arbitrium* is nothing other than a certain reason or *aspectus* or apprehension. Generically free choice belongs to the apprehensive faculty. Thus it is related to the reason as to its subjective part.[38] Here Fishacre is clearly moving away from Grosseteste's Augustinianism with its emphasis on the will and beginning to stake out an intellec-

35. Ibid.

36. Ibid., 2:74.

37. See Augustine, *De libero arbitrio* 2.5.48 (CCSL 29,245).

38. Fishacre, *In 2 Sent.* 24.1, ed. Long, 2:74.

tualist position, a position that will become identified with the Dominican school.

Therefore, when the Lombard defines free choice as the faculty of the reason and the will, it should be understood as follows: free choice is the *facilis potestas* (a ready or facile power, a play on the word *facultas*).[39] It belongs to the soul as apprehending and willing—that is to say, that apprehension and incomplete will which precede the act of free choice. Free choice, it is to be noted, is not the power by which the good is chosen. It is rather the will that chooses through the judgment of the latter. This act of choice is the completed will-act (*velle completum*), which follows the act of free choice, namely its judgment. Since, therefore, *liberum arbitrium* is the medium between the apprehension and incomplete will on the one hand and the completed will or consent on the other, it is defined by each of the extremes.[40]

With respect to the power of free choice, Fishacre inquires into the relationship between our natural freedom and grace, an issue wherein the Christian theologian must steer a careful course between the Scylla of Pelagianism and the Charybdis of Manichaean determinism. Fishacre concludes—correctly from an orthodox point of view—that left to our own powers, absent grace, we are capable only of the "deformed" act called "sin." Through grace alone can the human creature execute a "formed" act, pleasing in the sight of God.[41] Because the discussion comes only at the end of Grosseteste's treatise—and there only in sketchy form—Fishacre is here once again left on his own. So clearly and convincingly does he argue, moreover, that Richard Rufus, his frequent critic, here deigns to follow his teaching.[42]

39. Here Fishacre might have borrowed from William of Auxerre. See *Summa aurea* 2.10.3, ed. Jean Ribaillier (Grottaferrata: Collegium S. Bonaventurae ad Claras Aquas, 1982), 2:279; cf. Odon Lottin, *Psychologie et morale aux XIIe et XIIIe siècle* (Louvain: Abbaye du Mont-César, 1942), 1:68n1.

40. Fishacre, *In 2 Sent.* 24.1, ed. Long, 2:74.

41. Ibid., 2:75.

42. See Raedts, *Richard Rufus*, 214–15.

Having established the definition of free choice, Friar Richard next asks about its name: that is, why it is called *arbitrium*, why *liberum*, and why the former is used substantively and the latter adjectivally. Some say that *arbitrium* is named from the judgment of the reason, which follows the will, while others say it is from the judgment that precedes the determination of the will. The former opinion is held by Bernard, the latter by Augustine. However, the two are readily reconcilable, replies Fishacre, for the act of *liberum arbitrium* is both consequent upon the imperfect will and precedent to the perfect will or consent.[43] The act of free choice, consequently, is essentially an act of reason.[44] But why is it called *arbitrium* and not *iudicium*? Fishacre answers that the latter, when once the truth has been made manifest, is nonrescindable, whereas the former—used in the sense of arbitration—allows the will the liberty to follow it without imposing any necessity on it to do so. Therefore, because the reason can judge as it wishes, and the will is free to follow or not to follow the decision of the reason, this decision is rightly called "*arbitrium* and *iudicium*."[45]

But for what reason is this *arbitrium* called "free"? The common opinion—held by Augustine, Bernard, Peter Lombard, and "almost all the moderns" (*fere omnes moderni*)—is that it is so called from the will. This is true, replies Fishacre, insofar as the will *freely* follows the verdict of the judgment which precedes it. To this extent freedom belongs to the will. It must be added, however, that freedom is also predicated of the reason, for the latter is free to judge about whatever it wills, when it wills, and how it wills. Therefore, the power of *liberum arbitrium* is called "free" from its own act, which is the judgment, in which there is freedom and according to which it belongs to the reason *and* to

43. Fishacre, *In 2 Sent.* 24.1, ed. Long, 2:83–84.

44. On the point of the intellect sitting in judgment of the will Richard Rufus will strenuously disagree with Fishacre; see Raedts, *Richard Rufus*, 211.

45. Fishacre, *In 2 Sent.* 24.1, ed. Long, 2:84–85.

the will. Hence, the above-mentioned authorities were correct in what they said—but they had not said everything that needed saying.[46]

Finally, Richard asks, why speak about *liberum arbitrium* rather than *arbitrans libertas*? This is a question which rightly may be asked of those who say that liberty is rooted in the will and decision in the reason. The answer is that the power which the soul has of turning itself back on its own willing is an apprehension and a judgment of its will and is, therefore, an act of reason. The use of the substantive *arbitrium* underscores this preeminence of the cognitive element in free choice.[47]

Reversing Grosseteste's order of presentation, Fishacre concludes his chapter on the free choice of the will with two questions which logically should have come first: namely, whether free choice exists (in which he treats the arguments against and the arguments for) and then, from whom it is given. His explanation for why they did not come first is that they were not touched on by the Master of the Sentences, "as if," Fishacre says, "he were saying that they should not be asked." Here Fishacre's guide is the bishop of Lincoln. The dependence is close, and though Fishacre transforms his exemplar into his own style, adding arguments of his own, the conclusions are the same.

Fishacre's teaching on free choice, Lottin has remarked, is a very personal and original essay.[48] Its originality, moreover, becomes the more striking when seen in the context of both the dominant Parisian tradition and the nascent Oxford tradition. Although Fishacre elsewhere does not hesitate to borrow from both William of Auxerre and his Dominican confrere Hugh of St. Cher, even citing the former by name, there is no evidence of either's influence here.[49] As argued above, whatever doctrinal de-

46. Ibid., 2:85.

47. Ibid., 2:86.

48. Odon Lottin, "La notion du libre arbitre dans la jeune école dominicaine d'Oxford," *RSPT* 24 (1935): 275.

49. At first glance there is a similarity between Richard's and Albert the Great's

pendence there is in Fishacre's treatise is on Robert Grosseteste, but even at that the borrowings are confined principally to the question of the existence and source of free choice and are far from slavish.[50]

What conclusions may be drawn from this study? First, Fishacre's treatment of the free choice issue reveals that the influence of Grosseteste on Oxford masters was not confined to the Franciscans and seculars but extended as well to the Dominicans. Secondly, it provides further evidence of the power and independence of Fishacre's mind and argues for his inclusion as a major player in the emerging Oxford tradition. Lastly, and here I would like to be most tentative, Fishacre's teaching on free choice, with its emphasis on the reason as opposed to the will, provides some grounds for delineating the beginnings of a specifically Dominican philosophical tradition.

---

discussion of the structure of the human act. On further examination, however, it is discovered that there are significant differences; the third act for Albert is choice, for Richard it is a judgment; the fourth act for Albert is the motion which imprints the will, for Richard it is consent. See *Summa de homine* 5, ed. Auguste Borgnet, *Opera omnia* (Paris: Vives, 1896), 35:575; Odon Lottin, "École dominicaine," *RSPT* 24 (1935): 274–75.

50. Absent from both Fishacre's and Grosseteste's analysis was the influence of the whole of Aristotle's *Nicomachean Ethics*. Fishacre cites only the *Ethica vetus* (that is, books 2 and 3), and it would not be until the late 1240s that Grossteste would turn his hand to producing the first Latin translation of the complete *Ethics*. See Lewis, who calls Aristotle's influence on Grosseteste "marginal" ("First Recension," 13–14).

CHAPTER 12

Undoing the Past

Fishacre and Rufus on the Limits of God's Power

Peter Lombard asserted that "free choice does not refer to the present or the past, but to future contingencies."[1] The assertion provides the Dominican master Richard Fishacre, commenting on this text, with the occasion to ask a question which to the best of our knowledge no one at the Oxford *studium* had yet asked: namely, whether God is free to alter the past.[2] The treatment, which takes the form of a *quaestio*, is concise and nuanced, but not without its difficulties. As was not infrequently the case, moreover, it drew the fire of his contemporary, Richard Rufus.[3]

1. Peter Lombard, *2 Sent.* 25.1, ed. Ignatius Brady (Quaracchi: Collegium S. Bonaventurae ad Claras Aquas, 1971), 1:461.

2. The question itself dates back to Peter Damian (1007–1072), who had argued in his *De divina omnipotentia* that God can bring it about that a past event did not happen, the principle being that what is impossible in time is possible in eternity (PL 145,612); see Etienne Gilson, *History of Christian Philosophy in the Middle Ages* (New York: Random House, 1955), 616; David Knowles, *The Evolution of Medieval Thought* (London: Longmans, 1962), 96–97; and Frederick C. Copleston, *A History of Medieval Philosophy* (London: Methuen, 1972), 67.

3. Peter Raedts was the first to call attention to this question, and I derived much

Any restriction of God's power over the past, of course, would entail a denial of the divine omnipotence.[4] The extent of the power known as *potentia absoluta,* later to be embraced—famously—by Duns Scotus, is limited only by absolute impossibility, such as for example that governed by the principle of contradiction. But the authority to the contrary, from the Gospel of Luke, affirms that "no word shall be impossible with God."

The solution for Fishacre lies in a distinction: power over the past is of two kinds. There is first the power to reconstitute in being something that had ceased to be; the other is to cause that which in fact had being not to have been, to make it such, for example, that Caesar, having crossed the Rubicon, did not cross the Rubicon. The latter is not within God's power according to Fishacre, and on this point Rufus concurs. However, with respect to the former, there is another distinction that needs to be made: there are three different kinds of things that could conceivably be caused to be again. The first are those beings which, when corrupted, pass into "profound nothingness" (*penitus nihilum*), and Fishacre counts in this group time, light, every "successive" or series, and the souls of plants and animals.[5] To restore these things such that they are the same in number is within the power only of God, not of creatures.[6]

A second kind, when corrupted, is reduced to "pure matter,"

---

profit from reading his study; see *Richard Rufus of Cornwall and the Tradition of Oxford Theology* (Oxford: Clarendon Press, 1987), 217–20. Raedts also remains the most authoritative source for the life and works of Richard Rufus; see especially ibid., chapter 1, 1–13. Raedts dates the Rufus commentary ca. 1250 (5).

4. This question invites the celebrated distinction between God's ordained power (*potentia ordinata*) and his absolute power (*potentia absoluta*), but there is no mention of such a distinction either in Fishacre's treatment or Rufus's rebuttal thereof. For an exhaustive treatment of the origin and development of this distinction, see Lawrence Moonan, *Divine Power. The Medieval Power Distinction up to Its Adoption by Albert, Bonaventure, and Aquinas* (Oxford: Clarendon Press, 1994). Though Moonan has identified the distinction in Rufus's Balliol commentary at book 1, distinction 42 (ibid., 317–18), he found no such usage in Fishacre's Commentary.

5. Fishacre, *In 2 Sent.* 25.1.3, ed. Long, 2:118.

6. Ibid.

which lacks any seminal natures (*rationes seminales*), such that this matter possesses only a passive power. But a third kind, when corrupted, is released into matter that does retain seminal natures.[7] In one sense the reestablishment of this kind is within nature's power, but the reconstituted being is the same only in species, not in number, and at a time determined beforehand. Fishacre has in mind, for example, the regeneration of a tomato plant from last year's seed or the ubiquitous dandelion from seed propagated by an earlier plant. The due season for such regeneration cannot, however, be altered except perhaps by a saint performing a miracle or by an angel.[8]

But to restore the same in number from among the last class of things belongs to God alone, because this is in a manner of speaking creation. Moreover, it is a much greater miracle and bespeaks greater power to restore the same in number from matter in which there is not a residual seminal nature. But only the highest power can restore that which was reduced to absolute nothingness to the same in number.[9] If there is a possibility of this, God can do it, since he is able to do whatever is possible. Although Fishacre admits that he is unaware of any case where God has so acted, all of these modes are within God's power, but not within ours.[10]

Quite different is the question of undoing the past, that is, of making what was, like Caesar's crossing of the Rubicon, not to have been. Fishacre is clear that in his view neither human nor divine will is free to undo what has been done. Furthermore, the statement "Caesar crossed the Rubicon," having once been true, cannot be rendered false even by God. As to where this truth

7. Ibid.

8. Ibid. Examples of such miracles abound in the *Vitae fratrum*, compiled by Gerard Fracheto, OP, at the request of Humbert of Romans, the Dominican General. Though Fracheto's collection postdates Fishacre, he certainly would have heard many of the stories recorded there. For another collection of *exempla*, compiled by a younger contemporary of Fishacre's see Stephen L. Forte, "A Cambridge Dominican Collector of Exempla," *AFP* 28 (1955): 115–48; note especially no. 32.

9. Fishacre, *In 2 Sent.* 25.1.3., ed. Long, 2:118.

10. Ibid.

resides, Fishacre says it is in the human soul; but even should this historical memory be lost, that is, should this truth cease to exist in any human mind, the truth of this sentence would continue to live in Truth itself. On the strictly verbal level, therefore, God cannot undo a true proposition, whatever be its status in the souls of whomsoever.[11]

Such is Fishacre's brief exposition of the problem of God's power—or, more precisely in this context, God's freedom—over the past. Although Raedts is surely correct in his claim that "Richard Rufus ... develops [this question] far beyond Fishacre's rather short treatment,"[12] he admits his perplexity over Fishacre's third class of things, those namely that are reduced to their seminal natures.[13] The setting for this question must be sought in Fishacre's notion of *ratio seminalis*.

The potentiality of matter, claims Fishacre, is twofold: a passive potency, which is simply receptivity to form; and an active potency, which is something of form latent in matter. This latter was called by Augustine a "seminal nature" or "seminal reason" (*ratio seminalis*) and corresponds to causal natures in God.[14] Matter in the sense of passive potency is one in number, whereas matter in the sense of active potency is plural; there are in other words as many active potencies as there are forms.[15]

Furthermore, there are two ways in which seminal reasons can be brought from potentiality into actuality. The first is through causal reasons immediately, and when something of this kind, which is deemed unusual, happens through the prayers of a saint, it is called a miracle. The second is when something is educed into act through the mediation of other agents. This mediation

11. Ibid., 2:118–19.

12. Raedts, *Richard Rufus*, 217.

13. Ibid., n66.

14. Fishacre, *In 2 Sent.* 7.6, ed. Long, 1:140. In a subsequent chapter, Fishacre explicitly connects the Augustinian and Aristotelian doctrines; Fishacre, *In 2 Sent.* 7.8, ed. Long, 1:151

15. Ibid., 1:151–52.

in turn is either through nature alone—in which case the event is called *natural* and not miraculous—or through nature along with the principle which is the will; the coprinciple of the will may be either that of a good angel or a bad, and the agency of the latter accounts for what is called magic.[16]

Fishacre's point here seems to be that the angel, good or bad, cannot solely by willing it effect a change which is contrary to nature. However, the angelic will can speed the process of maturation so as to reduce from potency to act more quickly than nature alone would dictate. Such marvelous and unwonted (*mira et insolita*) happenings do not differ greatly from those produced by the magical arts. Miracles, on the other hand, in the true and proper sense are effected immediately from the causal reasons, absent nature and created will.[17]

The greatest miracles are those in which there is no *ratio seminalis* in the matter corresponding to the *ratio causalis* in the divine mind. The first woman, for example, did not have a seminal nature in the rib of the first man. Nature has no part to play in this kind of miracle.[18]

Other miracles, which are called "lesser," likewise reduce from potency to act through causal reasons alone, but these are actualities which nature would also be capable of producing: the multiplication of the loaves, for example, or the changing of the water to wine, both from the Gospel of John.[19] The lowest grade of miracles is that which takes place with the help of nature, namely (as above) those which can speed the natural process of maturation so as to reduce from potency to act more quickly than nature alone would dictate.[20]

What is worrying Fishacre in this passage are the astonishing feats recorded in the book of Exodus: the rods that were turned

16. Ibid., 1:140.
17. Ibid.
18. Ibid.
19. Ibid. In what sense nature would be able to effect these results is not clear to me.
20. Ibid.

into serpents by the pharaoh's magicians and the plague of frogs produced by the magicians.[21] In a subsequent chapter Fishacre adds the blossoming rod of Aaron and the ass that spoke to Balaam, both examples from the book of Numbers. Though in any given case the question whether the cause be created or uncreated cannot be answered, the principle for Fishacre is clear: of those things wherein dwell seminal reasons, angels as well as saints can effect the kinds of changes listed above; of those without such natures, only God can.[22] He thinks Adam's rib is an example of the latter; the others are *probably* examples of the former.[23] However, if Aristotle is correct that we can know only what is actual, it is not within our power to discern potencies, and hence we cannot assert which changes are within the power of the created will (that is, which things contain seminal reasons) and which are reserved to God's power alone.

With the remainder of Fishacre's taxonomy, however, Rufus has considerably greater difficulties. Of those things which, when corrupted, pass into absolute nothingness, namely time, light, every "successive" or series, and the souls of plants and animals, Rufus doubts (*de his forte est dubitatio*) that time and light pass into nothingness and flatly denies (*puto simpliciter esse falsum*) that animal and vegetable souls do.[24]

With respect to the last example, animal and vegetable souls,

21. Ex 7:12; 8:7. The apocryphal literature produced its own examples: Fishacre mentions Simon Magus, who made dogs sing (from the Acts of Peter) and Merlin, who was generated from an incubus, from a source I have not been able to discover.

22. Here, as elsewhere (e.g., *In 2 Sent.* 8.3), Fishacre exhibits a fondness for the distance metaphor: there is a finite distance between an active potency and act, and therefore the traversing of that distance requires only a finite power; whereas there is an infinite distance between pure matter (or pure nothingness) and act, and therefore, and so forth. ("Sed producere de potentia activa in actum non est potentiae infinitae, quia inter talem actum et talem potentiam non est infinita distantia. Sed potest hoc potentia finita voluntatis bonae, ut angeli, vel malae, ut diaboli; tamen simul cum natura," Fishacre, *In 2 Sent.* 7.8, ed. Long, 1:151.)

23. Ibid., 18.6, ed. Long, 1:373.

24. Appendix 12A, §3.

Fishacre had followed Grosseteste—perhaps uniquely among thirteenth-century scholastics.[25] With Grosseteste, Fishacre holds that animal souls were created *ex nihilo*, not generated by sexual transmission.[26] Furthermore, Fishacre provides four reasons in support of Grosseteste's view,[27] even extending the class to include vegetable souls as well. If therefore animal and vegetable souls were *ex nihilo*, they would have no preexistent matter to which they would return when corrupted, and hence this is an apt example for Fishacre to use.

Much closer to Aristotle's conception of nature than to Grosseteste's (and Fishacre's), Rufus opposes the immediate creation of animal life, wishing instead to limit the direct intervention of God in the world, and in fact devotes considerable space to the question in his Oxford commentary.[28] If then, in Rufus's view, animal souls are produced from their seminal principles, they would not be reduced to absolute nothingness upon corruption, but to matter.

Rufus's *dubitatio* regarding time and motion and light also betray very different concepts of these phenomena. The last of these, light, evoked from Fishacre a special *quaestio*, composed in the last years of his life and extant in only two manuscripts.[29]

25. Raedts first claims the uniqueness of Grosseteste's view on the creation of animal life, 162, then admits that Fishacre also held this view, but that "he is dependent on Grosseteste" (n32).

26. Fishacre, *In 2 Sent.* 15.1, ed. Long, 1:306. Cf. Robert Grosseteste, *Hexaëmeron*, ed. Richard C. Dales and Servus Gieben, ABMA VI (Oxford: Oxford University Press, 1982), 200. See also Richard C. Dales, *The Problem of the Rational Soul in the Thirteenth Century* (Leiden: Brill, 1995), 57.

27. Fishacre, *In 2 Sent.* 15.1, ed. Long, 1:306–7.

28. See Raedts, *Richard Rufus*, 163–69, for a good summary.

29. The question has been edited and published: see R. James Long and Timothy B. Noone, "Fishacre and Rufus on the Metaphysics of Light: Two Unedited Texts," in *Roma, magistra mundi. Itineraria culturae medievalis. Mélanges offerts au Père L. E. Boyle à l'occasion de son 75e anniversaire*, Textes et Études du moyen âge, ed. Jacqueline Hamesse (Louvain-la-Neuve: Fédération Internationale des Instituts d'Études Médiévales, 1998), 517–48. The *quaestio de luce* is not found in any of the remaining seven manuscripts that contain the second book of the Fishacre Commentary.

Though Grosseteste devoted considerable attention to light, Fishacre's question had never been asked by Grosseteste: namely, is light a substance or an accident?

Conflating the questions of whether light is body or spirit and whether substance or accident, Fishacre in the end decides that *light* is used equivocally of substance and accident, difficulties arising only when we fail to distinguish between the two usages. Sometimes *light* is the name given to the subtlest of bodily substances; sometimes the same name designates the accident caused by light, namely lighting up or illumination.[30]

However, in his most novel (and most vulnerable) position, Fishacre contends that the matter of light-as-substance neither emanates from the sun nor is bestowed by the air, but is unceasingly created by God on an as-needed basis. A parallel case is the soul, whose matter[31] is created *de novo*, though this does not entail a creation of a new nature that was not a part of the six days: indeed the matter of the soul (and of light) now being created is generically the same as the soul (and light) created in the beginning. There is, however, this difference between the two cases: the entire soul—form and matter—are created together and simultaneously; when light is made, only the matter is created, the form being generated by the luminous body. Thus the sun confers light on the matter which is the ongoing effect of the creative action of God.[32]

Indeed, some things that have been generated have only their matter from their *generans*, as is the case with human progeny, who receive only their matter, not their form, from their parents. Other things, namely angels, emanate directly from the creator as form-matter composites.[33] The principle of plenitude, there-

30. Ibid. 533–34, §19–20.

31. Fishacre, like the majority of his contemporaries, embraced a doctrine of spiritual matter (or universal hylomorphism); see R. James Long, "Richard Fishacre and the Problem of the Soul," 52 (1975): 267–69.

32. Long and Noone, *Metaphysics of Light*, 535, §24–25.

33. Angels, like human souls, are for Fishacre composed of form and matter: see

fore, would demand the existence of the only remaining possibility: beings whose matter is supplied by the creative act of God and whose form is provided by another creature, namely the sun.[34] If then light is totally form, its corruption leaves no matter to which to be reduced. Its corruption therefore is according to Fishacre's analysis into complete nothingness.

Here, too, Rufus is critical of Fishacre's views (*ista non placent*), especially his theory that God immediately creates the matter for the form which is light. Neither is it the case, he says, that matter is created without form, nor conversely.[35] They both need rather to be concreated by God.[36] In fact, Rufus turns Fishacre's plenitude argument on its head: since there is a being which has neither form nor matter from a creature (the angel), and a being which has only matter from a creature (the human being), receiving its form immediately from God, the *Timaeus* principle would suggest a third category to fill out the possibilities, namely one which has form only from a creature, that is, light which receives its form from the sun.[37] Light, whose path is intercepted by a solid object, either suddenly returns to its source or is preserved in some manner or other, but is not reduced to absolute nothingness, claims Rufus.[38]

Concerning Fishacre's view of time there is nothing unusual—nothing unusual that is for the reader of Aristotle. Time is the measure of motion,[39] and is caused by motion.[40] Time is a *succes-*

R. James Long, "Of Angels and Pinheads: The Contributions of the Early Oxford Masters to the Doctrine of Spiritual Matter," *FS* 56 (1998): 239–54.

34. Long and Noone, *Metaphysics of Light*, 35–36, §26–28.

35. Ibid., 543, §43.

36. Ibid., 542–43, §41–42.

37. Ibid., §42. I omit mention here of an equally strange theory on Rufus's part, namely, light as *forma-habitus*. This odd hybrid, which did survive its creator, was dubbed by Noone a "metaphysical novelty," *Metaphysics of Light*, 525.

38. Ibid., §27.

39. Fishacre, *In 2 Sent.* 2.4, ed. Long, 1:37.

40. Ibid., 1:31. Cf. Fishacre, *In 2 Sent.* 14.11, ed. Long, 1:301.

sio,[41] passing from the future through the present into the past.[42] Finally, time is an accident that inheres in the *mobile*, and like the *mobile*, its only reality is the present.[43]

Rufus's view by contrast is, to say the least, odd. Citing Augustine, Rufus finds matter to be the mutability of all mutable things, and thus matter is also the cause of change. But whatever lies within the potentiality of matter, God can restore; thus also time and motion.[44] Furthermore, if God can reconstitute every substance the same in number, a fortiori is he able to restore every accident (that is, time).[45] So far Rufus's arguments fall well within the harbor of traditional understandings.

However, at this point Rufus sets sail into the speculative deep. What if not even the present were real? What if the nature of time and of motion were sheer becoming? He admits his puzzlement, especially in the face of the authority of St. Augustine.[46] Nevertheless, he concludes that if becoming and succession were the very essence of time, then not even God could recover the past, just as he could not render the following statement true: what is not, is.[47] If becoming is the very essence of time, then time would recede into absolute nothingness.[48]

Rufus's next gambit is to consider time as a privation of eternity: more precisely, the prior and posterior of time is a privation of the simultaneity of eternity in Boethius's famous definition.

41. See Fishacre, *De creatione vel inchoatione mundi*, ed. R. James Long, in "The First Oxford Debate on the Eternity of the World," *RTPM* 65/1 (1998), 85–86.

42. Fishacre, *In 2 Sent.* 14.11, ed. Long, 1:292.

43. Ibid., *In 2 Sent.* 3.4, ed. Long, 1:80.

44. See Appendix 12A, §12.

45. Ibid., §13.

46. He recalls Augustine's taxonomy: the present of past events (memory), the present of present events (contuition, or simultaneous awareness), and the present of the future (anticipation); ibid., §15.

47. Ibid., §14–15.

48. Ibid., §22. Raedts summarizes the position as follows: "But if time's essence is becoming, then it is reduced to nothing, because 'becoming' is contrary to 'being.' On the other hand, if the substance theory of time has any justification, then it looks as if time cannot be reduced to nothing. So far the argument is clear." Raedts, *Richard Rufus*, 219.

Every privation, however, takes its origin from nothingness and is not incongruously returned to nothingness.[49]

Conclusion

The question of God's power over the past, as engaging as the issue is in itself, serves also to reveal more fundamental positions, especially as they highlight the degrees of engagement with the new science introduced by the Aristotelian translations. Rufus's years of experience in the Arts faculty at Paris had brought him a more intimate acquaintance and consequent sympathy with the natural philosophy of Aristotle than his Dominican colleague enjoyed. To the extent that Rufus has managed to understand and follow Aristotle's lead, his criticisms of Fishacre's views are well placed; to the extent that he ventures off on his own, which he does not infrequently, he ends in muddle and confusion.[50]

Finally, in contrast to Rufus, Fishacre is willing to ascribe more to divine intervention, thereby granting more to God's power. Though he stops short of affirming a *potentia absoluta* doctrine, he is paradoxically closer to that view, which would later be associated with the Franciscans, than his Franciscan colleague, Rufus.

APPENDIX 12A

Ricard Rufus, *In 2 Sent.* 25.1

The following text was edited from Oxford, Balliol College MS 62, fols. 166va–167ra (=*Ba*). Direct and *verbotenus* citations from the Fishacre Commentary are italicized. Paragraphs are numbered for ease of reference, and spelling has been standardized.

49. Ibid., §24.

50. At least two years in the grave when Rufus's commentary appeared, Fishacre never had the opportunity for rebuttal. One can well imagine, however, that, as Anselm did to Gaunilon, he would have pointed out some of the confusions of his fellow Oxonian.

§1. AD PRAESENS VEL AD PRAETERITUM REFERTUR. In secunda parte est. Et quaeritur an liberum arbitrium Dei possit in praeteritum. Quod si non, videtur Deus esse impotens.

§2. Respondetur quod *posse in praeteritum dupliciter est, scilicet vel posse facere ut id quod fuit non fuerit, vel posse facere ut res quae praeteriit iterum sit.* Primum non potest Deus facere. Nam hoc non est posse, quod satis docet Augustinus, *Contra Faustum* lib. 25, dicens: Hoc idem est ac si diceres: "faciat Deus, ut ea quae vera sunt eo ipso quo vera sunt, ut falsa sint.... *Quidquid praeteritum est, iam non est: quod si de ipso fieri aliquid potest, adhuc est, de quo fiat, et si est, quomodo praeteritum est?*"[51] Quis ergo dicat ut id quod iam non est, faciat non esse? Ergo nec quod factum est nec quod praeteritum est potest facere quod non sit praeteritum. Nec potest facere quod sit praeteritum, quia iam factum est praeteritum. "Huic veritati (quod praeteritum est praeteriit) Deus non potest adversari, in quo est summa et incommutabilis veritas, qua illustratur ut sit quidquid in quorumque animis verum est."[52]

§3. Hoc modo ergo non potest Deus in praeteritum, sed secundo modo potest. Distinguitur tamen ibi quod *rerum tria sunt genera: quaedam enim cum corrumpuntur, cedunt in pure nihil, ut anima vegetabilis et sensibilis in plantis et brutis.* Quod pure falsum est. Iterum, *ut tempus, motus, et lux, et omne successivum.* De his forte est dubitatio.

§4. *Quaedam vero cum corrumpuntur, resolvuntur in materiam puram, carentem omni ratione seminali, ut solum remaneat in ea potentia passiva.* Et istud puto simpliciter esse falsum. Nam secundum hoc redigerentur omnes formae generales in materia in pure nihil, de quarum numero sunt rationes seminales, nihil sic corrumpitur.

§5. *Quaedam iterum resolvuntur in materiam habentem rationes seminales, et tale praeteritum dicunt posse naturam reparare; idem quidem specie, non numero.* Sed intellige quod quidquid corrumpitur, hoc modo corrumpitur. Et non potest universaliter tale praeteritum natura reparare; nec idem specie nec numero.

§6. *Idem numero reparare solius Dei est,* et de materia in qua non est residua ratio seminalis ut dicunt idem numero reparare, magnum est miraculum. Sed valde maius est in penitus nihilum redactum, idem numero reparare. Quod si posse est, potest Deus qui potest omne quod posse est.

§7. Sed non est dubium quin Deus hoc possit eadem ratione qua primam creaturam de pure nihilo creavit.

§8. His ergo modis potest liberum arbitrium Dei in praeteritum, scilicet de materia in qua est residua ratio seminalis, idem numero reparare et etiam in pure nihilum redactum sine omni materia. Et primo modo istorum forte faciet in resurrectione.

51. Augustine, *Contra Faustum Manichaeum* 26.5 (CSEL 25,732–33).

52. Ibid., 733.

§9. Et quaeritur hic in primis qua [Ba, fol. 166vb] de causa non potest natura facere redire idem numero per viam generationis: verbi gratia, ex *a* igne generetur *b* aer. Quare non potest ex *b* aere generari *a* ignis, sed alius numero.

§10. Ecce ignis qui generabit ex *b* aere ignem generaret si possibile esset ignem sibi numero eundem. Generat autem quantum possibile est sibi propinquum, et aliquid sui, scilicet formam communicat generato. Ergo quia *a* nihil est ipsius generantis—nam *a* non est in actu—ideo iste generans alium numero generat ab ipso *a*. Et etiam a seipso generante. Generans enim generat aliud propter materiam; et non generat aliud nisi propter materiam. Unde si esset agens nullo modo patiens, et faceret de *b* aere ignem, posset indifferenter vel *a* ignem vel alium de ipso *b* facere. Hoc ergo potest Deus et natura non, quia generans physice partem suae substantiae communicat generato.

§11. Utrum autem Deus possit quodcumque praeteritum idem numero redire facere posset quaeri. Et videtur quod sic. Nam sive illud quod corrumpitur cedat in pure nihil—potest enim illud Deus ex pure nihilo creare, sicut et prius fecit—sive illud cedat in aliquid ens et manens. Nam sic est ipsum ens in potentia. Facilius autem est de ente in potentia facere ens in actu. Quaeritur ergo de motu et tempore an possit facere idem numero redire. Et videtur iterum quod sic. Nam omnia accidentia causantur in substantia ex materia, ut vult Philosophus,[53] et praecipue quantitas.

§12. Et idem videtur per Augustinum, *Confessionum* lib. 12: Materia est ipsa "mutabilitas rerum mutabilium."[54] Tempora autem fiunt rerum mutationibus dum variantur et vertuntur species. Ergo materia ipsa causa est temporis. Et de hoc dictum est alias. Quidquid autem est in potentiis materiae potest Deus idem reparare. Ergo tempus et motum.

§13. Item, omnem substantiam eandem numero potest reparare. Ergo et omne accidens. Nam si eandem causam numero, et eundum effectum.

§14. Contra: quidditas et substantia motus et temporis est ipsum fieri. Ergo si non potest Deus facere praeteritionem esse praesentialitatem, non poterit facere praeteritum praesens. Nec est tempus aliqua natura subiecta his rationibus: praeteritum, praesens, futurum.

§15. Contra istud videtur quod vult Augustinus, *Confessionum* lib. 11: "Tempora sunt tria ... praesens de praeteritis memoria, praesens de praesentibus contuitus, praesens de futuris expectatio."[55] Nescio. Sed si est tempus aliqua natura subiecta his rationibus, sicut velle videtur etiam Philosophus: signum idem est quod semper fertur secundum esse solum differens, sicut idem in foro et in theatro.[56] Et si instans est tota substantia temporis,

53. See Aristotle, *Phys.* 1.9 (192a15–16).

54. Augustine, *Conf.* 12.6 (CCSL 27,219).

55. Augustine, *Conf.* 11.20 (CCSL 27,207).

56. Vide forsitan Boethius, *In Categorias Aristotelis* 1 (PL 64,172).

non solum hoc potest Deus, sed et facit ut idem numero sit semper secundum esse solum fore et praeteritum esse. Si autem ipsum fieri et succedere sit substantia et quidditas ipsius temporis, non potest Deus facere praeteritum redire, sicut non potest facere ut istud sit verum: quod non est, est. Nec potest facere ut eo sit aliquid falsum, quo ipsum est verum. Non est enim veritati contrarius.

§16. Ait Augustinus, *Contra Iulianum* lib. 6: "Actus est qui opere ipso peragitur, et non erit; et si iterum fit, alterum fit."[57]

§17. Non potest autem Deus facere ut duo tempora sint simul. Nam hoc esset duo tempora esse unum tempus. Unde si potest Deus idem tempus numero reparare, hoc fieret alio tempore non exsistente.

§18. Item, quaeritur si ista possint cedere in pure nihil. Et videtur quod nulla creatura omnino cedat in pure nihil per Augustinum in libro *De immortalitate animae*: Deus "praesenti potentia tenet universum. Non enim fecit atque dicessit effectumque deseruit.... Et item illa effectoria vis vacare non potest quin id, quod ab ea factum est, tueatur.... Quod enim per se non est, si destituatur ab eo <per> quod est, profecto non erit."[58]

§19. Item, de corpore loquens ait. Non enim eius pars ad nihilum redigi sinitur, cum totum capescat vis illa effectoria [Ba, fol. 167ra] nec laborante nec deside potentia, dans ut sit omne quod per ipsam est in quantum est.

§20. Sed hic posset responderi quod Augustinus intelligit de eis quorum esse est in factum esse.

§21. Unde dici posset quod si substantia et quidditas temporis et motus est ipsum fieri et succedere, transit praeteritum in nihil, quia ipsum quidquid est ratio opposita enti est. Si autem aliquid subiectum est his rationibus illud non cedit in pure nihil.

§22. Sicut autem dictum est: si ipsum fieri est tota substantia temporis, tunc cedit tempus in pure nihil.

§23. Sed posito quod Deus vellet auferre omne tempus numquid istud redigeretur in pure nihil?

§24. Dicendum quod mutabilitas non maneret, potentia tamen materiae maneret, nec est mutabilitas creatura nec natura, sed privatio. Quod patet sic. Aeternitas est integra vitae possessio, tota simul.[59] Huius simultatis privatio est prius et posterius temporis vere et formaliter tam tempus quam motus mutatio vel mutabilitas est et privatio est. Nam immutabilitas verissimus habitus, verissima firmitas et stabilitas est. Ergo mutabilitas privatio. Omnis autem privatio originem ducit ex nihilo. Unde privationes in

57. Augustine, *Contra Iulianum Pelagianum* 6.19 (PL 44,860).

58. Augustine, *De immortalitate animae* 8.14 (CSEL 89,116).

59. Boethius, *De consolatione philosophiae* 5, pr 6.4. See *Les Auctoritates Aristotelis*, ed. Jacqueline Hamesse (Louvain: Publications Universitaires, 1974), 293, #86.

pure nihil redigi non est inconveniens. Sed natura, scilicet aliquid et ens numquam in pure nihil redigitur.

§25. Futurum et futuritio videtur aliquid esse in potentia materiae et praesens aliquid in actu et forma materiae. Praeteritum vero videtur dicere non aliquid et ens in actu materiae, sed forte aliquid in potentia materiae.

§26. De luce autem in medio et in obiecto interposito aliquo umbroso inter visum et obiectum, quocumque deveniat sive subito in suam originem redeat, sive alio quocumque modo salvetur, non credo quod cedat in pure nihil.

CHAPTER 13

The Virgin as Olive Tree

A Marian Sermon of Richard Fishacre and Science at Oxford

The manuscript catalogued as Cambridge, Trinity College B.15.38, contains among other things a collection of sermons by Oxford masters of the mid-thirteenth century. The first sermon in the codex[1] is attributed to Richard Fishacre, the earliest Dominican at Oxford from whom we have any substantial body of writings.[2]

The Fishacre sermon is in the form of a *similitudo* (Mary is

1. For a description See Montague R. James, *The Western Manuscripts in the Library of Trinity College* (Cambridge: Cambridge University Press, 1900), 1:505–10. Cf. Franz Pelster, "Eine Handschrift mit Predigten des Richard Fishacre, O.P. und anderer Oxforder Lehrer," *ZKT* 57 (1933): 614–18. Pelster dates the manuscript to the mid-thirteenth century, 615.

2. See R. James Long and Maura O'Carroll, SND, *The Life and Works of Richard Fishacre, OP. Prolegomena to the Edition of his Commentary on the "Sentences"* (Munich: Verlag der Bayerischen Akademie der Wissenschaften, 1999), 31–37. Cf. Franz Pelster, "Das Leben und die Schriften des Oxforder Dominikanerlehrers Richard Fishacre († 1248)," *ZKT* 54 (1930): 518–53; and Thomas Käppeli, OP, *Scriptores Ordinis Praedicatorum Medii Aevi* (Rome: Ad S. Sabinae, 1980), 303–6.

like an olive tree), a common device of the medieval preacher.[3] Common also was the theme the Mother of God. The subject seems to have been a particular favorite with Richard Fishacre. Of the twenty-five sermons attributed to him by Johann Schneyer, no fewer than fifteen are on Marian themes.[4] Even among Franz Pelster's more conservative—and probably more accurate—list of fifteen sermons, the majority are Marian.[5]

Fishacre's sermon, which is in Latin, was preached to clerics and, probably, judging by the content, to members of the university community. There are no salutations in the entire collection and the only rubrics to indicate an audience belong to several sermons attributed to Robert Grosseteste, where one finds *ad prelatos* in the margin twice and *ad religiosos* once.[6] Friar Richard's sermon is preserved in *reportatio* form and very possibly edited by the compiler of the collection. Such *reportationes* generally omit the initial and final formulae (the reader will observe how abruptly the *Ego autem sicut oliua fructifera* sermon begins and ends) and reduce the original homily to a skeletal argument; often the citations are truncated as well. This form of transmission, from which much of the vividness and robustness of the spoken sermon has been drained, likewise renders very difficult any discussion of style, at least as an argument for authorship.[7]

The sermon edited below takes its theme from the text of Psalm 51: "But I, as a fruitful olive-tree in the house of God <have

3. See Phyllis B. Roberts, *Stephanus de lingua-tonante: Studies in the Sermons of Stephen Langton*, Studies and Texts 16 (Toronto: University of Toronto Press, 1968), 89–93.

4. Johannes B. Schneyer, *Repertorium der lateinischen Sermones des Mittelalters*, in *Beiträge* 43.5 (Münster i. W.: Aschendorff, 1974), 147–49.

5. Pelster, "Eine Handschrift," 615–16.

6. Cambridge, Trinity Coll. MS B.15.38, fols. 38r, 40r, 41r.

7. Pelster, for example, wants to argue that Fishacre's frequent usage of *item* and *praeterea* as connectives, while common in *quaestio* literature, is rare in sermons and serves to connect the following six sermons in the codex to the same author; "Eine Handschrift," 615.

hoped in the mercy of God for ever; yea for ever and ever>."[8] In his division of the material, Fishacre asks first why Mary is compared to a tree and why to this kind of tree in particular; secondly, since some trees are domesticated and others wild (*siluestres*), why Mary is compared to the domestic tree, as in the phrase "in the house of God."

The first point of comparison is the singular eminence of the tree among all the adornments of earth, just as Mary excels all beings born of earth and heaven. Indeed, even while on earth her mind and heart extended to heaven.

Secondly, the tree is as useful as it is sublime: it provides shade for animals and an abode for birds. Likewise is Mary a protection for men and a dwelling place of angels, who are the "birds of heaven," adds the preacher. Whoever, therefore, fears the feverish desires of the flesh and the airy (*aereas*) powers, as of heat and storm, let him flee to the protection of this tree. This is, moreover, contrary to what is now more usually the case: that is, the more exalted a being the less useful it is, indeed often it is the more harmful.[9] Does Fishacre have in mind the moral uselessness and even scandalous ways of the nobility and higher clergy, the eminent of society?

Thirdly, the tree is likened to Mary with respect to its generative power. Citing the pseudo-Aristotelian *De vegetabilibus*,[10] Fishacre argues that the plant contains both the male and female element and hence reproduces itself without any outside assistance; likewise did Mary conceive the savior without help from

8. As has been established above, the Douay-Rheims version, since it was translated from the Latin, is more faithful to the Vulgate version used by Fishacre.

9. Cf. Augustine, *Conf.* 9.4, where, speaking of his literary activity at Cassiciacum, Augustine contrasts the "high cedars of the schools" (useless against the serpent) to the health-giving (and low-lying) herbs of the church (CCSL 27,137).

10. This treatise was regarded as the Stagirite's throughout the Middle Ages, although Albert the Great was obviously troubled by the inferior, muddled, and even contradictory nature of the text; see Albert, *De vegetabilibus libri VII* 1.9, eds. Ernst Meyer and Karl Jessen (Berlin: Georg Reimer, 1867), 32.

any male. And just as the tree produces its fruit without losing its integrity and without experiencing pain, so too does Mary. Here reflected is the pseudo-Aristotle's view that the plant is sexually mixed and hence able to fertilize itself.

Why is Mary compared specifically to the olive tree? Because, responds the preacher, the olive has by tradition been the symbol of peace. Just as the olive branch was a signal to Noah that the flood had ended, so too the appearance of Mary, like a green olive tree—symbol of hope and life—heralded surcease from a greater and much worse flood, namely the flood of vices.

In addition, just as there lies hidden in the root of the olive tree a bitterness, which the sweetness of its fruit belies, so too did Mary suffer secretly the death of her Son, while displaying outwardly naught but sweetness. These two features the church joins together when she sings (in the *Salve Regina*) *O dulcis Maria*—that is, "O sweet bitterness," Mary (*Marah*) meaning bitterness in Hebrew.

Thirdly, just as the olive, once planted, grows and nourishes without cultivation, so too Mary. Fishacre employs the apocryphal story, here attributed simply to a wise man (*philosopho*), of the infant Mary after her third birthday being left at the temple by her parents and growing to perfection without benefit of tutor or books.[11]

The olive tree is therefore not sterile but fruitful. Again, citing the *De vegetabilibus*, the preacher finds that just as the fruits of certain trees are composed of many parts—namely, the cortex or exocarp, the flesh or mesocarp, the pit or endocarp, and finally the seed—so too Mary had four corresponding parts: the cortex or skin, the flesh, the pit or *testa* (her virtuous soul), and finally

11. The feast of the Presentation of the Virgin Mary was observed as early as the eighth century in the Eastern Church and gradually established itself in the West in the late Middle Ages; Sixtus V made its observance universal in 1585. See Frank L. Cross and Elizabeth Livingstone, eds., *The Oxford Dictionary of the Christian Church*, 3rd rev. ed. (Oxford: Oxford University Press, 2005), 1332.

the seed inside the pit, Christ Jesus (Lk 8:11: "The seed is the Word of God").

Again, quoting the *De vegetabilibus*, that "forest trees produce more fruit than garden trees, but the fruit of the latter is better," Fishacre says that Mary, planted in the house of the Lord, had but one Son, a better fruit than all other women were able to produce, though others may have been more fruitful.

In his fourth and final citation of the *De vegetabilibus* our preacher says, with the pseudo-Aristotle, that forest fruits mature more slowly and garden fruits more quickly. Christ, therefore, is rightly called garden fruit, because he came to maturity instantly in Mary's womb. Thus does Jeremiah prophesy: "The Lord hath created a new thing upon the earth: a woman shall compass a man" (Jer 31:22), that is, in the center of her womb; and Friar Richard again taps Jeremiah for his concluding text: "The Lord called thy name, a plentiful olive-tree, fair, fruitful, and beautiful" (Jer 11:16).

What is of particular note in this charming celebration of the Virgin? I submit that the extensive and significant use that is made of the newly recovered Aristotelian science in a homiletic context is at least unusual—as unusual certainly as a contemporary preacher citing Einstein, Fermi, or von Neumann from the pulpit. In the few published sermons from this period there is nothing comparable. In a collection of eighty-four sermons delivered at the University of Paris in the academic year 1230–1231, Aristotle is cited but twice (the *De animalibus* and the *Metaphysics*).[12] And in eleven Marian sermons attributed to Fishacre's Franciscan contemporary at Paris, John of La Rochelle, the use of Aristotle is limited to a paraphrase from the *Eudemian Ethics*.[13]

12. Marie-Madeline Davy, *Les sermons universitaires Parisiens de 1230–1231*, Études de Philosophie Médiévale XV (Paris: J. Vrin, 1931), 168, 248.

13. John of La Rochelle, *Eleven Marian Sermons* [*by John de la Rochelle*], ed. Kilian F. Lynch (St. Bonaventure, N.Y.: Franciscan Institute, 1961), 80.

Not only is this extensive mining of the scientific Aristotle unusual, it also provides further support for Fishacre's authorship. Indeed, we find him advocating just such a methodology in the prologue to his *Sentences* Commentary.[14] For the rather commonplace rationale for the study of science as a propaedeutic to the study of sacred scripture, Fishacre finds a novel figure: the Old Testament tale of Abraham, who had first to sleep with the maidservant Hagar before his wife Sarah could conceive—the former representing science, the latter theology.[15]

Although he endorses such a relationship, Fishacre warns of the risks involved. There were those in his day, he admits with astonishment (*fateor mirabile*), who delighted solely in the embraces of a common serving girl and cared nothing for the mistress of the house though she was possessed of incomparable beauty. When they finally tore themselves away from the bosom of the secular sciences, moreover, they found themselves to be impotent with the queen of the sciences owing to their advanced age, just as David in his declining years bedded the beautiful Abisag for her warmth but did not know her carnally.[16]

In a *quaestio disputata* on the Ascension of Christ,[17] moreover, Fishacre makes use of the Aristotelian categories of natural place, natural motion, gravity, levity, and velocity to explicate this particular theological issue. The Ascension could have taken place, Friar Richard maintains, either by virtue of the soul alone (since the rational soul, noblest of creatures, is deserving of the highest place in the universe and will naturally be conveyed there unless impeded) or by virtue of the composite of glori-

14. R. James Long, "The Science of Theology according to Richard Fishacre: Edition of the Prologue to his *Commentary on the Sentences*," *MS* 34 (1972): 73–74. For the dating, see Long and O'Carroll, *Life and Works*, 39–42.

15. Long, "Science of Theology," 85–86.

16. Ibid., 86–87.

17. See R. James Long, "Richard Fishacre's *Quaestio* on the Ascension of Christ: An Edition," *MS* 40 (1978): 43–55. See chapter 14.

fied body and soul (since either the soul or the godhead could have retarded the instantaneousness of the body's motion). Fishacre concedes that in the final analysis the matter exceeds the capacities of the human intellect.[18] Even so, his argumentation in this *quaestio* provides us with incontrovertible evidence of his involvement with the physical sciences, an involvement which earned Matthew Paris's commendation of him as preeminent in theology and *in other sciences.*[19]

I am far from suggesting that Fishacre was alone in his interest in the new science. From the very beginning, in fact, the *studium* at Oxford exhibited a distinctly scientific orientation.[20] This interest in the sciences, of which Aristotle was the prince, was true not only of Fishacre, but of secular clerics like Alfred of Shareshill, Daniel Morley, John Blund, Adam of Bockenfield, and Robert Grosseteste; and Franciscans like Adam Marsh, Richard Rufus, and Roger Bacon. What has not yet been established is the extent to which this empirical orientation, which set Oxford apart from Paris, also manifested itself in university sermon literature. Obviously, this and similar collections[21] merit further study.

In addition to supplying further evidence of Fishacre's theological methodology, this sermon points up the value such pieces can have to the historian of theology or philosophy or even of science as sources for the dating and transmission of texts. From this sermon, for example, one discovers, by means of three *verbatim* quotations, that the translation of the *De vegetabilibus* still in vogue at Oxford in the 1240s was that of Alfred of Shareshill, not

18. Ibid., 54.

19. *Matthaei Parisiensis, monachi Sancti Albani Chronica maiora*, ed. Henry R. Luard, Rolls Series 57.5 (London: Longmans & Co., 1880), 16.

20. See especially Daniel A. Callus, "Introduction of Aristotelian Learning to Oxford" (repr. London: H. Milford, 1944), 3–55.

21. See, e.g., Oxford, Laud Misc. MS 511, which contains sermons by Fishacre and his successor in the Dominican chair at Oxford, Simon Hinton. See Franz Pelster, "An Oxford Collection of Sermons at the End of the Thirteenth Century (MS Laud Misc. 511, Sc. 969)," *Bodleian Quarterly Record* 6 (1929–1931): 168–72.

the so-called *translatio nostra* of Roger Bacon, who was delivering his lectures on botany during the same decade at Paris.[22]

Fishacre's sermon on Mary as olive tree, then, can be seen as more than a mere *tour de force* by a highly regarded master of theology. It bears witness—now in a new context, that of sermon literature—to Richard Fishacre's theological methodology: to make the fullest use of Aristotelian science in the service of the queen of the sciences. It invites us, moreover, to an examination of other known Oxford university sermon material to discover whether this incipient empirical tradition is generally reflected there. Finally, this sermon provides us with a case study of the potential importance of sermon literature for the intellectual historian.

APPENDIX 13A

The Edition

The text, which is contained on folios 24 recto and verso of the Trinity College codex, is in a very legible and not highly abbreviated Gothic hand with looped ascenders. I found it necessary to emend the text only once; I also corrected two obvious omissions in the text by the use of pointed brackets and without further explanation. Since it was a unique witness, I made the decision to follow the orthography of the manuscript faithfully, even when the scribe was not consistent (e.g., with respect to the *u/v* and *cio/tio* distinctions).

I acknowledge with gratitude the financial support of the American Council of Learned Societies and Fairfield University.

Fr. R. De Fisakre <Sermo "sicut oliva fructifera">

[fol. 24^{r}] "Ego autem, sicut oliua fructifera in domo Dei ..."[23] Tria hic uideamus: primo, quare Maria comparatur arbori et tali, et hoc est "ego si-

22. On the Bacon translation, see S. D. Wingate, *The Medieval Latin Versions of the Aristotelian Scientific Corpus, with Special Reference to the Biological Works* (London: Courier Press, 1931), 61–64. Another example is provided by David Greetham in "The Concept of Nature in Bartholomaeus Anglicus," *Journal of the History of Ideas* 41 (1980): 663n2. Greetham argues that the earliest citation of the *De proprietatibus rerum* seems to be in the sermons of Berthold of Regensburg, ca. 1240.

23. Ps 51:10.

cut oliua"; secundo, quia arborum quedam sunt steriles, quedam fructifere—quare fructifere et non sterili, et hoc est "fructifera"; tertio, quia fructiferarum quedam sunt domestice, quedam siluestres—quare domestice et non siluestri, et hoc est "in domo Dei."

De primo comparatur arbori ratione[24] eminentie singularis. Quippe cum ornetur terra duppliciter, scilicet mineralibus inferius—herbis, animalibus, et arboribus superius, inter hec omnia arbor est singulariter eminens; et certe sicut arbor excellit omnia terre nascentia, sic Maria omnes terrigenas. Nec mirum, quia canit Ecclesia: "Supra celigenas etheris omnes."[25] Unde Prov. XXXI: "Tu supergressa es universas."[26] Quippe in terra, mente et corpore pertingebat in celum. Eccli. XXIIII: "In Syon firmata sum et in ciuitate sanctificata similiter requievi."[27] Unde de illa arbore Dan. IIII: "Ecce arbor in medio terre," quia in terra promissionis que in quarta climate est, "et altitudo eius nimia,"[28] et cetera, quia ab omni terra clamatur ad eam: "Illos tuos misericordes oculos ad nos conuerte."[29]

Item, ratione communis utilitatis: licet enim arbor cetera excellat, communiter tamen est utilis, quia in ea est umbraculum animalium et conuersacio auium. Sic Maria sublimis est et vtilis. Est enim umbraculum hominum et conuersacio angelorum, qui sunt aues celi. Dan. IIII: "Subter eam habitabant animalia et bestie, in ramis eius conuersabantur uolucres celi, et esca uniuersorum in ea,"[30] scilicet diuinitas, qua reficiuntur angeli, et humanitas, qua reficiuntur homines. Ps.: "Panem angelorum manducauit homo."[31] Quicumque ergo timet feruentes carnis concupiscentias aut aereas potestates tamquam estum et aeris intemperiem, ad huius arboris fugiat umbraculum. Ys. IIII: "Super omnem gloriam protectio (scilicet est ista). Et tabernaculum est in umbraculum diei ab estu et in serenitate et in absconsione a turbine et a pluuia."[32] "Super omnem gloriam protectio," id est gloriosa protectio, quia ut dicit Anselmus: "Summa gloria est post Deum te uidere, a te protegi."[33] Sublimis ergo et utilis fuit. Econtra nunc de multis, quia quanto magis sublimes, tanto minus utiles, immo magis nocentes. Ys. I: "Principes tui infideles, socii furum."[34]

Item, ratione generatiue uirtutis. Quippe arbor habet in se uim generatiuam sine adminiculo extrinseco, que non est in animalibus. Vnde Aristoteles in *De vegetabilibus*: "Natura in plantis miscuit masculum et femi-

24. rationi MS.

25. "O quam glorifica luce coruscas" (Ancient Hymn), *Liber Usualis*, ed. Benedictines of Solesmes (Tournai: Desclée & Co, 1952), 1864.

26. Prv 31:29.

27. Eccl 24:15.

28. Dn 4:7.

29. "Salve Regina," *Liber Usualis*, 279.

30. Dn 4:9.

31. Ps 77:25.

32. Is 4:5–6.

33. I was unable to find the source in the works of Anselm.

34. Is 11:23.

nam."[35] Sic etiam Maria sine adminiculo maris genuit. Vnde Augustinus *De simbolo*: "Illa femina virum sine uiro concepit ut esset in ea qui fecerat eam."[36] Sed et hoc attende quod arbor fructum producendo nec integritatem perdit nec dolorem sentit. Sic nec Maria. Ys. VII: "Ecce uirgo concipiet et pariet filium,"[37] et item LXVI: "Antequam parturiret peperit "[38] Et nota: alie mulieres cum pariunt, perdunt integritatem et sentiunt dolorem. Ioan: "Mulier, cum parit, tristiciam" et cetera.[39] Ecclesia: Manens uirgo integra cum parit.[40] Non tamen sine dolore; Apoc. XII: "In utero habens clamat parturiens et cruciatur ut pariat."[41] Sed Maria sine utroque. Vnde merito arbori comparatur.

Item, quare tali arbori, scilicet oliue, siue potius olee? Primo, propter pacem indultam. Quippe oliua est pacis insigne. Vnde concessa pace de diluuio columba attulit ramum uirentis oliue, et "intellexit Noe quod cessassent aque" et cetera, Gen. VIII.[42] Sed maius et peius diluuium fuit ante Mariam (Osee IIII: "Maledictum et mendacium ... inundauerunt" et cetera)[43] et in isto diluuio erant homines longe a Deo, tanquam irato (Ps.: "Verumptamen in diluuio aquarum multarum ad eum," et cetera).[44] Sed apparente Maria tanquam virens oliua spes pacis et uite indulta est. Vnde ipsa dicit Eccli. XXIIII: "In me est omnis spes uite et uirtutis,"[45] qua illa illam inundationem viciorum sedauit.

Item, propter compassionem occultam. Quippe oliua in radice que latet habet amaritudinem, sed in fructu que patet habet dulcedinem. Sic Maria moriente Filio in occulto, scilicet in corde, habuit amaritudinem; Luc II: "Tuam ipsius animam pertransibit gladius."[46] Anselmus: "Quicquid crudelitas inflictum est corporibus martirum leue fuit aut potius nichil comparacione ipsius tue passionis."[47] Tunc uere fuit Maria, id est amarum mare, secundum illud Ruth primo: "Vocate me Maranth (id est amarum), quia

35. *Liber Aristotelis de vegetabilibus et plantis* 1.2.49, trans. Alvredus de Sareshel, in *Nicolaus Damascenus de plantis. Five Translations*, ed. H. J. Drossaart Lulofs and E. L. J. Poortman (Amsterdam: North-Holland Publishing Co, 1989), 524.

36. Augustine, *De symbolo*, cap. 5 (PL 40:643).

37. Is 7:14.

38. Is 66:7.

39. Jn 16:21.

40. See Lateran Council of 649, canon 3: "Si quis secundum sanctos Patres non confitetur ... Mariam ... incorruptibiliter eum genuisse, indissolubili permanente et post partum eiusdem virginitate, condemnatus sit," in *Enchiridion Symbolorum*, edition 31, ed. Henrich Denzinger and Karl Rahner (Freiburg im Breisgau: Herder, 1955), 121.256.

41. Apoc. 12:2.

42. Gn 8:10–11.

43. Osee 4:2.

44. Ps 31:6.

45. Eccl 24:25.

46. Lk 2:35.

47. Eadmer, *De excellentia Virginis Mariae*, cap. 5 (PL 159,567). On the attribution of the *De excellentia* to Anselm, see *Dictionnaire de Spiritualité* (Paris: Beauchesne, 1960), 4, col. 4.

ualde amaritudine repleuit me Omnipotens."[48] Sed nichil in manifesto nisi dulce. Sed quia frequenter "ex habundantia cordis os loquitur," Matt. XII,[49] numquid de corde eius amaritudine pleno maledictione et amaritudine plenum erat os eius? Nequaquam. Sed de dulci corde amaritudine pleno non erupit nisi illud dulce, de quo Augustinus in *Conf.*: "Fletus dulcis miseris."[50] Vnde Anselmus: "Quos fontes dicam erupisse de pudicissimis oculis? Quos fluctus credam perfudisse piissimum vultum? Quibus singultibus estimabo purissimum pectus uexatum, cum attenderes vnicum <filium> tuum innocentem coram te ligari, flagellari, mactari, cum audires: "mulier, ecce filius tuus," cum acciperes discipulum pro magistro, seruum pro domino?"[51] Et certe propter hec duo bene iungit Ecclesia canens: "O dulcis Maria,"[52] id est, O dulcis amara.

Item, propter perfectionem incultam. Sicut salices plantantur et crescunt sine diligentia cultoris, sic oliua et sic Maria. Nouimus enim narrante inde philosopho quod post triennium a patre et matre relicta in templo, sine exemplo et cuiusquam documento creuit ad perfectionem super omnes mulieres.[53] Vt de illa dici posset illud Iudith XI: "Non est talis mulier super terram in aspectu, in pulcritudine et in sensu uerborum."[54] Sed nunc multi multa exculti diligentia aut nullum aut modicum fructum faciunt. Vix modicum; Ys. XXVI: "Manda remanda, manda remanda ... modicum ibi modicum ibi."[55] Fuit ergo oliua non sterilis, immo fructifera. Sed Aristoteles *In vegetabilibus*: "Fructuum quidam sunt compositi ex partibus paucis, quidam ex multis, vt olee; habent enim corticem et carnem et testam et semen."[56] Certe sic fructus Marie habuit tales IIII^{or} partes. Habuit corticem et carnem; Iob X: "Pelle et carnibus" et cetera.[57] Et testam, illam scilicet uirtuosam animam; Ps.: "Aruit tanquam testa" et cetera.[58] Et semen infra testam, de quo Luc. VIII: "Semen est uerbum Dei."[59]

Item, est arbor domestica, non siluestris. Aristoteles *De vegetabilibus*:

48. Ru 1:20.

49. Mt 12:34.

50. Augustine, *Conf.* 4.5.10 (CCSL 27:44).

51. Anselm, *Oratio* 2, in *Omnia opera*, ed. Franciscus S. Schmitt (Edinburgh: Thomas Nelson and Sons, 1946), 3:8.

52. "Salve," *Liber*, 279.

53. See note 11 above. Cf. *The Gospel of Pseudo-Matthew*, caps. 4 and 6, in *The Ante-Nicene Fathers*, ed. and trans. Alexander Roberts & James Donaldson (Buffalo: The Christian Literature Publishing Co., 1886), 8:370–71.

54. Jdt 11:19.

55. Is 28:10.

56. *De veg. et plantis* 1.3.65, trans. Alvredus de Sareshel, in *Nicolaus Damascenus de plantis. Five Translations*, ed. H. J. Drossaart Lulofs and E. L. J. Poortman (Amsterdam: North-Holland Publishing Co., 1989), 526.

57. Jb 10:11.

58. Ps 21:16.

59. Lk 8:11.

"Siluestres magis fructificant quam ortenses, sed fructus ortensium sunt meliores."[60] Sic Maria, que non habuit nisi vnicum Filium in domo Dei plantata, fructum fecit meliorem quam omnes mulieres [fol. 24v] licet non plurem, quia alie mulieres faciunt fructum plurem. Sed ualde peiorem; Ad Eph. II: "Eramus natura filii ire."[61] Sed scribitur Eccli. XVI: "Melior est vnus timens Deum, quam mille filii impii."[62] Sic Christus, de quo Ys. XI: "Repleuit eum spiritus timoris Domini."[63]

Item, Aristoteles *De vegetabilibus*: Fructus siluestres tardius maturescunt et ortenses citius.[64] Sic igitur Christus qui bene dicitur fructus ortensis, qui statim etiam in ventre fuit maturus. Vnde Ier. XXXI: "Nouum creauit Dominus super terram, mulier circumdabit uirum,"[65] scilicet gremio vteri sui. Ideo dicit illa Eccli. XXIIII: "Quasi oliua speciosa in campis,"[66] non dicit "in siluis." Hec est de qua <Ier.> XI: "Oliuam uberem, pulchram, fructiferam, speciosam, uocauit Dominus nomen tuum."[67]

60. *De veg. et plantis* 1.4.95, trans. Alvredus, 531.
61. Eph 2:3.
62. Eccl 16:23.
63. Is 11:3.
64. See *De veg. et plantis* 1.7.130, trans. Alvredus, 527.
65. Jer 31:22.
66. Eccl 24:19.
67. Jer 11:16.

CHAPTER 14

Richard Fishacre's *Quaestio* on the Ascension of Christ

Fishacre's approach to theology via the secular sciences is admirably illustrated in an untitled and anonymous *quaestio* on the Ascension of Christ, which occurs at the end of Biblioteca Apostolica Vaticana MS Ottob. lat. 294.[1] On the evidence both external and internal, which I will review below, I feel confident in ascribing the piece to Fishacre. It is probable that his *Sentences* Commentary was composed between *circa* 1241–1245.[2] If so, I would tentatively place the *De ascensione* between 1245 and 1248, the year of Fishacre's death. The style, the rather unfinished nature of the text, and especially the character of the not infrequent errors, moreover, all suggest strongly that the original was in in the form of a *reportatio*.[3]

1. For a description see R. James Long and Maura O'Carroll, SND, *The Life and Works of Richard Fishacre, OP. Prolegomena to the Edition of his Commentary on the "Sentences"* (Munich: Verlag der Bayerischen Akademie der Wissenschaften, 1999), 185–97.

2. Ibid., 39–42.

3. There are a number of stylistic clues that would indicate that the piece resulted

The first and most obvious argument for the authorship of the work is its physical location, namely appended to a copy of Fishacre's *Sentences* Commentary.[4] The scribe of the *De ascensione*, furthermore, was one of several who labored over the latter. More significantly, the style of the piece, principally its cautious tone, is unmistakably Fishacre's. Like many an untenured faculty member he tends to abstain on issues that reflect a division of opinion. In the *Sentences* Commentary this hesitancy saves him from committing himself on such sensitive and complex issues as the plurality of forms.[5] In the *De ascensione* we read the same distinctive phrases: *sic dico, non tamen asserendo, sed magis mihi videtur; cui concedenti mihi videtur, non tamen assero; dici tamen posset, nisi aliquid melius videatur; non certum invenio et ideo non dico*; and so on.

Most telling, of course, are the close doctrinal similarities of the piece, amounting at times to literal parallelisms, to at least three distinctions (2.14, 4.44, and 4.47) in his *Sentences* Commentary.[6] Fishacre nowhere in his Commentary explicitly addresses the doctrine of the Ascension.[7] Nevertheless, it is abundantly

from the reciprocity of live debate and the reporting thereof: e.g., *ad hoc quod dicis* (§23), *cuius des subtilitatem* (§33), *responde* (§54) (for ease of reference I have assigned section numbers to the Fishacre text). The textual corruptions, moreover, that are likely to have resulted from oral transmission are noted in the apparatus.

4. The Vatican codex contains as well *adnotationes* on Augustine's *De haeresibus* (fols. 287r–294v), which I have argued on similar grounds are from the pen of Richard Fishacre; see R. James Long, "Richard Fishacre's *Super S. Augustini librum de haeresibus adnotationes*: An Edition and Commentary," *AHDLMA* 60 (1993): 207–8.

5. See R. James Long, "Richard Fishacre and the Problem of the Soul," *TMS* 52 (1975): 265–66. See chapter 9 above.

6. See Cambridge, Gonville and Caius Coll. MS 329/410, fols. 188ra–b, 515ra–518vb, and 530va–531ra. See also Cambridge, Trinity Coll. MS O.1.30, qq. 49–50, fols. 20v–21v, in R. James Long, "The Moral and Spiritual Theology of Richard Fishacre: Edition of Trinity Coll. MS O.1.30," *AFP* 60 (1990): 107–10.

7. Notice should be taken of a sermon on the Ascension ("Ascendit Deus in iubilatione") in Cambridge, Trinity Coll. MS B.15.38, fols. 35r–37r, which Schneyer has attributed to Fishacre (*Repertorium* [*Beiträge* 43.5 (Münster i. W.: Aschendorff, 1974), 148, no. 17]). The only reason given by Schneyer for his assigning the sermon to Fishacre, however, is that it follows a sermon on fol. 24r ("*Ego autem sicut oliva*")

clear from these passages that not only was the author raising the same physical and cosmological issues and reading the same sources (notably Aristotle) but he was in most instances also reaching precisely the same conclusions as in the *De ascensione*.[8]

As to the content of the *quaestio* it must be said at the outset that Fishacre approaches this doctrine with both originality and daring. The usual manner of treating the issue employed by his predecessors and contemporaries at Paris was by way either of a literal gloss on the scripture text or a meditation on the metaphorical content of the doctrine.[9] Although there are several allusions to Aristotelian science in an anonymous *quaestio* on the Ascension, which the Quaracchi editors have tentatively attributed to Alexander of Hales, the author's analysis takes a different tack and relies far less than Fishacre on the Stagirite.[10]

Since the Lombard did not include the doctrine in his *Sen-*

---

which bears Fishacre's name in the rubricator's hand (see my edition, "The Virgin as Olive-Tree: A Marian Sermon of Richard Fishacre and Science at Oxford," *AFP* 52 [1982]: 77–87; and in chapter 9 above). There are, moreover, arguments against Fishacre's authorship: 1) the marginal note (in a modern hand) on fol. 35r reading "*Dictum Lincolniensis 50*"; 2) a note in the same hand in the flyleaf following the item "*Ser. in Ascensione Domini*" reading "*Lincolniensis*"; 3) most importantly, the fact that the sermon has nothing in common with the treatment of the subject in both the *Sentences* Commentary and the *De ascensione*. The "*Ascendit Deus*" sermon, in fact, stands in sharp contrast to the "*Ego autem sicut oliua*" sermon, which makes extensive use of Aristotelian science (in this case the pseudo-Aristotelian *De plantis*) and clearly bears the impress of Fishacre's style and interests.

8. The parallel passages will be noted as they occur in the text. Though by no means do I claim to have found every relevant text, enough have been cited, I believe, to demonstrate quite convincingly Fishacre's authorship of the present *quaestio*.

9. See e.g., William of Auvergne, Sermon for the Fourth Sunday after Easter, in *Opera omnia* 2.2 (Paris, 1674; repr. Minerva, 1963), 265.

10. Alexander of Hales, *Quaestiones disputatae "Antequam esset frater,"* vol. 3 (Quaracchi: Collegium S. Bonaventurae, 1960), appendix 2, q. 3, 1469–78. See the note on this question: ibid., vol. 1, 23*. In addition, the compilation that circulated under the title *Summa fratris Alexandri* devotes seven chapters to the Ascension (Alexander of Hales, *Summa theologica* 3, tr. 7, q. 1, vol. 4 [Quaracchi: Collegium S. Bonaventurae, 1948], 278–92). Despite the occasional reference to Aristotle and two citations of St. Augustine in common with Fishacre, there is no evidence to suggest that the one work influenced the other. Since, moreover, a version of the *Summa* was in circulation about 1250, the dates of compilation of the two works are roughly contemporaneous.

tences, it was not incumbent on his commentators to raise the issue. Neither Alexander's glosses on the *Sentences*, a prototype of such works at Paris, or Fishacre's *Sentences* Commentary, as mentioned, contain any specific treatment of Christ's ascension. However, when Peter Lombard asks about the nature and location of Christ during the three days in the tomb (3.22), Thomas Aquinas finds occasion also to ask several questions about his ascension: namely "whether Christ ought to have ascended"; "whether the motion of the Ascension was forced (*violentus*)"; and finally, "whether Christ ascended above the heavens."[11]

Until Aquinas's careful and thorough discussion of the question, however, Fishacre's opuscule stands virtually alone with respect to the extent to which he makes use of the new science.[12] Invoking the Aristotelian concepts of natural place, natural motion, gravity and levity, vacuum and time, Fishacre asks by what power Christ's ascension took place, that is, was it by virtue of his divinity, his soul, or his body? That it was possible that Christ ascended by virtue of his divinity, Fishacre establishes by citing the authority of scripture. The possibility of the Ascension taking place by the power of Christ's soul, however, merits a lengthier discussion. Four arguments are advanced, all to the effect that the rational soul is deserving of the highest place in the universe, because it is the noblest of creatures; furthermore, it will naturally be conveyed to that place unless impeded.[13]

11. Aquinas, In 3 *Sent.* 22.3.1–3 (Parma, 7.232–35).

12. My examination of the works of Fishacre's contemporaries has admittedly not been exhaustive. Mention should be made, for example, of two anonymous questions (one possibly Alexandrine) on the Ascension in Prague, Univ. MS IV.D.13, fols. 211vb–213va (described by Bertrand G. Guyot, "Quaestiones Guerrici, Alexandri et aliorum magistrorum Parisiensium," *AFP* 32 [1962]: 86). The second was printed by the Quaracchi editors as Alexandrine material (see n. 10 above), but the first (listed as no. 216) seems to contain, according to Guyot's summary description, a scientific analysis not unlike Fishacre's. Also Guerric of Saint-Quentin has a question on the Ascension in Todi, Biblioteca Communale MS 71, fols. 59c-60b, which I have not had the opportunity to examine.

13. §1–5.

Does not the glorified body impede the soul, asks Fishacre? Decidedly not, is his response, and he formulates no fewer than nine arguments to prove it. Most of these arguments are *a fortiori* and offer little difficulty of interpretation. The third, for example, runs as follows: a sound albeit heavy body is more mobile than a light and infirm body (according to the authority of St. Augustine); but since Christ's soul is most robust, his body is perfectly sound; therefore, most mobile. In the seventh argument he rhetorically asks why, if by virtue of a heavenly body water is suspended in clouds (above its natural sphere), cannot the glorified body, which is heavenly by nature; or similarly (in the ninth argument), if the spirits of birds can keep their nonglorified bodies in the airy sphere, why cannot the soul of Christ bear his lighter body (because glorified) into the empyrean, the highest sphere of heaven?[14]

To the thesis that the soul by its very nature ascends, Fishacre presents two objections. First, it would seem that the souls of the damned *descend* into hell. Do they do so willingly, forcedly, or naturally? Eliminating the first two alternatives, it remains that certain souls descend of their own nature. Secondly, if the natural appetite of the angel is to be in heaven, its beatitude is diminished whenever it is sent thence on a divine mission; the implication is that this is unseemly.[15]

Fishacre resolves the difficulty by drawing a distinction; a place is said to be natural to a thing in two ways: 1) because the substance in question has a natural form by which it is inclined toward and desires that place (such being the case with the elements), and 2) because it has a natural form by which it desires that which is suitable to its nature (for example, the bird that is drawn to its nest but leaves it temporarily in search of food). The latter is the case with the rational spirit, which by its specific

14. §6–14.
15. §15–16.

form desires naturally whatever it sees as being in harmony with its nature, including the highest place, the empyrean heaven.[16]

Replying to the first objection regarding the souls of the damned, the Dominican distinguishes four ways in which a substance can be in a place: naturally and not voluntarily (for example, heavy bodies), voluntarily and not naturally (for example, angels when they are in the sublunar sphere), naturally and voluntarily (for example, the blessed spirits in heaven), and lastly, neither naturally nor voluntarily. It is to this last category that the souls of the damned belong. However, by what power they are retained there (since they are there only by force), Fishacre does not know, suggesting only that it may be the same power that suspends water in clouds, that is, above their natural place. Alternatively—Fishacre also hesitates to assert this—there may be a bonding between the damned spirits and the fires of hell, which is yet not altogether like the composition of body and soul in man. Thus it would be divine power that effects the bond and by the latter would they be forcibly detained.[17]

Responding to the second objection, that the beatitude of the angels is diminished when they are apart from their natural place, Fishacre posits a distinction between grace and nature. In the angels the latter is ennobled and, as it were, absorbed in its entirety by the former. Therefore, they delight more in the works of grace (for example, coming here below in response to the divine will) than in remaining in heaven in accordance with their nature. Nor is this contrary to their nature. There are indeed in the angels not contrary appetites but appetites for two things that are not simultaneously possible (that is, to be in heaven and here below at the same time). But the one appetite belongs to nature, the other to the informed will.[18]

16. §17–19.

17. §21–22.

18. To illustrate this distinction he cites the example of Christ's agony before his

Resuming his original division of the text, Fishacre raises the third possibility, namely, that it is solely by virtue of his glorified body that Christ could have ascended. In support of this option Fishacre marshals thirteen arguments, punctuated occasionally by objections, to which he then immediately replies. To the nobler body, runs the first argument, belongs the higher place; but the body of Christ is noblest; therefore, and so on.[19]

According to this line of reasoning, the opponent objects, the sun would be higher than all the stars (on the Aristotelian supposition that the sun is nobler). As a consequence of this absurd situation, the empyrean, that sphere of the heavens above the stellar sphere, would be occupied by a body, namely, the sun, and there would then be no room there for the body of Christ.[20]

He answers the objections by affirming the truth of his original proposition with respect to those heavenly bodies whose sole function is ornamental; it may be the case, however, that the proper working of the universe as a whole should dictate a different arrangement. Perhaps, he suggests, the sun is endowed by nature with a greater appetite for a *locus medius* than for the supreme position to which its nobility entitles it. The objection in any case is clearly not relevant to the body of Christ.[21]

His second argument is that the heavens were made for man, including his body, and according to sacred scripture are in his service. But this servitude should extend even to physical location. Therefore, man's natural position is above the heavenly bodies.[22]

death. The meaning seems to be that the two appetites are not divided against themselves, just as Christ's flesh, which willed not to die, did not in fact desire anything in opposition to the spirit (which willed the death of the body), "because the spirit willed that the flesh should so will." Or, Fishacre continues, it could be said that just as the deity, which has power over the humanity in Christ, permits it sometimes to sleep, to suffer, and in general to perform human acts, so also the informed will enjoys such sovereignty over the nature joined to it that it can temporarily disallow the functioning of its proper act (e.g., that it would actually desire, rather than avoid, the wood of the cross). Such an act is not contrary to nature, but above it (§23–24).

19. §25.

20. §26.

21. §27.

22. §28.

His third argument is particularly obtuse. Heaven is the natural dwelling place of the soul. Some souls, however, since man is capable of killing himself, are brought there by violent means.[23] Is it not reasonable to suppose, Fishacre asks, that the earthly substance can dwell in heaven naturally (in opposition to "violently") and also move there naturally?[24]

Fourthly, there is a greater difference between spirit and body than between one body and another. But the spirit dwells in the body naturally. Therefore, *a fortiori* a body should be able to inhabit another body—specifically the glorified body should be capable of dwelling in the celestial body.[25]

To these last arguments the following objection is raised. If the natural place of the entire earth is the same as for that of a single clod (*gleba*), and if the clod of earth which is the body of Christ is naturally on high, so too will be the entire earth—at least when it will have been glorified.[26]

Fishacre responds by stating that the proposition (which is, in fact, Aristotle's) is true only of a clod or atom of earth not united to another and especially to a nobler nature (as is the case with earth in the body of Christ). Also in the glorified human body the weight of the earthly element will be removed, which may not be true of the entire glorified earth—in which case their place will not be the same.[27]

The following eight arguments proceed in similar fashion and cause no particular difficulty. The thirteenth argument (in support of the Ascension taking place by virtue of the body) is, however, somewhat convoluted. Fishacre establishes first that the universe

23. Literally "this violence someone inflicts on it (i.e., the soul)"; I suspect the text is corrupt here, the original positing the opposition between *animal/infernum/violencia* and *corpus/celum/natura*. Thus, "if the soul can be borne to hell by violent means (i.e., suicide), *a fortiori* the body can be borne to heaven by natural means." This is merely a conjecture, and I have found no parallel text in the *Sentences* Commentary to support it.

24. §29.

25. §30.

26. §31.

27. §32.

consists of four concentric spheres: earth, air, the stellar heaven, and the empyrean. Because "heaven" is three-tiered (air, stars, and the empyrean), the phrase "heaven and earth" is frequently used by the sacred writers to signify every creature.[28] There is, however, a hierarchy among the bodies that adorn the universe, the opaque being the less noble, the luminous the more noble; within these categories, furthermore, the inanimate is less noble than the animate, such that the following classification results: opaque inanimate substances ornament the earthly sphere, opaque animate the air, luminous inanimate the stellar heaven, and therefore, by extrapolation, luminous animate substances (including especially the glorified body of Christ) adorn the empyrean heaven.[29]

In addition, just as the star is borne upward naturally, so also is the glorified body, because, as Augustine has it, God removes gravity from the elements composing such a body. Remembering, however, that fire is one of those elements, and that fire by nature is light, Fishacre adds that though Augustine is silent on this point, if the glorified body retains its fiery element, it will ascend naturally at least as far as the outer limit of the fiery sphere (that is, the stellar heaven). Because fire in the glorified body has been ennobled above the nature of the stellar heaven, moreover, it will ascend still higher ("just as if God were to make a nobler heaven above the stellar heaven, and each were to be light because made of fire, thus the nobler heaven would naturally ascend still higher if it were below").[30]

Even if both lightness and heaviness are removed from the glorified body, Fishacre continues, it still retains a natural appetite for that which is in keeping with its nobility, namely, the

28. In the Pentateuch alone see, e.g., Gn 1:1, 2:1, 2:4, 14:19, 14:22, 24:3; Ex 20:11, 31:17; Dt 4:26, 30:19, 31:28.

29. §33–39.

30. §42. See Fishacre: "Quod ibi non sit tempus, dicit Aristoteles in libro *Caeli et mundi*, loquens de loco super caelum stellatum quem ibi frequenter vocat locum spirituum sic," *In 2 Sent.*, 2, 4.3, ed. Long, 1:37.

highest position and one which contains the noblest being, and barring any impediment will be carried thence by its natural appetite. To illustrate this latter he chooses the example of fire, which here below has no natural figure, but only a "pineal" figure. In its proper sphere fire derives its round or spherical configuration from the heaven which contains it, or, if fire is itself a heaven, it naturally has a spherical figure. But because it has a natural form which seeks that which is in keeping with its nature, it gathers itself together now into a penetrative figure (that, the cone-shaped figure in which fire now appears), by which it seeks to penetrate to a higher place.[31]

The conclusion Fishacre draws from all of this is that Christ could have ascended either by virtue of his divinity by itself, or by virtue of his soul by itself, or by virtue of his body by itself. Granting the possibility of any of the above options, the Dominican now asks by what power Christ did in fact ascend. The objection is posed that it could not have been by all three powers simultaneously, for no action is common to God and creature. He answers by reminding his putative interlocutor that the action of ascending could have been an *actum* (that is, something done) on the part of God and an *actio* on the part of the creature (that is, Christ's soul and body) simultaneously; hence the possibility of ascending by all three powers.[32]

In typical scholastic fashion Fishacre argues in the first place that Christ did not in fact ascend by virtue of his body alone. Presenting arguments for the opposition, he says that it could be demonstrated that Christ ascended by virtue of his body, if he were borne on high instantaneously—which seems to be the case. First, if a stone were on high and the medium were a vacuum, it would fall instantaneously owing to the total lack of resistance; but nothing between earth and empyrean could offer any resistance

31. §43–44.
32. §45–47.

to the rarefied nature of Christ's glorified body; therefore, and so on. Secondly, light travels instantaneously owing to its subtlety; but the glorified body of Christ is subtler than light, which is evident because light finds resistance in doors and walls (whereas the risen Christ penetrated these);[33] therefore, and so on.[34] Arguing the contrary position, Fishacre formulates the following syllogism: Christ did not ascend by virtue of his body unless he did so instantaneously; but he did not ascend instantaneously; therefore, he did not ascend by virtue of his body. In support of the minor premise the Dominican argues that in instantaneous motion there is "prior and posterior" with respect to nature, but not to time; the senses, however, cannot perceive prior and posterior with respect to nature, but only with respect to time. But scripture clearly attests that the disciples "watched" him ascend.[35] Therefore, he did not ascend instantaneously and, therefore, not by the power of his body alone.[36]

Was Christ's divinity then in fact responsible for his ascension? Fishacre finds three arguments against such a thesis. First, Christ's ascension ought to arouse our own hopes of ascending to our eternal reward; however, we will not ascend by virtue of the Godhead conjoined with our nature, but by virtue of our soul; therefore, Christ ascends by the same power. Secondly, every motion takes place only with some resistance of the *mobile* to the *motor* or of the medium to the *mobile* or from both of these; but no finite power can offer any resistance to an infinite, indivisible *motor*. Therefore, just as in the case of the instantaneous fall of the stone through a vacuum, if Christ ascended by virtue of his divinity, such ascension would be instantaneous (the possibility of which has already been discounted). Lastly, local motion can be predicated only univocally; but if God moved a body

33. See Jn 20:19.

34. §48–49.

35. "Cumque intuerentur in caelum euntem illum" (Acts 1:10).

36. §50.

locally, he would share a category in common with a creature, which is impossible; therefore, and so on.[37]

To the second and third objections Fishacre has a response. The need of resistance for motion to take place obtains only for natural motion, not voluntary motion (which would be the case with a divinely caused ascension). Univocal predication, moreover, is avoided by once again positing the distinction between *actus* (predicated of God) and *actio* (predicated of the creature); only the latter is an accident, the former being identical with God's very being.[38]

Fishacre thus seems most inclined to the third option, namely, Christ's ascending by virtue of his soul. Motion, he asserts, is either natural, voluntary, or forced; but voluntary procession is solely from the soul. However, based on the authority of the text from Acts, the Ascension was gradual.[39] Thus, it evidently took place by virtue of the soul.[40]

Opposing arguments are presented as follows: gradual motion requires resistance; must we suppose, therefore, that in order to ascend gradually Christ increased the density of air, fire, and heaven itself (as he once did that of the sea)?[41] Such does not seem to be necessary, replies Fishacre, since no resistance (in howsoever solid a body) can be found to the glorified body.[42]

Tentatively (and characteristically) Fishacre offers his conclusion that Christ's gradual ascension took place either by virtue of the soul alone or by virtue of the composite of soul and body, such that the soul or the divinity would have retarded the instantaneousness (*subitatio*) with respect to the body.[43]

In the final analysis, however, the matter exceeds the capacities of human knowledge, as the Lombard says in his gloss on

37. §51–53.
38. §54–55.
39. Acts 1:10.
40. §56.
41. See Mt 14:25; Mk 6:48; and Jn 6:19.
42. §57.
43. §58.

the psalm text *Et ascendit super cherubim.*[44] In fact, according to Peter Lombard's gloss on another psalm, it would seem that it was by virtue of Christ's divinity that he ascended. Neither can Fishacre find anything conclusive to say about the gradual nature of the Ascension.[45]

Finally, posing a new question, the Dominican asks in what direction Christ ascended. Scripture seems to offer contrary views, that is, toward the east and toward the west. After considering several alternate views offered by the Lombard, Fishacre concludes the *quaestio* by suggesting a literal interpretation based on one of the suppositions of contemporary geography: namely, that Jerusalem (the site of the Ascension) occupies the midpoint between east and west in the belt or climate of the earth which we inhabit. When the sun makes its daily circuit, it is setting for those living in the east at the same time as it is rising for those in the west. If, therefore, Christ ascended straight upward from the midpoint (Jerusalem), he would be ascending toward the west for those living in the east and ascending toward the east for those living in the west.[46]

Curiously, Fishacre never cites Aristotle or his works by name in spite of his frequent and often unassimilated borrowings from the *Physics* and the *De caelo*. Since, moreover, he is generally conscientious about citing his sources—and, in fact, refers *nominatim* to Aristotle and his works with some frequency in the *Sentences* Commentary—we must assume that the omissions were by design. Possibly, to suggest an explanation, Fishacre felt that the Aristotelian propositions that were being appealed to were so familiar to his audience that there was no need to mention their author and no advantage in so doing, since in these matters Aristotle did not possess the authority of an Augustine (who, incidentally, is cited a dozen times).

44. Ps. 17:11.

45. §58–59.

46. §60–62.

What, in conclusion, can be said of the present question? To be sure, Fisahcre only imperfectly understood a scientific analysis that even at best remained the weakest and least developed branch of Aristotelian science. Indeed, at times his incomplete assimilation of the new science led the Dominican into quite wrong-headed conclusions: his contention, for example, that on the Last Day human bodies will ascend of their own accord, the original quantum of matter (Adam's seed) having been expanded to such a volume (the entire human race) that the inversely proportioned density will have become rarer than air or even fire.[47]

To the Oxford theologian reading the *Physics* and the *De caelo*, however, the doctrine of the Ascension must have naturally suggested itself as a test case for the viability of the new science, as the doctrine of the angels was destined to play a like role in the hylomorphic debates looming on the horizon. Conversely, the Aristotelian categories of natural place and natural motion, gravity, levity, and velocity apparently struck Fishacre as a novel and fruitful means of explicating a central tenet of the creed. At any rate the question on the Ascension provides further evidence of Fishacre's involvement with the physical sciences.[48]

That Fishacre answered the problems posed by Aristotle by appealing to Augustine, moreover, is not in the least surprising. His vision was still informed by traditional Christian Platonism and in that tradition Augustine remained the authority par excellence. Fishacre, to borrow his own imagery, was willing to entertain a dalliance with the handmaiden, science, but was loath to tarry in her chambers. The queen was waiting, and it was by her that Fishacre desired to bear fruit.

47. §34.

48. See also an article that appeared in the same issue of *MS* as the original version of this chapter and makes the same point respecting Fishacre's use of the science of his day: Walter H. Principe, "Richard Fishacre's Use of Averroes with Respect to Motion and the Human Soul of Christ," *MS* 40 (1978): 349–60.

APPENDIX 14A

The Manuscript and Edition

Only one copy of Fishacre's *quaestio* on the Ascension is extant: Biblioteca Apostolica Vaticana MS Ottob. lat. 294, fols. 294vb–296rb (*V*).[49] The same codex also contains a copy of Fishacre's *In IV libros Sententiarum* (fols. 1r–286v), which ends with book 4, distinction 8, and also an untitled and anonymous work containing *adnotationes* on Augustine's *De haeresibus* (fols. 287r–294v).[50] The latter, I have argued, is also from the pen of Fishacre.[51]

The manuscript is of English origin, in a small hand, and more than usually abbreviated. It has page, column, and (for the most part) line numberings in fives—the latter a peculiarity of a mid-thirteenth-century Oxford scriptorium which serves to identify the earliest Fishacre manuscripts.[52] Finally, two pieces of circumstantial evidence suggest that *V* and the closely related Paris, BNF MS lat. 16389 (*S*) were both produced during or shortly after Fishacre's lifetime.[53]

Since the text is a unique copy, I decided to preserve as faithfully as possible the orthography of the scribe, including the inconsistencies (e.g., *ignis* and *ingnis*). Whenever the spelling was so unusual or strange in appearance as possibly to engender confusion, I noted the more usual spelling in the apparatus (e.g., *opagum* for *opacum*). It will be noted that *tia or tio* becomes *cia* or *cio* following *i* or a liquid (e.g., *resistencia*). The puncuation and capitalization are mine.

I have emended with reluctance, and then only when I felt it necessary in order to preserve the sense. Obvious omissions and dittographies I have corrected in the text without further explanation by the use of pointed and square brackets, as follows:

< > signifies letters or words to be added;
[ ] signifies letters or words to be omitted.

49. See n. 1 above for a description and history. In addition, note the following: F. Ehrle, "L'agostinismo e l'aristotelismo nella scolastica del secolo XIII," *Xenia Thomistica* 3 (1925): 553; Franz Pelster, "Das Leben und die Schriften des Oxforder Dominikanerlehrers Richard Fishacre († 1248), *ZKT* 54 (1930):526–27. It was first identified by Arthur Landgraf in *Das Wesen der lässlichen Sünde in der Scholastik bis Thomas von Aquin* (Bamberg: Goerres-verlag, 1923), 105.

50. See R. James Long, "Richard Fishacre's *Super S. Augustini librum de haeresibus adnotationes:* An Edition and Commentary," *AHDLMA* 60 (1993): 207.

51. Ibid., 207–8.

52. Long and O'Carroll, *Life and Works*, 191. Unlike the Commentary and the *Adnotationes*, the work on the Ascension lacks the line numbering in fives.

53. *In 2 Sent.*, ed. Long, 1:32*–33*.

RICHARD FISHACRE

<De ascensione Christi>

§1. (fol. 294vb) Quesitum fuit de ascensione: qua uirtute Christus ascendit? Et primo utrum uirtute solius deitatis potuit ascendere. Et patet quod sic. Si enim illa manus Dei, scilicet Filius Dei, *tribus digitis appendit mo[bi]lem terre* (Is. 40),[54] quanto magis corpusculum assumptum? Num. 11: *Numquid manus Domini inualida est?*[55] Luc.: *Non*[a] *erit impossibile apud Deum omne uerbum.*[56]

§2. Quod autem uirtute anime, probatio. Nobiliori creature debetur locus superior. Ergo omni anime rationali debetur naturaliter locus suppremus.[57] Sed fertur unumquodque ad locum suum non prohibitum.[58] Ergo et cetera.

§3. Item, angelus[b] et anima natura sunt pares.[59] Ergo et locus naturalis eis par aut idem. Sed angelorum locus est celum. Ergo et animarum.[60]

§4. Item, quod omnibus inest, naturale est, ut dicit Augustinus.[61] Sed appetitus illius (fol. 295ra) bone[c] habitationis omnibus inest. Ergo est naturalis. Ergo secundum illum appetitum motus ad illum locum naturalis erit et illuc feretur nisi prohibeatur.[62]

54. Is 40:12.

55. Nm 11:23.

56. Lk 1:37.

57. Cf. Fishacre: "Item, materia et sua per se forma proportionantur, ita ut nobililoris materiae sit nobilior forma et e contrario. Sed forma corporis humani est nobilissima, scilicet anima rationalis. Ergo ipsum est nobilissimum. Ergo naturaliter ei debetur locus supremus," *In 2 Sent.*, 14, 9.2, ed. Long, 1:290.

58. See e.g., Aristotle, *De caelo* 1.8 (276a23–28).

59. See Augustine: "Animae sunt enim rationales, et illis superioribus officio quidem impares sed natura pares," *De libero arbitrio* 3.11 (CCSL 29, 294).

60. Cf. Fishacre: "Quorum est eadem natura idem est locus naturalis. Sed animae rationalis et angeli est eadem natura, quia ut dicit Augustinus: 'Sunt natura pares et officio dispares.' Ergo eorum est idem locus naturalis. Sed locus omnis compositi naturalis est locus naturalis praedominantis in ipso. Ergo cum homo compositus sit, et in eo pars praedominans sit anima, locus totius hominis naturalis est locus animae. Sed locus animae, ut ostensum est, est caelum. Igitur et locus totius hominis naturalis est caelum," *In 2 Sent.*, dist. 14, 9.2, ed. Long, 1:290.

61. See n. 62 below, where Fishacre gives as his source the *Unde malum*, the title under which the first book of the *De libero arbitrio* was known in the Middle Ages. I was, however, unable to locate the source of this quotation.

62. Cf. Fishacre: "Item, cum absque haesitatione animae locus naturalis sit caelum, habet naturalem caeli appetitum cuius indicium est manifestum: quod omnibus insitus est appetitus caeli. Quod autem inest omnibus est naturale, ut dicit Augustinus in libro *Unde malum*. Igitur anima humana naturaliter appetit locum supremum, qui, si non esset naturalis corpori nostro, accideret hominem numquam fore plene beatum, quia si corpus nostrum ibi non erit, non habet anima suum appetibile naturale; si ibi,

§5. Item, que tantum corpora sunt, ut mineralia, habent naturalem posicionem in infima[d]; que coniuncta[e] ex corpore et spiritu, in media, ut in superficie terre, in aqua, in aere, et in celo. Stelle animate secundum ethnicos angelique in medium uenientes induunt corpora. Ergo naturalis posicio spirituum nudorum erit in supremo. Ergo illuc naturaliter feruntur nisi prohibea<n>tur.

§6. Sed numquid potest corpus glorificatum cui est colligatum inpedire? Patet quod non. In[f] Christo glorificato corpus omnino subditur[g] spiritui.[h] Alioquin si haberet corpus inclusionem deorsum et anima sursum, iam non esset Christo plena quies uel habitudo, et fieret aliquando separatio corporis et spiritus. Quia nullum uiolentum[i] eternum, et nullus appetitus naturalis eternaliter [cum] frustra,[63] ergo ubique[j] uolet spiritus, ibi statim erit corpus, quod et dicit Augustinus.[64]

§7. Item, spiritus glorificati Christi est in ultimitate sue potencie et uirtutis.[k] Et <uirtus> corporis glorificati in Domino ad deorsum est aut[l] minor quam fuit aut nulla. Ergo uincet super corpus nec inpedietur ab eo.

§8. Item, anima corpus graue tam sanum et bene dispositum facilius mouet quam idem macilentum et leue et infirmum, ut dicit beatus Augustinus,[65] et patet. Sed Christi anima glorificata est robustissima, et corpus gloriosum in fine sanitatis et bone disposicionis. Ergo facillime mouebit quo uult.

§9. Item, angeli assumunt corpora corruptibilia et hec mouent facillime; sed non est anima Christi glorificata quouis angelo inpotencior, immo omnibus potencior, et corpus eius glorificatum corpore ab angelo assumpto nobilius et mobilius.[m] Ergo multo forcius et cetera.

§10. Item, Dan. 14: tulit [tulit] angelus Abacuc facillime a Iudea in Babilonem cum panibus et pulmento que omnia erant grauia.[66] Nec est anima Christi illo angelo inpotencior, et eius corpus illis leuius. Ergo et cetera.

---

scilicet in caelo, est corpus nostrum, non habet corpus suum appetibile, scilicet locum suum naturale," *In 2 Sent.*, dist. 14, 9.2, ed. Long, 1:290–91.

63. See Aristotle, *De caelo* 1.4 (271a33). Cf. Fishacre: "Item, locus naturalis corporis Christi est caelum. Alioquin cum locus naturalis animae eius sit caelum, concupiscet etiam caro eius contra spiritum, quia caro naturaliter appeteret locum suum naturalem; et tunc Christus miser esset. Sed idem est locus naturalis eius corporis et nostri, quia de nobis carnem accepit, sicut idem locus naturalis est totius terrae et unius glebae. Igitur corporis nostri locus naturalis est caelum," ibid., 1:290.

64. Augustine: "Certe ubi volet spiritus, ibi erit protinus corpus," *De civitate Dei* 22.30 (CCSL 48,862).

65. Ibid., 13.18 (CCSL 48,400). See Fishacre: "Item, spiritus onera non sentit, ut probat Augustinus sic: corpus sanum et pingue, licet multo maioris ponderis sit quam corpus macillentum et macrum, tamen ipsum anima supra modum facilius portat et ad nutum movet anima hoc quam illud. Quomodo hoc esse posset si pondere spiritus gravaretur?" *In 4 Sent.*, dist. 47 (*C*, fol. 530vb).

66. Dn 14:32–35.

§11. Item, nunc potest corpus animam[n] natura celestem deprimere inferius dum neutrum gloriosum. Quare non poterit tunc anima leuare corpus sursum cum utrumque erit gloriosum[o]?[67]

§12. Item, uirtute corporis celestis, que est uirtus corporis, aqua suspenditur in nubibus. Quare non uirtute spiritus naturaliter celestis corpus gloriosum aqua leuius eleuet<ur> sursum?[68]

§13. Item, ignis propter naturalem adherenciam cum graui combustibili fertur et manet deorsum. Quare non[p] corpus propter naturalem coherenciam[q] cum spiritu feratur et maneat sursum?[69]

§14. Item, si possunt spiritus auium sua corpora non gloriosa eleuare in celum aereum, quare non anima Christi corpus leuius in celum empireum?[70]

§15. Contra. Uidetur quod anime male descendant in infernum. Hoc aut est propter culpe pondus, que nichil est, aut propter illatam uiolenciam. Sed cuius? Non demonum. Quis enim et demonibus hanc facit uiolenciam cum et ipsi descendant? Nec bonorum angelorum; tunc enim eternaliter aliqui essent in inferno ad detinendum demones et animas ibi. Ergo per naturam aut propriam uoluntatem. Sed non hoc. Ergo propter naturam.

§16. Item, si naturalis appetitus angelorum est esse in celo, tunc cum angeli exeunt a celo, minus gaudent, quia contra appetitum naturalem exeunt.

§17. Solutio. Dupliciter dicitur locus alicui naturalis, scilicet uel quia istud locatum habet formam naturalem qua inclinatur et appetit illum (fol. 295rb) locum—et sic elementa sunt naturaliter in suis locis et feruntur ad ea—uel quia habet formam naturalem qua appetit omne congruum sue nature, ut decens et expediens sue nature—et sic auis naturaliter fertur ad nidum suum et naturaliter a nido ad colligendum cibum pro tempore.

§18. Sic dico—non tamen asserendo, sed magis mihi uidetur—quod spiritus habet naturaliter sibi deputatum locum suppremum, quia habet formam suam naturalem qua appetit omne congruum sue nature. Et locus suppremus talis est et ratione posicionis, quia nobilior est situs superior quam inferior, et ratione corporis ibi positi, scilicet substancie celi empirei, que

67. Cf. Fishacre: "Item, si potest corpus terrestre animas deprimere deorsum, non poterit aliquando anima corpus levare sursum?" *In 4 Sent.*, dist. 47 (*C*, fol. 530vb).

68. Cf. Fishacre: "Item, si opere naturae aqua suspenditur in nubibus super aerem, quomodo opere creatoris naturae non poterit corpus humanum habitare super caelum?" ibid.

69. Cf. Fishacre: "Item, secundum Platonem idem est spera ignis et caelum. Si igitur potest corpus ignis, scilicet corpus caeleste, esse in terra ut hic nobiscum per adhaerentiam cum sua materia, cuius ponderis virtus vincit super ignis levitatem, immo in profundissimo terrae, ut in inferno, et non poterit corpus terrestre esse in caelo propter adhaerentiam cum anima, cuius virtus vincit supra pondus corporis?" ibid.

70. See Augustine, *De civitate Dei* 22.11 (CCSL 48, 829). Cf. Fishacre: "Qui per pennarum levitatem donavit avium terrenis corporibus ut portentur in aere (etc.)" *In 4 Sent.*, dist. 47 (*C*, fol. 530vb).

est corpus nobilissimum[r] inter corpora continencia. Non[s] tamen est uerum[t] quod habeat spiritus rationalis specialem formam qua feratur ad illum locum uel inhabitet sicut terra, sed qua appetit omne quod uidet sue nature congruere.

§19. Cui concedenti[u] mihi uidentur (non tamen assero) supradicte rationes probantes quod est naturalis locus ille spiritibus rationalibus.

§20. Item, rationibus affirmantibus quod corpus glorificatum non inpedit spiritum assencio. Augustinus, *De ciuitate Dei* lib. 22: "Poterit Deus graue pondus auferre, ut in eodem elemento habitet uiuificatum corpus, in quo uoluerit uiuificans spiritus."[71]

§21. Ad obiectum contra dicebat quod eorum[v] que sunt in loco quedam sunt naturaliter in loco et non uoluntarie, ut corpora grauia[w]; quedam uoluntarie et non naturaliter, ut angeli boni aliquando sunt hic nobiscum; quedam naturaliter et uoluntarie, ut spiritus beati in celo; quedam non naturaliter nec uoluntarie, ut demones in inferno et dampnate anime, qui quia noluerunt tenere ordinem, ut dicit Augustinus, tenentur ab ordine.[72]

§22. Sed qua ui teneantur dampnati[x] spiritus in inferno, nescio. Dici tamen posset, nisi aliquid melius uideatur, quod illa uirtus detinet uiolenter illos spiritus naturaliter celestes que detinet aquas uiolenter superius—dico aquas que super celos sunt. Sed aquas detinet sursum, quia forte expedit et spiritus tales deorsum, quia decet et congruit. Licet enim deformes sint, tamen ornare possunt illam uilem habitationem et penalem, sicut latro ornat carc<er>em, ut dicit Augustinus, *De libero arbitrio*,[73] et eadem ui possunt detineri in illis ingnibus[y] qua ille ingnis in loco infimo.[z] Uel aliter (quod nec assero) dicit Augustinus, *De ciuitate Dei* lib. 21: "Adherebunt spiritus incorporei corporeis ingnibus cruciandi meris et ineffabilibus modis, accipientes ex ingnibus penam, non dantes ingnibus uitam."[74] Sic ergo uidetur quod aliqua sit colligatio spiritus dampnati cum illis ingnibus, licet non talis omnino qualis est anime cum corpore. Et tunc, ut uidetur, posset dici quod ministerio demonum illuc ueniunt et ibi uirtus diuina colligationem hanc facit cum illis ingnibus et ita uiolenter ibi per similem colligationem detinentur.

§23. Ad hoc quod dicis quod naturaliter sunt angeli in celo, uiolencia fit eis et minuitur eorum gaudium cum huc ueniunt, respondeo. Duo sunt: gratia uel uirtus et natura. Et opus gratie uel uirtutis non est uiolentum nec nature, sed secundum naturam et supra naturam[aa] ad eius melior<itat>em. Dici ergo potest quod in angelis est natura et gratia, et natura illa tota quasi absorpta

71. Augustine, ibid. (830).
72. Augustine, *De musica* 6.14 (PL 32,1187).
73. Aug., *De libero arbitrio* 3.9 (CCSL 29,292).
74. Aug., *De civitate Dei* 21.10 (CCSL 48,776).

a gratia est. Et ideo potest gratia super naturam, et ideo plus delectantur in operibus gratie ut atemperando diuine uoluntati huc ueniendo quam prout congruit sue nature (fol. 295va) illic manendo. Et ita huc uenire et non est contra naturam sed potius secundum naturam sicut opus uirtutis. Qui[bb] appetit illic manere, quia congruit sue nature, appetit pro tempore huc uenire, quia uidet Deum hoc uelle, et quia plus potest in eis amor Dei quam sui, mauult huc uenire cum uidet Deum hoc uelle quam illic manere. Et sicut non est ui<o>lencia nec contra naturam quod amat Deum plus quam se, sic nec opus ab amore egrediens et per hoc essent in angelis huc uenientibus appetitus non contrarii sed duorum incompossibilium,[cc] scilicet esse ibi <et esse hic>. Sed unus est nature et alter est uoluntatis informate.[dd] Nec sunt hec diuisa contra se propter hoc, quia uoluntas informata uult quod natura hoc uelit quod uult, sicut caro Christi, que noluit[ee] mori, non tunc cupit ac aduersus spiritum[75] qui uoluit carnem mori, quia spiritus uoluit carnem sic uelle.

§24. Uel posset dici, sicut uidetur dicere Damascenus[76] et Crisostomus[77] de Christo, quod deitas que potuit super Christi humanitatem nunc permitebat eam somni<a>re et pati et agere humana, nunc autem non. Sic uoluntas informata si potest super naturam sibi iunctam intantum ut actum suum ad tempus non sinat agere, scilicet appetere illud lignum[ff] tunc esse, hoc non est contra naturam sed supra naturam.

§25. Quod autem uirtute corporis solius glorificati potuit ascendere uidetur, quia nobilior<i> corpori debetur locus superior.[78] Sed corpus Christi nobilissimum. Ergo ei debetur locus suppremus.

§26. Contra. Secundum hanc rationem esset sol superior omnibus stellis. Item, cum locus suppremus [sic], scilicet celum empireum, sic plenus corpore esset, sic corpus Christi et extra empireum.

§27. Sed respondeo: prima est uera in corporibus ornantibus[gg] ad inuicem, ut in speris, [et in corporibus ornantibus ad inuicem] nisi utilitas contrarietur uniuersi. Forte enim soli est inditus[hh] naturaliter maior appetitus loci medii propter utilitatem uniuersi quam loci suppremi[ii] propter suam nobilitatem—quorum nullum inpedit—rationem de corpore Christi.

§28. Item, nobilius non fit propter innobilius. Sed celum et stelle sunt propter hominem, etiam propter corpus. Deut. 4: *Ne forte uideas solem et lunam et uniuersas stellas quas creauit Deus in ministerium cunctis gentibus.*[79] Igitur non seruiendum sideribus, sed ipsa potius[jj] seruiunt nobis. Ergo cum

75. See Gal 5:17.

76. John Damascene, *De fide orthodoxa* 58.5, trans. Burgundio of Pisa, ed. Eligius M. Buytaert (St. Bonaventure, N.Y.: Franciscan Institute, 1955), 217.

77. I was unable to find this reference in any of Chrysostom's authentic works.

78. See Aristotle, *De caelo* 2.13 (293a30–32).

79. Dt 4:19.

ministrorum sit[kk] etiam localiter subesse, Dominus: *Nisi sicut paruuli*,[80] secundum illud Gal 4: *Quanto tempore heres paruulus est, non differt a seruo, cum sit dominus omnium; sed sub tutoribus[ll] et a[u]ctoribus est usque ad prefinitum tempus a patre*.[81] Sed si nobilius, naturaliter superius.

§29. Item, anima, cum sit quiddam celeste, detinetur naturaliter in celesti habitatione, non uiolenter. Quidam hanc ei infert uiolenciam, cum possit homo se ipsum occidere. Quare ergo non potest terrenum naturaliter habitare in celo, et sic mouere potest illud[mm] naturaliter?

§30. Et maior est differencia corporis ad spiritum quam corporis ad quodcumque corpus, et habitat spiritus in corpore naturaliter. Quare non potest naturaliter <habitare> corpus quodcumque in quocumque?[82]

§31. Contra hec: "Idem est locus naturalis tocius terre et unius glebe."[83] Ergo si gle(fol. 295vb)ba corporis Christi naturaliter sursum est, et tota terra—saltem cum erit glorificata.

§32. Respondeo. Prima uera[nn] est de gleba uel athomo[oo] terre non unita alteri et nobiliori maxime qualis est terra in corpore Christi, et si non esset maior glorificatio terre in corpore Christi quam tocius terre erit, tunc idem esset eorum locus. Item, idem tocius et partis [idem] est locus, quia in utroque eadem est inclinatio.[84] Sed ut uidetur sentire Augustinus in fine precedentis pagine in auctoritate premissia uel ultima[m] auferetur terre in corpore glorificato humano pondus et forte non auferetur hoc toti terre glorificate.[85] Et ita non idem locus.

§33. Item, uniuersaliter coniuncta sunt grauitas et grossicies uel densitas, ut patet in elementis.[86] Et quod est grossissimum uel densissimum est grauissimum. Ergo subtillissimum corpus, scilicet gloriosum, cuius des subtilitatem,[pp] erit leuissimum.

§34. Item, quanto ex minori fit maius,[qq] tanto factum est subtilius:[87] ut

80. Mt 18:3.

81. Gal 4:1–2.

82. Cf. Fishacre: "Sed contra eos arguitur multipliciter ibidem ab Augustino (See *De civitate Dei* 22.4 [CCSL 48, 809–10]): Si potuit Deo agente spiritus, qui est tamen caelo nobilior, habitare in terra ut in terrestri corpore, quare non potuit eodem agente non violenter cogente corpus terrestre habitare supra caelos? Maior enim supra modum est differentia spiritus ad corpus quam unius corporis ad quodcumque aliud. Mirabilius est igitur spiritum habitare in corpore terreno quam corpus terrenum in corpore caelesti." *In 4 Sent.*, dist. 47 (*C*, fol. 530va–b).

83. Aristotle, *Phys.* 3.5 (205a10–11).

84. See Aristotle, *De caelo* 1.3 (270a3–5).

85. See n. 71 above. In fact, this passage is cited on the preceding page of the manuscript (fol. 295r), approximately a third of the way down in the second column. While not precisely "at the end of the preceding page," this method of cross-referencing suggests a unique copy.

86. See Aristotle, *De caelo* 1.6 (273b3–5).

87. See ibid., 3.7 (305b13–16).

si ex pugillo terre fiant centum, factum erit subtilius quam si ex ea tantum X fierent. Igitur cum uera humana caro non fit nisi de semine Adam, illud modicum factum est uehementer magnum. Et erit in die iudicii, cum erunt corpora tot humana completa, nullo addito illi materie seminis Ade, et subtiliora, si computes, quam si essent omnino ingnis uel celum. Ergo cum subtilius sit naturaliter superius, erunt corpora superius et supra celum stellatum. Et sic corpus Christi.

§35. Item, quanto leuius tanto mobilius, et quanto ponderos<i>us tanto inmobilius, ut patet in elementis. Et ideo spera terre omnino inmobilis, cum cetere spere elementorum moueantur. Sed corpus Christi est summe agile propter dotem agilitatis. Ergo summe leue.

§36. Item, opacum[rr] infimum, diafonum medium, et luminosa, ut ignis et stelle,[ss] sursum sunt; naturaliter ergo et corpus gloriosum ratione dotis[tt] que est claritas. Unde conparat Appostolus ea[uu] stellis, dicens I Cor 15: *Alia claritas solis, alia lune, alia stellarum; stella[m] enim a stella <differt> in claritate. Sic et resurrectio mortuorum.*[88]

§37. Item, ut ponit Plato[89] et Basilius,[90] "facit Deus,"[91] id est aufert ingni urendi qualitatem manente qualitate lucendi, quia lux ingnis emicat per oculos. Sed quare non similiter in elementis potest separare grauitatem aliis qualitatibus manentibus?[92] Augustinus, *Epist.* 73: "Ualet diuina potencia de ista uisibili atque tractabili materia corporum, quibuslibet manentibus, auferre quas uoluerit qualitates."[93]

§38. Item, uniuersaliter in sacramento altaris est accidens sine omni subiecto. Quare non potest fieri ut subiectum sit saltem sine aliquo accidente, scilicet grauitate?

§39. Item, non plus ponderat hostia consecrata quam prius cum fuit non consecrata et constat <quod> pondus in consecrata est non corporis Christi secundum <modum> accidencium; nec est in corpore Christi illud pondus magis quam illa albedo. Ergo cum pondus primum remaneat nec modicum additur ponderi post consecrationem, corpus Christi nullius ponderis est uel potest esse aliquando sine pondere. Quare non ergo in ascensione?

88. 1 Cor 15:41–42.

89. *Timaeus* 45B; probably quoted from Augustine, *De civitate Dei* 13.18 (CCSL 48,401).

90. Basil, *Hom. in Hexaëmeron* 6.3 (PG 29,122).

91. Possibly a reference to Gn 1:16 ("Fecitque Deus duo magna luminaria"), the text upon which Basil is here commenting.

92. See Fishacre: "Item si, ut dicit Basilius, Verbo Dei separabitur in igne lux ab ustione et, ut dicit Plato, dii qui hominem fecerunt secundum eum potuerunt separare ab igne urendi qualitatem et lucem relinquere quae per oculos emicaret, quare non poterit a resurgentium corporum terra auferre pondrositatem, natura terrae remanente?" *In 4 Sent.*, dist. 47 (*C*, fols. 530vb–531ra).

93. Augustine, *Epist.* 205.1 (CSEL 57,326–27).

§40. Contra. Eadem ratione uidetur quod non sit leue, quia non est aucta leuitas post consecrationem.

§41. Item, nullum uiolentum eternum,[94] quia si sol eternaliter esset sursum uiolenter, motus contrarius esset ei possiblis et potencia respectu talis motus frustra. Igitur cum corpus Christi sit in celo—et hoc eternaliter—non erit uiolenter. (fol. 296ra)

§42. Item, omnes spere integre sunt 4, scilicet terre, aeris, celi siderei, empirei. Hinc frequenter dicitur coniuncti<m> "celum et terra"[95] ut comprehendat<ur> "omnis creatura." Solum[vv] enim triplex est: aereum, sidereum, empireum. Aqua non habet speram, quia non undique tegit terram.[96] Unde apud phisicos una[ww] spera reputatur.[97] Angelis spera secundum sanctos non est nisi celum. Sunt autem inter ornancia corpora innobiliora[xx] opaga et nobliora luminosa; et opacorum inanimata innobiliora quam animata. Prima sunt ornatus terre. Secunda sunt naturalis ornatus aeris. Tercia, scilicet luminosa inanimata, sunt ornatus celi siderei. Ergo luminosa animata sunt ornatus celi empirei. Et sicut stella sursum feretur naturaliter, sic corpus gloriosum, quod, ut dicit Augustinus, auferet[ur] Deus grauitatem elementis componentibus corpus glorificatum.[98] Sed utrum leuitatem ingni in eodem corpore non dicit. Si ergo manet in eis leuitas naturalis et nulla grauitas, ascendit sursum naturaliter saltem usque ad locum suppremum spere ignis, et si non est alia spera ignis nisi celum sidereum, usque ad celi siderei suppremum. Et quia ingnis in illo corpore est nobilitatus supra[yy] naturam celi siderei, adhuc ascendet hinc, sicut si faceret Deus celum nobilius super hoc celum sidereum et esset utrum<que> leue, quia ingnis, pars celi nobilioris, si esset inferius, ascenderet[zz] superius naturaliter.

§43. Si autem aufert Deus leuitatem sicut et grauitatem, ut nec sit graue nec leue corpus glorificatum, tamen licet non haberet formam qua moueretur sursum sicut nec qua deorsum, habet tamen naturaliter inditum sibi appetitum eorum que congruunt sue nobilitati, scilicet situm[a] suppremum et continens nobilissimum, et isto appetitu naturali, ex quo nullum inpedimentum, feretur sursum, ut mihi uidetur—non assero tamen. Et si stella non est grauis uel leuis, si esset extra suum locum, consimili appetitu ferretur ad suum locum.

§44. Exemplum est ignis: non habet figuram naturalem,[99] maxime[b] figuram pinealem.[c] Unde in sua spera non habet figuram sed uel a celo continente[m] rotundam uel, si est celum, naturaliter habet figuram speralem;

94. See Aristotle, *De caelo* 2.14 (296a33–34).

95. See n. 28 above.

96. See Aristotle, *De caelo* 2.4 (287b1–14).

97. See ibid. (287b15).

98. Augustine, *De civ. Dei* 13.18, 22.11 (CCSL 48,401, 829–31).

99. See Aristotle, *De caelo* 3.8 (306b30–307b26).

nunc tamen hic figurat se figura pineali, quia non habet formam naturalem qua sic figuretur (tu<n>c enim sic figuaret ubique). Sed quia formam habet naturalem qua appetit congruencia sue nature, et ideo colligit se in figuram penetratiuam, qua penetret ad locum superiorem.

§45. Sic ergo patet quod uirtute et deitatis per se et anime per se et corporis per se potuit ascendere.

§46. Sed cum uirtute singulorum potuit ascendere ille, queritur qua uirtute ascendit. Non uirtute omnium simul, quia nulla actio Deo et creature communis est. Augustinus, *Epist.* 125: "Nichil omnino[d] a duobus idem fieri[e] potest."[100]

§47. Solutio. Illa actio posset esse actio creature et actum Dei. Sermo autem Augustini intelligitur in coequeuis agentibus ex quibus non fiat unum.

§48. Sed probatio quod uirtute corporis, si[f] ipsum fer<r>etur sursum subito, demonstraretur—quod sic uidetur. Lapis si esset sursum et medium uacuum, fieret lapis deorsum subito propter nullam medii resistenciam.[101] Sed nichil inter celum empireum et terram habet resistenciam ad subtilitatem corporis glorificati propter dotem subtilitatis. Ergo et cetera.[102]

§49. Item, lux pertransit inde huc subito ratione sue subtilitatis. Augustinus, *Ad Deogratias sacerdotem*: "Radius oculi non cicius peruenit ad propinquiora, tardius ad longinquiora, sed utraque interualla parili celeritate pertingit."[103] Sed corpus Christi gloriosum est hac luce subtilius, quod patet, quia lux inuenit in ostio uel in alio resistencian.

§50. Quod non est <uirtute corporis, nisi> corpus Christi subito ferretur de se. Sed Christus non ascendit subito; ergo non ascendit uirtute nature corporis gloriosi. Quod non ascendit (fol. 296rb) subito patet, quia in subito non est nisi prius et posterius natura, non <temp>ore.[104] Et sensus non discernit transitum lucis. Nunc autem uisus intuencium apprehendit eius ascensum inter prius et posterius natura sed tempore tantum, ut patet quia non discernit. Act.: *Cumque intuerentur in celum.*[105] Ergo non subito. Quod concedo.

100. Augustine, *Epist.* 14 (CSEL 34.1,33).

101. See Aristotle, *Phys.* 4.8 (215b1-6) and *De caelo* 4.4 (311b17–22). Cf. also Fishacre: "Item, ad hoc quod sit motus exigitur necessario aliqua resistentia in moto respectu motoris," *In 4 Sent.*, dist. 44 (*C*, fol. 518rb).

102. See Fishacre: "Item, demonstrat Aristoteles in *Physicis* quod quantumcumque spatium vacuum pertransiret lapis in instanti ... et ex hoc concludit si vacui ad plenum est infinita proportio, in infinitum citius pertransibit vacuum quam plenum. Ergo subito. Et causa huius subiti transitus est nulla resistentia medii vacui. Sed cum maxima sit subtilitas in corpore glorificato, patet quod nec in pariete nec in quolibet alio corpore invenit aliquam resistentiam. Ergo eadem ratione transibit subito," ibid.

103. Augustine, *Epist.* 102 (CSEL 34,548).

104. See Fishacre: Sed si corpus esse sic posset ubique in eodem instanti, hoc esset per prius et posterius natura, licet non tempore," *In 4 Sent.*, dist. 44 (*C*, fol. 518rb).

105. Acts 1:10.

§51. Item, non uirtute deitatis, quia si eius ascensio in spem ascendendi[g] suscitare debet,[106] restat ut ascenderit eadem qua nos uirtute ascendemus. Sed nos non propter unitam nobis deitatem sed propter animam. Ergo et ipse.

§52. Item, omnis motus est ex resistencia aliqua mobilis ad motorem aut medii ad mobile[m] aut ex utroque. Sed uirtutis finite ad infinitum et inpartibilem nulla omnino potest esse resistencia. Quod probari potest per crementum uirtutis, quia quanto maior uirtus tanto minor resistencia medii, sicut patet in descensu[h] lapidis per uacuum.[107] Ergo si sursum ferretur uirtute diuina, subito sursum esset.

§53. Item, cum mouere secundum locum non sit nisi uniuocum, si moueret Deus aliquod corpus, haberet cum creatura predica<men>tum positum unicum et commune—quod est impossibile. Igitur non ascendit uirtute deitatis.

§54. Responde: quod dicitur "non est motus ubi non est resistencia medii ad motorem,"[108] uerum tantum[i] in motu naturali, non uoluntario.

§55. Ad aliud "mouere secundum locum": de Deo dictum est motum esse actum Dei. De creatura uero dictum est esse actionem creature, et ita non uniuoce.

§56. Cui[j] "ascendit uirtute anime," que habet uirtutem particularem, quod etiam uidetur. Cum enim sit motus naturalis, uoluntarius et uiolentus. Sed processus uoluntarius est solum ab anima. Cum ergo Christi ascensus fuerit processiuus, patet quod fuit ab anima. Act. 1: *Cumque[que] intuerentur in celum euntem illum.*[109]

§57. Sed contra. Motus processiuus est super uiam habentem aliquam resistenciam. Numquid ergo sicut mare solidauit,[110] sic nunc aerem, ignem, et celum? Sed non uidetur, quia nulla ad corpus gloriosum in aliquo corpore resistencia.

§58. Solutio. Non assero, sed mihi uidetur quod potuit sic successiue asce<n>disse uirtute anime solius uel coniuncti ex corpore et anima, scilicet ut anima subitationem illi corpori retardaret uel deitas. Sed cuius uirtute factum sit, nescio, quia *ascendit super cherubin*,[111] *id est, ascensio eius "omnem modum sciencie excedit,"* ut dicit ibi *Glossa.*[112] Uidetur tamen quod uirtute deitatis; sic *qui ascendit super celum celi ad orientem*,[113] *Glossa*: "Oriens intel-

106. See Jn 14:3; Mt 24:28; and Mi 2:13.

107. See Aristotle, *De caelo* 4.6 (313b17–22).

108. For the doctrine that the void has no independent existence and therefore that movement through it is impossible, see Aristotle, *Phys.* 4.8 (214b12–216a24).

109. Acts 1:10.

110. See Mt 14:25; Mk 6:48; and Jn 6:19.

111. Ps 17:11.

112. Peter Lombard, *Commentarium in Psalmos* 17.12 (PL 191,190).

113. Ps 67:34.

ligitur Uerbum a Patre genitum, cuius uirtute ascendit."[114] Sed an uirtute anime et grauis interdum est, nec certum inuenio et ideo non dico.

§59. Utrum etiam ascendit motu processiue, nescio nec de hoc aliquid fixum inuenio. Nec necesse fuit solidari aerem, cum Christi corpus non habeat grauitatem.

§60. Sed qua ascendit? Uidetur quod per occidentem; Ps.: *Qui super occasum*.[115]

§61. Item, uidetur quod per orientem; Ps.: *Qui ascendit super celum celi ad orientem*.[116]

§62. Solutio. *Ascendit super occasum*,[117] id est, "mortem corporis quam resurgendo uicit."[118] Et ita fit hic mencio de resurrectione, non de ascensione." "'Ad orientem' uel 'ab oriente'; alia littera locum exprimit ubi resurrexit et unde ascendit, quia Ierusalem, ubi hec facta sunt, est in oriente. Uel 'ad orientem,' id est, ut lumen gratie nobis oriri faceret."[119] Uel quia ascendit uerso uultu ad orientem—quod nescio, licet uideatur Damascenus hoc dicere.[120] Uel ad litteram, quia terra promissionis est media habitabilis nostre—maxime Ierusalem in medio quarti climatis sita tenet[k] capitum.[121] Ibi est medius punctus inter orientem habitabilis nostre et occidentem. Et quando sol transit per meridionalem circulum illum, necessario occidit sol existentibus in puncto orientali et oritur existentibus in puncto occidentali. Et ita cum directe ad illud tendit[l] <et> ascendit, ascendit ad orientem et occidentem.

[a] bene MS.

[b] augustinus MS.

[c] bene MS.

[d] infona MS.

[e] coniucta MS.; this spelling occurs regularly.

[f] an MS.

[g] The scribe seems to have written *subdividitur*, then corrected it by expunction to *subditur*.

[h] spiritum MS.

[i] uiathicum MS.

[j] utique MS.

[k] ueritatis MS.

[l] ante MS.

[m] nobilius et mobilius: nobilior et mobilior MS; an example of perseveration (see "inpotencior … potencior" above).

[n] anima MS.

114. Peter Lombard, *Comm.* 67.36 (PL 191,618).

115. Ps 67:5.

116. Ps 67:34.

117. Ps 67:5.

118. Peter Lombard, *Comm.* 67.4 (PL 191,603).

119. Ibid.

120. John Damascene., *De fide orthodoxa* 85.2, trans. Burgundio, ed. Buytaert, 305–6.

121. For an example of the sort of geography which is framing Fishacre's thinking here, see Honorius of Autun, *De imagine mundi* 1.6 (PL 172,122–23).

[o] gloriosus MS.

[p] quare non: qualiter omnino MS.

[q] choerenciam MS.

[r] nobilissimus MS.

[s] nam MS.

[t] uno MS.

[u] concedente MS.

[v] torum MS.

[w] glaria MS. (possibly an error of oral transmission).

[x] dampnari MS.

[y] ignibus; this spelling is by far the more common.

[z] infinco MS.

[aa] secundum materiam et supra materiam MS.

[bb] cui MS (an error of oral transmission).

[cc] incompossibilem MS.

[dd] informare MS.

[ee] uoluit MS.

[ff] illud: illum linum MS.

[gg] ornans MS.

[hh] indicas MS

[ii] suppremum MS.

[jj] post MS.

[kk] sic MS.

[ll] autoribus MS.

[mm] *fort.* illuc *legendum est.*

[nn] natura MS.

[oo] achomo MS.

[pp] subtilitas MS. (Possibly an error of perseveration).

[qq] magus MS.

[rr] opagum MS.

[ss] stellas MS.

[tt] docis MS.

[uu] ca MS.

[vv] i.e., the "vault" (of the heavens); *forsitan* celum *legendum est.*

[ww] *forsitan* uniuersum *legendum est.*

[xx] in hora MS.

[yy] sic MS.

[zz] ascendit MS.

[a] sicum MS.

[b] *forsitan* magis *legendum est.*

[c] literally "pineal" or "shaped like a pine cone."

[d] oratio MS.

[e] f_n (?) MS.

[f] quia MS.

[g] ascendenti MS.

[h] decensu MS.

[i] c_ (?) MS.

[j] *forsitan* quod *legendum est.*

[k] tenit MS.

[l] tenit MS.

CHAPTER 15

Richard Fishacre's *"Super S. Augustini librum de haeresibus adnotationes"*

At the end of a Vatican codex containing an incomplete copy of Richard Fishacre's *Sentences* Commentary is an anonymous scholastic treatise on heresies, which purports to provide rational arguments both for and against the ninety heresies listed and described by St. Augustine in his *De haeresibus*. The work is followed without a break by Fishacre's *quaestio* on the Ascension of Christ.[1]

On several counts I feel confident in ascribing the treatise on heresies to Fishacre as well. The Oxford Dominican was not credited with such a treatise by any medieval or early modern bibliographer.[2] However, there occurs the following marginal note in a manuscript of the aforementioned *Sentences* Commentary: "Hic

1. See my edition, "Richard Fishacre's *Quaestio* on the Ascension of Christ: An Edition," *MS* 40 (1978): 30–55 (see chapter 14).

2. The last bibliographer to have mentioned the work was Thomas Käppeli, OP, who listed it as "anon., Richardi?" *Scriptores Ordinis Praedicatorum Medii Aevi* (Rome: S. Sabina, 1980), 3:305.

deest questio de eternitate uel increacione mundi, que scripta est una cum questione de luce in parvo volumine ante questionem de heresibus."[3]

Furthermore, the fact that the treatise on heresies is sandwiched between two authenticated works by Fishacre in the Vatican codex, though circumstantial, nevertheless affords additional supporting evidence of his authorship. Thirdly, there is the unmistakable Fishacrean style.[4] Both the hesitancy to commit to a position (*nec asserere presumo; asserere non audeo*; *non assero tamen*) and the frequency of the shibboleth *fateor* are characteristic of Fishacre.

Lastly, and most convincingly, there are several pieces of internal evidence. In discussing whether a number of ideas might be repugnant to the divine simplicity, Fishacre answers in the negative and adds: *sicut alias poterit patere*.[5] And indeed we find in book 2, distinction 7, chapters 8 and 9 of the *Sentences* Commentary a "fuller discussion" of this issue, namely the efficacy of secondary causes. Finally, there are at least six passages to which close parallels are to be found in the *Sentences* Commentary, five of these in distinction 47 of book 4.[6]

The parallel passages also lead one to conclude that Fishacre's *Adnotationes* was a magistral work, composed after the *Sentences* Commentary, completed in ca. 1245.[7] The work was completed

3. Cambridge, Gonville and Caius Coll. MS 329/410, fol. 170vb. See Franz Pelster, "Das Leben und die Schriften des Oxforder Dominikanerlehrers Richard Fishacre († 1248)," *ZKT* 54 (1930): 529, who first called attention to this note.

4. See Joseph Goering and R. James Long, "Richard Fishacre's Treatise *De fide, spe, et caritate*," *Bulletin de philosophie médiévale* 31 (1989): 106; R. James Long, "Richard Fishacre and the Problem of the Soul," *TMS* 52 (1975): 265–66; and Long, "Ascension of Christ," 31–32.

5. R. James Long, "Richard Fishacre's *Super S. Augustini librum de haeresibus adnotationes:* An Edition and Commentary," *AHDLMA* 60 (1993): 229, lines 32–33.

6. See text notes 46, 47, 48, 52, 53, and 55.

7. See R. James Long and Maura O'Carroll, SND, *The Life and Works of Richard Fishacre, OP. Prolegomena to the Edition of his Commentary on the "Sentences"* (Munich: Verlag der Bayerischen Akademie der Wissenschaften, 1999), 41.

within the three years before Fishacre's death in 1248. Indeed it is quite possible that the writing of the work was interrupted by his final illness.

The point of departure for Fishacre's treatise, as stated above, is Augustine's *De haeresibus*, itself little more than a catalogue of the heresies from the first Christian century to his own time.[8] A mere "potboiler" extracted from Augustine by the deacon Quodvultdeus,[9] the work achieved considerable popularity in the High Middle Ages, a fact attested to by the significant number of manuscripts of the twelfth and thirteenth centuries.[10]

Augustine's handbook aimed at the instruction of the clergy and the laity, giving a simple exposition of the errors of the heretics and the contrary teachings of the church.[11] Fishacre's *Adnotationes* ("annotations"), however, was a scholastic disputation, the aim of which was persuasion and the means, rational arguments.

Claiming that Augustine did not present "reasons" either for or against the heresies he enumerated, Fishacre asserts that he will attempt just that, that is, for each of the heresies in order he will give the heretics' reasons and the reasons of the Catholics against them.[12] In fact, of the ninety heresies in Augustine's work, Fishacre responds only to the first six, leading scholars to con-

8. In the tradition of Justin Martyr and Irenaeus, the immediate sources for Augustine's brief handbook were Epiphanius of Salamis, who wrote in Greek, and the Latin author Filatrius of Brescia: see Ligouri G. Müller, *The "De Haeresibus" of Saint Augustine. A Translation with an Introduction and Commentary* (Washington, D.C.: The Catholic University of America Press, 1956), 22–30. After attempting to find a Greek translator for a short synopsis of Epiphanius's voluminous *Panarion*, Augustine finally consented to translate the work himself: see Pierre Courcelle, *Late Latin Writers and Their Greek Sources*, trans. H. E. Wedeck (Cambridge, Mass.: Harvard University Press, 1969), 206–7.

9. The characterization is Peter Brown's (*Augustine of Hippo* [Berkeley: University of California Press, 1969], 412).

10. According to the editors of the text for the *Corpus Christianorum* some forty manuscripts can be dated to these two centuries; *Aurelii Augustini opera*, pars XIII,2, in CCSL, 46: xxviii–xxx.

11. Müller, *The "De Haeresibus" of Saint Augustine*, 7–8.

12. Long, "Fishacre's *adnotationes*," 222.

clude that the work is incomplete.[13] The abruptness with which the treatise leaves off, moreover, lends further weight to the view either that Fishacre never finished the treatise or, at the very least, that the scribe of the Vatican manuscript did not have a complete copy text.

The first heresy in Augustine's listing (and the earliest heresy of the Christian Church) was that of Simon Magus.[14] The Simonians (*Symoniani*) receive from Fishacre more attention than any of the others, the focus being on three of their teachings: that God did not make the world; that there is no resurrection of the body; and that free love (literally, the "common use of women") was licit.[15]

With respect to the Simonian claim that God did not make the world, there are two positions, says Fishacre: either the world was not made or that it was made by another than God (by an angel, for example, or even a devil). Against the first position, following arguments from the authority of scripture, Fishacre arrays some eighteen arguments, some demonstrable, some merely rhetorical. For example, Fishacre says that every man proceeded by generation from a prior man, otherwise there would be a first man, which is contrary to the hypothesis. But if every man is made, so too is every ass and ox and every noble part of the world. But living things are nobler than nonliving. Therefore, if living things were all made, so too was the world.[16]

Having demonstrated that the world was made, Fishacre's next move is to prove that it was made by God. After rehearsing arguments on behalf of the heretic, Fishacre concedes neither that

13. See Pelster, "Das Leben und die Schriften," 531, and William A. Hinnebusch, *The Early English Friars Preachers,* Dissertationes historicae 14 (Rome: S. Sabina, 1951), 365.

14. In fact, the relation of Simon Magus to the Simonians is one of the complicated questions of church history; see Müller, *The "De Haeresibus" of Saint Augustine,* 135.

15. For their teachings, see ibid., 134–35.

16. Long, "Fishacre's *adnotationes,*" 213.

angels created the world nor that they generated it as offspring nor even drew forth its first individuals from potency to act. With respect to the last position, Fishacre allows that it is a serious question (*gravis questio est*), because in fact Augustine seems to think that angels and other creatures can provide "occasions and opportunities" for the educing of forms; nevertheless they cannot themselves truly draw them forth. Fishacre hesitates—characteristically—to assert this, leaving the matter to a fuller discussion elsewhere, namely, in the *Sentences* Commentary.[17]

Regarding the second of the heretical teachings ascribed to Simon, that there is no resurrection of bodies, Fishacre delineates three different positions: that if human souls perish with the death of the body (like bovine souls), there is therefore no hope of resurrection for the body; that souls revolve in the heavens until such time as one should sin and then be consigned to a body as to a prison and that therefore the incarnate state is not the best state for the soul; and that bodies are terrestrial and therefore cannot remain in the heavens with their respective souls.

Postponing a discussion of the immortality of the rational soul, Fishacre musters against the apodasis of the first proposition twelve arguments of his own, in addition to the arguments of St. Paul, in favor of the resurrection of bodies. Without fully penetrating the Aristotelian metaphysics of the soul-body composite, Fishacre nevertheless argues in general that the human soul has "affection" for the body, and indeed for a particular body, and is incomplete without it.[18] For example: matter responds or

17. Ibid., 229.

18. In the *Sentences* Commentary Fishacre had raised the question as to whether this affection for the body constituted a specific difference between humans and angels. After some hesitation, he finally decided in the negative; *In 2 Sent.* 2.3, ed. Long, 1:64. Indeed, in the same distinction he quotes with approval Augustine's statement that the rational soul and the angel are equal with respect to their natures (though unequal with respect to their offices); but to be equal in nature is to have the same ultimate constitutive difference—that is, to belong to the same species; ibid., 63. We are very far here from Aristotle's view of the soul.

answers to (*respondet*) its proper form; since the rational soul is perpetual and since it is the proper form of the body, the body too will be perpetual. Also: some actions are proper to the soul alone, such as understanding; some to the body alone, such as falling when released from a height; still others to the body and soul conjoined, such as grieving, rejoicing, weaving, and building. But these actions of the composite can be meritorious or blameworthy, for which there is either reward or punishment. Since the composite, and not simply the soul, is worthy of reward, therefore there will be a resurrection of the body.[19]

There are, however, arguments for the heretical position, the first among them being that death is the privation of life and that, just as there is no retreat from privation to habit, neither is there a turning back from death to life. Therefore, there is no resurrection. This "turning back," responds Fishacre, does not take place naturally, but miraculously, as blindness to sightedness.[20]

To the third heretical position, that it is impossible for earthly bodies to dwell in heaven, Fishacre argues that either the terrestrial body is deprived of heaviness or else it is able to dwell on high, its heaviness remaining. The first possibility Fishacre argues at some length, marshaling eighteen arguments in all to the point that God can deprive a body of heaviness just as he can deprive light of the property of burning (a power Plato also had attributed to the gods).[21] Many of these arguments the Dominican master recycled from the obviously parallel issue of his question on the Ascension of Christ.[22]

That a body can be held outside of its natural place by the power of God is obvious; notwithstanding, Fishacre offers a number of rhetorical arguments to that end: for example, if by the work of nature water is suspended in the clouds above the air

19. Long, "Fishacre's *adnotationes*," 923.

20. Ibid., 233.

21. Ibid., 234–37.

22. See Long, "Ascension of Christ," 49–52.

(that is, outside of the natural place of water), how could it not be the case that by the work of the creator of nature the human body could dwell above the heavens? That a body can be held outside of its natural place by the power of the soul as well is less obvious, and Fishacre's considerations here are less convincing. If, for example, the earthly body can hold here below souls that are celestial by nature, why cannot the soul at some point retain the earthly body above, that is, in the heavens? And if an angel can be with a corruptible body, not united to it but assumed, wherever it wills, why cannot the soul be with a body that is united to it wherever it wills?[23]

For the heretic on this point Fishacre cites the authority of John Damascene (a passage which seems to suggest that bodily resurrection was limited to Christ) and then articulates seven arguments, to each of which he then responds.[24]

Returning to the second of the three Simonian positions, namely that souls have sinned in heaven and are thus temporarily committed to a body as to a prison, Fishacre summarizes the difference between our faith and the perfidy of Simon (*nostram fidem et Symonis perfidiam*) thus: that we say that the soul is naturally able to be united with body but in the Simonian view is united as a result of the fall. The latter will be proven false on two counts: by showing that the soul is not in the body violently as one would be in prison and by showing that it did not sin in heaven before it entered the body.[25]

On behalf of the first claim, that the soul is in the body naturally and not violently, Fishacre finds sixteen arguments, three of them virtually identical with arguments he posed earlier on behalf of the body's resurrection. Of the new arguments one of the most novel is an application of medieval spirit theory. Taking its origins from Galen's medicine, the theory responded to a felt

23. Ibid., 237–40.

24. Ibid., 242–43.

25. Ibid., 243–44.

need in Platonic psychology for a medium between the soul, an independent, immaterial substance, and the body. "Spirits," though belonging to the genus "body," were nevertheless the subtlest of bodies and helped explain interaction with the soul.[26] Fishacre's immediate source for the doctrine was undoubtedly the *De motu cordis* of his fellow countryman, Alfred of Shareshill.[27]

If the soul is not naturally able to be united to the body, says Fishacre, it is not bound to the body by its nature; therefore, it is bound through some other mediate nature which is either body or spirit. If that "mediate nature" itself be a body, we are left with the same problem: according to the classic "third man" argument, soul cannot be united with the latter body except through the mediation of yet another, and so on *in infinitum*. If the mediate nature be a spirit, then although that spirit be united to the body, it will be so either violently—and then it demands still another medium, and so forth *in infinitum*—or naturally, and then the soul will be united to that spirit violently. And so on, *ad absurdum*.[28]

In another argument, Fishacre speaks of the seven "simples," namely the four elements and the three spirits, which he terms —curiously—the vegetable, sensible, and rational.[29] Since these simples are all natural, so too will be anything composed of them. Thus, those things composed of the four elements comprise the

26. Ibid., 244–46.

27. See Clemens Baeumker, "Des Alfred von Sareshel (Alfredus Anglicus) Schrift *De motu cordis*," *Beiträge* 23.1–2 (Münster i. W.: Aschendorff, 1923); see also James J. Bono, "Medical Spirits and the Medieval Language of Life," *Traditio* 40 (1984): 91–130.

28. Long, "Fishacre's *adnotationes*," 244.

29. One plausible explanation for his use of the term "spirit" rather than "form" is that he is restricting himself in this context to the corporeal, the genus common to the elements and the spirits, which are bodies. There is also some warrant in the tradition for this terminology. Costa ben Luca, author of the *De differentia spiritus et animae*, speaks of certain "*virtutes animae*," specifically the vegetative, sensible and rational. The operations of the soul in the body are related to these powers, which in turn depend upon the constitution and operations of the spirits in the body, which he calls "secondary causes." See Bono, "Medical Spirits and Medieval Language," 96n17.

mineral class, the four elements and the "vegetable spirit" the plants, and so forth. Human beings are composed of all seven simples and therefore constitute a single natural species, the union of which components is not violent but natural. If not, the universe would lack the ultimate and completing species.[30]

Against the second claim, namely, that souls sinned in heaven before entering bodies, Fishacre musters a dozen arguments. His first argument is perhaps the strongest: without the human species the universe would be incomplete; but the body-soul composite would not come about except through the sin of the soul; therefore (absurdly) the completion of the universe is contingent upon sin. In addition (also absurdly), it would be better to spill one's seed on the ground rather than in the womb and more pious to procure sterilizing poisons, lest prisons be generated for new souls, which would be a source of torment for the parents.[31]

Supporting both of the aforesaid heretical positions, Fishacre uncovers seven arguments. The three arguments claiming that the soul is in the body naturally are all recycled from the part of the treatise where Fishacre argues against the resurrection of the body. Clearly Fishacre is not expending an excess of energy in constructing a case for the heretic.[32]

The last Simonian heresy to be disposed of is their view that free love—including fornication, adultery, and incest—is licit. Against this teaching Fishacre amasses, in addition to scripture, the largest number of arguments, twenty-nine in all.[33] Marriage first of all is a sacrament, the sign of the unity of Christ and his church. Adultery is a violation of this sacred symbol. But according to Roman law, to desecrate the royal standard is a capital crime. How much more serious is this offense![34]

No man, moreover, is willing to share his wife, and this uni-

30. Long, "Fishacre's *adnotationes*," 244.

31. Ibid.

32. Ibid., 248–49.

33. Ibid., 250–53.

34. Ibid., 250.

versal unwillingness is natural and indeed is part of the natural law. Therefore, this article of Simon's teaching is contrary to natural law. In fact, adds Fishacre, Simon seems not to have been willing to share his own woman, a prostitute by the name of Helena (whom he called Minerva, according to Augustine's account).[35]

Marriage between close relatives is forbidden by divine law, furthermore, because it is expeditious to love more people rather than fewer. Carnal intercourse is a powerful cause of this love as is the bond of consanguinity. Therefore, carnal love should be had with one with whom we are not already tied by blood.[36]

In addition, the primary end of sexual intercourse is the generation of offspring. But if the free use of women were permitted, women would be rendered sterile as rather frequently happened among prostitutes. There are finally several agrarian arguments: if feudal law forbids occupying land cultivated and sown by another, how much more so the uterus.[37] And so forth.

Fishacre ventures the opinion that Simon posited free love in order to gain followers, and that the root of this position is nothing more than vile pleasure. But there is a clear inconsistency here, says Fishacre. According to the Simonians, the soul is in the body for punishment. Thus, to seek pleasure from the prison is to make of it a nonprison and to resist the divine justice, which condemned the sinful soul to prison.[38]

Even here Fishacre finds arguments on behalf of the heretical positions, in fact five in all. There is first the well-worn example of Abraham and his relations with Hagar. This was by any other name fornication and adultery; yet since Abraham did them, they were not illicit. Sexual intercourse, moreover, is a natural act and not only not simply a concession, but indeed also a command

35. Justin Martyr is the earliest source of this story; see Müller, *The "De Haeresibus" of Saint Augustine,* 135. See Long, "Fishacre's *adnotationes,*" 251.

36. Long, "Fishacre's *adnotationes,*" 251.

37. Ibid.

38. Ibid., 253.

("Increase and multiply," Gn 1:28). Also Cain and Abel took their sisters to wife, and therefore incest was not illicit.[39]

Fishacre replies that Abraham's carnal knowledge of Hagar was by divine dispensation and no man can grant dispensations in these matters. Furthermore, sexual intercourse after the concupiscence acquired as a result of the sin of our first parents is about as natural as food suffused with poison. As limping is to walking, moreover, so in our present state is sexual intercourse to the same act before the Fall. It was a precept initially only until such time as mortals would have multiplied sufficiently; now it is a concession owing to the infirmity of the flesh, always within the limits of monogamous matrimony. The divine counsel, however, insists the celibate friar, was to celibate continence.[40]

The second heresy in Augustine's ordering is that of the Menandrians, after Menander, a disciple of Simon's.[41] Menander claimed that the world was not made by God but by angels. Fishacre, however, considers this particular spin on Simon's heresy to have been sufficiently refuted in his remarks above.[42]

He therefore passes on to the third heresy, that of the Saturninians, named for a certain Saturninus, who was responsible for having spread to Syria the Simonian doctrine of free love; he also posited that seven angels made the world, and without God's awareness.[43] Both of these teachings, Fishacre thinks, have also been adequately dealt with.[44] However, the claim that the world was made without God's foreknowledge or indeed that anything could be hidden from God captures his attention. Scriptural testimony seems at times to confirm this view, but there are both scriptural arguments as well as rational arguments opposed to it.[45]

39. Ibid., 254.
40. Ibid., 255.
41. See Müller, *The "De Haeresibus" of Saint Augustine* 135.
42. Long, "Fishacre's *adnotationes*," 255.
43. Müller, *The "De Haeresibus" of Saint Augustine,* 135–36.
44. Long, "Fishacre's *adnotationes*," 255.
45. Ibid., 256.

Aristotle says that we judge that we know something when we know the causes of that thing. He, therefore, who knows the first cause of all knows all in a most excellent manner. But God knows himself. Therefore, and so forth.[46] Furthermore, if God is something than which nothing greater can be thought (borrowing St. Anselm's formula), and to know all things is greater than to know only some things, therefore all things are known to God.[47] To these Fishacre adds another six arguments.

For the Saturninian he finds two arguments. First, we are ignorant of many things in our minor world, our microcosm. Were this not the case we would not consult physicians to learn of our inner disposition via urinalysis but would instead consult them only for a cure. Why is it also not the case that God is ignorant of many things in the macrocosm? Secondly, the knowledge of God is twofold: simple knowledge, by which he knows all things, and the knowledge of approbation, by which he knows the good. But since God is the agent or at least the coagent of every act, he knows with the knowledge of approbation everything that is done. He therefore approves of sin.[48] This *reductio ad absurdum* is aimed at establishing that there are some things of which God is ignorant.

To the first argument Fishacre simply denies parity: the soul does not create itself as God creates the world. The response to the second involves a distinction: action God knows by the knowledge of approbation, although Fishacre is aware that others feel differently; deformity, on the other hand, God knows only through simple knowledge so that he can be the avenger of that of which he is not the author.[49]

The fourth heresy is that of the *Basiliani*, named for Basilides, a Gnostic of the second century.[50] The followers of Basi-

46. Ibid.

47. Ibid., 256–57.

48. Ibid., 258.

49. Ibid.

50. Müller, *The "De Haeresibus" of Saint Augustine*, 136.

lides agree in all things with the Simonians, except they add that there are 360 heavens. The latter view is not, however, heretical, thinks Fishacre, and the determination of its truth he leaves to the natural philosophers, who have thus far reached no certitude in these matters.[51]

The fifth heresy is that of the Nicolaites, named for the deacon Nicholas and mentioned in the Apocalypse.[52] Nicholas, like Simon, was a libertine, who offered his own beautiful wife for the enjoyment of anyone who wanted her, and in addition ate food offered to idols. Since he had already offered sufficient refutation of libertinism, Fishacre here concentrates his attention on the issue of idolatry, specifically the consuming of food offered to pagan idols.[53]

Subsumed under the rubric of idolatry are two questions: first, whether it is licit to show *latria* to an idol; secondly, whether it is licit in order to save one's life to venerate idols by word only and not from the heart. Fishacre answers the first question in the negative and finds six arguments for his view. The five arguments he gathers for the licitness of offering *latria* to creatures, and hence to idols, all hinge on the similarity of creatures to God. So similar are we that we begin existence as an idea in the divine mind. Our similarity to God is greater, in fact, than a statue of Christ is to Christ the God-man who was crucified. But if honor is shown the statue of Christ, how much more licit is it to honor the creature, and hence an idol.[54]

Furthermore, even if it were a fault to practice *latria* in the heart toward an idol, it would not be a fault to do so externally, because divine veneration is solely mental. If God is a spirit, as John says in his Gospel, and he is to be worshiped in the spirit,

51. Long, "Fishacre's *adnotationes,*" 258.

52. Apoc 2:6. See Müller, *The "De Haeresibus" of Saint Augustine,* 137.

53. Long, "Fishacre's *adnotationes,*" 258–59.

54. Ibid., 259–60.

we detract nothing from him by venerating idols externally in the body.[55] To this same point Fishacre constructs the following case: take note first that there are many Manichees who say that it is illicit to eat meat. On this particular occasion there is present a weak Catholic who will be scandalized if you eat food that has been offered to idols. The question is: should you in this case eat the illicit meat? Yes, answers Fishacre, because by not eating it you confirm many Manichees in their error, even though by eating it you scandalize a single Catholic.[56]

Furthermore, in reply to the above objection Fishacre argues that it is not similarity that causes us to venerate the statue of Christ; the cause is rather that the statue is a sign signifying Christ, and it is to Christ that we pay *hyperdulia*. Though the creature is similar to God, it was not instituted as a sign and therefore veneration paid to it does not pass to God.[57]

But the heretic will say that in the scriptures fire, light, and a dove are made to signify God; is it therefore licit to worship these? To this Fishacre replies that signs are instituted for different ends: solely that the thing signified be understood; or that the thing signified also be venerated or even detested (as in a picture of Judas hanging). Since those names and objects in scripture were instituted for the sole purpose of signifying, that is, making known the divine reality, whoever shows *latria* toward it is guilty of idolatry. One can also say the same about tongues of fire and the dove—though Fishacre is not certain enough to make any assertions—insofar as they do not remain as such, but are immediately reduced to their matter.[58]

Regarding the giving of scandal to the infirm Catholic, Fishacre reverses his earlier position and says now that we owe more to the infirm believer than we do to many Manichees. Lest the weak think that by eating food we are worshiping idols, we should

55. Ibid., 261.
56. Ibid., 262.
57. Ibid., 260.
58. Ibid., 263–64.

refrain from eating. We are, he says, more bound to the one infirm believer than to many unfaithful Manichees, and it is worse that a person be turned and sin than that sinners should persist in their sin.[59]

The sixth heresy in Fishacre's catalog, and the final one in the extant fragment, is Gnosticism, also called Borboritism.[60] Augustine attributed two heretical teachings to the Borborites: that the soul is of divine substance, which would constitute a form of pantheism; and that there is a good god and an evil god.[61]

Having rehearsed the scripture passages that seem to support the position of pantheism, Fishacre finds a total of eighteen arguments against it. One of the arguments makes use of the Socratic paradox, "I know only that I do not know." Ignorance, however, cannot be attributed to God, not even the incarnate God.[62]

But what if the heretic should offer this analogy: just as light is from the substance of the sun without the sun's being diminished, so also are souls from God's substance. In addition, God can bring it about that the substance of the bread passes into the substance of his own body without his body suffering increase. In similar fashion, it seems that he is able to make souls from his substance without its diminution. To these arguments, moreover, Fishacre adds an additional five on behalf of the pantheist, then answers them all in turn.[63]

The analogy of the radiation of light from the sun being like the emanation of souls from God is without parity, responds Fishacre: what is a perfection for the sun, for God is an imperfection, because every mutation and transmutation is alien to the

59. Ibid., 265.

60. Named from the Greek word for slime or mud, the Borborites were an antinomian sect of Ophitic Gnostics, who flourished from the second to the fifth centuries. Augustine—and Fishacre—are wrong in ascribing the characteristics of this subset to all Gnostics. See Müller, *The "De Haeresibus" of Saint Augustine*, 138

61. Long, "Fishacre's *adnotationes*," 266–67

62. Ibid., 267–71.

63. Ibid., 271–72.

divine perfection. In addition, while God has power over bodies, so that he can transform the body of Christ into bread, he has no power over his own substance, because his power and substance are identical, and nothing has power over the deity, nor does it suffer transmutation.[64]

As to the second heretical teaching of the Gnostics, that there is a good and an evil god, Fishacre reminds his readers that other heretics had also posited two principles: namely the Heracleonites[65] and the Apellites.[66] There were as well varieties of dualistic teachings, like that of the Cerdonians.[67] They taught that there was one good god, the father of Christ, and also another, neither good nor evil who was the giver of the Old Law; others taught that there was one good god and the other simply evil. The latter identifies the position of the Borborites or Gnostics and also the Manichees.[68]

As with the other heresies he dealt with, Fishacre finds arguments for the dualists' position. First the arguments from authority: seven scriptural passages appear to confirm the view that there is an evil god as well as a good god. When in the very beginning

64. Ibid., 272.

65. Named from Heracleon, a Valentinian Gnostic (ca. 145–180); his writings, which survive only in fragments, reveal a strong allegorizing tendency in his scripture commentaries. See Müller, *The "De haeresibus" of Saint Augustine*, 143.

66. Sect founded by a disciple of Marcion, Apelles, a long-time resident of Rome and an associate of a female visionary, Philumene, whose revelations he recorded; in opposition to Marcion, Apelles held that there was in fact only one principle and that Christ lived and died in a real body formed of cosmic matter. Like Marcion, however, he saw an absolute opposition between the Old and New Testaments and taught that the only thing necessary for salvation was hope in the crucified. See Müller, *The "De haeresibus" of Saint Augustine*, 147.

67. Cerdo was a Syrian Gnostic who lived at Rome ca. 140 where, having foresworn his errors, afterwards secretly professed them; in his teachings, the creator God of the law and the prophets was different from the father of Jesus; the former was the known and Just, the latter the unknown and Good. It is unclear whether he headed a distinct sect or whether his followers were early absorbed into the school of Marcion, who was said to have joined himself to Cerdo soon after coming to Rome. See ibid., 145–46.

68. Long, "Fishacre's *adnotationes*," 272.

of the book of Genesis, for example, it is written that God created the heavens and the earth and also that darkness covered the face of the earth, it is not written that God created the darkness. This darkness is the evil god.[69]

The strongest of the rational arguments adduced in the heretic's favor is provided by the problem of evil. If God is good, he cannot be the cause of evil. But there is evil in the world. Therefore, its cause is the evil god. Fishacre's response to this objection is out of the pages of Augustine. Evil is a privation, an absence of an owed good. Therefore, it needs not an efficient cause but rather a deficient cause.[70]

After answering the eight arguments offered in favor of dualism, Fishacre mobilizes his own reasons. At work's end he has amassed twenty-three arguments, most of which hinge on the absurdity of positing two supreme principles. For example, the two together would be greater than either the one or the other, so that neither the one nor the other would be supreme. Also, being is not opposed to being but to nonbeing. If, therefore, the good god is wholly being and the evil god is opposed to the good god, the evil god must totally not exist, or must in other words be nothing.[71]

The section at which the treatise breaks off argues as follows: "If sin is a nature, as they say, then when sin is committed by someone, it becomes some nature. This nature is either from something or from nothing. If from nothing, then it is created, and every sinner is a creator. If from something, from what? One cannot be assigned."[72] Thus, abruptly, ends the treatise.

What are we to make of Fishacre's "annotations" on Augustine's *De haeresibus*? At first glance it seems a curious work. At the same time that his brother preachers across the English Channel were actively combating the Albigensian heresy,[73] Fishacre was

69. Ibid., 272–73.
70. Ibid., 273–74.
71. Ibid., 277.
72. Ibid., 279.
73. See Bernard Hamilton, *The Medieval Inquisition* (New York: Holmes and Meier Publishers, 1981), 36.

engaged with heresies that were at least a millennium old.[74] Even granted the fact that the British Isles were virtually untainted by heresy in the thirteenth century,[75] Fishacre's ambitious and probably incomplete project seems oddly detached from the exigencies of his world.

On the other hand, Augustine's work on heresies was not, for the Christian of the thirteenth century, a dead letter. Its very popularity would argue that not a few saw in the work something relevant to their age. The reason is embodied in a remark of St. Bernard's to the effect that the heretics of his day were but the "heretics of old" come back to work their evil.[76] It is for this reason that patristic texts, like Augustine's, were seized upon with such eagerness. Augustine, in describing the heresies of the early Christian centuries, was also describing the new heresies, the Cathars and the Waldensians, which were in reality the old ones in new guises.[77]

74. The most recent heresy mentioned by Fishacre is the Manichean, which was founded in the third century and continued into Augustine's day. See Müller, *The "De haeresibus" of Saint Augustine*, 159–72.

75. Indeed, John R. H. Moorman posits this as one of the reasons for the "failure" of the Dominicans in England: "the Preaching Friars existed to combat heresy, but this country seems to have been one of the few places in Europe where heresy did not exist. In a way, the *raison d'être* of the Dominicans was taken from them the moment that they landed at Dover in 1221," *Church Life in England in the Thirteenth Century* (Cambridge: Cambridge University Press, 1945), 398. Aside from the shaky assumption that the Dominicans failed (they boasted forty-eight priories and more than 1,600 friars by the end of the thirteenth century), the Dominicans always regarded preaching as their foremost responsibility and inquisitorial activity as an *impedimentum*; see William A. Hinnebusch, *The History of the Dominican Order: Origins and Growth to 1500* (Staten Island, N.Y.: Alba House, 1966), 1:57–58.

76. "They are foxes and little ones. The points in which we allege they are mistaken are indefensible, and not so much subtle as plausible, and then only to peasant girls and imbeciles, such as are all I have met of this way of thinking. I do not recall having heard anything in all their many statements which made any contribution to knowledge, but only trite sayings well-aired by heretics of old, yet crushed and exploded by our theologians," *Sermon 65:8*, in Bernard of Clairvaux, *On the Song of Songs*, trans. Kilian Walsh and Irene M. Edmonds (Kalamazoo, Mich.: Cistercian Publications, 1979), 3:188.

77. Most obvious is the connection between the Manichees and their latter-day reemergence in the Cathars. A polemic of the time was even entitled *Liber contra*

Thus Fishacre, in converting the Bishop of Hippo's compendium into a full-fledged scholastic disputation, was addressing his contemporaries, his brothers on the continent, and his concern was as much with the Albigensians as with Simonians, the Borborites, and the rest. Indeed, it is quite possible that he may have intended his *Adnotationes* to be a kind of source book of arguments, both authorial and philosophical, for the use of the brothers in heresy-infected areas, just as Thomas Aquinas's *Summa contra gentiles* was meant for the brothers preaching against Muslims, Jews, and heretics in Spain, according to one tradition at least.[78]

Long before coercion became the order of the day, the friars assigned to inquisitorial duties aimed at *persuasio* "persuasion," largely through preaching the word of God.[79] Intimately connected with preaching, however, was disputation, the working out of the arguments to be employed against the enemies of the faith. In the period between 1235 and 1270, heresiological literature reached its apogee.[80] During this period we find in fact several treatises written by Dominicans: the *Summa* attributed to Peter Martyr (ca. 1235),[81] the *Adversus Catharos et Valdenses* of Moneta of Cre-

---

Manichaeos; see Antoine Dondaine, "Durand de Huesca et la polémique anti-Cathare," reprinted in *Les hérésies et l'Inquisition, xiie–xiiie siècles*, ed. Yves Dossat (Aldershot, UK: Variorum; Gower Publishing Co., 1990), 228–76. Moreover, although Fishacre's disputation stops well short of the section on the Manichees (the lengthiest in Augustine's compendium), he mentions the group by name a total of seven times. For the connection between the Cathars and other early heresies, see Jaroslav Pelikan, *The Growth of Medieval Theology (600–1300)*, vol. 3 of *The Christian Tradition: A History of the Development of Doctine* (Chicago: University of Chicago Press, 1978), 238–76.

78. See James A. Weisheipl, *Friar Thomas d'Aquino: His Life, Thought, and Works* (Washington, D.C.: The Catholic University of America Press, 1983), 359. However, Jean-Pierre Torrell, after reviewing the evidence, rejects the thesis as being without solid historical foundation: *Saint Thomas Aquinas, The Person and His Work*, trans. Robert Royal (Washington, D.C.: The Catholic University of America Press, 1996), 1:104–7.

79. Hinnebusch, *Dominican Order*, 57.

80. Edina Bozóky, *Le livre secret des Cathares: Interrogatio Iohannis* (Paris: Beauchesne, 1980), 197.

81. This work has been edited by Thomas Käppeli in *AFP* 17 (1947): 320–35.

mona (1241),[82] the *Summa de Catharis et Pauperibus de Lugduno* of Raynier Sacconi (1250),[83] and the *Tractatus de hereticis* of Anselm of Alexandria (1267–1270).[84] Fishacre's contribution was to have taken its place among these, had it ever circulated.

That Fishacre's *Adnotationes* did not circulate is inferred both from the absence of surviving copies other than the Vatican fragment and from the fact that it is cited by no contemporary writer. What it provides us with, nevertheless, is evidence of a powerful mind, enlisting the latest in scientific understandings and philosophical insights in the service of religious orthodoxy. It is an example of *persuasio* at its best and is one more argument for the inclusion of Richard Fishacre among the major scholastic theologians of the first half of the thirteenth century.

82. Moneta's treatise, "Venerabilis Patris Monetæ Cremonensis Ordinis Prædicatorum S.P. Dominico Æqualis Adversus Catharos et Valdenses libri quinque," was edited by Tommaso Agostino Ricchini (Rome: ex typografia Palladis, 1743; repr. Ridgewood, N.J.: Gregg Press, 1964). At 560 pages in the printed edition, this *summa* was by far the most imposing work on heresies produced by a Dominican during this period. See Georg Schmitz-Valckenberg, *Grundlehren katharischer Sekten des 13. Jahrhunderts. Eine theologische Untersuchung mit besonderer Berücksichtigung von "Adversus Catharos et Valdenses" des Moneta von Cremona* (Munich: Verlag Ferdinand Schöningh, 1981), for an exhaustive analysis of Moneta's work.

83. This treatise has been edited by Antoine Dondaine in *Une traité néo-Manichéen du XIIIe siècle, le Liber de duobus principiis* (Rome: Institutum Historicum, 1939), 64–78. See also Edward Peters, *Heresy and Authority in Medieval Europe* (Philadelphia: University of Pennsylvania Press, 1980), 125–32, for an English translation of part of the text.

84. This work has also been edited by Antoine Dondaine in *AFP* 20 (1950): 308–24. See also Marie-Humbert Vicaire, "Dominique et ses Précheurs," in *Studia Friburgensia*, n.s. 55 (Paris: Èditions du Cerf, 1979), 119–20.

Selected Bibliography

Bataillon, L. J. "Exemplar, Pecia, Quaternus." In *Vocabulaire du livre et de l'écriture au moyen âge*, edited by O. Weijers, 206–19. Turnhout: Brepols, 1989.

Biffi, Inos. "Figure della teologia medievale: tra scrittura e teologia o gli inizi della scuola domenicana a Oxford di Riccardo Fishacre." *Teologia* 14 (1989): 59–86.

———. *Figure medievali della teologia*. Milan: Jaca Book, 1992.

Boyle, Leonard. "Pastoral Training in the Time of Fishacre." *NB* 80 (1999): 345–53.

Brown, Stephen F. "Richard Fishacre on the Need for 'Philosophy.'" In *A Straight Path. Studies in Medieval Philosophy and Culture: Essays in Honor of Arthur Hyman*, edited by Ruth Link-Salinger, Jeremiah Hackett, Michael S. Hyman, R. James Long, and Charles H. Manekin, 23–36. Washington, D.C.: The Catholic University of America Press, 1988.

———. "The Eternity of the World Discussions at Early Oxford." In *Mensch und Natur im Mittelalter. MM* 21/1, edited by Albert Zimmermann and Andreas Speer. Berlin: De Gruyter, 1991.

———. "The Reception and Use of Aristotle's Works in the Commentaries on Book I of the *Sentences* by the Friars Preachers in the Early Years of Oxford University." In *Aristotle in Britain During the Middle Ages*, Proceedings of the international conference at Cambridge, 8–11 April 1994, edited by John Marenbon, 351–69. Turnhout: Brepols, 1996.

Callus, Daniel A. *Introduction of Aristotelian Learning to Oxford.* Reprint. London: H. Milford, 1944.

———. "The Origins of the Problem of the Unity of Form." In *The Dignity of Science: Studies in the Philosophy of Science Presented to William*

Humbert Kane, O.P., edited by James A. Weisheipl. Washington, D.C.: Thomist Press, 1961.

———. "Richard Fishacre." In *New Catholic Encyclopedia*, 12:479. New York City: McGraw-Hill, 1967.

Catto, J. I. "Theology and Theologians 1220–1320." In *The Early Oxford Schools*. vol. 1: *The History of the University of Oxford*, edited by T. H. Aston. Oxford: Clarendon Press, 1984.

Chatillon, J. "De Guillaume d'Auxerre à saint Thomas d'Aquin. L'argument de saint Anselme chex les premiers scholastiques du XIIIe siècle." *Spicilegium Beccense* (Paris: J. Vrin, 1959): 209–31.

Dales, Richard C. "The Influence of Grosseteste's *Hexaëmeron* on the *Sentences* Commentary of Richard Fishacre, O.P. and Richard Rufus of Cornwall, O.F.M." *Viator* 2 (1971): 271–300.

———. *The Scientific Achievement of the Middle Ages.* Philadelphia: University of Pennsylvania Press, 1973.

———. "Discussions of the Eternity of the World During the First Half of the Twelfth Century." *Speculum* 57 (1982): 495–508.

———. "Time and Eternity in the Thirteenth Century." *Journal of the History of Ideas* 49 (1988): 27–45.

———. *Medieval Discussions of the Eternity of the World*. Leiden: Brill, 1990.

———. *The Problem of the Rational Soul in the Thirteenth Century*. Leiden: Brill, 1995.

Davenport, Anne A. "The Catholics, the Cathars, and the Concept of Infinity in the Thirteenth Century." *Isis* 88 (1997): 263–95.

Ehrle, Fr. "L'agostinismo e l'aristotelismo nella scholastica del secolo XIII." *Xenia Thomistica* 3 (1925): 550–57.

Eichinger, Alexander. "Optics and the Knowledge of Christ in Richard Fishacre." In *Intellect and Imagination in Medieval Philosophy*, Actes du XIe Congrès International de Philosophie Médiévale de la S.I.E.P.M, vol. 2, edited by Maria Pacheco and José Meirinhos. Turnhout: Brepols, 2006.

Fishacre, Richard. *In secundum librum Sententiarum. Part 1: Prologue, Distinctions 1–20.* Edited by R. James Long. Band 24. Munich: Verlag der Bayerischen Akademie der Wissenschaften, 2008.

———. *In secundum librum Sententiarum. Part 2: Distinctions 21–44, Appendices, Additiones.* Edited by R. James Long, Band 25. Munich: Verlag der Bayerischen Akademie der Wissenschaften, 2011.

———. *In tertium librum Sententiarum. Part 1: Prologue, Distinctions 1–22.* Edited by Alexander Eichinger, Hans Kraml, and Gerhard Leibold. Band 26. Munich: Verlag der Bayerischen Akademie der Wissenschaften, 2011.

———. *In tertium librum Sententiarum. Part 2: Distinctions 23–40.* Edited by Klaus Rodler, Band 23. Munich: Verlag der Bayerischen Akademie der Wissenschaften, 2003.

Gerardus de Fracheto, *Vitae Fraturm Ordinis Praedicatorum.* Monumenta Ordinis Fratrum Praedicatorum Historica. Edited by B. M. Reichert. Louvain: E. Charpentier and J. Schoonjams. 1896. English translation: *Lives of the Brethren of the Order of Preachers 1206–1259.* Translated by Placid Conway. Edited by Bede Jarret. London: Burns, Oates & Washbourne, 1924.

Gillon, L. -B. "L'esprit 'partie' de l'univers: Autour d'un texte de Richard Fishacre." *Studi tomistici* 1 (1974): 210–22.

Ginther, James. "Theological Education at the Oxford Studium in the Thirteenth Century: A Reassessment of Robert Grosseteste's Letter to the Oxford Theologians." *FS* 55 (1998): 83–104.

Goering, Joseph, and R. James Long. "Richard Fishacre's Treatise *De fide, spe, et caritate.*" *Bulletin de philosophie médiévale* 31 (1989): 103–11.

Grant, Edward. *Physical Science in the Middle Ages.* New York: Wiley, 1971.

Grosseteste, Robert. *Hexaëmeron.* Edited by Richard C. Dales and Servus Gieben. Auctores Britannici Medii Aevi VI. Oxford: Oxford University Press, 1982.

Hinnebusch, William A. *The Early English Friars Preachers.* Dissertationes historicae 14. Rome: S. Sabina, 1951.

Jewett, Margaret, and R. James Long. "A Newly Discovered Witness of Fishacre's *Sentences* Commentary: University of Chicago MS 156." *Traditio* 50 (1995): 342–45.

Käppeli, Thomas. *Scriptores Ordinis Praedicatorum Medii Aevi.* Rome: Ad S. Sabinae 1980.

Lawrence, C. H. *The Friars. The Impact of the Early Mendicant Movement on Western Society.* London: Longman, 1994.

Lewis, Neil. "The First Recension of Robert Grosseteste's *De libero arbitrio.*" *MS* 53 (1991): 1–88.

Long, R. James. "The *Problem of the Soul* in Richard Fishacre's *Commentary on the Sentences.*" Ph.D. diss., University of Toronto, 1968.

———. "The Science of Theology according to Richard Fishacre: Edition of the Prologue to His *Commentary on the Sentences.*" *MS* 34 (1972): 71–98.

———. "Richard Fishacre and the Problem of the Soul." *TMS* 52 (1975): 263–70.

———. "Richard Fishacre's *Quaestio* on the Ascension of Christ: An Edition." *MS* 40 (1978): 30–55.

———. "The Virgin as Olive Tree: A Marian Sermon of Richard Fishacre and Science at Oxford." *AFP* 52 (1982): 77–87.

———. "Richard Fishacre." *Dictionnaire de Spiritualité* 13 (1987): cols. 563–65.

———. "Richard Fishacre's Way to God." In *A Straight Path: Studies in Medieval Philosophy and Culture; Essays in Honor of Arthur Hyman*, edited by Ruth Link-Salinger, et al., 174–82. Washington, D.C.: The Catholic University of America Press, 1988.

———. "The Moral and Spiritual Theology of Richard Fishacre: Edition of Trinity College MS O.1.30." *AFP* 60 (1990): 5–143.

———. "Richard Fishacre." In *Medieval Philosophers*, edited by Jeremiah Hackett. *Dictionary of Literary Biography*, vol. 115, 195–200. Detroit: Bruccoli Clark Layman, 1992.

———. "Richard Fishacre's *Super S. Augustini librum de haeresibus adnotationes*: An Edition and Commentary." *AHDLMA* 60 (1993): 207–79.

———. "Richard Fishacre's Treatise *De libero arbitrio.*" In *Moral and Political Philosophies in the Middle Ages*, Proceedings of the Ninth International Congress of Medieval Philosophy, edited by B. Carlos Bazán, Eduardo Andújar, Léonard Sbrocchi, 2: 879–91. Ottawa: Legas, 1995.

———. "The Reception and Use of Aristotle by the Early English Dominicans." In *Aristotle in Britain During the Middle Ages*, edited by John Marenbon. Turnhout: Brepols, 1996.

———. "Of Angels and Pinheads: The Contributions of the Early Oxford Masters to the Doctrine of Spiritual Matter." In *FS. Essays in Honor of Girard Etzkorn*, edited by Gordon A. Wilson and Timothy B. Noone, 56 (1998): 237–52.

———. "The First Oxford Debate on the Eternity of the World." *RTPM* 65/1 (1998): 54–98.

———. "The Role of Philosophy in Richard Fishacre's Theology of Creation." *MM* 26 (1998): 571–78.

———. "The Cosmic Christ: The Christology of Richard Fishacre, OP." In *Christ among the Medieval Dominicans. Representations of Christ in the Texts and Images of the Order of Preachers,* edited by Kent Emery and Joseph Wawrykow. Notre Dame, Ind.: University of Notre Dame Press, 1998.

———. "Richard Fishacre." *Lexikon für Theologie und Kirche* 8 (1999): 1171.

———. "The Integrative Theology of Richard Fishacre, OP." *NB* 80, nos. 941/42 (July/August 1999): 354–60.

———. "Aquinas and the Cosmic Christ." In *Medieval Masters. Essays in Memory of Msgr. E. A. Synan,* Thomistic Papers VII, edited by R. E. Houser, 233–48. Houston: Center for Thomistic Studies, 1999.

———. "On the Usefulness of 'Augustinianism' as a Historical Construct: Two Test Cases from Oxford." *Medieval Perspectives. Southeastern Medieval Association* 26 (2001): 74–83.

———. "The Significance of Richard Fishacre's *Sentences* Commentary." *Bochumer Philosophisches Jahrbuch für Antike und Mittelalter* 6 (2001): 213–16.

———. "The Beginning of a Tradition: The *Sentences* Commentary of Richard Fishacre, OP." In *Medieval Commentaries on the "Sentences" of Peter Lombard,* vol. 1: *Current Research,* edited by G. R. Evans. Leiden: Brill, 2002.

———. "Richard Fishacre." In *A Companion to Philosophy in the Middle Ages,* edited by Jorge J. E. Gracia and Timothy B. Noone. Oxford: Blackwell, 2003.

———. "Richard Fishacre." In *The Oxford Dictionary of National Biography.* Oxford: Oxford University Press, 2004.

———. "The Philosophy of Richard Fishacre." In *Albertus Magnus und die Anfänge der Aristoteles-Rezeption im lateinischen Mittelalter von Richardus Rufus bis zu Franciscus de Mayronis,* Subsidia Albertina I, edited by Ludger Honnefelder, et al. Münster i. W.: Aschendorff, 2005.

———. "Interiority and Self-Knowledge according to Richard Fishacre." In *Intellect and Imagination in Medieval Philosophy,* Actes du XIe Congrès International de Philosophie Médiévale de la S.I.E.P.M., Recontres de philosophie médiévale 11, edited by M. C. Pacheco and J. F. Meirinhos. Turnhout: Brepols, 2006.

———. "Undoing the Past. Fishacre and Rufus on the Limits of God's Power." In *Laudemus viros gloriosos. Essays in Honor of Armand Maurer,*

C.S.B., edited by R. E. Houser, 60–74. Notre Dame, Ind.: University of Notre Dame Press, 2007.

———. "Lying with Hagar: The Role of Natural Philosophy in the Theology of Richard Fishacre." *TMS* 86 (November 2008): 47–64.

———. "The Division of the Waters (Gn 1, 6–7): The History of a Conundrum and Its Resolution by the Early Oxford Masters." In *Philosophy and Theology in the Long Middle Ages: A Tribute to Stephen F. Brown*, edited by Kent Emery, Russell Friedman, and Andreas Speer, 41–62. Leiden: Brill, 2011.

———. "Richard Fishacre." In *Encyclopedia of Medieval Philosophy*, edited by Henrik Lagerlund. London: Springer, 2011.

———. "Between Idolatry and Science: The Magical Arts in the Grosseteste School." In *Robert Grosseteste, His Thought and Its Impact*, Papers in Mediaeval Studies 21, edited by Jack P. Cunningham, 167–97. Toronto: Pontifical Institute of Mediaeval Studies, 2012.

———. "Adam's Rib. A Test Case for Natural Philosophy in Grosseteste, Fishacre, Rufus, and Kilwardby." In *Robert Grosseteste and His Intellectual Milieu. New Editions and Studies*, Papers in Medieval Studies 24, edited by John Flood, James R. Ginther, and Joseph W. Goering, 153–64. Toronto: Pontifical Institute of Mediaeval Studies, 2013.

Long, R. James, and Timothy B. Noone. "Fishacre and Rufus on the Metaphysics of Light: Two Unedited Texts." In *Roma, magistra mundi. Itineraria culturae medievalis. Mélanges offerts au Père L.E. Boyle à l'occasion de son 75e anniversaire*, edited by Jacqueline Hamesse. Textes et Études du moyen âge. Louvain-la-Neuve: Fédération Internationale des Instituts d'Études Médiévales, 1998.

Long, R. James, and Maura O'Carroll, SND. *The Life and Works of Richard Fishacre OP. Prolegomena to the Edition of his Commentary on the "Sentences."* Band 21. Munich: Verlag der Bayerischen Akademie der Wissenschaften, 1999.

Lottin, Odon. *La théorie du libre arbitre depuis S. Anselme jusqu'à S. Thomas d'Aquin.* Saint-Maximin: École de Théologie, 1929.

———. "La composition hylémorphique des substances spirituelles; les dèbuts de la contraverse." *RNSP* 34 (1932): 21–41.

———. "La notion du libre arbitre dans la jeune école dominicaine d'Oxford." *RSPT* 24 (1935): 268–83.

Martin, R. M. "Quelques 'premiers' maîtres dominicains de Paris et d'Oxford et la soi-disant école dominicaine augustinienne." *RSPT* 19 (1920): 556–80.

———. "La question de l'unité de la forme substantielle dans le premier collège dominicain à Oxford." *RNSP* 22 (1920): 107–12.

McEvoy, James. *The Philosophy of Robert Grosseteste.* 2nd ed. Oxford: Clarendon Press, 1982.

———. *Gli inizi di Oxford. Grossatesta e i primi teologi (1150–1250).* Milan: Jaca Book, 1996.

Mulchahey, M. Michèle. *"First the Bow is Bent in Study . . .": Dominican Education before 1350.* Toronto: Pontifical Institute of Mediaeval Studies, 1998.

O'Carroll, Maura E. "The Educational Organization of the Dominicans in England and Wales 1221–1348: A Multidisciplinary Approach." *AFP* 50 (1980): 23–60.

———. "Two Versions of a Sermon by Richard Fishacre, OP for the Fourth Sunday of Lent on the Theme: *Non enim heres erit filius ancille cum filio libere.*" *AFP* 54 (1984): 113–41.

———. *A Thirteenth-Century Preacher's Handbook: Studies in MS Laud Misc. 511.* Toronto: Pontifical Institute of Mediaeval Studies, 1997.

———. "Editorial: Why Richard Fishacre." *NB* 80 (1999): 319–20.

———. "'The Fishacre Tribe': The Family Origins of Richard Fishacre, OP." *NB* 80 (1999): 324–45.

———. "Who Is Richard Fishacre." *NB* 80 (1999): 320–23.

Pegis, Anton. "The Bonaventurean Way to God." *MS* 29 (1967): 206–42.

Pelster, Franz. "Der älteste Sentenzenkommentar aus der Oxforder Franziskanerschule. Ein Beitrag zur Geschichte des theologischen Lehrbetriebs an der Oxforder Universität." *Scholastik* 1 (1926): 50–80.

———. "Das Leben und die Schriften des Oxforder Dominikanerlehrers Richard Fishacre († 1248)." *ZKT* 54 (1930): 518–52.

———. "Eine Handschrift mit Predigten des Richard Fishacre, O.P. und anderer Oxforder Lehrer." *ZKT* 57 (1933): 614–17.

Peters, Edward. *Heresy and Authority in Medieval Euriope.* Philadelphia: University of Pennsylvania Press, 1980.

Principe, Walter H. "Richard Fishacre's Use of Averroes with Respect to Motion and the Human Soul of Christ." *MS* 40 (1978): 349–60.

———. "Early Explicit Use of Averroes by Richard Fishacre with Respect to Motion and the Human Soul of Christ." In *Actas del V congreso internacional de filosofía medieval, 1127–37*. Madrid: Ed. Nacional, 1979.

Raedts, Peter. *Richard Rufus of Cornwall and the Tradition of Oxford Theology*. Oxford: Clarendon Press, 1987.

Russell, Josiah C. *Dictionary of Writers of Thirteenth Century England*. London: Dawson and Sons, 1967.

Senner, Walter. "R. Fishacre, OP." In *Lexikon des Mittelalters* 7:821–22.

Sharp, Dorothea E. "The Philosophy of Richard Fishacre." *NS* 7 (1933): 281–97.

Sharpe, Richard. *A Handlist of the Latin Writers of Great Britain and Ireland before 1540: Additions and Corrections*. Turnhout: Brepols, 2001.

Sheehan, M. W. "The Religious Orders 1220–1370." In *The Early Oxford Schools*, vol. 1: *The History of the University of Oxford*, edited by T. H. Aston. Oxford: Clarendon Press, 1984.

Smalley, B. "Robert Bacon and the Early Dominican School at Oxford." *Transactions of the Royal Historical Society* (4th series) 30 (1948): 1–19.

Solomon, David M. "The Sentence Commentary of Richard Fishacre and the Apocalypse Commentary of Hugh of St. Cher." *AFP* 46 (1976): 367–77.

Southern, Richard W. *Robert Grosseteste: The Growth of an English Mind in Medieval Europe*. Oxford: Clarendon Press, 1986.

Sweeney, Leo, and Charles J. Ermatinger. "Divine Infinity according to Richard Fishacre." *TMS* 35 (1958): 191–235.

Van der Lugt, Maaike. *Le ver, le démon et la vierge. Les théories médiévales de la génération extraordinaire*. Paris: Les Belles Lettres, 2004.

Index of Names

Abraham, xi, 12, 126, 138, 201, 244–45
Adam of Bockenfield, 202
Adam Marsh, 50n7, 202
Adelard of Bath, 137
Albert the Great (Albertus Magnus), 47, 62, 97n39, 150, 152n11, 179n49, 182n4, 198n10, 259
Albumasar, 17, 86, 120
Alexander of Hales, vi, 2, 3n9, 49n3, 62n51, 65, 66n15, 69, 70n28, 72nn34–36, 75, 79, 86, 94, 114, 133, 169, 210–211
Alfred of Sareshill (Alfredus Anglicus), 137, 202, 242
Algazel, 68n19, 86
Alhacen, xiii–xiv, 17, 91, 94
Ambrose, 67, 84, 110, 111n2, 117, 123–24, 127–28, 130–31, 134
Anselm, 2–3, 5, 169n3, 170n11, 171–72, 191n50, 204n33, 205–6, 246, 256, 260
Aquinas, Thomas, 1–4, 11, 22, 45, 47, 78, 99, 148, 157, 167, 182, 211, 253, 259
Aristotle, xii, xv–xvi, 4n10, 7–8, 16–18, 20n40, 31, 34, 50, 52–53, 56–58, 60–61, 63, 66–69, 75–76, 86, 91–93, 99, 102n57, 104, 108–9, 113–14, 117, 119–22, 124, 126, 130n77, 133, 139, 140n24, 142–50, 157, 163, 165–67, 180n50, 184n14, 186–87, 189, 191, 193nn53–56, 194n59, 198–207, 210–11, 214–16, 220–24, 227n78, 228n86, 230nn94–99, 231nn101–2, 232nn107–8, 239, 246, 255–56, 258–59
Augustine, vi–vii, xin3, xiii, xv, 2–4, 7–9, 18, 19n35, 21n3, 22–23, 27, 31, 37–38, 40, 44–46, 50, 53, 56, 60, 64n5, 67, 75, 80–84, 93–95, 101, 104, 106, 108–9, 111–12, 114–16, 118–20, 122, 124–25, 127–28, 130–32, 135–36, 139n20, 140, 146–47, 149, 152–69, 171–72, 176, 178, 184, 190, 192–94, 198, 205–6, 209–10, 212, 216, 220, 221–26, 228–31, 233, 235–39, 244–47, 249–53, 258–59, 261
Averroes, 76, 86, 95, 99, 108, 221n48, 261
Avicenna (ibn Sina), 68n19, 86, 150–51, 152n10, 156

Bacon, Roger, 20n41, 50n7, 54n20, 62n51, 66n15, 86, 91n19, 100, 150, 202–3, 262
Bartholomaeus Anglicus, xvn18, 90n14, 203n22
Basil the Great, 84, 112–13, 115, 123, 128, 229
Bataillon, Louis, 19n38, 64n7, 88n2, 255
Baur, Ludwig, 15n17, 24, 25n16, 170n11, 173n25
Blund, John, 202
Bonaventure, xi, xii, 2, 5, 11, 13, 47, 54, 62, 75, 138n14, 182n4
Boyle, Leonard, vii, 144n38, 187n29, 255, 260
Brown, Peter, 237n9
Brown, Stephen, viii, xin3, xiin5, xvii, 12n1, 65n12, 77n57, 80, 255, 260

Callus, Daniel, 4n10, 7, 143n37, 152nn10–11, 169n7, 170n8, 173n25, 202n19, 255
Catto, Jeremy, 144n39, 256
Chatillon, Jean, 2–3, 256

Dales, Richard, 17n26, 25, 26nn23–24, 29n32, 31n38, 43n77, 50n5, 65nn9–13, 66nn14–15, 67nn16–18, 68nn20–21, 72n34, 74nn42–43, 75n47, 80n72, 128nn67–69, 130n76, 131nn80–81, 135n5, 137n13, 142, 143n32, 187n26, 256–57
Daniel of Morley, 137, 202
Davenport, Anne, 256
Dondaine, Antoine, 252n77, 254nn83–84

Ehrle, Franz, 222n49, 256
Eichinger, Alexander, xiii, xivn12, xvii, 256–57

Gaunilon, 5, 191n50
Gillon, L.-B., 257
Ginther, James, 32n42, 141n30, 257, 260
Goering, Joseph, xvii, 24n15, 25n21, 32n42, 141n30, 236n4, 257, 260
Grant, Edward, 73n38, 257
Grosseteste, Robert, viii, xii, 15n17, 17n26, 19n33, 21, 24–26, 29n32, 31, 32n42, 40n68, 49–50, 54, 65–69, 72n34, 74n43, 76, 79, 80n72, 85, 87, 89, 90nn11–13, 94, 97n39, 100, 111n2, 116–18, 124, 128nn67–69, 130n76, 131nn80–81, 135, 137–38, 141–43, 148, 155, 158, 169–74, 176, 180, 187–88, 197, 202, 256–57, 260–62

Hackett, Jeremiah, vii, xin2, 12n1, 50n7, 255, 258
Hagar, xi, 9, 12, 126–27, 201, 244–45, 260, 32n42, 85–86, 134, 140n26, 147–48, 152n11, 260
Hamesse, Jacqueline, vii, 130n77, 144n38, 194n59
Hinnebusch, William, 238n13, 252n75, 253n79, 257
Hinton, Simon, 202n21
Hugh of St. Cher, 26, 32n40, 34n49, 35n53, 36nn56–58, 38n62, 47n91, 179, 262
Hugh of St. Victor, 21n2, 126, 156
Humbert of Romans, 13n3, 183n8

Ibn Gabirol, 48, 60n46, 139n20, 152, 154, 157

John of La Rochelle, 150, 169, 200
John Damascene, 2–3, 4n12, 6, 54–55, 57, 58n40, 67, 75, 81, 84, 91, 93–95, 102, 104, 108, 123–24, 129, 174, 227, 233, 241

Käppeli, Thomas, 3n7, 196n2, 235n2, 253n81, 257
Kieckhefer, Richard, 21n1, 28n28, 35n55, 42n75
Kilwardby, Robert, vi, 32n42, 85–86, 134, 140n26, 147–48, 152n11, 260
Kraml, Hans, xvii, 257

Leibold, Gerhard, xvii, 85n91, 148n50, 257
Lewis, Neil, 170, 171nn12–13, 172nn17–20, 173nn21–23, 180n50, 257
Lombard, Peter, xii–xiv, xvii, 2, 4, 15, 18, 26–27, 33n45, 53, 55, 60, 64, 68, 73n39, 85, 89–90, 94, 117n20, 118n29, 132n91, 136n8, 138, 140, 144–45, 154, 158, 172n16, 174, 177–78, 181, 210–11, 219–20, 232n112, 233nn114–18, 259
Lottin, Odon, 48n1, 152n11, 169n3, 177n39, 179, 260

Maimonides, Moses, 17n26, 68n19, 69, 70nn28–30, 73n37, 78–79, 86
Martin, R. M., 152n11, 171n12, 260
Mary, xvii, 196, 198–200, 203; Mother of God, xvii, 197; Virgin, vii, xi, xv,

19n36, 196, 199n11, 200, 205n40, 205n47, 210n7, 258
McEvoy, James, 24n15, 25, 50nn6–7, 89, 90n11, 116n17, 137, 143, 261
Moneta of Cremona, 253, 254n82
Moonan, Lawrence, 182n4

Noone, Timothy, vii–viii, 93n28, 94n33, 97n39, 139n19, 144n38, 154n17, 187n29, 188n32, 189nn34–37, 258–60

O'Carroll, Maura, xivn15, xvnn17–19, xvii, 3n9, 18n30, 19n36, 51n10, 64n8, 88n5, 118n29, 150n1, 196n2, 201n14, 208n1, 222n52, 236n7, 260–61
Origen, 112
Oxford, v–viii, xi, 3–4, 19nn36–37, 20, 48–50, 62–63, 65, 77, 79, 85–87, 89, 93n28, 94, 100, 110, 116, 119, 137, 144n38, 148, 150, 152nn11–13, 168n2, 169, 173, 179–81, 187, 189n33, 190n41, 202–3, 210n7, 221–22, 235, 236n2, 255–62

Panti, Cecilia, 25, 141n30
Paris, Matthew, xvi, 202
Peckham, John, 62n51, 100, 152n11
Pegis, Anton, 1n1, 2n2, 261
Pelster, Franz, 20n39, 94n32, 152n13, 196nn1–2, 197, 202n21, 222n49, 236n3, 238n13, 261
Philip the Chancellor, 49n3, 70n29, 75, 77n53, 79, 114–15, 169
Plato, 4, 8, 18n28, 60, 69, 75–76, 84, 86, 149, 167, 225n69, 229, 240
Principe, Walter, 135n2, 221n48, 261

Raedts, Peter, 65n10, 77nn57–59, 78n64, 94n32, 97n39, 144n38, 168n2, 177n42, 178n44, 181n3, 184, 187nn25–28, 190n48, 262
Reynolds, Philip Lyndon, 135n2, 139n23, 141–42, 144, 147
Rodler, Klaus, xvii, 257
Roland of Cremona, 169
Rufus, Richard, v–viii, 17n26, 31n37, 32n42, 43–47, 49, 59–62, 65, 68n20, 74n43, 76n49, 77–80, 86, 94–100, 118n28, 124–27, 134, 137nn12–13, 144–45, 147, 168n2, 177–78, 181–82, 184, 186–87, 189–91, 202, 256, 259–60, 262

Scot, Michael, 22nn5–9, 26n25, 29n31, 41n71
Seneca, 14, 122n47
Sharp, Dorothea, 8n26, 59n41, 152n11, 155n22, 166n22, 262
Simon Magus, 34, 186n21, 238–39, 241, 244–45, 247
Smalley, Beryl, 20n41, 262
Solomon, David, 262
Southern, Richard, 25, 135n3, 169n5, 170nn8–10, 262
Sweeney, Leo, 33n46, 164n14, 262

Teske, Roland, 112n4, 135n4
Thomson, S. Harrison, 170nn10–11
Thorndike, Lynn, xvi, 22n8, 26n25, 29n31, 35n52, 41n71, 112n5
Tugwell, Simon, 13n3

Van der Lugt, Maaike, 31n38, 33n43, 35nn54–55, 262

Weisheipl, James, xviii, 97n39, 152n10, 253n78, 256
William of Auvergne, 22–23, 24nn13–15, 26, 27n27, 35n52, 47n91, 49n3, 114, 119n32, 150, 210n9
William of Auxerre, 2–3, 49n3, 94, 114, 168, 177n39, 179, 256
Wippel, John, 50n8, 54n21, 62n51
Witelo, 89n10, 100
Wood, Rega, 68n20, 76n49, 77n57, 97n39, 98n44

Subject Index

Accident (accidental), 52–53nn15–17, 90–92, 94–96, 98–99, 104, 107–8, 120, 156, 159, 172, 188, 190, 193, 219, 229
Act, 8–9, 29, 31–34, 38, 70–72, 78, 83, 85, 95, 102–3, 106, 108, 119, 129, 140–42, 159–60, 162–64, 186n22, 193–95, 219, 231–32, 239
Action, 26, 52, 58, 70–71, 80, 93, 104, 110, 119–20, 128, 158–60, 167–68, 176, 188, 217, 232, 240, 246
Actuality (actualize), 52, 57, 60–61, 140, 170, 184–85
Agency, 9, 23, 32–34, 38, 42, 185
Agent, 9, 24, 26, 31n39, 32, 56, 60n43, 70, 72, 76, 80, 119, 124, 140n24, 149, 184, 228n82, 231, 246
Analogy, xvii, 9, 59n40, 67, 99, 249
Angels: composition of, 49, 59–62, 94n30, 105, 139, 154, 188, 258; existence and nature of, 28–29, 32, 36–40, 47n91, 49–55, 58, 60–61, 93, 136n8, 151–53, 156, 189, 198, 204, 221, 223–24, 239n18; good and fallen, 32–34, 36, 38, 40, 185; individuation of, 53; place or location of, viii, 39, 55–58, 61, 79, 83, 127, 139, 143n34, 212–13, 223, 225–26, 230; power of, 37, 45–46, 161, 163, 166, 167n27, 171, 183, 185, 227, 238–39, 241, 245
Appetite, 155, 174, 212–14, 216–17
Apprehension, 176–77, 179
Arts, v, viii, xiii, 14, 21–22, 25–27, 29, 46, 50n7, 61, 65, 116, 185, 191, 260
Ascension (of Christ), vi–vii, xv, xvii, 19, 201, 208–11, 215, 218–23, 229, 233, 235, 236n4, 240, 258
Atheist, 5–6
Augustinianism, 176, 259

Being, 4–5, 8, 11, 14, 16, 34–37, 39, 43, 45, 49, 51n9, 55–57, 59, 67, 69, 71, 73–76, 78–79, 94, 113, 115, 133, 140, 163, 171–72, 182–83, 189, 190n48, 198, 217, 219–20, 243, 251

Cambridge, 19, 55n24, 63, 183n8
Cause (as substantive), 10–11, 28, 39, 46, 52 –53, 57, 60, 67, 69, 71–72, 76, 78, 86, 123, 148, 166, 173, 186, 190, 236, 242n29, 244, 246, 248, 251
Change, 52, 70, 72, 154–55, 185–86, 190
Contingency, 71, 181
Corporeity, 59, 76, 91
Creation, v, viii, xii–xiv, 12–16, 19n39, 20n40, 36, 63, 68nn19–20, 70–71, 73–77, 80, 82–83, 85–87, 89–90, 93, 97n39, 110, 126, 134–36, 138n14, 140, 148, 151, 161, 163, 166, 169n3, 183, 187–88, 190n41, 258
Creature, 2, 10, 13–14, 16, 26, 37, 50, 55–58, 60, 62, 72, 74, 78, 94, 96, 112, 154–55, 160, 166–68, 171–73, 175, 177, 182, 189, 201, 211, 216–17, 219, 223, 231–32, 239, 247–48

Demon, 22–23, 27–31, 34–45, 47n91, 51–52, 56, 120, 225–26; demoniacs, 37, 45; demonic magic, 23; demonic ministry, 24; demonic possession, 56; demonic power, 46; demonology, 23n10, 47
Demonstrations: *a posteriori,* 1; *a priori,* 5
Division of the waters, vi, viii, xvin20, 110, 118, 123, 260

Element, 16–17, 27n27, 34, 36–38, 45, 103, 121–22, 124–25, 127, 129–30, 132, 145, 148, 175, 198, 212, 215–16, 225–26, 228–30, 242–43
Emanation, 249
Eternity, v, vii, 19n39, 63–75, 77n57, 78, 80–84, 86, 89nn6–8, 144n38, 181n2, 190, 194, 236, 255–56, 258
Expansion, 135n2, 140–42, 144, 146, 148
Extension, 55n24, 58n40, 139, 143, 148

Faith, xii, xvi, 18, 20, 47, 60–61, 66, 87, 111, 113, 118, 126, 173, 241, 253
Food, 31, 135n2, 139n23, 141n29, 144n40, 145–46, 147n47, 212, 245, 247–48
Form, xiv, 9, 14, 31, 47, 50–52, 53n17, 54–55, 57–60, 92–109, 121, 136, 139–41, 142n31, 149–54, 157, 159, 161, 165–67, 184, 188–89, 192–93, 195, 212–13, 217, 223, 225–26, 230–31, 239–40, 242n29, 255; plurality of, 48, 58, 157, 209
Forma-habitus, 94, 97, 98n44, 99, 109, 189n37

Generation, 35–36, 53, 71, 74, 76, 82–83, 92, 151, 193, 238, 244
Genus, 42, 50n5, 54, 74, 242
God: creative act of, 119, 249, 251; eternity of, 67, 69–70, 74, 76, 85; existence of, xvii, 1, 5, 73; freedom, 171–72, 181, 184; image of, 26; invoking of, 30; knowability, 1–2, 6, 10, 166, 246; mercy of, 25, 198; nature of, 55, 57, 62, 70, 247; omniscience of, xi, 52, 70, 113, 166, 170, 245; power of, viii, 9, 16, 23–24, 26, 28, 31n37, 32 –33, 37, 40, 42, 44, 67, 70–72, 76, 93, 120, 126, 138, 145–48, 170, 181–91, 216–17, 238, 240, 245–46, 249–50; presence of, 57; revelation, 29; self-evidence, 1–2, 4, 11; simplicity of, 50; way to, v, vii, 1, 6; will of, 33–34, 36, 44, 70, 72–73, 78, 113, 115, 117, 123, 170 –72; wisdom of, xii, 13, 171
Good, 5, 14, 42, 69, 71, 172–74, 177, 246, 251
Goodness, 14, 36, 39, 69
Gravity, xv, 120, 201, 211, 216, 221

Habit (*habitus*), 94, 97, 98n44, 99, 102, 108–9, 160–61, 165, 189n37, 194, 240
Heresy, xv, xvii, 19, 63–64, 88, 235–38, 243, 245–47, 249–54, 261
Heretic (heretical), 40, 47n90, 66, 237–41, 243–44, 247–254
Hexaëmeron, xiv, 15, 17n26, 18–19, 25–26, 31n38, 61, 62n52, 65–68, 72n34, 77, 80n72, 84, 90, 111nn2–3, 112n6, 116–18, 124, 127–28, 130n76, 131nn80–81, 134–35, 137n13, 187n26, 229n90, 256–57
Hylomorphism, universal, 48, 54, 93n28, 139, 153–54, 188n31

Idea, 24n15, 60n44, 117, 165, 236, 247; innate ideas, 165
Idolatry, v, viii, 21, 47, 247–48, 260
Illumination, 9, 11, 92–93, 96, 188
Imagination, viii, xivn12, 59, 73, 78, 81, 256, 259
Immanence, 8
Individuation, 50, 53
Innatism, 8
Intellect, viii, xivn12, 5n16, 8–10, 39,

52n11, 54, 79, 83, 106, 160n4, 161, 163–67, 175–76, 178n44, 202, 256, 259
Intelligence, 15, 158, 160–61, 163
Interiority, vi, viii, 158, 259

Judgment, xi, xvin22, 46, 47n90, 59n41, 123, 172, 176–79

Knowledge, xi–xiv, 1–2, 6–7, 20, 26–27, 34, 42–43, 46, 65n12, 99, 115–16, 126–27, 137, 143, 160, 163, 165–66, 181, 219, 245–46, 252n76, 256; self-knowledge, vi, viii, 158, 161, 259

Levity, xv, 201, 211, 221
Light, v, vii, xvin20, 7, 9–11, 13, 16–17, 19, 54, 56, 64, 72, 74, 79, 88–100, 116, 119, 121, 134, 141–42, 144n38, 147, 154–55, 163, 166, 171, 182, 186–89, 216, 218, 240, 248–49, 260
Location, 39, 55, 58n40, 59, 122, 209, 211, 214

Magic, magical arts, v, viii, xvi, 21–23, 25–30, 32–33, 35, 38, 41n71, 42n75, 46, 47n90, 112n5, 185–86, 260
Magus, 22n5, 27, 29–30, 40–41, 44; magi, 22, 24–25, 27–29, 31, 32n40, 36, 38, 42–44
Matter: spiritual, 54–55, 59, 61–62, 94n30, 105, 139, 154, 188, 221, 258; prime, 143. *See also* Hylomorphism
Memory, 158, 160–61, 163–65, 184, 190n46
Metaphysics, v, vii, 4, 49–51, 62, 70, 78n64, 86–90, 94, 97–98, 100, 141–44, 163, 187n29, 188n32, 189nn34–37, 200, 239, 260
Miracle, 23n11, 27, 29, 31–34, 46, 115, 120, 123, 140, 147, 183–85
Motion, xv, 67, 70, 72, 78, 81, 97, 113, 122, 125, 133, 155, 180n49, 187, 189–90, 201–2, 211, 218–19, 221, 261
Multiplication, 33, 140–42, 146–47

Nature, xvi, 6, 8, 13, 19, 23–24, 26–34, 36, 38, 40, 42, 44–47, 49–50, 52, 54–56, 58, 64, 70, 72–75, 78–79, 86, 90–91, 93–94, 96, 98–100, 113, 115, 117, 120, 123, 125–26, 135nn2–3, 137, 139–42, 145–47, 149, 151, 153, 155–56, 170n11, 173–74, 183, 185–88, 190, 203n22, 211–18, 220, 225–27, 231, 239n18, 240–42, 251
Necessity, contingent, 170

Optics, xiii, xivn12, 100, 256

Paris, 3nn8–9, 20, 22, 24, 27, 63–65, 77n57, 79, 87, 114–15, 169, 173, 179, 191, 200, 202–3, 210–11, 260
Participation, 4, 164n14
Philosophy, v, vii–vii, xi–xii, xiv, xvi, 2, 8n26, 12, 18, 20–21, 26n25, 48nn1–2, 50n6, 59n41, 68n20, 90n11, 97n39, 116n17, 118n27, 124–26, 137, 143, 152n11, 154n17, 155n22, 166n22, 202, 255–56, 258–62; Christian, 168; 181n2; of knowledge, 7; medieval, 20; natural, vi, xv, 9, 18, 20n40, 32n42, 46, 49, 61, 96, 124, 126, 134, 148–49, 191, 260
Physics, 92, 97n39, 117, 136
Place, xv, xvin20, 16–17, 53n17, 54n20, 55–61, 72–73, 79, 88–89, 92, 113–14, 116, 119, 121–22, 124–25, 141, 198, 201, 211–15, 217, 221, 240–41, 252n75
Plurality of forms, 48, 58, 152, 157, 209
Potency (potencies), 31–33, 47, 139–42, 167, 184–86, 224, 229–30, 239
Potentiality, 8, 61, 71, 139, 142, 148, 184, 190
Power, vi, viii, xiv, 9, 14, 22–24, 26–27, 31n37, 33–34, 36–42, 44, 46, 51n9, 66, 70, 72, 97, 111–12, 115–16, 120–21, 123,

Power *(cont.)*
125, 138, 145, 158, 160–61, 163, 168n2, 169, 174–84, 186, 191, 198, 211, 213, 217–18, 240–41, 242n29, 250, 259
Principle, 14, 31n37, 32, 54, 58, 71, 92, 94–96, 99, 115, 119, 123, 125, 133, 140, 142, 148, 151, 152n13, 176, 181n2, 182, 185–89, 250–51

Quality, 47n91, 100–102, 104, 107, 229
Quantity, 34, 105, 119, 139n23, 143nn34–35, 146, 193

Reason, xii, 27, 55n24, 57–58, 60, 67, 70, 72, 74–75, 78, 87, 112, 118, 124, 168n2, 169, 172–80
Reasons (natures): causal (*rationes causales*), 31–33, 140, 184–85; seminal (*rationes seminales*), 31–32, 34, 80–81, 140–41, 184–86, 192
Revelation, 27–29, 250n66
Rib, Adam's, vi, xvin20, 32–33, 134–36, 138, 140–41, 144–46, 148, 185–86, 260

Scholastic (scholasticism), 3, 22, 49n2, 126, 150, 168n2, 187, 256
School, v, viii–ix, 12n2, 21, 26, 48, 55n24, 118, 137–38, 144n39, 148, 152, 168–69, 177, 198n9, 250n67, 262
Schoolmen, 12n2, 114, 168
Science, v–viii, xi–xiii, xvi–xvii, 4n10, 12–13, 15, 19n36, 22nn4–8, 23, 47n90, 116, 126–27, 152n10, 191, 196, 200–202, 211, 221, 255, 258, 260; applied, 23; Aristotelian, 133, 203, 210, 221; natural, xi, 20–21, 23, 73n38, 138, 202, 221, 257; sacred, 116, 137–38, 203; secular, 201, 208
Scripture(s), xii, xv, 13, 18, 36, 45–46, 56, 68, 93, 111, 115, 118, 125, 137, 138n14, 156, 201, 210–11, 214, 218, 220, 238, 243, 248–49, 250n65
Soul: activity of, 8, 10, 13–14, 35, 141, 151, 155, 163–65, 167, 240, 242–43; of Adam, 156, 163; animal (sensible) soul, 35, 39, 151, 153, 175–76, 182, 186, 239; of Christ, 211–12, 217–19; creation of, 93, 135–36, 246; form of the body, 150, 188; immortality of, 55; interaction with body, 155; matter of, 93, 188; nature of, 7–9, 11, 26, 33, 35, 97, 139, 141, 149–56, 158, 160, 163–64, 166–67, 167, 174, 242, 246, 249; place of, 211–13, 215, 218, 239, 241; plurality (duality) of, 151, 153, 157–58; powers (faculties) of, 97, 158, 160, 162, 174–77, 179, 202, 241; problem of, vi–vii, 8, 93, 141, 236; rational (human) soul, 26, 33, 37, 50–52, 56, 60–61, 68, 73–74, 76, 87, 93–94, 14, 151, 153–54, 156, 184, 201, 240; single, 76; union with body, 242–43; vegetative, 152, 182, 186–87
Subject, xiv, 23, 91, 99
Subsistence, 91
Substance, 45, 48n1, 49–57, 59, 70, 72, 80, 90, 93–102, 104–9, 120, 138n16, 139, 146, 149–50, 153, 155, 157, 188, 190, 193–94, 212–13, 215–16, 225, 242, 249–50, 260

Theology, xi, xiii, xv–xvi, 2, 12, 20n40, 21, 47, 50, 116, 120, 126, 148, 169–70, 173n24, 201–3, 208
Time, xv, 53n17, 65n12, 66–68, 71–76, 78–79, 85–87, 92, 136, 181n2, 182, 186–87, 189–90, 211, 218, 256
Tradition, xiin8, 20–21, 31n39, 35, 38, 46, 65n10, 68, 75, 94n32, 100, 106n58, 118n29, 137n13, 144n38, 148, 150, 168n2, 179–80, 182n3, 199, 203, 221, 237n8, 242n29, 253, 259, 262

Unity, 59, 152, 162, 243, 255

Vacuum, xv, 16, 91–92, 109, 117, 119, 126, 211, 217–18, 231n102
Velocity, 16, 201, 221
Vision, xiv, 10, 37, 119, 157, 221

Will, 25–26, 32–33, 38, 40–42, 44–45, 58, 70–71, 78, 117, 123, 158, 162, 164–65, 168n2, 169–70, 172–80, 183, 185–86, 213, 214n18
Wisdom, xi–xii, xiv, 13, 47n90, 70, 77, 166
World, v, vii, xiii, xvi, 4, 13–15, 19, 20n40, 22n4, 26n23, 46, 51n9, 63–73, 74n42, 75–79, 85–87, 89, 99, 113, 116, 126–27, 137, 144n38, 187, 190, 238–39, 245–46, 251–52, 255–56, 258

Hagar's Vocation: Philosophy's Role in the Theology of Richard Fishacre, OP was designed in Adobe Caslon Pro and composed by Kachergis Book Design of Pittsboro, North Carolina. It was printed on 60-pound Natures Book Natural and bound by Thomson-Shore of Dexter, Michigan.